Steamship Nationalis

Steamship Nationalism is a cultural, social, and political history of the S.S. *Imperator*, *Vaterland*, and *Bismarck*. Transatlantic passenger steamships launched by the *Hamburg-Amerikanische Packetfahrt-Aktien-Gesellschaft* (HAPAG) between 1912 and 1914, they do not enjoy the international fame of their British counterparts, most notably the *Titanic*. Yet the *Imperator*-class liners were the largest, most luxurious passenger vessels built before the First World War. In keeping with the often-overlooked history of its merchant marine as a whole, they reveal much about Imperial Germany in its national and international dimensions. As products of business decisions shaped by global dynamics and the imperatives of international travel, immigration, and trade, HAPAG's giant liners bear witness to Germany's involvement in the processes of globalization prior to 1914. Yet this book focuses not on their physical, but on their cultural construction in a variety of contemporaneous media, including the press and advertising, on both sides of the Atlantic. At home, they were presented to the public as symbolic of the nation's achievements and ambitions in ways that emphasize the complex nature of German national identity at the time. Abroad, they were often construed as floating national monuments and, as such, facilitated important encounters with Germany, both virtual and real, for the populations of Britain and America. Their overseas reception highlights the multi-faceted image of the European superpower that was constructed in the Anglo-American world in these years. More generally, it is a pointed indicator of the complex relationship between Britain, the United States, and Imperial Germany.

Mark A. Russell is Associate Professor at the Liberal Arts College of Concordia University in Montreal. He is the author of *Between Tradition and Modernity: Aby Warburg and the Public Purposes of Art in Hamburg, 1896–1918* (2007).

Routledge Studies in Modern European History

www.routledge.com/history/series/SE0246

Steamship Nationalism

Ocean Liners and National
Identity in Imperial Germany and
the Atlantic World

Mark A. Russell

Routledge
Taylor & Francis Group

LONDON AND NEW YORK

First published 2020
by Routledge
2 Park Square, Milton Park, Abingdon, Oxon OX14 4RN

and by Routledge
605 Third Avenue, New York, NY 10017

First issued in paperback 2021

Routledge is an imprint of the Taylor & Francis Group, an informa business

British Library Cataloguing-in-Publication Data
A catalogue record for this book is available from the British Library

Library of Congress Cataloging-in-Publication Data
Names: Russell, Mark A. (Mark Allen), author.
Title: Steamship nationalism : ocean liners and national identity in Imperial
Germany and Atlantic world / Mark A. Russell.
Description: Abingdon, Oxon ; New York, NY : Routledge, 2020. |
Series: Routledge studies in modern European history |
Includes bibliographical references and index.
Identifiers: LCCN 2019054846 (print) | LCCN 2019054847 (ebook) |
ISBN 9780367136437 (hardback) | ISBN 9780429027710 (ebook)
Subjects: LCSH: Ocean liners–Germany–History–20th century. |
Steamboat lines–Germany–History–20th century. | Nationalism–Germany–
History–20th century. | Germany–Foreign relations–1871-1918. |
Germany–History–1871-1918.
Classification: LCC HE601.G3 R87 2020 (print) | LCC HE601.G3 (ebook) |
DDC 387.2/432094309041–dc23
LC record available at https://lccn.loc.gov/2019054846
LC ebook record available at https://lccn.loc.gov/2019054847

ISBN 13: 978-1-03-223650-6 (pbk)
ISBN 13: 978-0-367-13643-7 (hbk)

DOI: 10.4324/9780429027710

Typeset in Times New Roman
by Integra Software Services Pvt. Ltd.

For my parents, Ross and Elizabeth Russell, and my wife Leslie-Stéfanie Stoianov.

Contents

Figures

Acknowledgements

Many people have contributed to this project. It grew out of an interest in the life and work of Aby Warburg and I am grateful to Dr. Dorothea MacEwan for her assistance as Archivist of the Warburg Institute where my research began. Mr. Peter Maaß, in the archive of Hapag-Lloyd AG, kindly granted permission to access the company's papers and provided assistance in doing so. Frau Elisabeth Wilker of the *Hochschule für bildende Künste* in Hamburg helped guide me through the holdings of its library. Dr. Julia Haas and Dr. Jonathan Cayer provided assistance in organizing my research in its early days, and the Fonds Québécois de la Recherche sur la Société et la Culture generously funded it. Hapag-Lloyd AG; the German Maritime Museum; The Mariners' Museum, Newport News; and the Hoboken Historical Museum all granted permission to publish images from their collections. The faculty and students of the Liberal Arts College of Concordia University, my academic home, have provided a stimulating environment in which to think and write. Most importantly, the patient encouragement of my wife, Leslie-Stéfanie, kept the wind in my sails (or coal in my bunkers) and helped me bring this project into dock, while my parents, Ross and Elizabeth, have always encouraged me to achieve by loving example.

Introduction

On the morning of 23 May 1912, the latest in a long line of monuments constructed by the German Empire was christened amid considerable national and international interest. Yet this monument was unlike any other. For many Germans, it was a wonder of the modern age – a powerful symbol of the nation's achievements in industry, engineering, and technology. For others, it was the embodiment of all the evils wrought by political, social, and cultural transformation.[1] Some said it expressed the character of the German people in a manner similar to Cologne Cathedral and Sanssouci, the palace of Frederick the Great.[2] But there were those who thought it "appeared as a typical manifestation of the new Germany, with its huckstering, and obtrusive manners, more a snobbism than a symbol of German competence."[3] The Kaiser was fascinated by this expression of the ambition, ingenuity, and might of an Empire in which he believed power rested with himself, the Prussian nobility, and a powerful military complex. And yet Hamburg's mayor, Johann Heinrich Burchard, echoed the feelings of many when he described the new wonder as "above all ... the product of a flourishing, self-conscious German middle class."[4] Although extolled as a symbol of German unity, Social Democrats denounced the modern leviathan as an expression of class inequality and lamented that ten men were killed and one hundred injured while constructing it. With this in mind, how could Germany be proud of what it had wrought?[5]

The monument in question was the *Imperator*, the new flagship of the *Hamburg-Amerikanische Packetfahrt-Aktien-Gesellschaft* or HAPAG, then the world's largest shipping company. The vessel that slid down the ways into Hamburg's harbour on that May morning – just over five weeks after the sinking of the *Titanic* – embodied a dramatic departure in German shipbuilding. In fact, the *Imperator* was the world's largest vehicle of any type: almost twice the size of the largest German warship, it displaced 52,117 gross tons, measured nearly 919 feet in length, bunkered 8,500 tons of coal, and could accommodate 4,594 passengers – 908 of them in first-class cabins.[6] Its crew of 1,180 hands was commanded by a commodore and four captains. And the *Imperator* was but the first of a trio of passenger steamships commissioned by HAPAG, each larger than the one before. The second, christened *Vaterland*, was launched in Hamburg on 3 April 1913. The third, which took the name *Bismarck*, slid down

Figure I.1 The *Imperator.*
Source: Bain Collection, The Library of Congress, Washington, D.C.

the ways into the Elbe River on 20 June 1914. Known collectively as the *Imperator*-class liners, these vessels were intended to transport passengers and freight across the Atlantic between Hamburg and New York.

Transatlantic passenger shipping during its golden age – from approximately 1880 until the onset of travel by jet airplane in the 1950s – has long been the subject of keen popular interest. Britain's passenger fleet, in particular, is the focus of widespread and sustained fascination; its premier passenger liners, including Cunard's *Lusitania* and White Star's *Titanic*, have captured the imagination of an international public. By comparison, HAPAG's *Imperator*, *Vaterland*, and *Bismarck* enjoy nothing like this sort of fame, even in Germany. Of course, this is partly due to the fact that they did not share the terrible fate of the British vessels. But more profoundly, the nature and events of modern German history have turned the attention of scholars, and the general public, to subjects other than the nation's merchant shipping. That said, there is a small body of literature in English and German that testifies to an interest in the *Imperator*-class liners. In particular, the trio's namesake has been referred to as a major development in maritime architecture and design; declared the finest first-class hotel to sail the North Atlantic during the Belle Époque; and been situated as a prototype of the modern transatlantic liner that appeared following the First World War.[7] And yet, in my experience, most people have never heard of the *Imperator*. Reference to its British counterparts, especially the *Titanic*, is almost always an obligatory and unfailing means of introducing the German vessel. Nonetheless, this book is motivated by the conviction that the *Imperator*-class liners will reward serious study by scholars working on modern German history, maritime history, Atlantic history, and the history of transnationalism and globalization prior to 1914. It contributes to positioning these vessels for such study.

Much of what has been written about HAPAG's trio in English and German has appeared in histories of transatlantic passenger shipping intended for enthusiasts and the general public.[8] And most of this literature devotes its attention to British companies and their fleets. Furthermore, when German steamers and shipping lines feature in English-language publications, they are often treated tangentially; in most instances they are afforded a limited amount of consideration in studies dealing principally with Britain. And, when this is the case, it most often occurs without reference to secondary or primary sources in German.

Many of the titles intended for a popular audience are nostalgic tributes to a bygone era and a storied means of transportation. Fascination with transatlantic liners from the Belle Époque resides partly in the impression that "living in those simpler times would have been easier than dealing with the uncertainties of our modern age."[9] Non-professional histories are often structured around the "biographies" of individual vessels. Many concentrate on technical detail and description sometimes in the manner of a catalogue. Recurring themes include milestones in the attempt to make ever speedier crossings of the Atlantic; tales of maritime disaster; and the exploits of individual captains. And many publications are essentially picture histories. A particularly impressive example, unusual for its exclusive focus on the *Imperator*-class liners, is Peter Zerbe's *Die Grossen Deutschen Passagierschiffe*.[10]

Other works of popular history are more critical and scholarly in conception and method. Some authors write about transatlantic liners not simply from a nautical but from a cultural, social, and political perspective and present them in the context of major historical phenomena. These include the First World War and changing patterns of experience with relation to space and time in the nineteenth and early-twentieth centuries.[11] There are histories of individual shipping lines and the eminent personalities involved in their founding and operation.[12] The life and work of Albert Ballin (1857–1918), managing director of HAPAG from 1899 until his death, has been the subject of particular interest, especially for German authors.[13] In addition, the interior design and outfitting of the transatlantic liners of several nations continues to attract considerable interest. Several publications document the development of the on-board environment as it transitioned from the maritime functionalism of the mid-nineteenth century to the outfitting of passenger vessels in a variety of sumptuous historical revival styles to match the luxury hotels of the Belle Époque.[14]

The quality of popular literature varies considerably as do the intentions of its authors. Many publications are the products of sound conception and research and are sources of reliable facts and figures. Several are filled with valuable information in the form of reproduced paintings, posters, photographs, newspaper articles, publicity material, and a variety of ephemeral items published by shipping lines. And yet no matter the appeal and constructive function of this literature, scholars are bound to criticize its habitually nostalgic bent; its often unexacting nature; its lack of critical and interpretative framework; its sometimes glaring errors of historical fact; and the lack of substantial historical context in many accounts or its treatment in an impressionistic, uncomplicated manner in others. Furthermore, many authors eschew primary-source research and the critical examination of sources to rely on and recycle the work of a limited number of other writers. In fact, information published by a small number of authors including John Malcolm Brinnin, Philip Dawson, John Maxtone-Graham, and Arnold Kludas is widely and repeatedly employed and recycled.[15]

To be sure, popular literature does not have a monopoly on the history of transatlantic passenger shipping; there is a comparatively small body of scholarship on the subject. Some of these publications, such as Arnold Kludas's invaluable five-volume reference work devoted to the history of German merchant shipping on all oceans, are structured around a traditional focus on the vessels themselves.[16] Yet in keeping with the renewal and expanding nature of professional maritime history in recent years, scholars have begun to employ a range of perspectives and methods to open the study of transatlantic shipping to insightful economic, social, and cultural analyses. Those with an interest in business and economic history have brought serious scrutiny to the operations of steamship companies including HAPAG.[17] And there has been a turn from ships to human experience.[18] This includes investigation of the lives and social structure of steamship crews and the manner in which passengers recorded their experience of crossing the Atlantic.[19] Yet one of the major problems with professional maritime history in general – despite its increased interdisciplinary nature linking it to a variety of scholarly themes and perspectives – is the extent to which it continues to be practiced apart from other disciplines. Transatlantic passenger shipping is a still more isolated topic. As Dagmar Bellmann has recently emphasized, it has even failed to attract significant attention in areas of study defined as "Atlantic History" and "Seafaring."[20]

It is, therefore, hardly surprising that the *Imperator*-class liners have received so little consideration in the field in which this book situates them: modern German political, social, and cultural history.[21] Of course, Imperial Germany's development as a maritime power continues to be the subject of much interest. Kaiser Wilhelm's famous proclamation that Germany's "future lies upon the water" is treated as emblematic of the Empire's ambitions to world-power status.[22] And yet the comprehensive nature of this statement uttered, in fact, aboard one of HAPAG's passenger steamers – the *Prinzessin Victoria Luise* – is largely ignored. Historians have focused overwhelmingly on the building of the Imperial Navy, especially in the context of growing Anglo-German antagonism prior to 1914. The construction of a battle fleet has also been analysed from the perspective of domestic politics and popular nationalism.[23] But this almost exclusive focus on the naval component of the German Empire's maritime ambitions and achievements neglects the extremely important non-military means by which Germany projected its power across the world's oceans while fostering and sustaining global engagement in a variety of forms.

That said, the merchant marine has not been completely ignored by historians of modern Germany. There are a small number of high-quality publications devoted to the subject. For example, the essays collected in the volume entitled *Übersee* and edited by Volker Plagemann are an important resource.[24] More recently, the *Imperator* has featured in Bernhard Rieger's study of the relationship between technology, politics, and culture in modern Germany.[25] Albert Ballin has also attracted the attention of scholars working on German history.[26] And yet, as previously noted, the exigencies of this history have determined the focus of much research such that the merchant marine is not a priority. Furthermore, the writing of Germany's history is indicative of a general phenomenon in historiography: ocean-going steamships feature much less in the composition of national histories than do railways, as the latter are more amenable to history conceived nationally.

It is true that historians of modern Germany "have clung to the internalist paradigm more stubbornly than elsewhere."[27] But many are turning from national to transnational paradigms and perspectives. There is also an ever-increasing amount of scholarship analysing Germany's role in the so-called first wave of globalization that occurred in the decades following 1850. Yet even as perspectives and paradigms change, the fact that the ocean-going steamship was the epoch-making means of communication remains largely ignored by all except scholars specifically concerned with maritime history.[28] The latter are keenly aware of the vital contribution made by the shipping industry to the development of the global economy and international integration prior to the First World War.[29] Yet they lament the fact that even "in the literature on global connectedness, or globalization, the industry that, more than any other, has made this possible is usually invisible."[30]

What, then, does the study of the merchant marine and transatlantic passenger shipping have to tell historians of modern Germany? Broadly speaking, it reveals much about the nature of the German Empire in both its national and international dimensions. The development of a merchant fleet, driven by capitalist innovation, was a major feature of German modernization. Studying its history can only complement our knowledge of the dynamic processes of industrial, economic, and technological change that played a significant role in shaping modern Germany. Moreover, as with industrial architecture, the construction of Germany's largest passenger liners was an undertaking in which the economic, political, and cultural spheres came into direct contact "extending beyond the exchange of ideas to collaboration on a practical level."[31] Consequently, transatlantic passenger liners offer concise, but nonetheless complex case studies of the tangible impact of modernization and modernity on German society.

Furthermore, ocean-going shipping is fundamentally an international and transnational phenomenon. As I have indicated, it has become more common for historians of Germany to adopt and expand upon ongoing research concerning global economic development, colonialism, the history of international migration, and the phenomenon of transnational cultural exchange. Much of this is driven by a desire to understand the several ways in which the German Empire was embedded in the world beyond and apart from the diplomatic and military spheres. At the same time, historians are becoming increasingly attuned to the fact that, over the past two centuries, Germans "have had a particularly lively imagination of the world beyond the nation."[32] As Michael Geyer explains, cross-border projections shaped "the national project right into the everyday habitus, mentality and world pictures of ordinary Germans."[33]

If anything, merchant and passenger shipping bears witness to the extent to which Imperial Germany participated in the various processes of globalization prior to 1914. The Hamburg–New York service for which HAPAG commissioned the *Imperator*-class liners was only one of many routes plied by the vessels of several German shipping companies around the globe. One of the themes repeatedly touched upon in media representation of HAPAG's liners on both sides of the Atlantic was their importance as agents that facilitated connections between continents and peoples. And it must not be forgotten that these vessels were hybrids of international and transnational competition, exchange, and cooperation in business, trade, technology, and culture. They were the products of business decisions informed by global dynamics and were a response to the imperatives of international migration, travel, and trade; their physical structures and technology were shaped by foreign innovation and experience; and their interiors were designed and constructed by international teams of architects and firms. Furthermore, international associations and treaties regulated their construction and operation. In sum, the *Imperator*-class liners offer a concise study of the ways in which the German Empire was embedded in the world.

Yet HAPAG's giant new steamships also played a revealing role in the nation's political and cultural life. That is the particular focus of this book. As such, its principal concern is not with the construction and physical form of these vessels. Instead, the following chapters concentrate on the manner in which the *Imperator*-class liners were pictured in a variety of media; their focus is on the representation, or cultural construction of these steamships and their role as popular signs and symbols that spoke to Germans about the nature, achievements, and ambitions of their nation. The symbolic dimensions of nationhood play an important role in objectifying a nation's identity; they raise collective consciousness, reinforce awareness of the nation, and affirm national values. And, of course, the nation is symbolized and narrated in a variety of forms including history, literature, the visual arts, and music.[34] Monuments to national heroes and events of national significance constitute particularly powerful representations of the nation. This book looks beyond the customary and expected repertoire of national symbols and monuments to present and analyse the manner in which transatlantic passenger steamships functioned in this capacity.

An important recent contribution to scholarship on the Imperial Navy has provided a productive inspiration for this study. In addition to its military, political, and strategic importance, Jan Rüger has demonstrated that the German battle fleet was a powerful cultural symbol. As part of the rapid expansion of public life in the 1890s, German naval rituals became a form of public theatre for domestic and foreign consumption. Furthermore, with the mass circulation of information and images in the popular press, and a growing market for entertainment and consumer goods, the German navy was turned into a commodity; a whole range of products – including tobacco, children's games, and clothing – linked naval themes with consumer desires. In this manner, the Imperial Navy provided important material for strengthening collective identity at home and for projecting an image of the newly founded Empire abroad.[35]

This book demonstrates why and how the same must be said of Germany's largest, and most luxurious transatlantic passenger liners. The *Imperator*, *Vaterland*, and *Bismarck* were highly visible, widely discussed entities in Germany's popular culture. In 1907, on the sixtieth anniversary of its founding, HAPAG described itself not only as a symbol of the German Empire but as a national institution whose interests and successes were intimately bound up with those of the entire nation. It also claimed that its fleet and the global reach of its enterprise had attracted extensive popular interest. By then the world's largest shipping company, HAPAG proudly announced that it was the subject of "innumerable essays and articles in newspapers, journals, textbooks, and literature."[36] A perusal of Germany's popular print media from the period reveals this was indeed the case: HAPAG, and its premier transatlantic liners, were presented to Germans in a wide variety of text and image.

Reports on the construction, outfitting, interior design, launch, sea trials, maiden voyages, and seemingly all events of any significance related to the *Imperator*-class liners appeared in several organs of the German press. The trio also featured in popular and professional journals and literature; on a range of merchandise such as calendars, postcards, travel guides, and diaries; and in an array of sophisticated advertising and public-relations material. The ceremonies that marked their launch were large, lavish, carefully planned public spectacles intended not only for a national but an international audience. Indeed, the success of HAPAG's vessels "was determined to a great extent by early public-relations men."[37] In an era that saw the rapid expansion of the mass media, popular entertainment, and consumerism, it might be said that the attention afforded the *Imperator*-class liners was a manifestation of the cult of media celebrity that appeared on both sides of the Atlantic.

Close textual and visual analysis of the various forms in which the *Imperator*-class liners appeared reveals a striking fact: that they were often and explicitly construed, pictured, and presented to the German public as national monuments. And many Germans responded to them as such and in ways that reveal the complicated and contested nature of German national identity at the time. Numerous national monuments were erected following the Empire's founding in 1871 through to the outbreak of the First World War. Mostly works of architecture, statuary, and images painted on the walls of public buildings, they have attracted serious scholarly attention for approximately fifty years.[38] Some studies range widely over time and type, while others focus on specific monuments.[39] And much of this research has been guided by an interest in the construction and contestation of German national identity prior to 1914. What this book argues is that the *Imperator*-class liners must be included in the canon of Germany's national monuments.

To be sure, the claim that Germans were proud of the *Imperator* as emblematic of their nation's ambitions and achievements is not new.[40] But it is an assertion most often made as an unsubstantiated claim – a fact to be taken for granted – in publications treating social and political context in an impressionistic manner. Furthermore, the paintings, posters, photographs, newspaper articles, and advertising material reproduced in popular literature on transatlantic liners are most often employed as illustrations; they are not analysed as meaningful artefacts of cultural, political, and social history in their own right.

In contrast, this book adopts an empirical approach to closely read, and carefully analyse the manner in which HAPAG's vessels were allegorized as national monuments and how they were presented as material for collective identification. In addition, the events in which they took centre stage – most importantly, the ceremonies that accompanied their launch – are reconstructed and analysed to clearly demonstrate how they functioned as platforms for symbolic nation building designed for a national audience. As a result, a precise picture emerges of how the *Imperator*-class liners featured as part of the "optical characteristics" of Imperial Germany, how they achieved their status as national monuments, and how they became one of several cultural phenomena informing day-to-day interpretations of national identity.[41]

We are not left, however, only with words and images circulating in a sphere of representation detached from social experience. There are several cases in which we know the identity of the journalists, commentators, writers, and artists who composed the texts and produced the images examined in the subsequent pages. Some of these people were prominent figures in Imperial German culture – influential individuals who have been the subject of scholarly study in their own right. Whether they admired or disliked the *Imperator*-class liners in their role as national symbols, the social and cultural experience of many commentators can be assembled and connected to their opinions. Furthermore, some of the events in the careers of these vessels can be reconstructed from a variety of sources such that we encounter people not just writing about the liners but acting around and aboard them.

Proceeding in this manner what we find is complexity. Of course, national symbols are not arbitrary; they are formed in line with the culture of their community. But they do not impose static meaning. Nor do they create unity or cohesion, as people do not share the same experience or understanding of their community. Instead, they provide a means by which meaning is created, meaning that is diverse, complex, and ambiguous.[42] As with any symbol, the *Imperator*, *Vaterland*, and *Bismarck* were neither monolithic nor univocal.

Vessels of steel, they were also symbolic vessels bearing a variety of meanings. When construed as national monuments, a range of different interpretations were projected onto them from a variety of perspectives and by commentators representing divergent political, social, and cultural positions. What this book emphasizes is that transatlantic passenger shipping played a more important role in the discourses of German national identity than previously understood. Studying this role contributes to a sophisticated picture of how Germans created and contested an understanding of their nation through and around the issues of technology, art, and design.[43] More generally, it reinforces the fact that national cultures "are not clear-cut or unified phenomena; they are dynamic systems, fields of conflict, contestation, and struggle."[44]

But of course, transatlantic liners were intended to travel beyond national borders and connect nations. Apart from promoting reflection upon the achievements and ambitions of the German Empire, the publicity and media coverage surrounding many liners played a role in making Germans cognizant of the world beyond their nation's borders. Furthermore, as vehicles of transatlantic communication, the symbolic working of the *Imperator*-class liners was not confined to a single national culture. Along with other ocean-going vessels, they were interpreted on both sides of the Atlantic as emblematic of increasing international cooperation and exchange; of the technological sophistication of the Western world and the progress of its civilization; of societies increasingly shaped by consumerism; and of class inequality.[45] Building its particular portrait of the *Imperator*, *Vaterland*, and *Bismarck* as national monuments, this book also points to the range of symbolic functions they fulfilled and emphasizes the truly complex nature of their symbolic working.

In so doing, the final chapters look beyond Germany's borders and across the Atlantic. There is considerable interest in cultural exchange between Germany, Britain, and America prior to the First World War.[46] In fact, the Atlantic world is now studied as an interconnected "transcultural space" with cross-cultural borrowing in both directions.[47] A particular subject of interest is Anglo-American perceptions of the German Empire and the print media's important role in informing the way Britons and Americans thought about Germany.[48] The connection between these nations "was often based on imagination" and there was a host of circulating literary and visual constructions of the "other." These promoted "an ongoing understanding, if not knowledge" of those on the opposite side of the North Sea and the Atlantic Ocean.[49]

Yet absent from the study of transatlantic cultural exchange and perception is serious consideration of how the means of transportation that facilitated communication between the continents featured, in their own right, as part of the phenomenon. Even before they set sail on their maiden voyages, the construction and commissioning of the *Imperator*-class liners was followed with considerable interest in the popular and professional press in Britain and America: they were extensively, and often enthusiastically reported on in newspapers; analysed in trade publications and popular journals; and written about in books on travel, maritime history, and new developments in passenger shipping. Tens of thousands of people turned out in Southampton and New York to greet their arrival and go aboard them to inspect their fittings and interiors, especially on the occasion of their maiden voyages. This meant that, chiefly in the United States, many German liners were better known than in Germany.[50]

Writing in 1913, Albert Ballin expressed the opinion that "in foreign ports nothing more impressively represents a nation, nothing more conspicuously represents its trade and industry, than a highly developed merchant fleet."[51] An examination of the English and American print media proves the truth of this statement. Construed as national symbols in Germany, the *Imperator*-class liners also communicated to the world beyond the nation's borders in a manner similar to the manufactured goods, and delegations to international exhibitions, that carried an influential image of the Empire abroad. These vessels were meaningful objectifications of Germany that, as this book demonstrates, provided not only Germans, but also Britons and Americans with important reference points – in physical reality, and in text and image – for picturing, imagining, and understanding the German Empire.

To be sure, just as in Germany, close analysis reveals that the *Imperator*, *Vaterland*, and *Bismarck* functioned as complex symbols. They constituted only one facet of the amalgam of multiple images of Germany that the American and English press offered its readers.[52] In both countries, the representation of HAPAG's liners occurred in the context of a host of articles treating political, social, economic, and cultural news from, and about the Empire. Nonetheless, analysing the way in which these vessels were pictured in the English and American media highlights the complexity of Anglo–German and American–German relations in an atmosphere of increasing nationalism and internationalization. It also pinpoints particular ways in which English and American commentators imagined their identity in comparison with, and in opposition to, the Germany they saw embodied and symbolized in the *Imperator*-class liners. Finally, in as much as the representation of foreign nations in various media fostered the growth of global consciousness in the Atlantic world prior to 1914, chapters five and six offer a concise study of this phenomenon.

Of course, the history of HAPAG cannot be written without, in large measure, writing that of the Norddeutscher Lloyd AG (NDL), its principal German counterpart. Founded in Bremen by Hermann Heinrich Meier in 1857, NDL operated a global network of shipping services. The two companies engaged in collaboration and competition from their early days and, by 1914, HAPAG possessed the world's largest fleet and NDL its third largest. These giant concerns merged in 1970 to form the premier German shipping company Hapag-Lloyd AG based in Hamburg and Bremen. Consequently, NDL appears frequently in the following chapters, and especially the first, not only as a necessary component of HAPAG's history, but also to provide essential context and a point of comparison and contrast. Its liners also caught the attention of Germans, Britons, and Americans and played a role in representing Germany to the Atlantic world. Several NDL vessels, including the *Kaiser Wilhelm der Große* which was christened by the Emperor in May 1897, received an enthusiastic reception in the United States. And in some cases, the company responded more readily than HAPAG to progressive contemporary trends when it came to the interior design of its premier passenger liners. This was the case, for example, with the *George Washington*, which was launched in 1908 and to which we will return in chapter four.

Yet by 1914, NDL was losing rank on the North Atlantic, especially in the cabin-class passenger trade. It was being rapidly outclassed by HAPAG, Cunard, and White Star in respect to the competitiveness of its steamers, and it was to the liners of these companies that the Atlantic world turned its attention. The financial difficulties that NDL suffered, especially from 1908, meant that it was not in a position to build two liners of just over 30,000 tons each until 1913. These were not completed until after the First World War and, in terms of their technology, size, and design, were "the end of the past, whereas the giant HAPAG trio were the development of the future."[53] The *Imperator* was more than twice the size of the largest vessel commissioned by NDL. Consequently, in the years covered by this book – 1910–1914 – it was the *Imperator*-class liners that attracted the greatest amount of popular attention at home and abroad.

–

The first and second chapters provide necessary historical context. Chapter one presents a concise history of HAPAG until the time of the *Imperator*'s launch. The trio of liners was but one component of the company's transatlantic services that were themselves one division of a transportation enterprise operating around the globe by 1914. Furthermore, HAPAG was only one shipping line among several that constituted Germany's merchant marine. The company's history is narrated in terms of the social, political, economic, and cultural contexts in which it unfolded at the national and international levels. Thus, however succinctly, the first chapter connects HAPAG's evolution to the historical phenomena that influenced its growth and in which it played a meaningful role. These include the international revolution in communications and transportation that characterized the second half of the nineteenth century; the economic and industrial development of the German Empire and its increasing engagement in a global economy; the phenomenon of transatlantic emigration; and the history of German colonialism. The chapter also critically examines the influence of HAPAG's managing director, Albert Ballin, in shaping the direction and expansion of the company from the 1890s.

In so doing, chapter one makes a start at bringing the history of HAPAG together with topics and themes currently pursued by scholars who are expanding the study of modern German history beyond long-standing foci and concerns. The principal purpose of the chapter is to stress the international and transnational orientation of HAPAG and the German Empire. As Michael Geyer explains, the common perception is that Germany "reached into the world as an exceptionally violent force."[54] And yet a significant contemporary trend in scholarship seeks to demonstrate the various ways in which Imperial Germany engaged constructively with the world. The history of HAPAG is an outstanding illustration of this reality. At home, and especially in the United States, the *Imperator*-class liners were interpreted as embodiments of Germany's positive engagement with the world beyond its borders.

Chapter two provides a portrait of the *Imperator* and a precise account of its career. In fact, much of the book is devoted to the *Imperator*. As the first of the trio to be launched, and with the longest service history prior to August 1914, it was the liner that received the greatest amount of attention in Germany and abroad. The *Vaterland* completed only three round trips to New York before the outbreak of war. The *Bismarck* was launched but lay unfinished in Hamburg until the end of hostilities. Physically speaking, while not identical, the three liners were sufficiently similar to allow the general characteristics of the class to be described through a focus on the *Imperator*. While emphasizing important differences in the design and outfitting of the vessels, along with variance in their representation in Germany and the Atlantic world, a focus on the *Imperator* avoids much unnecessary repetition. It also allows for a concise, but detailed and in-depth case study solidly grounded in a wealth of previously unconsidered historical sources.

In particular, chapter two examines the circumstances informing the decision to build the *Imperator*; investigates divisions within HAPAG about the wisdom of doing so; explores how the vessel came to be christened as it was; provides essential details about its construction and service history; and offers an assessment of its success as a transatlantic liner and business venture. A thorough description of the *Imperator* is drawn not from secondary literature but from company advertising published in German and English. The focus is on understanding what contemporaries could have known about the vessel based on how it was marketed and represented to them.

A proudly German firm, HAPAG branded itself as a genuinely international corporation and, in keeping with this, the chapter also emphasizes that the *Imperator*'s purpose and symbolism was transnational. It was allegorized in a variety of ways in the Atlantic world, ways that informed and fused with its construction and reception as a national monument. In particular, the chapter analyses how the liner was pictured as emblematic of the technological sophistication of the Western world and the progress of its civilization. It also scrutinizes its promotion as a luxury item – an experience to be "consumed" – by early-twentieth-century societies animated by the dream, and shaped by the reality of increased prosperity and leisure. It does this, however, while emphasizing a fact that deserves more consideration in writing about the *Imperator*: that it was intended not only to carry the wealthiest patrons in first-class cabins and suites, but also to transport people of all social classes including the poorest European emigrants in steerage. Sources from the period allow a glimpse into the experience of all social groups as they travelled aboard the liner.

Chapters three and four scrutinize the ways in which the *Imperator*, *Vaterland*, and *Bismarck* were construed, considered, and contested as national monuments in Germany. The third chapter analyses the form and content of a variety of texts and images principally from the popular print media through which the majority of Germans encountered the liners. It examines various tropes, analogies, metaphors, compositional strategies, and forms of imagery employed to present them as emblematic of the characteristics and achievements of the German Empire. It also reconstructs the most concentrated and elaborate presentation of all three liners as national monuments: the ceremonies that accompanied their launch. In particular, the chapter closely analyses the most recoverable, and one of the most significant aspects of these ceremonies: the speeches that marked the christening of the vessels. What these reveal, and what the chapter emphasizes throughout, is the complex, multi-faceted nature of HAPAG's liners as national monuments. A variety of meanings were projected onto what became sites of competing interpretations of Germany. More than that, the liners' very authority as national monuments was contested. This is distinctly revealed by the way in which the *Imperator* was received by organs of the Social Democratic press and among the working-classes in general.

Chapter four both expands and focuses the image of HAPAG's vessels as contested national monuments. It turns to another way in which German commentators pictured and perceived them: as ambassadors to the Atlantic world and especially America. In particular, the chapter examines the *Imperator*'s first-class interiors as sites where the nation's commercial, cultural, and political spheres came into direct contact over and through the subject of art and design. There are numerous publications treating the social, political, and cultural dynamics of the German Empire through the medium of its fine and applied arts.[55] But there is little discussion of passenger steamships as works of architecture and design from the perspective, and in the context of Germany's dynamic cultural politics.

The chapter analyses how and why the *Imperator* attracted the attention of prominent figures including the architect and designer Bruno Paul; the art historian and critic Karl Scheffler; the architect Fritz Schumacher; and the pioneering art and cultural historian Aby Warburg. These individuals are well known to historians, but their interest in the *Imperator* is not. In fact, Warburg was hired by HAPAG to provide advice on the pictorial decoration of the vessel's first-class interiors. What this chapter explores is why these artists and intellectuals opposed a current of popular enthusiasm to mount serious criticisms of the *Imperator* as a floating ambassador of Germany. In contrast to the interior decoration of the liner as conceived and executed by HAPAG, all pictured or imagined the way in which its first-class public spaces should be designed and decorated if it was to present their image of Germany to the transatlantic world: that is, not that of an Old-World realm characterized by its aristocracy and imperial monarchy, but the image of a modern, progressive society and economy shaped by an industrious, forward-thinking middle class.

Ultimately, chapter four both enriches our understanding of the *Imperator*'s symbolic function and reveals a dimension to Wilhelmine movements for social and cultural reform that has not been explored.

As a result, the following question arises: how were the *Imperator*-class liners actually received, pictured, and written about in Britain and America? This is what chapters five and six investigate through written and visual depictions of the vessels in various media, especially the popular press. What becomes immediately clear is that all three liners were widely received and discussed as floating monuments to the achievements and ambitions of Germany. Chapter five analyses the nature of English interest in HAPAG's vessels with reference to several phenomena: the challenge posed to British military might by the building of a German navy; the importance of merchant and passenger shipping in the construction of British national identity; and the way in which the German merchant marine, and HAPAG in particular, was seen to encroach upon Britain's international power and prestige. What we find is that English responses to the *Imperator*-class liners were mixed: along with anxiety, criticism, and occasional expressions of nationalist pugnacity went genuine admiration for the vessels as well as for what Germany had achieved in shipbuilding, engineering, industry, and technology.

Of course, Anglo–German relations and rivalry in the years before 1914 have traditionally and correctly been seen by historians in diplomatic, strategic, and economic terms. But chapter five emphasizes that there is much to be learned about English perceptions of the German Empire by directing attention to the role played by merchant and passenger shipping in these relations and this rivalry. More specifically, by placing reporting on the *Imperator, Vaterland*, and *Bismarck* within the broader context of press coverage of Germany, the chapter supplements recent scholarship on Anglo–German relations. This has sought to nuance a long-standing concentration on rivalry with an emphasis on the various economic, social, and cultural points of contact that informed relations between the two nations.

Chapter six examines media coverage of the *Imperator* and its sisters in the United States. Once again, by placing press coverage of the vessels within the broader context of media interest in various aspects of Imperial Germany, the chapter emphasizes the complex, multi-faceted image of the Empire that was presented to Americans. But it also draws a comparison between the way in which the English and American press pictured HAPAG's liners. What we find is that, in contrast to much of what was said in Britain, American representations were less coloured by anxiety about Germany's status as an expanding maritime, naval, and world power. Instead, with their enthusiastic interest in German innovation, American journalists were more prepared to celebrate the *Imperator, Vaterland*, and *Bismarck* as the peaceful products of an ambitious, progressive, modern nation shaped by an enterprising, forward-thinking middle-class – in other words, a nation much like their own. In conjunction with chapter five, this chapter emphasizes that, in addition to their role as national monuments at home, HAPAG's vessels also served as influential German ambassadors to the Atlantic world. Both chapters also highlight some of the significant ways in which Germany participated in the processes of economic, social, and cultural globalization prior to 1914.

Douglas R. Burgess points to an important reason why transatlantic passenger liners have received little consideration as national monuments: few if any physical traces of them survive.[56] This is especially the case with those launched by the German Empire. Clearly, their remains do not ornament Germany's cities nor mark its landscape as many other time-worn statues and structures still do. The service life of most liners was approximately a generation: the *Imperator*, *Vaterland*, and *Bismarck* were all sold for scrap by 1940. And yet they have left a large amount of ephemera in their wake that has, ironically, outlasted these steel giants. This volume of paper reveals the extent to which HAPAG's passenger steamships featured in the popular culture of the German Empire, achieved the stature of national monuments, and served to carry and project an image of Germany to the Atlantic world. The *Imperator*-class liners were transformed into signs as complex and more powerful than the steel vessels they signified. Analysing how they were pictured in a variety of media reaching beyond borders and across the Atlantic reminds us of the composite nature of signs and their complicated and contested workings. It also accentuates the complex and myriad ways in which national identity is constructed, represented, interpreted, and contested in a national and international context.

Notes

1   See the opinions of Gorch Fock in Jörgen Bracker, "Dampfer Imperator; das reisige Friedenschiff', in Volker Plagemann, ed., *Industriekultur in Hamburg: des Deutschen Reiches Tor zur Welt* (Munich, 1984), 64.
2   Max Leser, "Ausklang", in HAPAG, *Imperator Auf See: Gedenkblätter an die erste Ausfahrt des Dampfers am 11. Juni 1913* (Hamburg, 1913), u.p.
3   Hugo Freiherr von Freytag-Loringhoven quoted in Lamar Cecil, *Albert Ballin: Business and Politics in Imperial Germany, 1888–1918* (Princeton, NJ, 1967), 110.
4   "Der Stapellauf des Imperator", *Hamburger Nachrichten*, 23 May 1912.
5   "Zum Stapellauf des 'Imperator'", *Hamburger Echo*, 23 May 1912.
6   Technical data on passenger liners commissioned during this period often varies from publication to publication. The figures provided here are those released by HAPAG at the time of the *Imperator*'s maiden voyage.
7   See for example J. Kent Layton, *The Edwardian Superliners: A Trio of Trios* (Stroud, 2013); Philip Dawson, *The Liner: Retrospective and Renaissance* (New York and London, 2005); Douglas R. Burgess, *Seize the Trident: The Race for Superliner Supremacy and How It Altered the Great War* (New York, 2005); Arnold Kludas, *Die Geschichte der deutschen Passagierschiffahrt* (Hamburg, 1988), vol. 3; John Maxtone-Graham, *The Only Way to Cross* (New York, 1972); John Malcolm Brinnin, *The Sway of the Grand Saloon* (London, 1971).
8   See note 7 and the following: Nils Schwerdtner, *German Luxury Ocean Liners. From Kaiser Wilhelm der Grosse to AIDAstella* (Stroud, 2011); Christine Reinke-Kunze, *Die Geschichte der Reichs-Post-Dampfer* (Herford, 1994); Eberhard Mertens, *Die HAPAG-Riesen der Imperator-klasse* (Hildesheim and New York, 1974); Frank O. Braynard, *Leviathan: The Story of the World's Greatest Ship* (5 vols.) (New York, 1972–1981).

9 Layton, *The Edwardian Superliners*, 9.
10 Peter Zerbe, *Die Grossen Deutschen Passagierschiffe: Imperator, Vaterland, Bismarck* (Hamburg, 1999).
11 See for example Burgess, *Seize the Trident* and Douglas R. Burgess, *Engines of Empire. Steamships and the Victorian Imagination* (Stanford, CA, 2016).
12 On German shipping lines, see for example Reinhold Thiel, *Die Geschichte des Norddeutschen Lloyd 1857–1970 in fünf Bänden* (Bremen, 2007); Susanne Wiborg and Klaus Wiborg, *1847–1997:Unser Feld ist die Welt* (Hamburg, 1997).
13 See for example Peter-Franz Stubmann, *Mein Feld ist die Welt. Albert Ballin. Sein Leben* (Hamburg, 1960); Susanne Wiborg, *Albert Ballin* (Hamburg, 2000); Eberhard Straub, *Albert Ballin. Der Reeder des Kaisers* (Berlin, 2001).
14 See for example Matthias L. Trennheuser, *Die innenarchitektonische Ausstattung deutscher Passagierschiffe zwischen 1880 und 1940* (Bremen, 2011); Philip Dawson and Bruce Peter, *Ship Style: Modernism and Modernity at Sea in the 20th Century* (London, 2010); Anne Wealleans, *Designing Liners. A History of Interior Design Afloat* (London, 2006).
15 Brinnin, *The Sway*; Dawson, *The Liner*; Maxtone-Graham, *The Only Way*; John Maxtone-Graham, *Liners to the Sun*, 2nd edn. (Dobbs Ferry, NY, 2000); Arnold Kludas, *Die Geschichte der deutschen Passagierschiffahrt* (5 vols.) (Hamburg, 1986–1990). An exception is Stephen Fox, *Transatlantic: Samuel Cunard, Isambard Brunel, and the Great Atlantic Steamships* (New York, 2003).
16 Kludas, *Die Geschichte der deutschen Passagierschiffahrt*. Much of this is recapitulated in English in Schwerdtner, *German Luxury Ocean Liners*.
17 See for example, Frank Broeze, "Albert Ballin, the Hamburg-Bremen Rivalry and the Dynamics of the Conference System", *International Journal of Maritime History* 3 (1991), 1–32; Frank Broeze, "Albert Ballin, The Hamburg-American Line and Hamburg: Structure and Strategy in the German Shipping Industry (1886–1914)", *Deutsches Schiffahrtsarchiv* 15 (1992), 135–58; Frank Broeze, "Shipping Policy and Social Darwinism: Albert Ballin and the *Weltpolitik* of the Hamburg-America Line 1886–1914", *The Mariner's Mirror* 79 (1993), 419–36.
18 See for example Bernhard Klein and Gesa Mackethun, eds., *Sea Changes: Historicizing the Ocean* (New York, 2004).
19 See for example Leon Fink, *Sweatshops at Sea. Merchant Seamen in the World's First Globalized Industry, from 1812 to the present* (Chapel Hill, NC, 2011); Dagmar Bellmann, *Von Höllengefährten zu schwimmenden Palästen. Die Passagierschiffahrt auf dem Atlantik (1840–1930)* (Frankfurt and New York, 2015).
20 Bellmann, *Von Höllengefährten*, 19f.
21 Exceptions include Bernhard Rieger, *Technology and the Culture of Modernity in Britain and Germany, 1890–1945* (Cambridge, 2005); Niall Ferguson, *Paper and Iron: Hamburg Business and German Politics in the Era of Inflation, 1897–1927* (Cambridge, 1995); Volker Plagemann, ed., *Übersee: Seefahrt und Seemacht im deutschen Kaiserreich* (Munich, 1988); Cecil, *Albert Ballin*.
22 Christian Gauss, *The German Kaiser as Shown in His Public Utterances* (New York, 1915), 181.
23 There is a large amount of literature on the Imperial Navy. A recent bibliography can be found in Jan Rüger, "The Navy and the Sea", in Matthew Jefferies, ed., *The Ashgate Research Companion to Imperial Germany* (Farnham, 2015), 399–412.
24 See note 21.
25 Rieger, *Technology*.
26 Cecil, *Albert Ballin*; Gerhard A. Ritter, "The Kaiser and His Ship-Owner: Albert Ballin, the HAPAG Shipping Company, and the Relationship between Industry and Politics in Imperial Germany and the Early Weimar Republic", in Hartmut Berghoff, Jürgen Kocka, and Dieter Ziegler, eds., *Business in the Age of Extremes: Essays in*

Modern German and Austrian Economic History (Washington, D.C. and Cambridge, 2013), 15–39; Gerhard A. Ritter, "Der Kaiser und sein Reeder", *Zeitschrift für Unternehmensgeschichte* 42 (1997), 137–62.

27 Sebastian Conrad, "Wilhelmine Nationalism in Global Contexts. Mobility, Race, and Global Consciousness", in Sven Oliver Müller and Cornelius Torp, eds., *Imperial Germany Revisited: Continuing Debates and New Perspectives* (New York and Oxford, 2011), 282. Maritime historians have also been criticized for a limited focus on national maritime histories; see Lewis R. Fischer, "Are We in Danger of Being Left with Our Journals and Not Much Else: The Future of Maritime History", *The Mariner's Mirror* 91 (2011), 366–81.

28 But see Michael B. Miller, *Europe and the Maritime World: A Twentieth Century History* (Cambridge, 2012).

29 This is the argument made in Gelina Harlaftis, Stig Tenold, and Jesús M. Valdaliso, eds., *The World's Key Industry: History and Economics of International Shipping* (Houndmills and New York, 2012).

30 Gelina Harlaftis, Stig Tenold, and Jesús M. Valdaliso, "Introduction", in Harlaftis, Tenold, and Valdaliso, eds., *The World's Key Industry*, 2.

31 Matthew Jefferies, *Politics and Culture in Wilhelmine Germany: The Case of Industrial Architecture* (Oxford and Washington, D.C., 1995), 6.

32 Michael Geyer, "Where Germans Dwell: Transnationalism in Theory and Practice", *German Studies Association Newsletter* 31 (2006), 32.

33 Geyer, "Where Germans Dwell", 32.

34 See Stefan Berger, Linas Eriksonas, and Andrew Mycock, eds., *Narrating the Nation: Representations in History, Media and the Arts* (New York and Oxford, 2008).

35 Jan Rüger, *The Great Naval Game: Britain and Germany in the Age of Empire* (Cambridge, 2007).

36 HAPAG, *Die Hamburg-Amerika Linie: Im Sechsten Jahrzehnt Ihrer Entwicklung 1897–1907* (Berlin, 1907), 11.

37 William H. Miller, *The First Great Ocean Liners in Photographs* (New York, 1984), 9.

38 For a foundational study, see Thomas Nipperdey, "Nationalidee und Nationaldenkmal in Deutschland im 19. Jahrhundert", *Historische Zeitschrift* 206 (1968), 529–85.

39 These are too numerous to list here; for a bibliography, see Hans A. Pohlsander, *National Monuments and Nationalism in 19th Century Germany* (Oxford, 2008).

40 See for example Walter Kresse, "Jeder Hamburger, nein jeder Deutsche ist stolz auf die Hamburg-Amerika-Linie", in Plagemann, ed., *Industriekultur*, 69–71.

41 I have borrowed the term "optical characteristics" from Rudy Koshar, *From Monuments to Traces. Artifacts of German Memory, 1870–1990* (Berkeley, CA, 2000), 75.

42 See for example Anthony P. Cohen, *The Symbolic Construction of Community* (Abingdon: Routledge, 1985).

43 See Rieger, *Technology*.

44 Paul Michael Lützeler and Graduate Students, "The St. Louis World's Fair of 1904 as a Site of Cultural Transfer: German and German-American Participation", in Lynne Tatlock and Matt Erlin, eds., *German Culture in Nineteenth-Century America. Reception, Adaptation, Transformation* (Rochester, NY, 2005), 59.

45 See Burgess, *Engines*.

46 More recent studies include Richard Scully, *British Images of Germany: Admiration, Antagonism and Ambivalence, 1860–1914* (Houndmills, 2012); Dominik Geppert and Robert Gerwarth, eds., *Wilhelmine Germany and Edwardian Britain: Essays on Cultural Affinity* (Oxford, 2008); Frank Trommler and Elliot Shore, eds., *The German-American Encounter: Conflict and Cooperation between Two Cultures, 1800–2000* (New York and Oxford, 2001); Thomas Adam and Ruth Gross, eds., *Traveling between Worlds: German-American Encounters* (College Station, TX, 2006); David

E. Barclay and Elisabeth Glaser-Schmidt, eds., *Transatlantic Images and Percep-tions: Germany and America Since 1776* (New York and Cambridge, 1997); Alexan-der Schmidt, *Reisen in die Moderne. Der Amerika-Diskurs des deutschen Bürgertums vor dem Ersten Weltkrieg im europäischen Vergleich* (Berlin, 1997).

47 See Adam and Gross, eds., *Traveling*.

48 See Martin Schramm, *Das Deutschlandbild in der britischen Presse 1912–1919* (Berlin, 2007); Geppert and Gerwarth, eds., *Wilhelmine Germany*.

49 Christof Mauch, "Oceans Apart? Paradigms in Geman-American History and Histor-iograpy", in Adam and Gross, eds., *Traveling*, 11; Christiane Harzig, "Gender, Trans-atlantic Space, and the Presence of German-Speaking People in North America", in Adam and Gross, eds., *Traveling,* 168.

50 Miller, *The First Great Ocean Liners*, 35.

51 Albert Ballin, "Der Triumph der deutschen Seeschiffahrt unter Wilhelm II", *Neue Hamburger Zeitung*, 11 June 1913.

52 On this point, see Schramm, *Das Deutschlandbild*.

53 Edwin Drechsel, *Norddeutscher Lloyd Bremen, 1857–1970: History-Fleet-Ship Mails* (2 vols.) (Vancouver, 1994–1995), 411.

54 Geyer, "Where Germans Dwell", 32.

55 These are too numerous to list here. An excellent overview of the cultural and artis-tic history of the German Empire, with bibliography, is Matthew Jefferies, *Imperial Culture in Germany, 1871–1918* (Houndmills, 2003).

56 Burgess, *Engines*, 293.

1 "My field is the world"

HAPAG, Hamburg, Germany, and the globe

I

Mein Feld ist die Welt. This was the motto HAPAG adopted at the height of its success under the leadership of Albert Ballin, managing director of the company from 1899 until his death in 1918. Passers-by read it over the main entrance to the company's headquarters in Hamburg; it appeared on advertising produced for the German, European, British, and North American public; was carved on sculptural reliefs adorning the interiors of HAPAG liners; and decorated the menus, passenger lists, and other ephemera presented to those who travelled aboard them. But this proud assertion – My Field is the World – found its most dramatic and pugnacious expression on the figurehead that dominated the *Imperator*'s prow. This was the two-ton, bronze figure of an eagle boasting a wing span of fifty-two feet. With head stretched out before it, beak open in a menacing cry, wings splayed and swept back, and heavily articulated feathers emphasizing a muscular form, it was the epitome of a predatory creature. On its head, the giant bird wore a small crown and, with its massive talons, grasped a comparatively small globe encircled by a banner bearing HAPAG's motto. Eighteen rays emanated from the globe which, along with the creature's massive wings, bound the ensemble to the *Imperator*'s stem. It is hardly surprising that this martial beast, designed by the Berlin sculptor Bernhard Kruse, provoked considerable commentary, both positive and negative, on both sides of the Atlantic.[1]

On the 150th anniversary of the company's founding, HAPAG looked back on the *Imperator*'s launch as the actual and symbolic highpoint of its history before 1914.[2] However its motto was received, few would challenge the fact that Germany's pre-eminent shipping line could legitimately make this claim when the liner departed on its maiden voyage to New York in 1913. By that time, HAPAG was one of the nation's greatest industrial enterprises and the largest shipping company in the world. It is best described as a "worldwide transport concern" offering an array of freight and passenger services to destinations around the globe.[3] A history published by the company in 1907 offers an impressive portrait. Its pages present the image of a pioneering, complex, highly organized, thoroughly modern, future-oriented, and incredibly

Figure 1.1 The *Imperator*'s figurehead.
Source: Bain Collection, The Library of Congress, Washington, D.C.

successful transportation and industrial enterprise of enormous dimensions and far-reaching influence. Moreover, HAPAG described itself as playing a major role in the economic and industrial development of Germany and the entire Atlantic world. The company also claimed that its endeavours constituted a significant share of the Empire's world-power status and it was proud of the fact that it opened Germany to the world, and the world to Germans. It is difficult not to be impressed by HAPAG's global reach after only fifty years of operation. A partial list of the destinations to which its vessels steamed in 1914 includes Halifax, Montreal, Baltimore, Boston, New York, New Orleans, Philadelphia, San Francisco, Mexico, Brazil, Argentina, Columbia, Venezuela, Togo, Djibouti, Aden, Calcutta, Singapore, Manila, Hong Kong, Shanghai, and Yokohama. The company also offered leisure cruises to northern Europe, around the Mediterranean, to the Near East, and to the West Indies.[4]

When launched in May 1912, the *Imperator* was christened with an address by Hamburg's mayor. Giving succinct expression to opinion published in the popular press, Johann Heinrich Burchard celebrated the liner as symbolic of HAPAG's history and successes; of the industriousness and prosperity of Hamburg, its home port; of German achievements in engineering, economics, culture, and even politics; and of Germany's commitment to international communication and exchange. The details of Burchard's address are closely analysed in chapter three. But the following pages take their prompt from Hamburg's mayor: they sketch the historical facts, circumstances, and developments that he felt the *Imperator* symbolized and embodied. In this way, the chapter provides necessary context for understanding the multi-faceted symbolic importance that the trio of liners assumed in Germany and the Atlantic world.

A concise account of HAPAG's history from its modest beginnings in 1847 through to the *Imperator*'s launch provides the chapter's framework. During the first fifty years of its existence, the company was primarily a North Atlantic shipping line. Nonetheless, the history of such a large enterprise is incredibly complex, as is the history of German merchant shipping in general.[5] It can also be abstruse for non-specialists when recounted from the perspective of business history, or seen through the complicated dynamics of HAPAG's relations with other domestic and foreign shipping lines. The following pages concentrate on essential facts and figures to highlight HAPAG's place and role in the development of Germany's merchant and passenger shipping on the Atlantic before 1914. The shipping industry made a vital contribution to the development of the global economy. In fact, "our world could not function without the complex system of maritime transport sustaining international and regional trade."[6] What the following pages emphasize is that HAPAG's evolution was part of, and helped propel the international revolution in transportation, communications, and information technologies that drove globalization. It also played a major role in creating an integrated world market in the decades from 1850 to 1914.

This chronological narrative is punctuated and enriched by an examination of the local, national, and international contexts in which HAPAG operated, and the structural forces that shaped its development. The chapter provides a concise portrait of the particular environment in which the company was founded and headquartered: the Free and Hanseatic City of Hamburg. It also offers an assessment of HAPAG's relationship with the German government to demonstrate how its growth and success was facilitated by the Empire and its ambition to become a major maritime power. In addition, the following pages provide a succinct introduction to the ways in which the company, in keeping with much of the enterprise of its home port, engaged with the world beyond Germany's borders and was shaped by global dynamics. The late nineteenth and early twentieth century was "an era of worldwide interaction and exchange."[7] The chapter emphasizes that HAPAG's passenger and cargo business was but one facet of a German economy increasingly oriented towards global markets and shaped by international commerce; situates the company's role in the phenomenon of transatlantic and global travel and migration; and highlights the stake that it had in Germany's colonial expansion after 1884. In so doing, emphasis is placed on the fact that, from the 1880s, the development of German society "must be interpreted in the context of the globalization processes" that were ongoing at the time.[8] German history unfolded in an international context and HAPAG was an organization that connected the local and the global. Along with much of Germany's merchant marine, it was at the leading edge of the nation's global engagement, a fact often overlooked in studies of this phenomenon.[9] Seeing HAPAG in all these interconnected contexts enriches an understanding of the numerous instances in which the *Imperator*, *Vaterland*, and *Bismarck* were construed as national monuments at home and abroad. It also highlights the extent to which they were positioned and able to function as such.

It has been said that the liners were Albert Ballin's *Geisteskinder*, or brainchildren.[10] At the very least, he was a major driving force behind their construction and played a significant role in their design. More importantly, during his lifetime and in the century since his death, journalists, biographers, and historians have often treated Ballin and HAPAG as virtually synonymous. In 1918, Hamburg's Social Democratic newspaper, the *Hamburger Echo*, declared that to write Ballin's biography was to write "the history of the *Hamburg-Amerika Linie* and German maritime imperialism."[11] As he was the subject of considerable press interest in Germany, Britain, and America, Ballin returns time and again in subsequent chapters. But in the pages that immediately follow, his role in developing HAPAG's strategy, and driving its dramatic growth from the 1890s, is sketched in terms of his overall motivations and goals. Was he a patriot who put the interests of Germany's merchant marine ahead of those of HAPAG, or a ruthless businessman who waged commercial warfare to the point of endangering the financial well-being of his own firm? Was he responsible for stoking international tensions in the years before the outbreak of the First World War, or did he recognize the danger of the Anglo-German antagonism and seek to mitigate it? These are the questions that continue to inform thinking about Ballin's life and work.

Finally, the chapter turns to the most important aspect of HAPAG's global enterprise: the services it offered to the United States and especially its passenger service to New York. While the company operated a complex network of services on the Atlantic, none were as literally and symbolically important as its trunk line to New York. This was what the *Imperator*-class liners were meant to serve and particular attention is paid to HAPAG's contribution to the development of the modern transatlantic liner. More importantly, the decision to construct a trio of giant new liners is set within the international competition, especially with Britain, to commission not the fastest, but the largest and most luxurious passenger steamers the world had yet seen.

II

The *Hamburg-Amerikanische Packetfahrt-Aktien-Gesellschaft* was founded on 27 May 1847 by a group of Hamburg ship owners and merchants boasting a capital of 300,000 marks.[12] Referring to the leather or linen packages in which the overseas mail was transported, "packet" was a synonym for post in English shipping terminology. It was also used to describe a vessel transporting mail between two ports at regular intervals. As governments generally entrusted mail to the most reliable carriers with the best quality vessels, the use of the term *Packetfahrt* (packet crossing) in the new company's title was intended as a clear indicator that it was worthy of the public's trust.

HAPAG was created in response to increased demand for a fast and reliable service between Germany and the United States in the context of growing transatlantic trade and emigration. Before the middle of the eighteenth century, Hamburg's trade focused on the North Sea and the Baltic. After that time, it began to take on global dimensions. As the colonial ties of European powers weakened and were disrupted, the city forged important trading and investment ties with Britain and the United States. Nearly 500 ships were sailing under the Hamburg flag by the 1850s, many conducting business in the West Indies and South America. Julius von Eckhardt, a member of Hamburg's Senate in the 1870s, recalled that there were "dozens of older gentlemen" in the city who knew "every town on the Mississippi" and had been "twenty times in London" but had never visited Berlin.[13]

HAPAG's founding assured Hamburg a larger share in the expanding North American market. In particular, the company's intention was to build, buy, or charter sailing vessels for a passenger and freight service to New York. Until its creation, legislation passed by Hamburg's government and designed to control the potential disease and disorder that came with emigrants passing through its port meant that Bremen took the lead in the human component of Germany's transatlantic shipping. HAPAG came into being after Hamburg relaxed its regulations on emigrant traffic and the new enterprise quickly introduced a regularity and organization previously lacking in the city's shipping industry.

The first vessel it commissioned was the *Deutschland*, a Hamburg-built, wooden sailing ship of 538 tons.[14] Launched in 1848, and joined that same year by the *Nord-Amerika*, *Rhein*, and *Elbe*, the *Deutschland* established the first regular service from Hamburg to North America. On its maiden voyage to New York in October of that year, flying the red and white flag of its home port, the vessel carried a full complement of sixteen passengers in first-class quarters and seventy-four people in second-class and steerage.[15] On average, the *Deutschland* completed the westward crossing in forty days; twenty-nine were normally required for the return voyage.[16] Of course, HAPAG was not alone in this endeavour and faced significant competition, most importantly from Britain. The British and North American Royal Mail Steam Packet Company had been offering regular transatlantic service from Liverpool since its founding by Samuel Cunard in 1840. It would be reformed in 1879 as the Cunard Steamship Company and the years between 1840 and 1870 have been described as the period of Cunard domination on the North Atlantic.[17] An important reason why the German lands lagged behind Britain in the development of transatlantic liner services was the absence of sufficient capital and state subventions.[18] To be sure, HAPAG's beginnings were modest and its achievements limited under its first director, Adolph Godeffroy (1814–1893), who led the company until his retirement in 1880.

Nonetheless, Godeffroy proudly reported to HAPAG's shareholders that the accommodation provided to both cabin-class and steerage passengers aboard the *Deutschland* was "as pretty and comfortable" as one could desire.[19] Contemporary lithographs depict the vessel's spacious public rooms; these were comfortably, if not luxuriously, appointed. From its inception, HAPAG prided itself on treating passengers as clientele, not human cargo. And yet the experience of crossing the Atlantic in the mid-nineteenth century was anything but comfortable. Charles Dickens' account of his voyage to Halifax and Boston aboard Cunard's *Britannia* in 1842 is one of the best descriptions of the cramped, malodorous, noisy, and unstable conditions of an Atlantic crossing at this time. Much of his account deals with the pitching of the vessel in a heavy sea and the consequent seasickness of its passengers. Commenting that the *Britannia*'s saloon was not unlike a gigantic hearse with windows, Dickens also described his stateroom as an "utterly impracticable, thoroughly hopeless, and profoundly preposterous box."[20] Of its berths he wrote that "nothing smaller for sleeping in was ever made, except coffins."[21] Dickens also made the particular point that the attractive lithographic images of the *Britannia*'s seemingly large and comfortable staterooms that he had seen in London bore no resemblance to what he encountered on board.[22]

HAPAG continued to commission sailing vessels that were built in Hamburg and Bremerhaven until the late 1850s. But the second half of the nineteenth century was a period of substantial, epoch-making innovation in shipping technology. Pioneered in Britain, steam power began to replace sail in Europe and America in the 1850s and was widely adopted in the 1870s and 1880s. In 1892, steamships surpassed sailing vessels as a percentage of the German merchant fleet's carrying capacity. This occurred more rapidly in Hamburg and Bremen than it did in smaller German seaports such as those on the Baltic Sea. Steam power permitted ocean-going vessels to effectively counteract the forces of wind and tide and allowed them to travel directly to their destinations instead of following the longer routes dictated by prevailing winds. As a result, scheduled transatlantic services could be established. Use of steam power was one of the most important events in the revolution that transformed transport technology which, in turn, contributed to the integration of the world economy.[23] Also significant was the greatly increased efficiency of ocean travel affected, at mid-century, by the shift from wooden to iron hull construction and the replacement of the paddle wheel by screw propulsion.

Hamburg's Sloman Line was the first to transition from sail to steam power in the form of the iron-hulled *Helena Sloman* that completed its first transatlantic crossing in 1850. In June of that year, Leipzig's *Illustrirte Zeitung* praised the vessel's safety, its ability to overcome the forces of nature, and the comfort of its interiors.[24] These were the very concerns repeatedly emphasized in publicity and press reporting on passenger steamships, on both sides of the Atlantic, down to the time of the *Imperator*. HAPAG's first iron-hulled, steam-powered vessels were built in 1855 by the shipbuilding and engineering firm Caird & Company. An established Scottish enterprise, Caird constructed almost fifty vessels for the German merchant marine over the next twenty years.[25] The

Hammonia and *Borussia* displaced just over 2,000 tons apiece and, as with all early steamships, were equipped with sails as a form of secondary propulsion. Each liner carried the mail and 510 passengers in total, 310 of them in steerage quarters. Manned by exclusively German crews, they sailed at an average speed of twelve knots and could complete a westward crossing of the Atlantic in sixteen days. And, most importantly, they enabled HAPAG to offer a monthly steamship service to New York from June 1856. Motivated by a concern not to be overtaken by domestic and English competitors, HAPAG had made sufficient additions to its fleet by 1858 to enable it to offer two sailings a month with departures on the first and fifteenth.[26]

What followed was a rapid increase in the company's passenger and cargo traffic to the United States. In fact, as early as 1860, HAPAG could boast that it was second only to Cunard in passenger carriage on the North Atlantic.[27] And its fortunes continued to improve when, in the following year, the United States awarded it the contract to carry the American mail between Southampton and New York. With the outbreak of the Civil War in 1861, there was a decline in the number of passengers and tonnage the company transported across the Atlantic. To be sure, the economic situation in America always played an important determining factor in HAPAG's fortunes. But its business quickly rebounded after the cessation of hostilities. This was aided by the opportunity

Figure 1.2 Gustav W. Seitz. The *Hammonia* and *Borussia*. Lithograph. No date.
Source: The Mariners' Museum, Newport News, VA.

to profit from losses suffered by the American merchant marine during the conflict. By 1865, HAPAG was offering weekly sailings to New York and, in 1867, the *Cimbria* and a new *Hammonia* entered service. Also built by Caird & Company and displacing over 3,000 tons apiece, they were the largest German steamships afloat and could cross the Atlantic in ten days with 678 passengers, accommodating fifty-eight in first-class quarters, 120 in second-class, and 500 in steerage.

Yet HAPAG was not the only major German shipping line plying the North Atlantic in the years preceding the founding of the German Empire in 1871. Norddeutscher Lloyd, its principal domestic competitor, was founded in Bremen by Hermann Heinrich Meier in 1857. The word Lloyd in the new company's name was "simply a marketing ploy, borrowed from the famous British insurance company and shipping registry to bestow instant history and legitimacy on the new line."[28] Bremen's ties to America were actually older and stronger than Hamburg's; its ships had been trading with Boston and Baltimore since 1783.[29] In 1827, the port of Bremerhaven was established at the mouth of the Weser River to provide Bremen with docking facilities on the North Sea. Taking advantage of these, NDL grew to become one of the world's great shipping concerns before 1914, offering services to North and South America, Australia, and Asia.[30]

The history of these two great shipping companies is one of competition and cooperation; theirs was a dynamic relationship that served as a major impetus to the development of Germany's merchant marine. They merged in 1970 to form the premier German shipping company Hapag-Lloyd AG which is based in Hamburg and Bremen. Its orange shipping containers are now familiar sights on docks, in freight yards, and on rail lines and auto routes around the globe. But the two companies were directly intertwined as early as 1859 when HAPAG took on some of NDL's mail obligations. In the 1860s, they coordinated sailings from Germany to avoid costly competition and jointly leased property in Hoboken, New Jersey, for the construction of piers and passenger facilities. And yet, especially from 1898, suspicion and animosity instead of goodwill reigned between Bremen and Hamburg as the two companies competed for ever larger shares of Germany's overseas trade. Unsurprisingly, the extent to which HAPAG and NDL were rivals is diminished by Hapag-Lloyd; company publications prefer to stress a long history of cooperation.[31] And yet it was largely as a result of competition that, on the eve of the First World War, the two lines circled the globe both directly and through shipping firms in which they had financial interest. In fact, many of the smaller German lines were absorbed by them. Others, such as the *Hamburg Südamerikanische Dampfschifffahrts-Gesellschaft* and the *Deutsche Dampfschifffahrts-Gesellschaft Kosmos*, lost market share to these giants.

Yet as HAPAG, NDL, and the German merchant fleet grew from the 1850s, most of its vessels were not built in domestic shipyards. Iron shipbuilding was still in its infancy in Germany even in the early 1880s, and it was common, until that time, for German steamers to be built in Britain. In fact, until the mid-1870s, HAPAG owned only three small vessels constructed in German yards. The appeal of British shipbuilders resided in their experience and skill; their lower construction costs; and their ability to build vessels more rapidly than German yards. The latter lacked adequate facilities and equipment, and what they possessed was often of British design and manufacture. Furthermore, it took time for the German steel industry to adjust to the requirements of ship building, and the higher construction costs in domestic yards were partly the result of import duties on the large amount of material that had to be obtained abroad.[32] German shipyards lacked requisite know-how and it was common to import British engineers and skilled labour. It was also usual for German engineers to gain practical experience in Britain. For example, having trained in Germany, Robert Zimmermann (1851–1912) worked for several British shipbuilders in the 1870s and 1880s before returning home to become director of shipbuilding at Vulcan, the firm that built the *Imperator*.[33] HAPAG even had trouble finding German engineers to man their steamships. And yet it resisted hiring English ones as was the custom of other German lines. Ultimately, it obtained the services of "one of the few experts in marine engineering then to be had in Germany" and was able to train crews for its new steamer services.[34]

Notwithstanding the state of German shipbuilding in the three decades following 1850, HAPAG participated in the rapid transformation of communication and transportation technologies that characterized these years. And it is noteworthy that the company presented its history not simply as that of a German firm but as part of the greater, multinational story of ocean navigation.[35] In an official account published in 1906, HAPAG described its participation in more general, international developments indicated by chapter titles. These included "The Introduction of Steam as a Motive Power"; "The Introduction of Twin Screw Steamships"; "The Era of the Great Freight Carriers"; and "The Latest Achievements in Modern Shipbuilding."[36] Furthermore, HAPAG's adoption of steamships, the expansion of its fleet, and the growth and consolidation of its North Atlantic services were part and parcel of what is now considered the first wave of globalization.

As Sebastian Conrad writes, there is "general agreement that the period between 1850 and the First World War was a time during which the development of global interlinkages and structures reached a zenith."[37] Of course, the realities and effects of globalization were not everywhere the same. But it is said that the level of global integration attained before 1914 was, in many respects, not achieved again until after the Second World War. And, as maritime historians have emphasized, the international shipping industry constituted "an important catalyst" to these developments.[38] Of course, a great deal of the progress made in transportation, communication, and international economic exchange in the nineteenth century happened under British leadership. But at the cutting edge of Germany's global engagement, HAPAG and the merchant marine played an important role in the multinational processes of innovation that facilitated globalization. Its vessels, and those of other German shipping lines, participated in opening the seas to international trade and commerce and provided a major impetus to the integration of the world economy before 1914.[39] Along with railways, trams, telegraphy, and eventually automobiles, German steamships and those of other nations also altered patterns of experience; increasingly touted as quintessential creations of the modern age, they contributed to the impression – especially strong among the European and American middle classes – that the world was both shrinking and accelerating at a rapid rate.

In 1868, HAPAG disposed of its last sailing vessels to become entirely a steamship concern operating a fleet of twenty-five vessels. Two years later, it moved into Deichstrasse 7, the first headquarters that it owned in Hamburg. As with the American Civil War, war with France in 1870–1871 had a negative impact on transatlantic trade; while completing sixty-four round trips to the United States in 1869, HAPAG steamships made only forty-two in 1870.[40] And yet the damage done to German merchant shipping by the Franco-Prussian War was limited and, in 1871, the company's steamers undertook fifty-two voyages to New York as well as three to New Orleans. In addition, HAPAG began operating on a new route to the West Indies which included a local service to Haiti and Mexico.[41] In 1871, its vessels carried 39,150 passengers and 155,000 tons of cargo across the Atlantic. In that same year, NDL carried many more passengers but much less cargo, transporting 65,548 of the former and 77,800 tons of the latter.[42]

HAPAG's annual reports reveal its enthusiasm for the opportunities that appeared to be opening to it as the result of German unification in 1871 and the company commissioned several vessels for its new service to the West Indies.[43] This initiative was part of the large increase in investment that occurred in the shipping industry across the Atlantic world during the early 1870s. Between 1871 and 1873, twelve new shipping lines were founded in Britain, Belgium, Germany, Holland, Norway, and the United States. Four of these were headquartered in Hamburg. The *Hamburg Südamerikanische Dampfschifffahrts-Gesellschaft* was established in 1871 and offered service to Argentina, Brazil, and Central America. By 1914, this was a "thriving company" operating a fleet of freighters and forty-two passenger liners.[44] Also founded in 1871, the *Deutsche Dampfschiffs-Rhederei zu Hamburg*, which was known as the *Kingsin Linie* from 1881, operated Germany's first freight service to East Asia through the Suez Canal. The *Deutsche Dampfschifffahrts-Gesellschaft Kosmos* was established in 1872 and provided shipping services to the west coast of South America. Finally, the Adler Line operated services to New York from 1872 but, facing financial difficulties, was purchased by HAPAG in 1875.

German merchant tonnage grew rapidly after 1870 and, by 1900, there were 256 German steamship companies. Most were small, with only fifteen firms operating more than twenty ships. As Gerhard A. Ritter notes, the concentration of German shipping in the hands of a limited number of companies was the result of the dominance of Hamburg and Bremen. This was especially the case because their ports functioned as embarkation points for emigrants from central, east, and south-eastern Europe. It was also the consequence of the importance placed upon establishing shipping lines with regularly scheduled service to fixed ports of call on pre-determined and published dates. This was in contrast to the tramp services that were common in Britain, services in which ships without fixed routes or schedules were available to load any cargo travelling to and from any port.[45]

With the founding of the Empire in 1871, Germany's government passed laws that directly affected the merchant marine. These included rules for the prevention of collisions at sea and the regulation of industrial relations aboard ship by the *Deutsche Seemannsordnung* of 1872. But the German state actually did very little to organize and regulate merchant shipping. It was left to the German Lloyd – the classification society founded in Hamburg by ship owners and builders in 1867 – to register vessels, develop and administer regulations concerning safety, and conduct inspections. This body worked in cooperation with the *See-Berufsgenossenschaft* which was founded in 1887 to establish rules for accident prevention and to conduct inspections to ensure the compliance of shipping companies.[46]

Yet while Germany's merchant marine expanded in the early 1870s, HAPAG's fortunes stagnated for many years following 1873. Along with NDL, the company suffered from the loss of vessels at sea; increased competition for the emigrant passengers who constituted the majority of people it transported; and as the result of the extended international economic recession that began in that year. With the purchase of the Adler Line in 1875, HAPAG eliminated a rival that had engaged it in costly competition for emigrant passengers. But although this takeover came with seven first-class transatlantic steamers, the company lagged behind NDL in terms of the number and quality of its liners and the volume of business it conducted with the United States. In fact, with the purchase of the Adler Line, HAPAG found itself with more vessels than it could profitably employ and saddled with a sizable debt.[47] Plans to build new steamers were put on hold.

Adolph Godeffroy's retirement as managing director in 1880 did little to improve the situation. Between 1880 and 1885, HAPAG was directed by Oscar Ruperti (1836–1924) and William O'Swald (1832–1923), individuals unsuited to meet the challenges facing the company and advance its interests. In fact, Arnold Kludas has written that HAPAG was practically leaderless in the 1880s.[48] Shareholders regularly complained about the weakness of its management and this finally resulted in the appointment of John Meyer (died 1902) as HAPAG's director in 1885. Yet the difficulties facing the company in this year were still substantial. In fact, when the German government awarded the Imperial mail services to Australia and East Asia to NDL, HAPAG did not even tender for the contract.

Particularly stiff competition for emigrant passengers was a persistent problem. Between 1880 and 1886, this came especially from an English steamship company known as the Carr Line. Founded in 1879, its vessels carried emigrant passengers and cargo from Hamburg to Baltimore, Philadelphia, and New York.

In Hamburg, the company was represented by Albert Ballin who was instrumental in ensuring it could offer cheaper emigrant fares than both HAPAG and NDL. The Carr Line amalgamated with Robert Sloman's Union Line in 1886 to form the Carr-Union Line. It was only by combining its schedules with the Union Line, and purchasing the steamers belonging to Carr in 1888, that HAPAG was finally able to end what was a costly rate war. It also hired Ballin to head its passenger department and began to manage this aspect of the company's business itself instead of relying on independent agents.

Despite the difficulties confronting HAPAG, the 1880s were a decade of significant developments in German shipbuilding. Ultimately, these helped reverse the company's fortunes and significantly transformed the merchant marine. In fact, the growth of German shipbuilding was so rapid that, by the 1890s, the Empire's shipyards were launching vessels in every respect equal to the best that British yards could produce. Simply put, modern shipbuilding began in Germany in the 1880s. This was motivated by several factors including rapid economic growth and the construction of numerous canals and railway lines connecting the German interior to Hamburg and Bremen. More importantly, in 1873, the Admiralty stipulated that all vessels of the German Navy were to be built in domestic yards. They were to be constructed, as far as possible, by domestically produced machinery using German materials. And they were to employ German-made auxiliary equipment and fittings. As Philip Dawson explains, government naval contracts alone were insufficient to sustain the long-term growth of shipbuilding in the Empire. But the intention was, in part, that they "would place the shipbuilders and their suppliers of machinery, equipment and fittings in a more competitive position to secure other work on their own merit."[49] Furthermore, from the mid-1880s, the German government began granting subventions to companies carrying mail. On 6 April 1885, the Reichstag passed legislation to establish a *Reichspostdampfer-Dienst* to Australia and East Asia and the contract was offered to NDL later that month. Along with such contracts and subventions came the obligation to build vessels in German yards.[50]

New construction was facilitated by the lifting of import duties on shipbuilding materials and the emergence of giant industrial concerns such as the *Allgemeine Elektrizitäts Gesellschaft* and Siemens. As Dawson indicates, "electrical equipment and machinery from these firms was soon to find their way aboard not only German ships, but also those of Britain and other nations."[51] Also important was the significant expansion of professional training in shipbuilding.[52] The latter occurred especially under Wilhelm II and was conducted in institutions such as the *Königlich Preußische Technische Hochschule* in Berlin, which was founded in 1879.[53] Furthermore, the 1880s saw considerable innovation in shipbuilding technology. This included new steam engines producing three and four times more power than earlier models to propel double-screw drive systems.

All of this resulted in the establishment of larger shipyards with more modern facilities. By 1895, more than 31,000 people were employed in these yards.[54] And these developments began to reverse a situation in which both HAPAG and NDL had remained "reticent to entrust orders for their larger and more prestigious liners to fledgling domestic builders" for many years after 1871.[55] It was in the 1880s that HAPAG commissioned the first ocean-going passenger liners built in German yards. The *Rugia* was constructed by Vulcan in Stettin, and the *Rhaetia* by the Reiherstiegwerft in Hamburg. Launched in 1882 and 1883 respectively, these were single-screw vessels of approximately 3,500 tons and were part of an increase in ocean liner construction without which, as Lawrence Sondhaus argues, German shipyards "would not have been as well prepared later to accommodate the Tirpitz plan."[56] But the 1880s were not simply characterized by increased confidence in domestic shipbuilders and the expansion of production. Up until that time, German companies were content to commission vessels of moderate size and power that could not match those launched by their British rivals. After 1880, they began to commission first-class passenger liners.

Yet in this respect neither HAPAG's *Rugia* nor *Rhaetia* could match the *Elbe* that was launched by NDL in 1881. Although built in the Glasgow yards of John Elder & Company, it was Germany's first *Schnelldampfer*, or express steamer. It was also the largest and most technologically advanced German vessel of its time. Express steamers were designed to carry cabin passengers in comfort and to transport freight faster than any other type of ocean-going vessel. To be designated an express steamer in 1890, a vessel had to achieve an average speed of 17.55 knots; in 1910, the requisite average was 23.4 knots.[57] Displacing 4,500 tons, the *Elbe*'s reciprocating engines drove a single screw to deliver an average speed of sixteen knots. On its third voyage, the vessel completed the crossing from Southampton to New York in eight days, a record for that route.[58] Furthermore, its cabin-class public spaces, principally its dining saloons, were more spacious and more luxurious than had previously been seen aboard German steamers. Between 1881 and 1890, NDL commissioned eleven express steamers of similar specifications to the *Elbe*, the last being the *Havel*. These were collectively known as the "river class," as all took their names from German waterways. With these liners, NDL offered the fastest and most comfortable service from Germany to New York.

To be sure, the *Elbe* was smaller and slower than the British vessels that dominated express-steamer traffic on the North Atlantic in the early 1880s. Yet it was at this time that Germany began to challenge Britain's shipbuilding superiority and offer serious competition on the North Atlantic. In 1885, the *New-York Tribune* published a letter from a London correspondent describing that the "jealousy with which the English companies regard their German rivals is notorious."[59] It is important to remember that most of NDL's river-class steamers were built in Glasgow by John Elder & Co. and its successor, the Fairfield Shipbuilding & Engineering Co. And even after the 1880s, HAPAG had many of its vessels built in British yards. Bernhard Huldermann explained that Ballin did not want to rely solely on German engineers and engineering and was always keen to learn what was newest and best in British shipbuilding.[60] But in 1892, when Fairfield required exceptionally wide steel plates for the rudders of Cunard's *Campania* and *Lucania*, it was forced to turn Krupp AG in Essen. British steel mills had declined the job as impossible.[61]

Great advances continued to be made in German shipyards through the 1890s in terms of their equipment, expertise, efficiency, and building capacity. In early 1914, the English journal *Shipbuilding and Shipping Record* reported that Blohm & Voss, the builder of the *Vaterland* and *Bismarck*, had more tonnage in its Hamburg yard than any in the world. It also pointed out that there were fourteen German shipyards employing more than 1,000 men each. By 1914, Blohm & Voss boasted a workforce of 10,000 while Vulcan employed over 13,000.[62] Furthermore, the journal opined that German shipbuilding yards of any consequence were now probably better equipped than most British yards. When it published photographs of the *Vaterland* under construction, *Shipbuilding and Shipping Record* pointed out that the images "demonstrate very clearly the splendid equipment which the yard possesses and which, moreover, is a noteworthy feature with the big German yards."[63] By this time British shipbuilders were purchasing German technology. For example, in the early 1900s, Germany was manufacturing the world's largest harbour cranes and these were employed in the construction of White Star's *Olympic* and *Titanic*. The *Deutsche Maschinenfabrik A.G.* published images of its 260-ton wharf crane at work on the *Imperator* to advertise its wares in Britain.[64]

The launch of the *Elbe* in 1881 also marked the beginning of a period of rapid growth for the German merchant marine. As Stephen Fox indicates, the aggregate tonnage of the Empire's merchant fleet surpassed that of the United States in 1884 and that of France in 1889.[65] During the 1880s, HAPAG and NDL steamers carried almost 1.3 million passengers to New York. This was approximately the same total as the four principal British lines: Cunard, White Star, Inman, and Guion.[66] The bulk of this traffic was assumed by NDL. By 1884, the number of passengers it carried annually to Manhattan rose by over 40,000 to reach 100,764.[67] The following year, NDL transported 108,174 passengers across the Atlantic while HAPAG vessels carried only 42,158.[68] NDL's passenger traffic reached its highpoint in 1891 when it sailed with 214,000 passengers.[69] And the presence of Germany's merchant marine grew not only on the North Atlantic. The *Afrikanische Dampfschiffs-Aktiengesellschaft*, commonly known as the *Woermann-Linie* after its founder Adolph Woermann (1847–1911), was established in 1885 and the *Deutsche Ost-Afrika-Linie* in 1890. Headquartered in Hamburg, these companies operated passenger and cargo services between Germany and East, West, and South African ports.

As its ocean traffic increased, HAPAG became ever more anchored on German soil, first and foremost in Hamburg. In 1890, the company relocated from Deichstraße to new headquarters at 18–20 Dovenfleth. Designed by Martin Haller (1835–1925), the city's most prominent architect and builder of its city hall, the four-story structure boasted a stylish Neo-Renaissance façade with a tower positioned at one corner. In just ten years, this new headquarters proved too small and, in 1903, the firm moved once again into its offices at Alsterdamm 25. This thoroughfare has been known as Ballindamm since 1947. A large and imposing sandstone structure directly adjacent to the Inner Alster Lake, the building was designed by Haller and Hermann Geissler in the Neo-Renaissance style. It was originally called the Hapag-Haus and was renamed the Ballin-Haus in 1997. HAPAG referred to it as a "business palace."[70] The company's motto, *"Mein Feld ist die Welt,"* appeared over the main entrance which was flanked by four sandstone caryatids representing Africa, Asia, America, and Australia. On the roof was an early work in bronze by the sculptor Ernst Barlach (1870–1938). Standing seven meters tall, it depicted Neptune bearing his trident and being borne over the waves in a chariot. Unfortunately, the sculpture was destroyed during the First World War. In the 1920s, the architect Fritz Höger was commissioned to enlarge and remodel the building to the way it appears today.

With its imposing presence, HAPAG was a striking symbol of, and a major contributor to a dynamic, globally orientated city undergoing rapid social and economic transformation. At the beginning of 1890s, the company informed prospective American travellers to Hamburg that they would disembark "in one of the most beautiful cities of the European continent," its streets alive with "teeming thousands, among whom all parts of the globe are represented."[71] By 1871, the Free and Hanseatic City of Hamburg had existed as a republic for several centuries and thought of itself as having a unique political and cultural identity in the German lands. Joining the North German Confederation in 1867, the city's history in the last quarter of the nineteenth century is one of political, bureaucratic, and economic harmonization with a unified Germany. It was the seat of "a highly dynamic entrepreneurial culture," and the city thrived in the late nineteenth and early twentieth centuries as did the other great port cities of Europe, Britain, and America including Antwerp, Rotterdam, Liverpool, London, and New York.[72] In fact, just after 1900, Hamburg was the largest continental port and, in Europe, was surpassed only by London.[73]

For Mayor Burchard, celebrating the *Imperator* at its launch meant not only toasting Hamburg's historic role in Germany's maritime development, but extolling its commercial and industrial successes and their contribution to the nation at large. Niall Ferguson has described the liner, along with the *Vaterland* and *Bismarck*, as symbols of the "economic giganticism" of big business in Hamburg and of the "addiction" of the city to expansion.[74] HAPAG was representative of an elite group of companies that "regarded increasing turnover, high profits and (particularly in the shipping industry) high investment as the norm."[75] These firms constituted "the most tightly-knit and highly organized concentration of capital in Germany."[76] HAPAG came to dominate Hamburg's shipping and was connected, through a range of agreements and joint ventures, with almost all other steamship companies that called its port home. In conjunction with the expansion of the city's shipping business went the rapid growth of shipbuilding. The major firms – Blohm & Voss and Vulcan – boasted average annual output growth rates of approximately nine percent between 1885 and 1914.[77] Hamburg was also home to metal processing firms and an engineering sector that was dominated by a handful of large enterprises. Manufacturing and industry concentrated on the processing of imported raw materials including foodstuffs, wood, and mineral ores, along with the production of goods for export and domestic consumption. In addition, the city boasted sophisticated capital and money markets. Several banks including Berenberg and H.J. Merck & Co. played a major role in the development of shipping and industry. While the house bank of HAPAG was the Norddeutsche Bank, the company was an important client of M.M. Warburg & Co. which was headquartered in Hamburg. Ballin also had a close relationship with its director, Max Warburg, who became a member of HAPAG's board in 1911.[78]

Of course, Hamburg's transformation into a modern industrial and commercial centre was but one facet of the growth of Germany, between 1871 and 1914, into the world's second strongest industrial power after Britain, and its maturation into a world leader in science and technology. Although characterized by two decades of deflation and uneven development from 1873, the German economy grew steadily from 1895. In what is known as a second industrial revolution, significant German investment in research and development, university-based science, and the establishment of technical institutes aided the rapid expansion of domestic industries. In addition, powerful banks accelerated economic growth by "injecting capital into high-growth-sectors like coal, steel, transportation, utilities and heavy engineering."[79] These sectors were dominated by industrial empires including Krupp and Thyssen in steel, Siemens and AEG (Germany's General Electric Company) in electrical engineering, and BASF and Bayer in chemicals. Exporting highly manufactured articles, these giant concerns became emblematic of Germany on both sides of the Atlantic.[80]

Periods of strong economic growth commonly led to the expansion and intensification of the services offered by shipping lines, and HAPAG was widely recognized as representative, not simply of Hamburg's but of Germany's coming of age as an industrial, commercial, and economic power of international stature.[81] As we will see, this was one of the ways in which the *Imperator*-class liners, in particular, were construed in the German and foreign media. And this symbolic role was something that HAPAG proudly emphasized. In an official history published in 1907, the company described its development as commensurate with "the march of German trade" and presented itself as "a shining symbol of German commercial spirit and ability."[82] It also emphasized that, while benefitting from the Empire's positive economic development, the company's growth outstripped the general progress of the nation by far.[83] This was a bold claim given that, in the short span of time between 1871 and 1914, Germany became the world's second strongest industrial power.

Much more than industry, it was trade, and its expansion around the globe, that was fundamental to Hamburg's prosperity and the growth of Germany's merchant marine in the late nineteenth century. In fact, industry was dependent upon trade in Hamburg. Although situated on the Elbe River, approximately sixty-five miles from the North Sea, the city became Germany's most important gateway to the world. HAPAG was a self-consciously global enterprise, but so was much of Hamburg's merchant community and it played a significant role in economic globalization. Hanseatic merchants had established extensive trade links across the globe long before Germany was a unified nation. By 1866, the city maintained a network of 279 consular outposts around the world, many of them in Latin America.[84] Hamburg developed particularly strong commercial concerns in Brazil, Chile, and Venezuela. And the city's foreign commerce was not disrupted by German unification in 1871, nor the Empire's turn to economic protectionism in 1878–1879. In fact, the government-subsidized building of a free port, which Hamburg retained upon entry into the Customs Union in 1888, ensured that German tariffs did not disrupt its trade. By 1913, as much as forty-two percent of German imports, and thirty-eight percent of exports passed through Hamburg's port; by 1914, its share of total world trade was approximately 4.5 percent.[85] The volume of commerce conducted through Hamburg is also measurable by the tonnage of seagoing vessels that entered its port: in 1890, this amounted to 5,200,000 tons, four times greater than the tonnage that called at Bremen, the second largest port in Germany.[86] And this number doubled in the years before 1914.[87] It should be noted, however, that while Hamburg traded with African, Asian, and Australasian markets, most of its commerce was with continental Europe and its largest foreign trading partner was Britain. Nonetheless, the enormous volume of trade that passed through the city fostered the development of the transport sector such that by 1914 Hamburg's merchant marine alone amounted to 1,372 sea-going vessels, or over a third of German merchant tonnage.[88] By 1913, there were more than 160 regular shipping services connecting Hamburg to the world with approximately 620 departures per month.[89]

In addition to the industrial development and the expansion of international trade that fostered its growth, Mayor Burchard noted in his christening address that Germany's merchant marine had an important champion in the person of Kaiser Wilhelm II who ascended the imperial throne in 1888. His enthusiasm for everything naval and maritime is well known.[90] It was in a speech to the North German Regatta Association in 1901, aboard HAPAG's *Prinzessin Victoria Luise*, that the Kaiser uttered the famous phrase "our future lies on the water." As Albert Ballin noted, it was "the Emperor's high and noble mission to increase, promote, and protect Germany's power at sea – the merchant marine not less than the navy."[91] Wilhelm's interest in Germany's maritime future extended to the passenger steamers launched by HAPAG and NDL; we will see that this was especially the case with the *Imperator*-class liners. At the launch of these vessels, the Kaiser was praised for fostering the Empire's maritime development and orienting Germans, as never before, to the sea. In 1913, on the twenty-fifth anniversary of his ascension to the throne, Ballin praised the great strides made by German merchant shipping and explained that they were significantly aided by the attitude and practical engagement of a ruler who clearly understood the necessity of developing Germany's overseas trade.[92]

But the Kaiser's interest in transatlantic steamships originated many years before the *Imperator*'s launch. In 1887, while HAPAG planned to have two new vessels constructed in England, then Prince Wilhelm urged the company to contract Vulcan to build at least one of them and the *Augusta Victoria* was launched at Stettin in 1888.[93] In the following year, as Kaiser, he attended the British Naval Review at Spithead and the story is often told of his experience aboard White Star's passenger liner *Teutonic*. Launched in 1889, the *Teutonic* was the first merchant vessel designed for quick conversion to an armed cruiser equipped with twelve guns. The intention of Wilhelm's British hosts was to impress him with this fact. But during two hours spent aboard the vessel he proved more interested in its first-class passenger lounges and dining room. Impressed by the liner's fittings, Wilhelm apparently said to a member of his entourage that "We must have some of these."[94] Several authors suggest that these words were the spark that provoked the dramatic advances made in German passenger shipping during the 1890s. As Stephen Fox explains, it is a "good story, crisp and personal," that "entered the literature of transatlantic history and has been passed along from book to book ever since."[95] And yet, in reality, it is not certain that Wilhelm was speaking of the *Teutonic* as a passenger liner instead of as a potential warship.

It is easy to overestimate the Kaiser's personal and tangible influence on the German merchant marine's rapid growth in the two decades before the First World War. What is certain, however, is that the forces driving it were much greater than his enthusiasm and practical involvement. And many were in place long before Wilhelm ascended the throne. These included the ambitions of, and rivalry between HAPAG and other German shipping lines; the dramatic pace of German industrialization; and the growth of an economy increasingly oriented to world markets. Furthermore, the German government understood the importance of fostering the development of the merchant marine and establishing regular trade connections with overseas markets. Imperial Germany's *Weltpolitik* – what might be described as a foreign policy that expanded beyond Europe in an effort to promote Germany to world-power status – put an emphasis on the oceans. These were understood as an arena in which the Empire could prove that it ranked among the great nations and where the merchant marine was an important means of achieving Germany's "place in the sun." At the launch of HAPAG's *Deutschland* in 1900, Bernhard von Bülow, then German Foreign Secretary, gave a speech in which he claimed that "progress in marine engineering underlay both the nation's economic rise and its new bids in colonial and world politics."[96]

In addition to the rhetoric, there were several concrete ways in which the affairs of HAPAG, and Germany's merchant marine in general, were advanced by political decisions made by the German government. Direct subsidies were mostly limited to NDL's mail contract for the services it operated to Asia and Australia. Yet the business of shipping lines was influenced by government action on customs regulations, emigration and immigration, as well as colonial policy. Berlin also invested large sums in infrastructure including canals, docks, and harbours.[97] The expansion of the free port of Hamburg in the 1880s and the opening of the Kaiser-Wilhelm-Kanal in 1895 were particularly important initiatives. In addition, German shipping lines were the recipients of many indirect benefits: shipbuilding materials were imported into Germany free of duties and government railroads transported raw materials to shipyards while charging only the cost of handling.

Yet we must be careful about overstating the degree to which the German government was directly involved in HAPAG's business and operations. It needs to be emphasized, for example, that the company operated without government subsidies. This is despite the many claims to the contrary that were made at the time, especially in the English press. Albert Ballin was opposed to such subsidies; in 1907, *The New York Times* reported his belief that they "paralyze individual energy, and endanger the spirit of enterprise, and affect the decline, if not the ruin, of trade."[98] He made it clear that HAPAG had never received state subventions with one exception: from 1900 to 1904 the company ran two steamers in the subsidized mail service to East Asia. But HAPAG had been so dissatisfied with this experiment that it withdrew from the service "preferring to remain unaided but also unhampered."[99] It is important to note that subsidies granted shipping lines by the German government were exclusively used for postal services to East Africa, East Asia, and Australia. They were not used to finance the building of passenger liners.

Ultimately, although critical of the support that the British government provided Cunard, Ballin had no reason to believe German shipping would be disadvantaged by the aid its rivals received from their respective national governments.[100] An article published in 1911 by the German naval officer and journalist Count Ernst von Reventlow in *Cassier's Magazine* demonstrated exactly what Ballin believed: that Germany's merchant shipping had no need of government subsidies to be competitive and successful.[101] To prove his point, the author provided statistics from 1909 showing that German subsidies were absolutely and proportionally lower than those of Britain, France, Italy, Japan, Russia, Austria-Hungary, and Spain. Most of all, what Ballin feared was the idea that HAPAG, and Germany's global commerce, should be governed by incompetent government bureaucracy.

Much more than from government subsidies, Germany's merchant marine benefitted from the reorganization, growth, and modernization of the Imperial Navy under Admiral Alfred von Tirpitz, Secretary of State for the Navy from 1897 to 1916. Between 1898 and 1912, a series of five Navy Bills was passed by the Reichstag authorizing the expansion of the German battle fleet. The ultimate goal was to create a force capable not only of challenging France and Russia but also of confronting the Royal Navy with the aim of forcing Britain to make diplomatic concessions. Another important impetus to the construction of a battle fleet was the belief that, as the percentage of the nation's sea-borne trade increased, Germany required the means to defend its maritime interests as well as its territories abroad.[102] As the *Jahrbuch für Deutschlands Seeinteressen* explained in 1914, a strong navy would ensure the advance of German shipping, trade, and economic well-being.[103] This was certainly the thinking of Ballin who believed such a force would protect his nation's position in Europe, defend its overseas possessions, and open new regions to German trade.[104] Interestingly, Hamburg was long opposed to excessive German naval ambitions, fearing they would provoke conflict and result in economic disaster. In fact, until the early 1890s, the sons of leading Hanseatic families traditionally joined the officer corps of the merchant marine and not the Imperial Navy.[105] But Tirpitz's visit to Hamburg in September 1897 played a crucial role in converting the local commercial and political elite to his plans for naval construction. So did the advocacy of Ballin and Adolph Woermann who, along with other powerful business leaders such as Hermann Blohm and Carl Laeisz, belonged to the Hamburg chapter of the Navy League. In fact, Ballin played an active role in advocating for a strong navy in the early stages of its development.

Legislation passed to ensure the future of the German Navy guaranteed business for domestic shipyards. This enabled them to risk enlarging and improving facilities necessary for the production of vessels of ever-increasing size, including those of the merchant marine. By the time of the *Imperator*'s launch, several German shipyards were engaged in the construction of warships. Vulcan received numerous naval contracts; between 1871 and 1911, it constructed 110 such vessels, more than any other German yard. Many of these were battleships, cruisers, and torpedo-boats for the Imperial Navy. But the company also built warships for the Chinese, Japanese, Russian, and Greek navies.[106] As a result, it was well prepared to construct postal steamers for NDL and transatlantic liners for HAPAG. While at work on the *Imperator*, Vulcan was also constructing the battleship *Friedrich der Große* which was launched in June 1911. Blohm & Voss, the company that built the *Vaterland* and *Bismarck*, specialized in the construction of cruisers and also completed a large number of steamers for the merchant marine.[107]

Beyond benefitting from improvements to German shipyards prompted by the building of a battle fleet, HAPAG found itself working in concert with the Imperial Navy. Not only were several of its liners designed for quick conversion to auxiliary cruisers, but its vessels were frequently chartered as troop transports. In 1900, they carried German soldiers to suppress the Boxer Rebellion in China. During the Herero Wars in Southwest Africa, between 1904 and 1908, HAPAG and NDL steamers were chartered by the German government. Both the English and American press took note of this relationship with varying degrees of anxiety. In 1912, Commodore W.H. Beehler, an American naval attaché in Berlin, Vienna, and Rome from 1899 to 1902, emphasized "the intimate connection between the German navy and the merchant marine."[108] He claimed, in fact, that all German merchant ships were "virtually vessels of the German navy."[109] Given Ballin's friendly and much-publicized relationship with the Kaiser, and the fact that the company was represented by the government around the globe, it was easy to see HAPAG as an arm of the German state.

From 1908, Ballin would begin to question the wisdom of further expanding the German navy. By that time, he believed the Empire had sufficient naval resources to ensure its position in Europe and to defend its overseas possessions. He also felt that constructing a large navy would be financially ruinous and lead to domestic political problems.[110] And yet, as we will see in chapter five, HAPAG was seen by Britons as embodying a great deal of Germany's challenge to the "British-dominated maritime status quo" that characterized the decades before 1914.[111] In June of that year, the British shipping magnate Sir Owen Philipps stated in the *Daily Mail* that "the fight for world supremacy is being waged by German ships and British ships in every ocean."[112] And in a letter penned in 1915, Ballin claimed he had been conducting open warfare against British shipping for many years. He had, in his words, "captured one trench after the other," always renewing the attack as soon the necessary resources could be mustered.[113]

Written in wartime, Ballin's choice of words offers an inaccurate vision of Germany's engagement with the world before 1914. Beyond the diplomatic and military spheres, this interaction is now seen by historians as in many ways positive and constructive. It was a productive engagement to which HAPAG made significant contributions. In a speech given in Hamburg in 1888, Kaiser Wilhelm II praised the city's merchants for reaching out into the world in the following terms: "You are the ones who connect our fatherland with invisible ties to distant parts of the globe, trade with our products, and more than that: you are the ones who transmit our ideas and values to the wider world."[114] The very same can be said of HAPAG as it introduced a service to South America in 1896; sent its first freighter to Penang, Singapore, Hong Kong, Shanghai, Yokohama, and Kobe in January 1898; bought Hamburg's *Kingsin Linie* and took over its operations in China that same year; and initiated a service to Cuba and Mexico in 1902. By the time of the First World War, HAPAG had added services between Italy and New York, and between New York, Brazil, and East Asia. More than representative of Germany's industrial and commercial prowess, the company facilitated the peaceful, productive orientation of its society and economy towards the world.

III

Between 1886 and 1897, HAPAG restricted its activity to the Atlantic. After 1897, the company transformed itself from an Atlantic shipping line into a global one, rapidly expanding and diversifying its network of services, breaking into several new trading regions, and sailing to all continents except Australia by 1910.[115] HAPAG described its history as participating in the global development of trade and commerce. "Is it not," one company publication of 1908 proudly stated,

> principally to the great shipping companies that the rise of German trade and industry is due? They have cooperated untiringly, as pioneers, in the

endeavour to push German commerce to a leading place among emporiums of the world, and to render the commercial navy of Germany one of the mightiest and most respected.[116]

But in addition to self-congratulation, much of the publicity produced by HAPAG emphasized the extent to which its success depended on the larger issues of global commerce; foreign economies, industry, and agriculture; trade tariffs; international emigration; and conflict in Central and South America, the West Indies, and other locations around the globe.[117] Those who encountered company advertising in Germany, Britain, and America were presented with a compelling picture of the extent to which it was connected to the wider world. Whether it be a synopsis of how economic developments in East Asia had a direct impact on the company's business; a listing of the global services it offered; or a poster with a map portraying the routes plied by its vessels around the world, it was clear that HAPAG was an enterprise with a global reach.[118]

Germany's rapid industrialization and economic growth occurred within the context of increasing international exchange in which capital enjoyed great mobility and "countries became dependent on trade to an extent unmatched until generations later."[119] In fact, as Cornelius Torp has emphasized, the level of world trade before 1914 "was comparable with that of the 1970s and 1980s."[120] German entrepreneurs and industrialists supported *Weltpolitik* as a program for market acquisition, and the Empire's exports more than quadrupled between 1872 and 1913 as it developed business relationships with Latin America, China, and Ottoman Turkey. Of course, Germany was more connected to Europe, Britain, and America than it was to the rest of the world. But the increase in its volume of trade beyond the North Atlantic world was dramatic. Exports to East Asia rose by 547 percent; to South America by 567 percent; and to all German colonies by no less than 1,400 percent.[121] Industries producing electrical, metal, chemical, and consumer goods manufactured large amounts for export and, by 1914, foreign trade accounted for thirty-four percent of national income, a level attained once again only in the 1960s.[122] And, with improvements in transportation and the increasing integration of the global economy, transporting a ton of wheat from New York to Mannheim in 1900 cost no more than shipping it from Berlin to Kassel.[123]

Needless to say, a large proportion of Germany's foreign exports were transported by ocean-going merchant steamships. While much writing about HAPAG has focused on the glamorous aspect of its business – namely, its transatlantic passenger liners – it must not be forgotten that most of the company's revenues were generated by the transportation of freight. Before 1903, its freighters accounted for the predominant share of its ocean tonnage; following that year, vessels carrying both passengers and freight comprised the most.[124] It was in the 1890s that HAPAG introduced its so-called "P," "A," and "B" steamers, vessels of various sizes that, although they carried cabin passengers and emigrants, were designed to transport greater amounts of freight. Because of this, and because their modest speed meant they were more efficient to operate than an express steamer, these vessels became the real revenue earners of HAPAG's North American service. As the company claimed, the *Pennsylvania*, launched in 1896 as the largest freighter in the world, carried more freight to America in one voyage "than the entire sailing force of the line in its early days took across in one year."[125] Although they never became famous, these steamers formed the commercial backbone of the company's fleet.[126]

HAPAG's development both fostered, and was a response to international trade, exchange, and integration. This is also directly evident in the vessels it commissioned. International bodies and treaties regulated their outfitting and operation. The *Imperator* was constructed according to the regulations of the *Germanischer Lloyd*, a classification society based in Hamburg that ensured technical and engineering compliance with safety standards. It also conformed to rules established by the *See-Berufsgenossenschaft*, which were addressed to accident prevention. Yet the liner was also designed in compliance with German, English, and American laws that regulated the outfitting of vessels carrying travellers and emigrants.[127] Furthermore, even following the decision to have new additions to its fleet built in German yards, the company's ships were hybrids of international exchange and cooperation in design, engineering, and technology. Several foreign-made products went into the construction of HAPAG's liners, and German shipbuilding continued to benefit significantly from British innovation up until 1914. For example, the *Imperator* was fitted with British equipment and technology including the Stone-Lloyd hydraulic system for operating bulkhead doors. As the English journal *Engineering* emphasized in 1914, when it came to engineering, political frontiers were "but faint lines."[128] The Institution of Naval Architects, founded in 1860 and headquartered in London, represented marine designers and engineers of all maritime nations. Recognizing the great strides made by German merchant shipping from the 1880s, it held its first meetings in Germany in 1896. As we will see in chapter four, the interiors of the *Imperator*-class liners were designed and constructed by international teams of architects and firms.

HAPAG's liners were also insured by both German and British underwriters.[129] Given the rise in insurance costs following the sinking of the *Titanic* in April 1912, HAPAG worked in conjunction with British and American companies to form a combine for the protection of fleets on a mutual basis.[130] And in an effort to maintain the financial health of the shipping business in the Atlantic world, the company participated in international agreements regulating the number of steerage passengers carried by the lines of several nations. These were designed to lessen the detrimental effects of competition and to divide profits. It is also worth noting that a proportion of HAPAG's shares were owned by foreign investors. Furthermore, HAPAG invested heavily in European shipping, and especially in Austrian, Belgian, Dutch, and Italian lines. It did the same outside of Europe, in Argentina and Brazil for example.[131] The company also offered joint services with foreign shipping concerns.

While emphasizing the international dimensions and global engagement of the German economy, we must be careful not to overstate the case. It should be remembered that while Britain and the United States were privileged markets for its industrial products, most of Germany's exports were to other European nations. Furthermore, while it exported large quantities of manufactured goods, the Empire also depended heavily on the import of foodstuffs, raw materials, and industrial products. And it is well known that many sectors of German industry did not profit from international trade and supported a policy of protectionism. In fact, the German customs tariff of 1879 and the imposition of further tariffs in the 1880s were part of a general movement to protectionism in Europe excluding Britain. Chancellor Caprivi's trade treaties briefly moved Germany back towards free trade in the 1890s and meant greater involvement in the global economy. But following Chancellor Bülow's assumption of office in 1900, the Empire returned to a policy of protectionism until the outbreak of the First World War.

This protectionist trade policy was not simply the consequence of domestic power constellations; it was a reaction to the challenges of globalization.[132] And that is the point to be made: in the period between 1850 and 1914 goods, people, information, and capital moved across borders and oceans as never before. From 1890, international trade was contained within protectionist regimes. But no matter its turn to protectionism in the decades preceding the First World War, the German Empire was evermore oriented towards an international market and bound up with global structures and dynamics that extended beyond business decisions into the everyday lives of many Germans.

Indeed, beyond its importance to Germany's international trade and commerce, HAPAG's expansion around the globe served to advance the extent to which Germans became evermore aware of the world beyond their borders and were increasingly apprised of how their society was affected by international events and developments. The company was one of many that not only established economic and trade links across the world's oceans but also disseminated "information, images, and ideas about foreign lands throughout Germany."[133] The publicity given to foreign affairs increased dramatically at the end of the nineteenth century and more Germans were better informed about events occurring all over the globe. It was during this time that "the rhetoric of 'world' became almost ubiquitous: world politics, world economy, world powers, world empires, were catchwords of the day."[134] This is evident in various forms of popular culture including advertising, travel literature, popular fiction, and even board games with a colonial theme.[135] In a word, Germans were becoming ever more globally conscious in the decades just prior to 1914, and the way the German nation was "defined, understood, and practiced" owed much to the global context and interactions on the global scale.[136] As Sebastian Conrad emphasizes, "the belief that even distant events could affect the local situation was widespread among the educated classes."[137] Contemporary commentators also perceived that improved international transportation and communication was breaking down cultural barriers and offering a better understanding of societal and cultural difference.[138] A degree of standardization in industry, technology, weights and measures, fashion, culture, and law even produced a sense of synchronicity and homogenization; some observers even held that different cultures were becoming similar as the result of the diffusion of western modernity.[139]

As raw materials and manufactured goods were increasingly moved around the globe, so were people. Mass mobility was one of the principal features of globalization, and the phenomenon of economic migration was an important means by which Germany was connected to the world beyond its borders. Between 1890 and 1914, the movement of persons into and out of the nation occurred on an unprecedented scale. In fact, as Thomas Mergel argues, Germany was a society of migration.[140] By the middle of the 1890s, the demand for labour outstripped national supply, and this resulted in a large amount of foreign workers entering the country from neighbouring states, such as Holland, Poland, and Italy, to be employed in industry and agriculture.[141] Consequently, German seaports and industrial centres were acquainted with an "impressive number of people coming from elsewhere."[142] This movement of labour was an international phenomenon that changed the idea of the nation in Germany. Large sections of its society responded defensively and aggressively to the presence of foreign workers and, instead of dissolving borders, mass mobility served to intensify popular nationalist movements. This is one example of the fact that, as Conrad has argued, transnational interrelationships, global events, and interlinkages on an international scale actually contributed to the strengthening of national demarcation, the popularity of ideas concerning national distinctness, and the emergence of mass nationalist associations.[143] In short, the intensified nationalism of Wilhelmine Germany was partly a product of increased globalization.

But if these years saw an influx of foreign labour into Germany, they were also a time in which Germans increasingly explored the world beyond their borders, a time when global travel was becoming more accessible to the ordinary tourist. HAPAG played an important role in this respect, most interestingly as a pioneering force in the cruise industry and the rise of leisure tourism. In fact, cruising became an integral part of the company's operations, while NDL's attempts in this field were not nearly as extensive nor successful. HAPAG developed the cruise component of its operations partly as the result of a need to find employment for transatlantic steamers that were otherwise laid up during the winter months. The modern leisure cruise was inaugurated in January 1891 when HAPAG dispatched the *Augusta Victoria* on a voyage around the Mediterranean carrying 241 passengers and lasting several weeks.[144] Advertised as being for health and pleasure, the company's cruises extended to Scandinavia from 1894. In 1900, HAPAG took delivery of the *Prinzessin Victoria Luise* from Blohm & Voss, the first ship designed exclusively for cruising. It was intended to cater to the very rich, carrying them to Norway's fjords, around the Mediterranean, and to the West Indies. Modelled on the royal yachts of Europe, the vessel boasted an Imperial suite and 119 staterooms, each fitted with a bedroom, private drawing room, and full bath. In 1904, it was joined by another cruise ship, the *Meteor*. As early as 1907, HAPAG explained that it organized independent tours for small groups to the most various parts of the earth, established permanent connections with countries to which it is difficult to travel, compiled tour books and provided tickets for the railway and shipping companies of the various European and non-European travel zones, giving advice in all matters of travel.[145]

The company mounted its first round-the-world cruise aboard the *Cleveland* in 1909. It offered travellers checks to its customers in various denominations that could be used aboard its vessels, in hotels, in shops, or cashed by several "correspondents located in all civilized countries."[146]

HAPAG advertised its cruises in several languages to an international clientele, and especially in the United States. In fact, many of the company's cruises began in New York and those in the Mediterranean, for example, were often multinational affairs in which German ships, manned by German crews, carried large numbers of American travellers on voyages organized by Thomas Cook of London. From 1905, HAPAG operated its own extensive network of travel agencies in Europe and America. Its Berlin offices were the hub of this operation with subsidiaries located in Beirut, Cairo, Constantinople, Corfu, Haifa, Interlaken, Jaffa, Jerusalem, London, Mentone, New York, Paris, and Port Said. From 1907, with the aid of a rail connection between Berlin and Naples, HAPAG could carry tourists to the Egyptian pyramids in little more than 100 hours.[147] At least one company poster juxtaposed a snowy Berlin with the sun-drenched and sandy Sphinx.

Of course, the clientele for these cruises was very small. Nonetheless, they played an important role in the increasing interaction of Germans with the world through the medium of travel. They also shed light on how Germans experienced foreign societies and cultures, and the ways in which they understood themselves in relation to them. Mediterranean cruises, for example, afforded Germans a means to define themselves, and the achievements of their society, against what was often perceived as the backwardness of southern Europe and the "Orient." HAPAG advertising promoted the exotic nature of the destinations to which it carried travellers: Madeira, Gibraltar, Algiers, Genoa, Naples, Malta, Athens, Constantinople, Palestine, and Egypt. It foregrounded the vestiges of the illustrious past that were to be found there. But it also sustained images of a modern, rational, technologically advanced West that stood in contrast to a backward, superstitious East. Company advertising employed Orientalist tropes of a world that time had forgotten but to which German, European, and American travellers had access, thanks to "modern ingenuity."[148] Advertising posters frequently employed images of turbaned and bearded men, veiled women, camels, ancient monuments, and architecture that appears unchanged since biblical times.

Furthermore, travellers who recorded their experiences often commented negatively, and in derogatory tones, on the technology, religion, and social customs of southern Europeans. And they employed such impressions to articulate difference. Although Germany possessed no colonies in the

Mediterranean, the experience of travelling to the countries that bordered it helped Germans justify imperialism and the domination of others as a "necessary bringing of order to chaos."[149] In fact, the cruise ships themselves provided an important point of comparison and a reminder to Germans of their technological and cultural superiority; the vessels were a means of validating German and Western superiority and were perceived as monuments to national greatness. For the engineer Karl Radunz, advances in sea travel were unequivocal proof of the technological prowess of the West.[150]

Yet most of those who travelled aboard HAPAG liners were not middle-class Germans seeking leisure. Writing about transatlantic passenger liners often focuses on the design and decoration of their first-class accommodation and public spaces. However, it was transatlantic emigration, not cabin-class travel that accounted for the largest share of HAPAG's passenger business, just as it did for all major shipping lines plying the North Atlantic. One of the important characteristics of globalization was the large-scale migration of impoverished classes and the company's development must be seen, in large measure, as a response to the imperatives of international migration and especially emigration from Eastern Europe. Along with Britain's Cunard and White Star Lines, HAPAG and NDL transported fifty percent of all emigrants to North America between 1850 and 1914.[151] As Ballin simply said: "Without steerage passengers I would be bankrupt within a few weeks."[152] As we will see in the following chapter, the *Imperator* and other premier passenger liners were specifically designed to transport large numbers of poor European migrants.

From the early nineteenth century until 1914, approximately forty-four million Europeans emigrated from the continent to the United States and other overseas destinations.[153] Industrial and economic development in Germany after 1850 meant that German emigration decreased. Between 1871 and the First World War, just under 2.9 million Germans left their homeland. But during the same period, approximately 5.8 million Europeans, mostly from Russia and the Austro-Hungarian Empire, departed the continent's shores, many from German ports including Hamburg and Bremen, and many aboard German vessels.[154] As a result, Hamburg was "acquainted with an enormous number of people in its midst who were on the move."[155] Before the 1890s, HAPAG took little or no responsibility for steerage passengers awaiting transit from Hamburg. Often having travelled long distances, emigrants from Eastern Europe crowded the city's lodging houses, sometimes waiting weeks for their departure. In 1892, the company finally constructed barrack-style accommodation for its emigrant passengers. But their unhygienic conditions attracted bad publicity, and when a cholera epidemic broke out in Hamburg that same year many blamed Russian migrants.[156] As a result, municipal authorities closed the city's port to emigrants from Eastern Europe, and the number of steerage passengers carried by HAPAG dropped sharply between 1892 and 1894. These restrictions on emigrant traffic were only lifted when the company threatened to relocate its head office to Bremen and its cargo and passenger departments to Nordenham on the Weser River.[157]

In the wake of the cholera epidemic, the German government built border-control stations along the eastern frontier of the Empire to inspect and govern the flow of immigrants from Russia and Eastern Europe. Constructed in 1894, these were subsequently handed over to HAPAG and NDL for joint administration and financing. And to finally solve the problems generated by large numbers of emigrants passing through Hamburg, HAPAG constructed facilities to house them on the dockland island of Veddel. The land for these *Auswandererhallen*, along with a contribution to the cost of their construction, was provided by the city government. When it opened in December 1901, the *Hamburgischer Correspondent* described the complex as "like a little city, surrounded by a high palisade fence."[158] This "little city" stood on approximately 25,000 square metres of land and was serviced by its own rail station so that emigrants arrived and departed without entering Hamburg. It comprised dormitories, canteens, a baggage shed, and a delousing facility maintained by a staff of HAPAG employees. Accommodation cost two marks per night for adults, but those unable to pay were accommodated free of charge.[159] Here emigrants washed, had their clothes disinfected, and were submitted to a medical examination. These procedures and precautions were not, however, undertaken first and foremost considering the well-being of steerage passengers. Instead, they were meant to ensure that only healthy individuals went aboard ship so that HAPAG would not incur the cost of returning those who were denied entry to the United States. At the same time, the company sought to minimize the indignity of this experience by providing the *Auswandererhallen* with food and dry-goods stores, a beer garden, a music hall, a barber shop, a church, and a synagogue.

HAPAG was aware that this initiative would attract international attention and presented a model of the *Auswandererhallen* at the World's Fair in Paris in 1900. It did the same at the fair held in St. Louis four years later. Company advertising described the complex as "the world's largest hotel" and its facilities were recognized as exemplary at the International Hygiene Exhibition in Dresden in 1911.[160] They were enlarged several times until 1907 at which point the complex could accommodate 5,000 emigrants at any one time.[161] In 1913, 170,000 people passed through the *Auswandererhallen*, the largest number to do so in a single year. They remained in operation until 1934 and were re-opened as an emigration museum known as *Ballinstadt* in July 2007.[162]

In addition to the mass migration of impoverished classes, much of globalization in this period was defined by colonialism. The building of Germany's short-lived colonial empire began in 1884. Before losing them at the end of the First World War, Germans settled and controlled colonies in South-West Africa (now Namibia); in East Africa (today parts of Tanzania, Burundi, Rwanda, Cameroon, and Togo); in East Asia (Shandong province and Kiautschou in China); and in the Pacific Ocean where they held German Samoa, German New Guinea, the Marshall Islands, and islands in what is now Micronesia. Several of these colonies were at first privately administered through chartered companies until a Colonial Department was established in the

Foreign Office in 1890. This was the fourth-largest colonial empire of its day following those of Britain, France, and the Netherlands. Trade interests were one of the most important factors motivating its creation, and the calls of merchants for a more robust German presence abroad provided the justification for Berlin to promote imperial expansion. Colonies would provide Germany with raw materials and act as markets for goods manufactured at home. Furthermore, a new wave of German emigration began in the 1880s, and there were those in government who saw the opportunity to create new settlements and a colonial "New Germany," as opposed to having Germans assimilate into North American society.

Hamburg was "in many ways the precocious face of German expansionism."[163] In a speech made aboard the *Vaterland* on the occasion of its sea trials, Ballin stated that the ground work for Germany's colonial empire had been laid by the entrepreneurial Hanseatic spirit.[164] Not all the city's merchants were eager to embrace colonial ventures. But many were involved, in government and the private sector, in the processes of German imperialism and several were important advocates for a colonial empire.[165] Others established colonial communities and trading stations including the Godeffroys in the South Pacific, the O'Swalds in East Africa, and the Woermanns in West Africa. By 1884, the *Woermann Linie* was already an important element of the German presence in West Africa and provided regular service between Hamburg and this region. As Germany's colonial policy developed in the early 1880s, it often followed private connections established by Hamburg merchants earlier in the century.

Of course, Germany's colonial empire never lived up to the expectations with which it was invested. In 1912, it was home to approximately 18,000 Germans.[166] In 1913, the nation's exports to Romania were "three times greater than exports to all the German colonies combined."[167] And, to be sure, the impact of German colonialism on the colonized was characterized by economic exploitation, cultural destruction, and racially driven violence. But while very different, the impact of colonialism on Germans was also wide-ranging. In the words of Birthe Kundrus, it was "part of the broad spectrum of thoughts and experiences of German society."[168] Germans displayed "a remarkable and explosive curiosity in foreigners and in the foreign;" global consciousness was fostered by colonialism and featured in the reality of many Germans.[169] While it formed part of political and administrative planning, businessmen, engineers, scholars, and missionaries travelled extensively in the non-European world. The effects of colonialism also extended to sectors of the working classes that were becoming increasingly dependent on structures of global demand. Furthermore, colonialism's traces were found in literature, film, social science, medicine, advertising, urban geography, legislation, infrastructure planning, retail trade, military strategy, and popular leisure activity such as parlour games.[170] Colonialism also inspired German intellectuals to "be at the forefront of a host of nascent academic disciplines such as ethnology, anthropology, zoology and oceanography."[171] In Hamburg, it resulted the founding of the Museum for Ethnology in 1879, the Institute of Maritime and Tropical Diseases in 1900, and the Hamburg Colonial Institute in 1908. As one of several German institutions devoted to studying the "colonial" sciences and training colonial officials, the Colonial Institute was the forerunner of the University of Hamburg that was founded in 1919.

HAPAG and other German shipping lines had a financial stake in the acquisition of overseas colonies. Ballin, in fact, belonged to the Colonial Society which was founded in 1887 to promote German colonialism and was headquartered in Berlin. The Empire required reliable steamship connections for mail and freight, and vessels of the merchant marine also carried administrators, soldiers, sailors, and merchants to colonial outposts.

From 1901, HAPAG operated a postal service to Kiautschou in China. In 1907, the company extended its services to Africa when it took over a quarter of the *Woermann Linie's* trade to the continent, although the latter's ships remained under its own management. By 1914, HAPAG and the *Woermann Linie* maintained thirteen services from Hamburg to West Africa, twelve of which were devoted to freight with one carrying passengers to Douala in Cameroon. The company also provided service to the German colonies in South-West Africa. In so doing, it was one of many Hamburg firms that pioneered and pursued connections between Germany – including within the exploitative and violent phenomenon of colonialism – and the rest of the world.

IV

NDL became the world's largest steamship company in the 1890s. Yet it was succeeded by HAPAG in 1897 when, by its own account, the company moved 73,089 people and 2.3 million tons of freight around the globe.[172] In 1900, it owned the largest German fleet while NDL transported the largest number of passengers. And HAPAG grew rapidly over the next decade: it more than tripled its tonnage of shipping, grew its share capital from forty-five million to 125 million marks, and increased its profits from 9.7 million to 37.3 million marks.[173] By 1913, the company boasted fixed assets of 289 million marks, liquid assets of fifty-four million marks, and net profits equal to seventeen percent of its share capital.[174] In 1897, HAPAG's shore facilities were valued at 4.4 million marks; by 1907, this had increased to 18.5 million marks.[175] That said, it did not own its harbour facilities in Hamburg; it paid for their construction and leased them from the city.[176] But it purchased property on Unter den Linden in Berlin, in 1906, for its tourist and passenger offices. By 1908, it had offices in Bremen, Breslau, Cologne, Dresden, Frankfurt a.M., Hanover, Leipzig, and Munich. Others were located in Antwerp, Brussels, Cherbourg, Copenhagen, Florence, Genoa, Liverpool, London, Lucerne, Monte Carlo, Naples, Nice, Paris, Rome, Southampton, Vienna, and Zürich.

By 1914, Germany boasted the second-largest merchant fleet in the world and one of the most modern. It far surpassed those of France and the United

States.[177] On the eve of the First World War, the Empire possessed 2,160 steamships and 2,400 sailing vessels.[178] And, by 1914, HAPAG boasted a fleet of 194 ships and approximately 1,500,000 tons. By that time, the company owned over fifty percent of all shipping registered in Hamburg.[179] In size, it rivalled the largest German industrial enterprises and banks. And no company outside Germany "existed with even a vaguely similar liner network" to that of HAPAG.[180] In 1906, the company claimed that an assembly of its steamships "in one vast splendid armada of commerce would illustrate as well as anything could the stupendous growth of the world's facility for transportation by water of passengers and freight."[181]

HAPAG's annual reports for 1912 and 1913 present an impressive picture. It maintained seventy different services to all continents except Australia, called at more than 300 ports, and had a payroll of 29,000 people.[182] A large, two-page map of the world published in the journal *Hansa* in January 1914 indicates the routes plied by the company's ships. It depicts the globe criss-crossed by an impressive number of lines that become a veritable tangle on the Atlantic Ocean between Europe, North and South America, and Africa.[183] In fact, HAPAG was conducting so much business that its fleet was not adequate to its needs. In Britain, *The Marine Engineer and Naval Architect* stated that the company had chartered vessels for as many as 124 voyages in 1913.[184] And this business was incredibly diversified. Even in Britain, most shipping lines operated in only one field or sector. In fact, Ballin spoke disparagingly of the fragmentation of British shipping.[185] The only company comparable to HAPAG in diversification and reach at this time was NDL.

It is important to understand these impressive facts and figures in context and look beyond HAPAG's expert self-promotion. In 1914, the British merchant fleet was four times the size of Germany's. Although never plunged into a debilitating crisis, HAPAG suffered the adverse effects of the international economic slumps that occurred in the early 1890s and again in 1902–1903. It profited from the Russo–Japanese War (1904–1905), making significant revenue from the sale of several steamers to Russia and by supplying its fleet with coal.[186] Bernhard Huldermann even described the War as a rebirth for HAPAG.[187] But in response to the American financial crisis of 1907, HAPAG was forced to lay up fifteen vessels, suspend the construction of others, and cancel some of its services. Furthermore, as Frank Broeze has indicated, the company was actually less financially successful and less profitable than several of the smaller specialist shipping lines headquartered in Hamburg. Between 1900 and 1913, HAPAG's financial performance "consistently fell below companies such as Hamburg-Süd, Kosmos, and the Austral Line." The dividends paid by these companies in the decade before 1914 were "on average, between 2 and 3 percent per year higher" than those paid by HAPAG.[188] As we will see in the following chapter, there were those in its senior management who thought the decision to build the *Imperator*-class liners was unwise at a time when the sums annually invested by HAPAG exceeded its financial capacity.[189]

As noted in the introduction to this chapter, these liners have been described as Albert Ballin's *Geisteskinder*. Without doubt, the most momentous development in HAPAG's history in the three decades before the First World War occurred in 1886 when Ballin was hired to head its passenger department and revitalize its passenger services to North America. Born in Hamburg as the youngest of nine children in a Jewish family, Ballin was raised in modest circumstances. From the age of seventeen, he worked for Morris & Co., an emigration agency in which his father was a partner. The firm booked passengers from Germany through British ports to the United States; emigrants were carried to Britain in small vessels where they took passage on liners to America. In HAPAG, Ballin's rise was meteoric. In 1888, he was promoted to a directorship and became managing director in 1899. He held this position until his death in 1918.

All histories of the firm acknowledge Ballin's profound contribution to HAPAG'S spectacular growth and success and his important influence on everything from its global strategy to the design of its transatlantic liners. Niall Ferguson has correctly described him as "a bold business innovator."[190] And it is largely true that the form and direction that the company took from the 1890s was mostly "his creation and the product of his genius."[191] Ballin's appointment to a directorship in 1888 coincided with a shift in the firm's leadership from patriarchal structures to management in a modern sense.[192] He challenged the modest expectations of its previous directors, and their reluctance to take risks, with cosmopolitan sensibilities and a global vision; a keen understanding of the international nature of shipping; and a determination to expand the company and compete seriously with domestic and foreign rivals. Ballin freed HAPAG from the conservative approach it adopted beginning with the difficult years in the early 1870s and stimulated a desire to innovate in shipbuilding and experiment with new ideas. He presided over a huge expansion of the company's fleet and share capital, increased its gross income by a factor of seven, and drove much of the technical development of the line.[193] In addition, Ballin possessed a genius for advertising; as Gerhard Ritter has written, "more than any other major businessman of his time, he also recognized the necessity of public relations and advertising."[194] At the end of the 1890s, Ballin established the first public relations department to be found in any major German company: HAPAG'S literary bureau.[195]

Many commentators, biographers, and historians have seen Ballin and HAPAG as virtually synonymous. But this was definitely not the case; he was not, as *The Manchester Guardian* stated in 1914, "the supreme controller" of HAPAG's fortunes.[196] The company employed several extremely competent directors who exercised considerable independence in their respective spheres of responsibility. Furthermore, considerable tension existed between Ballin and his fellow directors as the result of his policy of enormous expenditure and the costly rate wars to which he committed HAPAG. And these tensions were common knowledge. To take one example, in 1908, *The New York Times* reported that disagreement among the company's directorship had resulted in the cancellation of the order for a new liner to be christened *Europa* (launched in 1912 as the *Imperator*) "which was to astonish the world"; the closure of offices in London and Paris; and even the replacement of Ballin as managing director by Emil Boas, the company's general manager in the United States. The paper claimed that Ballin's replacement had been expected by the international shipping industry for the last six months.[197] As we will see in the following chapter, discord among HAPAG's directorship extended to the wisdom of building a liner as large and costly as the *Imperator*.

To be sure, a more nuanced and accurate understanding of the influence Ballin exercised in his position as managing director does not diminish the fact that it was profound. Yet biographers and historians disagree about the particular nature of his vision, motivations, and goals. One problem is accurately ascertaining what these were; Ballin often provided little insight into the vision that informed his policies. In addition, HAPAG's annual reports were factual, "containing only comments on the activities and results of the company in the context of current circumstances."[198] Most importantly, much of Ballin's *Nachlaß* was destroyed or dispersed after his death in 1918.

Biographies published in the 1920s, by men who worked alongside him, offer the image of a German patriot who put his nation's interests before those of his company. In these accounts, Ballin is portrayed as a man who sought to resolve conflicts with domestic competitors for the benefit of all German shipping interests. Cooperation with NDL increased when Heinrich Wiegand became its director in 1892. From 1893, the companies even began to advertise together. Publicity in New York, for example, promoting the "German Mediterranean Service" detailed sailings offered by both lines to Gibraltar, Algiers, Naples, and Genoa.[199] In the eyes of early biographers, Ballin was also keenly aware that HAPAG's well-being was bound up with that of foreign shipping firms. As a consequence, he was an important motive force behind the organization of conferences and syndicates that regulated competition in international shipping. One of the more important examples of such agreements was the *Nordatlantischer Dampfer-Linien Verband*, or North Atlantic Conference. This was constituted in 1892 by HAPAG, NDL, the Antwerp-based Red Star Line, the Holland-America Line, and France's Compagnie Générale Transatlantique. Its purpose was to fix quotas with respect to the number of steerage passengers carried by each line in order to prevent rate wars that were damaging to all.[200]

In 1908, Ballin was instrumental in bringing the Conference together with British, American, and Canadian shipping lines to form the Atlantic Conference. Headquartered in Cologne with a secretary to arbitrate disputes, this great transatlantic shipping pool set common prices, divided steerage passengers between the carriers, and assigned specific ports to different lines. The purpose of the agreement was

> to fix quotas for each company according to the size of their fleet and pre-vious business; to fix prices according to the quality of the service and

accommodation required; to collect part of the fares in a "Pool" from which compensation was paid to those lines which had not reached their full quota.[201]

Lamar Cecil's important biography of 1967 offers a more detached account of Ballin's career than those published shortly after his death. But like the biographers before him, Cecil depicts Ballin as a man of mediation and diplomacy, a magnate who subordinated his own business interests to the well-being of Germany's merchant marine. Similarly, and more recently, Gerhard Ritter has emphasized that HAPAG's managing director understood the financial and commercial advantages of associations and regulation; any hostility he demonstrated in dealing with other shipping lines was but one facet of a strategy whose ultimate goal was to create a firm foundation for negotiations that would benefit all parties.[202]

A very different portrait was presented by Frank Broeze in a series of articles published in the 1990s. These shifted the substance of writing on Ballin from hagiography to critical evaluation. In them, the author argued that the persistent portrait of HAPAG's managing director as a man of consensus and compromise is the result of effective company propaganda. Far from pursuing cooperation and conciliation, Ballin was a ruthless businessman of overweening ambition who waged "commercial warfare" to realign "international relations into constellations more congenial to the interests and requirements" of his company."[203] Associations and conferences were "not objectives but tactics to be employed and exploited by the company."[204] Consequently, when HAPAG's interests were not served by these agreements, the company withdrew from them. Ultimately, Ballin was never satisfied with any agreement with other domestic or foreign shipping lines and always aimed to increase HAPAG's share of the industry. Max Schinckel, the long-standing chairman of the company's board of control, believed that it was Ballin's aim to take over all other Hamburg shipping lines as well as those based in Bremen.[205] And, from the late 1890s, NDL became the particular target of his expansionist ambitions. It "was hunted everywhere" by HAPAG.[206] As early as 1897, Ballin succeeded in obtaining a share of Germany's East Asian mail contract and "demonstrated his willingness to attack Lloyd wherever it was established."[207] He also claimed that the *Imperator*-class liners entitled HAPAG to a larger share of the steerage pool established by the Atlantic Conference. But NDL refused to recognize this claim and, on 31 January 1914, HAPAG withdrew from the Conference. It was at the behest of the Kaiser that talks were begun to settle the differences between the companies. Yet ultimately, in Broeze's opinion, Ballin's ambitions were such that he would have driven HAPAG to financial ruin if not for the outbreak of war in August of that year.

The fact that many contemporaries saw Ballin as waging a ruthless commercial war with other domestic and foreign shipping interests is clear from the substantial press reporting that was devoted to him on both sides of the Atlantic. Unsurprisingly, the portrait that was painted in the international press over several years was changing, complex, and sometimes contradictory. We will look at this again, especially in chapters five and six. But a distinct and recurring facet of Ballin's image was that of a tough-minded captain of industry for whom agreement and conciliation were but tools to furthering his own interests. To take one of many examples, in early 1914, readers of *The New York Times* were informed in Ballin's own words that he was interested in syndicates and international agreements only so long as they served the goals of HAPAG. Readers were also apprised of the company's antagonistic relations with other shipping lines; in fact, those with NDL were said to be so acrimonious that the latter was "prepared to risk everything to accomplish Ballin's defeat." The paper "feared that any other result might mean the eventual absorption of the North German Lloyd by the Hamburg-American, which is said long to have contemplated the subjugation of its great rival."[208]

In 1908, J. Russell Smith, a professor at the University of Pennsylvania, published a book on ocean transportation in which he described HAPAG as a ruthless competitor killing small rivals in a manner similar to an "American trust."[209] His text included a long quote from a complaint against HAPAG that was brought before the Interstate Commerce Commission. This was made by Peter Wright & Sons, a shipping firm based in Philadelphia, in the wake of its attempt to constitute a service between that city and Copenhagen. Advised by HAPAG to withdraw the service, and having suffered damaging competition following its refusal to do so, the American company accused its German rival of "maintaining monopolies in restraint of trade." It stated that, after "years of aggressive tactics," HAPAG stood as "the absolute dictator of German-American trade." It also claimed that no steamship company in the United States or elsewhere "dares to question its lofty supremacy; such temerity would be followed immediately by attempted extermination."[210]

Unsurprisingly, the press in Germany, Britain, and America often cast the company and its managing director in a still more profound role: as a symbol and embodiment of Germany's bid for world-power status. The part that Ballin and HAPAG played in the Empire's rise as a world power, and the extent to which the company contributed to the tensions that erupted in the First World War, was and is a subject of considerable interest. Broeze believes that "in pursuing his unrestricted shipping *Weltpolitik* Ballin was a greater disturber of the peace than any other ship owner at the time."[211] Douglas R. Burgess has argued that competition between Germany and Britain to build the largest and most luxurious transatlantic liners paralleled the naval race and aided the disintegration of relations between the two countries.[212]

Many German contemporaries saw things the same way. Some cast international developments in merchant shipping in terms of a profound rivalry between nations. In 1911, the German author Adolph Goetz described the history of HAPAG as a struggle, not only against foreign shipping companies, but against the states that backed them. He went further to describe the competition between the merchant marines of different nations as a conflict critical to the well-being of societies and peoples.[213] Others implicated Ballin as directly responsible for stoking international tensions. As the keel of the *Imperator* was being laid down in 1910, the journalist Georg Schröder warned that HAPAG's desire to expand its fleet was likely to lead to war with England. "Germany," he asserted, "has made an enemy of the whole world through HAPAG, that is, through Ballin."[214] In the spring of 1914, Walter Freyer, a former president of the Hamburg ship officers' union, published *Im Kampf um den Ozean: Seeroman*.[215] In the novel, a ruthless shipping magnate named Moritz Bebacher brings Germany and England to the brink of war as the result of his unprincipled behaviour. Recognizing a portrait of himself, Ballin actually helped publicize the book by bringing a successful libel suit against its author. As Lamar Cecil notes, "the term *Ballinismus* was coined by Ballin's foes to describe a policy characterized by complete ruthlessness."[216] Even among HAPAG's directorship, there were those who felt that Ballin's "insensate determination to drive the HAPAG forward" could lead to problems with England.[217] And during the First World War, Ballin was criticized in the German press for leading the country into the conflict.

It is hardly surprising that commentators in Britain and the United States should see Ballin as representative of Germany's expansionist aims. Chapters five and six examine this in more detail. But it is interesting to note here that, with the launch of the *Imperator* and *Vaterland*, England's *Daily News* claimed that HAPAG had "declared war on the world." It continued saying that "if our claim to rule the waves is threatened, this threat comes not from the German dreadnoughts but from Herr Ballin."[218] Upon his death in 1918, *The New York Times* stated that, under his directorship, HAPAG shouldered a great responsibility "in inducing Germany to make the gamble for world domination." But it also claimed that Ballin had stimulated "the course of peaceful maritime development all over the world." It added that the growth of Germany's merchant marine had been "accomplished without arousing animosity in other countries."[219]

This opinion from *The New York Times* is indicative of the fact that the role played by HAPAG in stoking the international tensions that led to war is complex and difficult to define precisely. So is Ballin's identity in its multi-faceted, even conflicted nature as German, Jew, patriot, and cosmopolitan. [220] Ballin's nationalist sentiments were well known. He publically expressed support for Admiral Tirpitz and the building of a German battle fleet that he believed provided security for the Empire's merchant shipping. He was a member of the Navy League and HAPAG contributed funds to this interest group whose aim was to arouse popular interest in, and enthusiasm for the construction of the Imperial Navy. He supported the semi-authoritarian structures of the German state and was critical of what he perceived as the Liberal attachment to parliamentary politics, believing that they were ineffectual. Of particular interest in the English and American press was what was perceived as Ballin's close relationship with the Kaiser, and what was thought to be his ability to influence the Imperial government. Wilhelm visited Ballin's Hamburg home in 1905 and on his desk stood a portrait of the Kaiser with a handwritten dedication: "To the farseeing, untiring pioneer of our German trade and export."[221] In 1906, *The Washington Post* reported on rumours appearing in the German press that Wilhelm had selected Ballin to succeed Bernhard von Bülow as Chancellor and that he was to be ennobled.[222]

Yet despite what contemporaries thought, historians now understand that Ballin's influence on the Kaiser was very limited. Broeze calls their relationship an "empty friendship."[223] Moreover, Ballin was critical of Wilhelm's faults and the narrow-mindedness of government ministers and bureaucrats. In his opinion, the highest position Chancellor Bethmann-Hollweg could competently fill at HAPAG was that of librarian.[224] Wanting trade to be unhindered by politics, Ballin was an opponent of government subventions and the agrarian protectionism of the Conservative party. Furthermore, he was an Anglophile who clearly believed there was a difference between commercial rivalry and a naval arms race, and was critical of the latter. In fact, Ballin was involved in the project of détente that Germany actively pursued during the decade prior to 1914.[225] From 1908, he found himself ever more at odds with Tirpitz's position and applied himself to ending military tensions believing "economic rationality and a common interest in peace" would prevent war.[226]

Ballin even began a campaign for Anglo-German naval talks, meeting the merchant banker Sir Ernest Cassel in London in 1908 and 1909, and reporting to the Kaiser about the possibility of a fleet agreement. The two men acted as unofficial intermediaries for their respective nations before the establishment of formal dialogue. When negotiations in February 1912 failed to reach an agreement whereby Germany would recognize English naval superiority, Ballin conferred with Britain's Secretary of State for War, Richard Haldane, and First Lord of the Admiralty, Winston Churchill, in an attempt to understand the stumbling blocks to Anglo-German rapprochement. Yet informal negotiations collapsed in March 1912. He and Cassel attempted to resume talks in early 1914, but war erupted in August of that year. Ballin was devastated by these events, and especially the entry of Britain into the conflict on 4 August. Clearly, he and his company had not intentionally led Germany into a war that would do so much damage to their enterprise. But in aggressively pursuing private commerce and the interests of HAPAG, *Ballinismus* contributed to the real and imagined antagonism between Britain and Germany in the years before the First World War.

V

In 1907, HAPAG described the Atlantic as "the most important highway of modern global trade." It stated that, upon it, the company employed "its largest and most capacious, its most expensive, most luxurious, and speediest steamers."[227] While true, HAPAG actually employed a variety of vessels on its North American routes. It sailed freighters carrying only cargo, for example, and ships that were principally cargo vessels but also accommodated steerage passengers. These could be run at a profit in times of economic recession and a decline in emigrant traffic. It also commissioned liners of moderate size and speed with quarters for passengers of all classes and substantial cargo capacity. And it employed express steamers with accommodation for all classes and much less storage for cargo.

Just prior to the First World War, HAPAG's services to the United States constituted the most important part of its enterprise. From 1910 until July 1914, while the company continued to expand globally, it redirected the majority of its investments to the North Atlantic, especially in the form of the *Imperator*-class liners. Although HAPAG transported only thirty percent of its total world-wide tonnage of freight on these waters, much of it consisting of grain, it carried sixty percent of its passengers.[228] It was here that the company employed the largest proportion of its fleet and earned most of its profits. No less important, this is where its prestige was most at stake.[229] In fact, from 1893, the company referred to itself as the *Hamburg-Amerika Linie*. The legally established name of the company – *Hamburg-Amerikanische Packetfahrt-Aktien-Gesellschaft* – was never changed. But it had little appeal for Ballin who introduced *Hamburg-Amerika Linie* in the hope of branding the company with a shorter and more recognizable name similar to "Lloyd" by which the North German Lloyd was commonly known around the world.[230]

HAPAG operated a complex network of services on the North Atlantic, its ships sailing to ports including Baltimore, Boston, Galveston, Halifax, Montreal, New Orleans, Newport News, and Philadelphia. But none of these services matched the profitability of its traditional trunk line to New York. As previously noted, by 1893, HAPAG was carrying more passengers to New York than NDL. It carried more first-class passengers from Germany to Manhattan than any other competitor for the first time in 1906.[231] In that year, the company offered three passenger services between Hamburg and New York: an express service carrying American and European mail; a passenger service with larger vessels of less speed calling at Plymouth, Dover, and Cherbourg; and a direct service between the two cities.

It was the desire to build ever larger and faster express steamers travelling to New York that provoked considerable competition between Britain and Germany from the 1880s. HAPAG often led the way, and played a critical role in perfecting the express steamer and luxury liner. Speed was a requisite of success for transatlantic shipping lines; the duration of crossings between the English Channel and New York was keenly followed in the Anglo-American press and played an important role in the public's perception of the major steamship companies. One of the developments permitting the construction of swifter transatlantic liners was the increased use of steel, instead of iron, as a construction and structural material during the 1880s. It had long been resisted as too expensive, of uncertain quality, and because it was difficult to handle.[232] And yet steel was strong, elastic, and reduced a hull's weight; a vessel built of steel could be fourteen percent lighter than a similar one of iron.[233] This meant less expenditure on fuel, as well as greater stability and safety in rough seas, and in the event of collision. Steel also permitted the construction of larger vessels with higher decks that facilitated the design of more elaborate cabins, private suites, and grander public spaces.

Equally important was the introduction of new propulsion mechanisms consisting of steam turbines driving double, triple, and eventually quadruple screws. In the early twentieth century, these were fitted to passenger liners, freighters, and warships to replace reciprocating engines that employed pistons. The turbine engine consisted of a geared propulsion system supplied with steam from water-tube boilers turning rotating blades to drive a propeller shaft. Before the First World War, turbines were still coal fired and vessels were loaded with tons of it before each voyage in what was a very dirty process. By 1890, HAPAG estimated that its vessels had consumed 15,000,000 tons since its founding.[234] The journalist Egon Erwin Kisch reported that it took twenty hours for coal elevators to bunker the *Vaterland* with almost 9,000 tons.[235] It was not until after the First World War that passenger liners employed oil fuel. That said, the steam turbine was cleaner and more efficient than a reciprocating engine and gave high-power output without vibration, something that was advantageous both in terms of a vessel's durability and the comfort of its passengers. Turbines also used less coal at greater speeds, weighed much less, and occupied less space than reciprocating engines, thus increasing a vessel's cargo capacity.

Constructed of steel, the *Imperator* was Germany's first turbine-driven, quadruple-screw liner. But HAPAG'S first express steamer, and the company's first true luxury liner, was launched many years earlier in 1888. The *Augusta Victoria* was built by Vulcan and christened in honour of the German Empress. It was Germany's first double-screw liner and the first express steamer built by a German yard. Measuring 460 feet in length, displacing 7,661 gross tons, and equipped with three funnels, it was also the largest vessel constructed in Germany to that date. HAPAG claimed that its launch was heralded throughout the nation "as an event of unusual significance" as it demonstrated that the Empire's shipbuilding industry "was well able to cope with the English rival."[236] Its first-class interiors were designed in the French Rococo style by NDL's house architect, Johann Poppe (1837–1915), and received critical acclaim from the travelling public.

On its maiden voyage to New York, with Ballin on board, the *Augusta Victoria* crossed from Southampton in just seven days at a speed averaging almost twenty knots. *The New York Times* claimed that while docked in Hoboken, requests to visit the vessel came "pouring in" to HAPAG's offices. As a result, the company decided to host an on-board reception, and it was estimated that nearly 30,000 visitors toured the ship on the afternoon of 22 May 1889.[237] HAPAG commissioned other liners of this type in quick succession between 1889 and 1891, contracting both German and British yards. The most famous were the *Columbia, Normannia,* and the *Fürst Bismarck.* These attracted a considerable number of cabin-class travellers and played a critical role in ensuring the success of HAPAG's passenger services to the United States.

By the early 1890s, the company possessed the most modern fleet of all European shipping lines. As Nils Schwerdtner writes, in "a giant leap they had overtaken most of their opponents and taken one of the first ranks in North Atlantic shipping."[238] But it is also true that the greatest expansion of the entire German merchant marine happened during the 1890s. More passenger vessels were launched in that decade than any other. And just prior to 1900, it was NDL, with its commitment to making express passenger service its priority, that commissioned the world's largest and fastest passenger liner. By this time, the transatlantic liner had "matured into the design it would retain through all future improvements."[239] Built by Vulcan and named in honour of Wilhelm II's grandfather, the *Kaiser Wilhelm der Große* was launched on 3 May 1897 in the presence of the Kaiser. Some historians consider it to be the first transatlantic super liner, and it was the first of a quartet of similar vessels that NDL christened in honour of the Hohenzollerns.[240] Measuring 655 feet in length, displacing 14,349 gross tons, equipped with four funnels, and able to carry 1,970 passengers, the *Kaiser Wilhelm der Große* made the crossing to New York in five days and seventeen hours, breaking the record held by Cunard's *Lucania* since 1894 and capturing the Blue Riband. This was the unofficial and intangible award presented to the merchant vessel that recorded the highest average speed for a transatlantic crossing in the westbound direction. As Matthew S. Seligmann explains, holding the award "was an important indicator of commercial success."[241] The *Kaiser Wilhelm der Große* marked both the beginning of the era of four-funnel steamers and the beginning of German dominance on the North Atlantic. In fact, its maiden voyage on 19 September 1897 initiated a decade in which the Empire's liners outclassed those launched by British companies, at least in terms of speed, until Cunard's *Lusitania* and *Mauretania* entered service in 1907.

The *Kaiser Wilhelm der Große* made HAPAG's express steamers, including the *Augusta Victoria*, a second choice for European and American cabin-class passengers. In response, the company built the four-funnel *Deutschland* which entered service in 1900. Measuring 684 feet in length, displacing 16,502 gross tons, and accommodating 2,050 passengers, it was the largest passenger liner of its time. Although it boasted a gymnasium and a grill-room restaurant that freed first-class passengers from scheduled meals, HAPAG described the vessel as decorated "less grandiosely" than its previous express steamers. And yet at a price of 12.5 million marks, the *Deutschland* cost more than half of what HAPAG had spent building its first four express steamers.[242] It captured the Blue Riband the very year it entered service and held the title until 1906 when it was taken by NDL's *Kaiser Wilhelm II*. Its swiftest crossing to New York was made in five days, seven hours, and thirty-eight minutes.[243]

The prestige value of express steamers like the *Deutschland* was enormous. And yet the liner was not the success HAPAG hoped for. The obsession with speed entailed high running costs, as well as uncomfortable hull vibration and excessive noise from high-speed engines.[244] In fact, this vibration was such that it caused the rupture of the vessel's cast-iron stern frame less than two years after its launch. As a result, the *Deutschland* was popularly known as The Cocktail Shaker.[245] The emphasis on speed also meant that new express steamers, which were expensive to build and operate, were quickly outdated due to the rapid pace of technological innovation.[246] Furthermore, HAPAG found that the *Deutschland* and its other express steamers were not economical. While they transported mail, their capacity for freight was considerably diminished as a result of the large amount of space afforded passenger accommodation, large engines, and enormous coal bunkers. The *Deutschland* consumed 574 tons of coal daily. As Shwerdtner emphasizes, the high speed of this and other express steamers "resulted in equally high coal consumption and, not being equipped to handle much cargo, they had to be well-booked to generate any profit at all."[247] Moreover, these vessels were profitable only between April and October when affluent Americans and Europeans crossed the Atlantic.

Despite the high costs and low profits, express steamers permitted HAPAG to be a successful competitor in the Atlantic passenger business. But it was not long before the company turned to building larger liners of more moderate speed. The greater capacity of larger, if slower vessels for passengers and freight meant higher financial yields that made operating them more economical. Moreover, the preference of transatlantic cabin-class passengers was changing from swift crossings to spacious and comfortable accommodation combined with high-quality service. As early as 1902, HAPAG claimed that increasing numbers of its clientele were attracted not to the *Deutschland* but to the slower steamers *Blücher* and *Moltke* that the company launched in 1901. At the same time in England, the White Star Line was having success attracting cabin-class passengers with its slower, yet larger, more spacious, and more comfortably outfitted liners including the *Oceanic*, the *Celtic*, and the *Cedric* that were launched between 1899 and 1902.

Consequently, HAPAG decided to shift its focus from building the fastest steamers on the Atlantic to building liners designed to meet the changing demands and expectations of the valuable cabin-class sector of their market. It made size, comfort, luxury, and dependability its priorities. "The ship of the future," the company explained, "must be a new luxury ship" characterized by "spaciousness, beauty, and safety."[248] After the *Lusitania* captured the Blue Riband in 1907, *The Washington Post* reported that HAPAG was content to let it remain in the hands of Cunard.[249]

It must be remembered that HAPAG continued to commission vessels for other routes. In 1904 and 1905, for example, it bought or built several steamers for its Mexican, South American, and East Asian services. But along with domestic and foreign competitors, the company committed itself to an especially ambitious programme of construction for the crossing to Manhattan, and launched several vessels prior to the outbreak of war in 1914. It was able to do this in spite of the financial crisis of 1908. While NDL was harder hit and not in a position to build two vessels of over 30,000 tons each until 1913, HAPAG quickly regained its financial health and raised new capital to expand its fleet. The company made enormous profits between 1911 and 1913, amounting to about 187 million marks.[250] As a result, the tonnage of Germany's premier passenger liners grew enormously and quickly. While it doubled between 1897 and 1907, it tripled between the launch of NDL's *Kronprinzessin Cecilie* in 1906 and that of the *Imperator* in 1912. The average length of transatlantic liners also grew from 400 to 900 feet. With this dramatic increase in size, the harbours of Hamburg, Southampton, Liverpool, and New York were repeatedly dredged to accommodate new liners.[251]

HAPAG's decision to make size, comfort, and luxury its priorities first took form in the *Amerika* and the *Kaiserin Auguste Victoria*. These entered service in 1905 and 1906 respectively and the company claimed they announced a new era in Atlantic travel.[252] At 700 feet in length and displacing 24,581 tons, the *Kaiserin Auguste Victoria* was the largest liner afloat and could carry over 1,000 cabin-class passengers and 2,300 emigrants in steerage. Both vessels offered extra space and comfort to all classes, and first-class accommodation was among the most luxurious on the Atlantic. As HAPAG explained, "in the splendid spaciousness of the *Amerika* and *Kaiserin Auguste Victoria* are apartments of such noble size and elegance that they would fit into any palace of the Old World."[253] The interiors of the *Amerika* were designed by Charles Frédéric Mewès (1860–1914), the French architect of the Ritz hotels in London and Paris. Mewès had a significant impact on the design of modern luxury liners; he conceived of them as defined by their interiors and passenger accommodation, not by the structural constraints of the vessel. His vision would find its most complete expression in the *Imperator*-class liners.

The Cunard Line's *Umbria* and *Etruria* were among the first liners promoted to the public as floating hotels when they were launched in 1884. Each featured a dining room, music room, ladies salon, barber shop, and improved sanitary facilities for their cabin-class passengers.[254] But HAPAG began offering on-board accommodation and service comparable to that of luxury hotels such as New York's Waldorf Astoria, the Paris Ritz, and the Berlin Adlon. One English journalist credited the "secret of German success" in the Atlantic passenger trade to the fact that its companies established a new standard whereby liners accommodated themselves to the demands of passengers and not vice versa.[255] The *Amerika* was outfitted with electric elevators, libraries, a palm court, a winter garden, hydropathic baths, and gymnasiums. These became standard features aboard luxury liners for the next two decades. The first-class dining room aboard the *Kaiserin Auguste Victoria* was provided with individual tables, instead of long trestles, thus creating a hotel-like atmosphere. And with extra-tariff Ritz-Carlton restaurants under the independent direction of César Ritz, both liners offered à-la-carte meals of Parisian cuisine and with "all the attractions of the best hotels."[256] Yet comfort was not entirely limited to cabin-class clientele. For the first time, emigrant passengers could book cabins in third-class accommodation.

HAPAG claimed that its new liners could only be surpassed if "floating islands" were put to sea.[257] And, to be sure, they received high praise in the press on both sides of the Atlantic. In 1906, London's *Daily Mail* reported that

Figure 1.3 Unidentified artist. The *Amerika*. Lithograph. No date.
Source: The Mariners' Museum, Newport News, VA.

"the *Amerika* embodies the highest perfection in respect of construction, furnishing and outfitting." Being operated "with the care and vision which once was the exclusive national property of the British," the paper claimed that "the *Amerika* will undoubtedly find numerous imitators among the shipbuilders of all nations, even if an increase in extravagant luxury seems scarcely possible."[258] As we will see in chapter six, the *Kaiserin Auguste Victoria* elicited high praise from President Theodore Roosevelt himself and 30,000 people greeted the vessel in New York upon the completion of its maiden voyage.[259]

Yet it was not long before HAPAG's liners were surpassed by those of its British competitors. Entering service in 1907, Cunard's *Lusitania* and *Mauretania* were the first turbine-driven superliners. Measuring 787 and 790 feet in length, they displaced over 31,000 tons each and, with a speed of twenty-five knots, were not only larger but also faster than their German rivals. Arnold Kludas has argued that, until they entered service, the liners commissioned by all shipping companies amounted to a succession of small ships.[260] The *Lusitania* and *Mauretania* broke boundaries in terms of their size and the spaciousness of their interiors, boundaries that were rapidly and dramatically extended in the short time before the First World War. Their cabin-class interiors were not designed by naval architects but by the interior designers Harold Peto (1854–1933) and James Miller (1860–1947). First-class accommodation offered Edwardian-era hotel luxury with lounges, salons, dining rooms, libraries, smoking rooms, and private parlours sumptuously decorated in a variety of historical-revival styles.

Of course, British shipping companies were not the only ones competing with HAPAG for cabin-class passengers. NDL commissioned liners which, if smaller than their Cunard rivals, were nonetheless prestigious. The *Kronprinzessin Cecilie* was launched in 1906. At just over 19,000 tons, its maiden voyage in 1907 seems to have attracted little attention outside Germany, as the interest of the Atlantic world was captured by Cunard's latest vessels. The *George Washington* was launched in 1908 and, displacing 25,570 gross tons, was Germany's largest liner. It was the first in a planned series of vessels intended to update and replace NDL's ageing fleet and was to be complemented by two liners of just over 30,000 tons: the *Columbus* and the *Hindenberg*. But the financial difficulties suffered by NDL, especially from 1908, meant that it was not in a position to build these vessels until 1913. The First World War put a halt to their construction. In any case, as Edwin Drechsel explains, the competition mounted by HAPAG and Cunard was "unbeatable by NDL in any foreseeable future and meant a declining of passenger traffic."[261] The Compagnie Générale Transatlantique launched the *France* in September 1910 as the flagship of the nation's merchant marine. Sailing between Le Havre and New York, it displaced just over 24,500 tons and measured 713 feet in length. Thus, while it was twice the size of any previous passenger liner flying the French flag, it had no pretension to being the largest, nor the fastest liner on the Atlantic. Yet it received high praise for its cabin-class public rooms that were decorated in a pastiche of historical-revival styles including Louis XIV, French Empire, and Moorish. In fact, the vessel proved so successful that the company set out to build four successively larger and more luxurious liners.

Yet all of these vessels were surpassed by White Star's trio of Olympic-class steamers of 45,000 tons. While Cunard's *Mauretania* and *Lusitania* were still express steamers of the Blue-Riband category, White Star made comfort and luxury more important than speed. Launched in 1910 and 1911, the first-class interiors of the *Olympic* and *Titanic* were modelled on stately European homes, palaces, and grand hotels. They boasted spa-like facilities, gymnasiums and, for the first time on transatlantic liners, indoor pools. A letter posted by a first-class passenger on 19 June 1913 provides a vivid impression of the *Olympic*:

> ... this is the finest boat in the world – not quite as fast as the Mauretania and Lusitania, but infinitely more luxurious and comfortable. The rooms are big and luxuriously furnished, and the restaurant is a model of excellence. It is a better restaurant, service considered and everything considered, than there is in all New York.[262]

White Star felt that cabin-class passengers would pay for the luxury and comfort of its new liners instead of opting for the faster, but smaller and less comfortable Cunard vessels.

Albert Ballin believed Germany's shipping lines had no choice but to respond to the introduction of the new British steamers if they were to avoid relegation to the second rank of carriers on the Atlantic. It was in this context that HAPAG made the decision to build a trio of passenger liners larger and more luxurious than anything its competitors had ever commissioned. This was an aggressive move to regain some of the valuable cabin-class custom that Cunard's *Lusitania* and *Mauretania* had already captured and that White Star's new liners were bound to do. And yet, even considering the size to which HAPAG had grown in its relatively short history, it was also a risky move, as building and operating such vessels would entail enormous expenditure. It was not a risk that everyone in HAPAG's senior management agreed was worth taking.

Yet once the decision was made and construction begun, it was inevitable that these liners would attract considerable national and international attention, especially in Britain and America. HAPAG had grown to such size and importance as a German and global enterprise that its transatlantic steamers were already construed as representative of the German Empire. But they were also anticipated, interpreted, and viewed as embodiments of forces transforming the western world at large. Their role as national monuments was but one aspect of their symbolic functioning in this sphere.

Notes

1 For the *Imperator*'s eagle see Arnold Kludas, *Die Geschichte der Hapag-Schiffe* (2 vols.) (Bremen, 2007–2008), vol. 2, 184ff.

2 See Susanne Wiborg and Klaus Wiborg, *1847–1997: Unser Feld ist die Welt: 150 Jahre Hapag-Lloyd* (Hamburg, 1997), 12–15.

3 Wiborg and Wiborg, *1847–1997*, 15.

4 HAPAG, *Die Hamburg-Amerika Linie: Im Sechsten Jahrzehnt Ihrer Entwicklung 1897–1907* (Berlin, 1907), 53–9.

5 For a manageable summary see Walter Kresse, "Die Deutsche Handelsschiffahrt", in Volker Plagemann, ed., *Übersee. Seefahrt und Seemacht im deutschen Kaiserreich* (Munich, 1988), 143–52.

6 Frank Broeze quoted in Gelina Harlaftis, Stig Tenold, and Jesús M. Valdaliso, "Introduction", in Gelina Harlaftis, Stig Tenold, and Jesús M. Valdaliso, eds., *The World's Key Industry: History and Economics of International Shipping* (Houndmills and New York, 2012), 2.

7 Sebastian Conrad, *Globalization and the Nation in Imperial Germany* (Cambridge, 2010), 1.

8 Conrad, *Globalization*, 45f.

9 Sebastian Conrad acknowledges the importance of steamships for transnational connections and trade but devotes only one paragraph to the subject. See Conrad, *Globalization*, 35.

10 This word is used by Bernhard Huldermann, *Albert Ballin* (Oldenburg and Berlin, 1922), 176.

11 Quoted in Susanne Wiborg, *Albert Ballin* (Hamburg, 2000), 11.
12 Wiborg and Wiborg, *1847–1997*, 20. The sum is recorded as 465,000 marks in HAPAG, *Sixty Years of Ocean Navigation and the Half Century Anniversary of the Establishment of the First Line of Steamships Flying a German Flag* (New York, 1906), 9.
13 Quoted in Richard J. Evans, *Death in Hamburg: Society and Politics in the Cholera Years* (London, 2005), 4.
14 Facts and figures for all HAPAG vessels discussed in this chapter are derived from Kludas, *Die Geschichte der Hapag-Schiffe*.
15 HAPAG, *Sixty Years*, 13.
16 HAPAG, *Sixty Years*, 13.
17 See Stephen Fox, *Transatlantic: Samuel Cunard, Isambard Brunel, and the Great Atlantic Steamships* (New York, 2003).
18 Arnold Kludas, *Die Geschichte der deutschen Passagierschiffahrt* (5 vols.) (Hamburg, 1986–1990), vol. 1, 11.
19 Quoted in HAPAG, *Souvenir of the Hamburg-American Line* (Berlin, 1908), u.p.
20 Charles Dickens, *American Notes* and *A Child's History of England* (London, Edinburgh, and New York, n.d.), 8.
21 Dickens, *American Notes*, 10.
22 Dickens, *American Notes*, 8.
23 See David M. Williams and John Armstrong, "An Appraisal of the Progress of the Steamship in the Nineteenth Century", in Harlaftis, Tenold, and Valdaliso, eds., *The World's Key Industry*, 43–63; Heide Gerstenberger and Ulrich Welke, *Vom Wind zum Dampf: Sozialgeschichte der deutschen Handelsschiffahrt im Zeitalter der Industrialisierung* (Münster, 1996).
24 See Kludas, *Die Geschichte der deutschen Passagierschiffahrt*, vol. 1, 14f.
25 Kludas, *Die Geschichte der deutschen Passagierschiffahrt*, vol. 1, 94.
26 Kludas, *Die Geschichte der deutschen Passagierschiffahrt*, vol. 1, 22.
27 Kludas, *Die Geschichte der Hapag-Schiffe*, vol. 1, 26.
28 Fox, *Transatlantic*, 367.
29 Fox, *Transatlantic*, 367.
30 See Edwin Drechsel, *Norddeutscher Lloyd Bremen, 1857–1970: History-Fleet-Ship Mails* (2 vols.) (Vancouver, 1994–1995); Wiborg and Wiborg, *1847–1997*.
31 See Wiborg and Wiborg, *1847–1997*.
32 See Kludas, *Die Geschichte der deutschen Passagierschiffahrt*, vol. 1, 102; Ernst von Reventlow, "The Shipbuilding Industry of Germany", *Cassier's Magazine: An Engineering Monthly* 40 (1911), 786.
33 Fox, *Transatlantic*, 379.
34 HAPAG, *Souvenir*.
35 HAPAG, *Sixty Years*, 6.
36 HAPAG, *Sixty Years*.
37 Conrad, *Globalization*, 29.
38 Gelina Harlaftis, Stig Tenold, and Jesús M. Valdaliso, "Epilogue: A Key Industry or an Invisible Industry", in Harlaftis, Tenold, and Valdaliso, eds., *The World's Key Industry*, 265.
39 This is the argument made in Harlaftis, Tenold, and Valdaliso, eds., *The World's Key Industry*.
40 Kludas, *Die Geschichte der Hapag-Schiffe*, vol. 1, 40.
41 Wiborg and Wiborg, *1847–1997*, 51.
42 Wiborg and Wiborg, *1847–1997*, 50.
43 Wiborg and Wiborg, *1847–1997*, 54.
44 Nils Schwerdtner, *German Luxury Ocean Liners: From Kaiser Wilhelm der Grosse to AIDAstella* (Stroud, 2013), 192.

45 Gerhard A. Ritter, "Der Kaiser und sein Reeder Albert Ballin, die HAPAG und das Verhältnis von Wirtshaft und Politik im Kaiserreich und in den Ersten Jahren der Weimarer Republik", *Zeitschrift für Unternehmensgeschichte* 42 (1997), 142.

46 Dagmar Bellmann, *Von Höllengefährten zu schwimmenden Palästen. Die Passagierschiffahrt auf dem Atlantik (1840–1930)* (Frankfurt and New York, 2015), 50.

47 Kludas, *Die Geschichte der Hapag-Schiffe*, vol. 1, 46.

48 Kludas, *Die Geschichte der deutschen Passagierschiffahrt*, vol. 1, 100.

49 Philip Dawson, *The Liner: Retrospective and Renaissance* (New York and London, 2005), 50.

50 Reventlow, "The Shipbuilding Industry", 786.

51 Dawson, *The Liner*, 50.

52 See Fritz W. Achilles, "Vom Binnenland zum Weltmeer. Die Infrastruktur des Reiches", in Plagemann, ed., *Übersee*, 53–7.

53 See Kurt Illies, "Schiffbau in Forschung und Lehre", in Plagemann, ed., *Übersee*, 135–9.

54 Lawrence Sondhaus, *Preparing for Weltpolitik: German Sea Power before the Tirpitz Era* (Annapolis, MD, 1997), 186f.

55 Dawson, *The Liner*, 50.

56 Sondhaus, *Preparing*, 187.

57 Bellmann, *Von Höllengefährten*, 38.

58 Fox, *Transatlantic*, 370.

59 Quoted in Fox, *Transatlantic*, 377.

60 Huldermann, *Albert Ballin*, 176f.

61 Fox, *Transatlantic*, 378.

62 "The Rise of German Shipbuilding", *Shipbuilding and Shipping Record* 4 (7 January 1914), 16.

63 "The Biggest Hamburg-Amerika Liner", *Shipbuilding and Shipping Record* 3 (18 June 1914), 747.

64 See for example *The Shipbuilder* 7 (October 1912), 74; *The Shipbuilder* 9 (August 1913), 86.

65 Fox, *Transatlantic*, 377.

66 Fox, *Transatlantic*, 377.

67 Kludas, *Die Geschichte der deutschen Passagierschiffahrt*, vol. 1, 125.

68 Gerhard Ahrens and Renate Hauschild-Thiessen, *Die Reeder: Laeisz, Ballin* (Hamburg, 1989).

69 Kludas, *Die Geschichte der deutschen Passagierschiffahrt*, vol. 1, 125.

70 HAPAG, *Die Hamburg-Amerika Linie*, 119.

71 HAPAG, *The New Twin-Screw Express Steamers of the Hamburg-American Packet Company* (New York, n.d.), 16.

72 Niall Ferguson, *Paper and Iron: Hamburg Business and German Politics in the Era of Inflation, 1897–1927* (Cambridge, 1995), 47.

73 There are several essays on the history of Hamburg's port facilities in Plagemann, ed., *Übersee*.

74 Ferguson, *Paper*, 31 and 48.

75 Ferguson, *Paper*, 47f.

76 Evans, *Death*, 33.

77 Ferguson, *Paper*, 42.

78 HAPAG, Jahresbericht für die am 26. März 1912 stattfindende ordentliche Generalversammlung der Aktionäre (Hamburg, 1912).

79 Brett Fairbairn, "Big Business, Technology, and the State", in James Retallack, ed., *Imperial Germany 1871–1918* (Oxford, 2008), 74.

80 Fairbairn, "Big business", 75.

81 Frank Broeze, "Albert Ballin, the Hamburg-America Line and Hamburg: Structure and Strategy in the German Shipping Industry", *Deutsches Schiffahrtsarchiv* 15 (1992), 146.

82 HAPAG, *Hints to Cabin Passengers of the Hamburg American Packet Co.* (New York, n.d.), 1.

83 HAPAG, *Die Hamburg-Amerika Linie*, 139.

84 Sebastian Conrad, *German Colonialism: A Short History* (Cambridge, 2012), 25.

85 Ferguson, *Paper*, 33.

86 Evans, *Death*, 29.

87 Evans, *Death*, 29.

88 Ferguson, *Paper*, 38.

89 Ferguson, *Paper*, 32f.

90 For a brief account see Michael Salewski, "Der Dreizack gehört in unsere Faust. Wilhelm II. und die See", in Plagemann, ed., *Übersee*, 43–6.

91 "Kaiser's Aid to German Sea Power", *Manchester Guardian*, 12 May 1914.

92 "Der Triumph der deutschen Seeschiffahrt unter Wilhelm II", *Neue Hamburger Zeitung*, 11 June 1913.

93 In 1897, the name *Augusta Victoria* was corrected to *Auguste Victoria*.

94 This remark was recorded in Bertram Hayes, *Hull-Down: Reminiscences of Windjammers, Troops and Travellers* (New York, 1925), 67f.

95 Fox, *Transatlantic*, 362.

96 Quoted in Bernhard Rieger, *Technology and the Culture of Modernity in Britain and Germany, 1890–1945* (Cambridge, 2005), 243.

97 Fox, *Transatlantic*, 378.

98 Albert Ballin, "Growth of Port of New York as a Shipping Centre", *The New York Times*, 6 January 1907; "Ship Subsidies Are Costly", *The Washington Post*, 30 January 1903.

99 Ballin, "Growth of Port".

100 "Flying across Ocean", *The Washington Post*, 11 September 1907.

101 Reventlow, "The Shipbuilding Industry".

102 See Rainer Postel, "Dem Handel mußte die Flagge folgen. Deutsche Seehandels- und Flottenpolitik", in Plagemann, ed., *Übersee*. 32–6.

103 "Die deutsche Kriegsmarine im Jahre 1913/14", *Jahrbuch für Deutschlands Seeinteressen* 16 (1914), 24.

104 See for example "Die Flottenvorlage vom Standpunkt der Handelsinteressen Deutshlands", *Hamburgischer Correspondent*, 6 January 1900; "Kriegsflotte und Welthandel", *Hamburger Nachrichten*, 27 February 1900.

105 Sondhaus, *Preparing*, 223.

106 Reventlow, "The Shipbuilding Industry", 793. For a history of Vulcan see Manfred Höft, *Der Vulcan in Stettin und Hamburg: Schiffswerft, Lokomotivfabrik, Maschinenfabrik* (2 vols.) (Bremen, 2013–2015).

107 Reventlow, "The Shipbuilding Industry", 796.

108 W.H. Beehler, "Germany as a Sea Power", *The Century Magazine* 84 (July 1912), 398.

109 Beehler, "Germany", 399.

110 Lamar Cecil, *Albert Ballin: Business and Politics in Imperial Germany, 1888–1918* (Princeton, NJ, 1967), 159ff.

111 Frank Broeze, "Shipping Policy and Social-Darwinism: Albert Ballin and the Weltpolitik of the Hamburg-America Line, 1886–1914", *Mariner's Mirror* 79 (1993), 419.

112 Quoted in Broeze, "Shipping Policy", 423.

113 Quoted in Huldermann, *Albert Ballin*, 324.

114 Quoted in Matthew Jefferies, *Hamburg: A Cultural and Literary History* (Oxford, 2011), 181.
115 Broeze, "Albert Ballin, the Hamburg-America Line", 135–58.
116 HAPAG, *Souvenir.*
117 HAPAG, *Die Hamburg-Amerika Linie.*
118 See for example HAPAG, *Die Hamburg-Amerika Linie.*
119 Brett Fairbairn, "Economic and Social Developments", in Retallack, ed., *Imperial Germany*, 73.
120 Cornelius Torp, "Imperial Germany under Globalization", in Sven Oliver Müller and Cornelius Torp, eds., *Imperial Germany Revisited: Continuing Debates and New Perspectives* (New York and Oxford, 2011), 297.
121 Broeze, "Albert Ballin, the Hamburg-America Line", 157, note 125.
122 Conrad, *Globalization*, 42.
123 Conrad, *Globalization*, 35.
124 HAPAG, *Die Hamburg-Amerika Linie*, 48.
125 HAPAG, *Sixty Years*, 32.
126 HAPAG, *Die Hamburg-Amerika Linie*, 74.
127 Staatsarchiv der Freien und Hansestadt Hamburg (hereafter St. A.H.) 621-1 HAPAG – Reederei 2656 Band 3. Verträge und Vereinbarungen zu Schiffsneubauten Band 3: D "Imperator" 1910–1914 MUG 128A 04 05 A – Bau-Offerte und Bauvertrag.
128 "The Hamburg-Amerika Liner 'Vaterland'", *Engineering* 97 (22 May 1914), 712.
129 See "Underwriters and the Imperator", *The Times* (London), 4 April 1913; "Further Insurances on the Imperator", *The Times* (London), 26 April 1913; "Insuring the Vaterland", *The Times* (London), 9 May 1914.
130 "Big Ship Era", *The Observer* (London), 6 April 1913.
131 For details see Broeze, "Shipping Policy".
132 See Torp, "Imperial Germany", 297–312.
133 Conrad, *German Colonialism*, 25.
134 Sebastian Conrad, "Transnational Germany", in Retallack, ed., *Imperial Germany*, 225.
135 Conrad, *Globalization*, 47.
136 Sebastian Conrad, "Wilhelmine Nationalism in Global Contexts. Mobility, Race, and Global Consciousness", in Müller and Torp, eds., *Imperial Germany*, 294.
137 Conrad, *Globalization*, 50.
138 Conrad, *Globalization*, 55.
139 Conrad, *Globalization*, 54.
140 Thomas Mergel, "The Kaiserreich as a Society of Migration", in Müller and Torp, eds., *Imperial Germany*, 268.
141 See Mergel, "The Kaiserreich", 274f.
142 Mergel, "The Kaiserreich", 277.
143 Conrad, *Globalization*.
144 For a contemporaneous account see H. Weth, *Die Orient-Reise der "Augusta Victoria" vom Januar bis März 1891* (Hamburg, 1891).
145 HAPAG, *Die Hamburg-Amerika Linie*, 114.
146 HAPAG, *Europe. First Class Cabins* (New York, 1914), 14.
147 HAPAG, *Die Hamburg-Amerika Linie*, 112.
148 HAPAG, *Across the Atlantic* (New York, n.d.), 25.
149 Jason Tebbe, "Excursions on the 'Middle Sea': Germans Cruising in the Mediterranean", Presentation at the German Studies Association Annual Conference, Louisville, Kentucky, 22–25 September 2011, 7.
150 Karl Radunz, *100 Jahre Dampfschiffahrt, 1807–1907: Schilderungen und Skizzen aus der Entwicklungsgeschichte des Dampfschiffes* (Rostock, 1907), 185.

151 Bellmann, *Von Höllengefährten*, 54.
152 Quoted in Hans-Hermann Groppe and Ursula Wöst, *Über Hamburg in die Welt. Von den Auswandererhallen zur Ballinstadt* (Hamburg, 2007), 21.
153 Harlaftis, Tenold, and Valdaliso, "Epilogue", 266.
154 Ferguson, *Paper*, 38.
155 Mergel, "The Kaiserreich", 277.
156 Jefferies, *Hamburg,* 193; see also Evans, *Death.*
157 See Cecil, *Albert Ballin*, 51f.
158 Quoted in Groppe and Wöst, *Über Hamburg*, 27.
159 Jefferies, *Hamburg*, 202.
160 Groppe and Wöst, *Über Hamburg*, 46.
161 Groppe and Wöst, *Über Hamburg*, 34.
162 Jefferies, *Hamburg*, 203.
163 Matthew Fitzpatrick, *Liberal Imperialism in Germany: Expansionism and Nationalism, 1848–1884* (New York and Oxford, 2008).
164 "Die Prinzenfahrt des Riesendampfers 'Vaterland'", *Hamburgischer Correspondent*, 11 May 1914.
165 See Fitzpatrick, *Liberal Imperialism.*
166 Birthe Kundrus, "From the Periphery to the Centre: On the Significance of Colonialism for the German Empire", in Müller and Torp, eds., *Imperial Germany*, 253.
167 Conrad, "Transnational Germany", 227.
168 Kundrus, "From the Periphery", 255.
169 Kundrus, "From the Periphery", 256.
170 Kundrus, "From the Periphery", 255.
171 Jefferies, *Hamburg*, 185.
172 HAPAG, *Die Hamburg-Amerika Linie*, 8.
173 HAPAG, *Die Hamburg-Amerika Linie*, 12.
174 Ferguson, *Paper*, 39.
175 HAPAG, *Die Hamburg-Amerika Linie*, 128.
176 HAPAG, *Die Hamburg-Amerika Linie*, 128.
177 See Heinrich Walle, "Förderung alles dessen, was zur Hebung des deutschen Seewesens beitragen kann. Das Seeverkehrswesen", in Plagemann, ed., *Übersee*, 71–9.
178 See Walle, "Förderung", 75.
179 Broeze, "Albert Ballin, the Hamburg-Bremen Rivalry", 2.
180 Broeze, "Albert Ballin, the Hamburg-America Line", 147.
181 HAPAG, *Sixty Years*, 6.
182 Ferguson, *Paper*, 38.
183 "Hamburg-Amerika Linie in 50 Hansa-Jahren 1864–1913", *Hansa: Deutsche nautische Zeitschrift* 51 (3 January 1914), 24f.
184 "The Imperator", *The Marine Engineer and Naval Architect* 36 (December 1913), 155.
185 Broeze, "Albert Ballin, the Hamburg-America Line", 148.
186 See Andreas Hamann, "Die Kohleversorgung russischer Seestreitkräfte auf ihrem Wege nach Ostasien durch die Hapag-Reederei", *Deutsches Schiffahrtsarchiv* 26 (2003), 101–10.
187 Huldermann, *Albert Ballin*, 145.
188 Broeze, "Shipping Policy and Social-Darwinism", 421.
189 Johannes Merck, "Meine Erinnerungen an die Hamburg-Amerika Linie und an Albert Ballin, 1896–1918" (1920). St.A.H. 622-1/62 Merck II 8 Konv. 2b., 99.
190 Ferguson, *Paper*, 38.
191 Cecil, *Albert Ballin*, 22.
192 Wiborg, *Albert Ballin*, 41.
193 Ferguson, *Paper*, 39.

194 Gerhard A. Ritter, "The Kaiser and His Ship-Owner: Albert Ballin, the HAPAG Shipping Company, and the Relationship between Industry and Politics in Imperial Germany and the Early Weimar Republic", in Hartmut Berghoff, Jürgen Kocka, and Dieter Ziegler, eds., *Business in the Age of Extremes: Essays in Modern German and Austrian Economic History* (Washington, D.C. and Cambridge, 2013), 19.

195 Wiborg, *Albert Ballin*, 31.

196 "Herr Ballin and His Rival", *The Manchester Guardian*, 4 February 1914.

197 "Ballin Will Retire from Hamburg Line", *The New York Times*, 18 July 1908.

198 Broeze, "Shipping Policy", 421.

199 Wiborg and Wiborg, *1847–1997*, 95.

200 One of the best sources on this topic is still Erich Murken, *Die großen transatlantischen Linienreederei-Verbände, Pools und Interessengemeinschaften bis zum Ausbruch des Weltkrieges. Ihre Entstehung, Organisation und Wirksamkeit* (Jena, 1922).

201 Eduard Rosenbaum, "Albert Ballin: A Note on the Style of His Economic and Political Activities", *Leo Baeck Institute Year Book* 3 (1958), 263.

202 Ritter, "The Kaiser", 26; see also Ritter, "Der Kaiser".

203 Broeze, "Shipping Policy", 419.

204 Broeze, "Albert Ballin, the Hamburg-Bremen Rivalry", 11.

205 Broeze, "Shipping Policy", 421.

206 Broeze, "Albert Ballin, the Hamburg-Bremen Rivalry", 16.

207 Broeze, "Albert Ballin, the Hamburg-Bremen Rivalry", 14.

208 "Ballin Defends Rate War Attitude", *The New York Times*, 2 February 1914.

209 J. Russell Smith, *The Ocean Carrier* (New York and London, 1908), 311.

210 Smith, *The Ocean Carrier*, 312 and 314f.

211 Broeze "Shipping Policy", 432.

212 Douglas R. Burgess, *Seize the Trident: The Race for Superliner Supremacy and How It Altered the Great War* (New York, 2005).

213 Adolph Goetz, *25 Jahre Hamburgische Seeschiffahrtspolitik* (Hamburg, 1911).

214 Georg Schröder, *Fiasko! Die deutsche Politik des Wahnsinns: Ballin gleich Deutschlands Tragödie ...* (Hamburg, n.d.), 16.

215 Walter Freyer, *Im Kampf um den Ozean: Seeroman* (Leipzig, 1914).

216 Cecil, *Albert Ballin*, 164.

217 Cecil, *Albert Ballin*, 164.

218 Quoted in Cecil, *Albert Ballin*, 95.

219 "Ballin, Germany's Shipping King, Dies", *The New York Times*, 11 November 1918.

220 Wiborg, *Albert Ballin*.

221 Ahrens and Hauschild-Thiessen, *Die Reeder*, 52.

222 This was reported by cable from Berlin in "Kaiser Has a Good Friend in Big Steamship Owner", *The Washington Post*, 19 August 1906.

223 Broeze, "Albert Ballin, the Hamburg-Bremen Rivalry", 30.

224 Ahrens and Hauschild-Thiessen, *Die Reeder*, 53.

225 See for example, Holger Afflerbach, *Der Dreibund. Europäische Großmacht-und Allianzpolitik vor dem Ersten Weltkrieg* (Wien, 2002).

226 Ritter, *The Kaiser*, 30.

227 HAPAG, *Die Hamburg-Amerika Linie*, 68.

228 Bellmann, *Von Höllengefährten*, 52.

229 Broeze, "Albert Ballin, the Hamburg-Bremen Rivalry", 17.

230 Broeze, "Albert Ballin, the Hamburg-America Line", 152, note 1.

231 HAPAG, *Die Hamburg-Amerika Linie*, 40.

232 Fox, *Transatlantic*, 292f.

233 Fox, *Transatlantic*, 293.
234 HAPAG, *Souvenir*.
235 Wiborg and Wiborg, *1847–1997*, 161.
236 HAPAG, *Across the Atlantic*, 4.
237 "The Augusta-Victoria", *The New York Times*, 23 May 1889.
238 Schwerdtner, *German Luxury Ocean Liners*.
239 Fox, *Transatlantic*, 254.
240 William H. Miller, *The First Great Ocean Liners in Photographs* (New York, 1984), 2.
241 Matthew S. Seligmann, "Germany's Ocean Greyhounds and the Royal Navy's First Battle Cruisers: An Historiographical Problem", *Diplomacy and Statecraft* 27 (2016), 163.
242 HAPAG, *Die Hamburg-Amerika Linie*, 70.
243 HAPAG, *Die Hamburg-Amerika Linie*, 70.
244 The *Deutschland*'s instability was also the effect of its great length to beam ratio.
245 Schwerdtner, *German Luxury Ocean Liners*, 32.
246 Kludas, *Die Geschichte der deutschen Passagierschiffahrt*, vol. 2, 162.
247 Schwerdtner, *German Luxury Ocean Liners*, 22.
248 HAPAG, *Die Hamburg-Amerika Linie*, 74.
249 "Germany 'Stands Pat'", *The Washington Post*, 24 November 1907.
250 Broeze, "Albert Ballin, the Hamburg-Bremen Rivalry", 21.
251 Burgess, *Seize*, 128.
252 HAPAG, *Die Hamburg-Amerika Linie*, 79.
253 HAPAG, *Sixty Years*, 49.
254 Dawson, *The Liner*, 52f.
255 Quoted in John Malcolm Brinnin, *The Sway of the Grand Saloon* (New York, 1971), 335.
256 HAPAG, *Sixty Years*, 50.
257 HAPAG, *Sixty Years*, 47.
258 Quoted in Kludas, *Die Geschichte der deutschen Passagierschiffahrt*, vol. 3, 72–5.
259 Ahrens and Hauschild-Thiessen, *Die Reeder*, 48.
260 Kludas, *Die Geschichte der Hapag-Schiffe*, vol. 2, 159.
261 Drechsel, *Norddeutscher Lloyd*, 411.
262 Quoted in Miller, *The First Great Ocean Liners*, 56.

2 "One of the greatest marvels devised by the human spirit"

The transnational career, image, and appeal of the *Imperator*-class liners

I

The title of this chapter is taken from the response of a Swiss journalist to the *Imperator*. It continues as follows:

> A monstrously colossal machine that has ceased to be a ship, that has become a swimming city, an invincible fortress, a monster for which our language lacks a name. Scarcely anything else is as able as this colossus – that upon black foundations bears a glimmering white city of palaces towering above the wastes of the empty waves from continent to continent – to create new bridges to the imagination. By achieving the possible it opens the way to what one must have considered unfeasible only a decade ago.[1]

Looking back from the twenty-first century, this evocative, almost poetic praise of a coal-fired steamship no doubt strikes many readers as unusual. To be sure, most commentary on the *Imperator* was not as extravagant in terminology and tone. And yet the sentiments to which this text gives expression were not uncommon; they can be found time and again in newspaper reporting and popular commentary on the *Imperator* published on both sides of the Atlantic.

What this quotation highlights is the way in which contemporaneous observers emphasized the spectacular qualities of new technology. It is a dramatic demonstration of how writers often poeticized and aestheticized new machines and mechanisms in order to capture and relay these qualities.[2] It is also a clear example of the mixed emotions that gigantic creations in metal often evoked in those who confronted them. On the one hand, this journalist saw the *Imperator* as a literally monumental, mechanical symbol of human progress that knew no limits as it confronted the forces of nature and which generated a mixed response of awe and "unease." On the other hand, the liner was a dazzling and enticing embodiment of social fantasies with respect to leisure, prosperity, well-being, and luxury consumption.

Although motivated by this response, the following pages offer a more sober description and history of the *Imperator*-class liners. They explain why the vessels were built and the costs involved; examine the names chosen to christen them; provide details about their construction, outfitting, and interior design; and present an overview of their careers. While writing about these liners is often adulatory, this account offers a more comprehensive and accurate assessment by including critical opinions. For example, it emphasizes that there were voices within HAPAG that questioned the wisdom of building them. The unpublished *Nachlass* of Johannes Merck (1855–1934), one of the company's directors, is invaluable in this respect. His papers also prompt, in conjunction with recent scholarship, a sober assessment of the economic viability of the *Imperator*-class liners and their success as a business venture.

It is important to understand that the *Imperator*, *Vaterland*, and *Bismarck* were not identical. While the first was built by Vulcan in Hamburg, the others were built by Blohm & Voss and were successively larger than the *Imperator*. The *Vaterland* displaced 54,282 gross tons, was 950 feet in length, and boasted bunkers for 9,000 tons of coal and holds for 12,000 tons of cargo. It was designed to carry 3,909 passengers, approximately 685 fewer than the *Imperator*. The *Bismarck*, designed as the world's largest passenger liner, displaced 56,551 gross tons, measured 956 feet in length, and was intended to carry over 3,500 passengers. It was not launched until after the First World War when it became the property of Britain's White Star Line. Yet to avoid tiresome repetition, most of the following discussion focuses on the *Imperator* as representative of the trio while indicating important differences with the *Vaterland* and *Bismarck* where it is instructive to do so.

There is a body of literature and scholarship from which facts and figures about the *Imperator* can be drawn and re-presented. Yet this chapter mostly avoids doing so. Instead, the information it provides is taken from primary sources, especially the sophisticated brochures and booklets that HAPAG published in Germany and America to accompany the commissioning of its new liners. The aim is not to ensure all the facts and figures – with respect to financial cost, engine power, tons displaced, and number of passengers carried, for example – are absolutely correct. In fact, the literature on transatlantic passenger liners is often in disagreement about these facts. Instead, the intention is to present the information that HAPAG made available on both sides of the Atlantic at the time; it is to establish what the public could have known about the liners as they were constructed, commissioned, and entered service.

HAPAG advertising in German and English emphasized that the *Imperator*-class liners set new international standards for size, technological sophistication, safety, and luxury. These themes were taken up by the print media in Germany, Britain, and America during a period in which the type and volume of reporting on transatlantic liners turned them into media stars on both sides of the ocean. Of course, technology was often discussed in nationalistic terms at the time; its possession and advancement were seen as signalling the international leadership of particular nations.[3] The presentation, reception, and role of the *Imperator*-class liners as symbols of the German Empire are the subject of the following chapters. But this chapter widens the focus to establish an international context for discussion of the vessels as national monuments. Examining newspapers, popular journals, advertising, and books published on both sides of the Atlantic, it emphasizes that HAPAG's new liners were not simply, nor always, perceived as representative of German achievements and ambitions. More often, they were discussed from the point of view expressed in 1912 by the *Hamburger Fremdenblatt*. The construction of a vessel such as the *Imperator*, it proclaimed, was not "the business solely of a single shipyard, a shipping company, a city, or even a nation." Instead, it was the concern of "civilized man."[4]

Transatlantic passenger liners were frequently construed as emblematic of the technological sophistication of the Western world and the progress of its civilization. When NDL's *Kaiser Wilhelm der Große* entered service in 1897, *Scientific American* described its speed, comfort, and provisions for safety as "an eloquent tribute to the engineering genius of these latter years of the nineteenth century."[5] In 1912, Commodore W.H. Beehler of the United States Navy stated that "modern ship-building expresses so much of modern scientific progress."[6] Material published by Cunard advertising the *Aquitania* before its maiden voyage to New York in 1914 read "like a fairy-tale of modern achievement."[7] The same was true of the *Imperator*-class liners, as the print media on both sides of the Atlantic made much of their size, speed, and technological sophistication.

The commentary analysed in this chapter reveals popular attitudes to modern technology; the compression of space and time fostered by a revolution in communications and transportation; and humanity's rapidly evolving relation to nature.[8] Much of this writing and many of the images that accompany it express an approving and enthusiastic response. At the beginning of a century that was "spectacularly ambitious about the possibilities of reason and science," the *Imperator*-class liners were construed as creations of human ingenuity that opened new worlds of power and freedom as they provided a source of control over the environment and suggested ways to determine the future.[9] But this was not always the case. Along with optimism came notes of ambivalence with respect to modern technology, the conquest of the natural world, and the processes of modernization in general.[10]

In addition to their reception as embodiments of modernity and progress, the *Imperator*-class liners were also widely discussed as monumental commodities. New ways of imagining and presenting ocean travel in advertising and the press emerged in the late nineteenth century. Travelling across the Atlantic was increasingly connected with comfort, well-being, and stylish accommodation in floating hotels.[11] This chapter scrutinizes the *Imperator*'s promotion as a luxury item – an experience to be "consumed" – by early-twentieth-century societies animated by the dream, and shaped by the reality of increased prosperity and leisure. It does this, however, while emphasizing a fact that deserves more consideration in writing about the *Imperator*: that it was intended not only to carry the wealthiest passengers in first-class cabins and suites but also to transport people of all social classes including the poorest European emigrants in steerage. Sources from the period allow a glimpse into the experience of all social groups as they travelled aboard the liner.

In sum, the following pages offer a composite and contextualized portrait of the *Imperator*-class liners drawn from contemporaneous sources and voices. They provide a picture not simply of what the vessels were but, more importantly, how they were perceived and what ideas and visions were projected upon them as they were represented to a popular audience on both sides of the Atlantic. Setting the *Imperator*, *Vaterland*, and *Bismarck* into an international context enriches an understanding of their multi-faceted symbolic working as national monuments. It also highlights the extent to which they were positioned to function as literal and symbolic ambassadors of Germany to the Atlantic world.

II

HAPAG'S decision to build a trio of passenger liners larger and more luxurious than anything its competitors had ever commissioned was made in 1908. The company reasoned that a trio was necessary to maintain a weekly service between Hamburg and New York. The vessels were intended to make the crossing between April and October, each liner completing ten round trips. This was an aggressive move designed to challenge NDL in all classes of passenger carriage and express freight. In fact, HAPAG's decision stoked a conflict between the two lines over the quota of steerage passengers allotted to each by the Atlantic Conference. To ensure the commercial success of its new trio, HAPAG knew it was vital to increase its share from forty-three percent of German traffic; it wanted its Bremen rival to accept parity with respect to the number of steerage passengers carried. But when NDL refused, HAPAG temporarily terminated all agreements not only with it but also with the Atlantic Conference.[12] As a result, the English press warned of a costly rate war for all companies in the North Atlantic trade.[13] The situation was finally resolved through the intervention of the German government and an agreement reached by which HAPAG increased its quota of steerage passengers while NDL gained in the carriage of freight and cabin passengers.[14]

HAPAG's decision to build the *Imperator*-class liners was also calculated to challenge Britain's White Star and Cunard Lines in the cabin-class passenger business.[15] While international agreements regulated the number of steerage passengers shipping companies could transport, this was not the case with cabin-class passengers. In particular, the company was motivated by a desire to regain some of the valuable first-class custom that Cunard's *Lusitania* and *Mauretania* had captured. A report prepared by HAPAG's "Imperator Commission" demonstrates how keenly it felt the advances made by Cunard and White Star in attracting a large share of the first-class passenger trade. But it was also sensitive to the fact that NDL had made similar gains and explicitly states the company's desire to capture cabin-class passengers from NDL.[16] As the *Frankfurter Zeitung* reported, HAPAG was seeking supremacy over its Bremen rival.[17]

If aggressive, the decision to commission a trio of giant liners was also risky. Constructing and operating vessels on this scale entailed enormous expenditure. At the time of the *Imperator*'s commissioning, HAPAG projected its cost to be 24,894,000 marks.[18] It would ultimately spend thirty-eight or thirty-nine million marks on the liner, far surpassing the cost of anything the company had previously launched. It valued the *Vaterland* at thirty-six million marks.[19] In total, the *Imperator*-class liners cost approximately 125 million marks, or forty percent of HAPAG's total assets. By comparison, company figures indicate that the *Deutschland*, launched in 1900, cost 12.5 million marks to build. Total construction costs for the express steamers *Augusta Victoria, Fürst Bismarck, Columbia,* and *Normannia,* launched between 1889 and 1891, amounted to twenty-four million marks.[20] And it is worth remembering that the *Imperator, Vaterland,* and *Bismarck* were not the only vessels HAPAG commissioned during these years. In 1912, in addition to the *Imperator,* the company brought seven freighters and one cruise ship into service. While the *Vaterland* was being completed in early 1914, HAPAG had nineteen steamers under construction.[21]

In public, the company expressed every confidence that operating a trio of such large liners would prove successful. In 1914, Dr. Ernst Foerster, one of its naval architects, explained the decision to commission them to *The New York Times.* He emphasized that it was "because of their steadiness, their safety, their speed, their economy, and their luxury." "The economy of the big ship," Foerster explained, "lies in the fact that the larger is the displacement the less is the cost of power per ton."[22] Some American commentators concurred with this assessment. Reproducing an article published in *Scientific American, The Washington Post* argued that from an economic standpoint, and with respect to potential revenue, "there is every inducement to build these transatlantic liners in ever-increasing sizes."[23] It argued that the larger the liner, the lower the cost of carrying a given number of passengers and a given tonnage of freight.

It has long been acknowledged that Albert Ballin was the principal driving force behind the decision to construct the *Imperator* and its sisters. But there were dissenting voices within HAPAG that questioned the wisdom of doing so and that challenged the reasoning of the company as expressed by Foerster. Johannes Merck, one of its directors from 1910 to 1915, was opposed to the trio because he felt they were too large and too expensive to generate positive earnings. He claimed that the *Imperator*-class liners were built without a proper cost–benefit analysis and accused Ballin of ordering the preparation of superficial calculations with respect to the profitability of the new vessels. These were intended to provide a favourable assessment but "were of no more worth than the paper they were written on."[24] "It was absolutely necessary to determine in advance," Merck explained, "through the most thorough considerations in every respect, whether this giant new risk would pay off. Each of our experts should have been asked and been required to candidly provide their opinion." But unfortunately, this was not the case. The new liners were not expected to break even, and it was understood that they would be subsidized by HAPAG's freight business. And although the company made huge profits between 1911 and 1913, Merck believed that the sums which were invested annually in new construction exceeded the company's financial capacity.[25] But "Ballin was stuck on the idea. He wanted to see it through and did not want to hear any dissent."[26] Ultimately, "heavy hearts carried out Ballin's wishes."[27]

More than ill-considered, Merck saw the construction of the *Imperator*-class liners as reckless.[28] In his memoirs, he blamed Ballin's hubris for commissioning vessels that were ultimately unprofitable and damaged the interests of HAPAG. According to Merck, Solomon in all his splendour "was an orphan boy compared to Ballin."[29] Such statements support Lamar Cecil's scepticism about the accuracy and reliability of Merck's opinions which he believed were born of "the violent antipathy he felt toward Ballin." Yet at the same time, Cecil describes Merck's *Nachlass* as "of the greatest value" and notes it is one of few accounts to provide insight into Ballin's relations with his colleagues.[30] More to the point, Merck's views on the wisdom of building the *Imperator*-class liners cannot be easily dismissed, as he was not the only voice to raise such concerns. Emil Boas, director of HAPAG's American operations, objected to the building of the *Bismarck* before the *Imperator* and *Vaterland* had proved their profitability.

In addition, commentators in the English and American press expressed a range of opinion, from the cautious to the critical, on the wisdom of building giant liners. In Britain, just prior to the *Imperator*'s maiden voyage, *The Times* suggested the vessel would probably be successful. But it explained that "except perhaps on one trip in each direction in the height of the respective seasons, even new and splendid New York liners do not run with a full complement of passengers at full rates."[31] *The Observer* suggested the *Imperator* represented the limit of commercial earning power while *The Nautical Gazette* questioned whether the commissioning of such gigantic liners was justified "by the needs of the world's commercial requirements." In its opinion, they were actually the product of their builder's "desire to excel and to have an advantage over competitors."[32] In 1911, *The Washington Post* commented that, in building such vessels, shipping lines were "preparing to assume extraordinary risks" on the speculation that the volume of transatlantic travel would enjoy an "enormous increase" in the near future.[33] When a correspondent of *The Baltimore Sun* questioned an official of NDL on the matter, the latter expressed his doubts as to whether HAPAG'S new liners would make money. But he was certain that the public would admire them and that they were invaluable advertisements for the company. "Every newspaper in the country," he explained, "will probably have something about the largest ship in the world while it is in this country."[34] As we will see, this anonymous commentator was correct on all counts.

Of course, the names *Imperator*, *Vaterland*, and *Bismarck* loaded the vessels with the significance of national monuments. But it was not uncommon for transatlantic liners to be christened in a manner that made them appear as representatives or ambassadors of the German state. NDL named its largest vessels after members of the royal family: *Kaiser Wilhelm der Große* (1897); *Kaiser Friedrich* (1898); *Prinzessin Irene* (1900); *Kronzprinz Wilhelm* (1901); *Kaiser Wilhelm II* (1903); and *Kronprinzessin Cecilie* (1906). HAPAG had done likewise with the *Augusta Victoria* (1888) and *Prinzessin Victoria Luise* (1900). Its *Deutschland* (1900) was more boldly and broadly symbolic. But what is unusual is that while ships were traditionally referred to as feminine, the *Imperator*-class liners were not. In its publicity material and press releases, HAPAG insisted on referring to the vessels as male rather than female: *der Imperator* instead of *die Imperator*. It seems as if they were too large and too symbolically important to be "tainted" by feminine associations.

Yet the names of all three liners were by no means determined from the moment it was decided to build them. In 1909, *The New York Times* reported that Ballin had sent a telegram to Chancellor von Bülow stating that HAPAG would "like to name its next large transatlantic liner after him."[35] The paper claimed Bülow had accepted the honour. And yet it seems that Ballin originally intended the *Imperator* to be christened *Europa*. In fact, before its launch, it was often referred to as such in the Anglo-American press.[36] In 1911, HAPAG's New York offices commissioned the German-American maritime artist Fred Pansing to paint the new liner. His rendition of the still-to-be-completed vessel bears the name *Europa* on its bow.[37]

The reasons for the choice of *Europa* are unclear. HAPAG originally intended to use the name for what became the *Kaiserin Auguste Victoria*. As the latter formed a pair with the *Amerika*, the intention was to give symbolic expression to the link between the two continents.[38] The name *Europa* may also have been intended to reflect the cosmopolitan vision and nature of HAPAG. But it may simply have been a tactic to attract as much of the general European travelling and emigrant public as possible. It is hardly surprising that the christening of German liners was often governed by business and marketing calculations. For example, HAPAG's decision to name its liners *President Lincoln* or *President Grant*, or in honour of an American city, was taken with the intention of attracting America-bound immigrants. According to William Miller, this was a successful strategy; many immigrants chose to book passage aboard liners with American names in the assumption that "their entry process and naturalization would be better achieved" as a result.[39]

Ultimately, the name *Imperator* seems to have been the choice of the Kaiser. In June 1910, Wilhelm travelled to Hamburg where he presented Ballin with a bronze bust of himself.[40] He also attended an illustrated lecture that provided details and revealed plans for the liner's construction. The Kaiser became so interested in the vessel that he was invited to christen it.[41] Johannes Merck claims that Ballin was at first disappointed when Wilhelm chose the name *Imperator*, inspired by his title Wilhelm Imperator Rex.[42] And it is clear that HAPAG did not wish to give the impression of a simple and direct connection between the German Emperor and the liner. In at least one instance, company advertising implied the name *Imperator* referred to the vessel's mantle as "Emperor of the Oceans."[43]

In 1912, American newspapers reported that the *Imperator*'s sister ship would be christened *Advent*.[44] In Britain, *The Times* speculated that it might be named *Hamburg*.[45] But the vessel that was to become the *Vaterland* was, just like its predecessor, more commonly referred to as *Europa* before its launch. For example, an artist's impression of the liner published in 1913 in the American journal *"Shipping" Illustrated* bears this name.[46] Merck relates that, in this instance, it was Ballin who chose to christen the liner *Vaterland*. The *Berliner Tageblatt* reported that HAPAG considered several names for the last of the trio including *Hamburg*, *Hansa*, *Monarch*, and even *HAPAG*. But it was reported that the Kaiser insisted that it must be christened *Bismarck*.[47]

III

HAPAG signed a contract for the *Imperator*'s construction with Vulcan in March 1910. The keel was laid down as hull number 314 in its Hamburg yards on 18 June of that year.[48] The vessel rose on its stocks at the same time as White Star's *Olympic* and *Titanic* were being built in Belfast by Harland &Wolff. Ballin announced that the *Vaterland* would also be built by the British company and even commissioned it to prepare plans.[49] But ultimately the liner, along with the *Bismarck*, would be constructed by Blohm & Voss in Hamburg.

Of course, extensive planning preceded the laying of keels. For example, five books of specifications were printed before the *Vaterland*'s construction, the longest being 242 pages in length. An incredibly detailed set of drawings was also prepared.[50] Painstaking preparation in drafting offices was then transferred to the clamour and energy of the building yard, as thousands of hands went to work on the vessel. The *Hamburger Echo* reported that approximately 1,800 men were employed in constructing the *Vaterland*.[51] But the public was offered relatively little specific information until after a liner was launched. With respect to the *Imperator*, one American commentator noted that "elaborate precautions had been taken to preserve the secrecy which had attended the construction of the vessel."[52] And yet, as we will see, this did not stop the German, and especially the Hamburg press, from reporting on the liner as it rose on its stocks. Its particular fascination was with the *Imperator*'s enormous size.

Descriptions of the vessel under construction were often colourful. In April 1911, the *Hamburger Fremdenblatt* described the sight as "gigantic and tremendous." The many steel ribs of the liner's frame rose high in the air like the bones of a prehistoric creature of unimaginable proportions. But it was also a mountain of iron and steel, the paper explained, a creation of the god Hephaestus who had moved his workshop to the banks of the Elbe.[53] We might further imagine the scene with the aid of Thomas Mann's description of the Blohm & Voss shipyard in *The Magic Mountain*:

> the confusion of the yards, the mammoth bodies of great ships, Asiatic and African liners, lying in dry-dock, keel and propeller bare, supported by props as thick as tree trunks, lying there in monstrous helplessness,

swarmed over by troops of men like dwarfs scouring, whitewashing, hammering; there were the roofed-over ways, wrapped in wreaths of smoke-like mist, holding the towering frames of rising ships, among which moved the engineers, blue-print and loading scale in hand, directing the work-people.[54]

Fortunately, several photographs have been preserved of all three liners under construction.[55] These give a vivid impression of the enormity and complexity of the task.

When the *Imperator* was launched on 23 May 1912, it weighed approximately 27,000 tons. It was then towed to a fitting-out berth where its boilers and engines were installed, its superstructure and interiors constructed, and its funnels added. This process took almost a year. Else Grüttel, one of the few journalists who can be identified as female, wrote a short account of her visit to the liner at this time in which she describes 3,000 men at work on the vessel. What struck her most was the "melody of dock work" which she described as a noise so incredible that it was difficult to know how people could think and communicate in such an environment.[56]

While Vulcan was at work on the *Imperator*'s hull, HAPAG was busy preparing its advertising campaign. As the maritime author R.A. Fletcher described the situation in 1913, steamship companies "would fare ill were it not for the publicity department."[57] He explained that shipping lines usually placed simple announcements of sailing dates in the daily press. But these stimulated

Figure 2.1 The *Imperator* in the Vulcan yard just prior to its launch.
Source: German Maritime Museum, Bremerhaven.

Figure 2.2 The *Imperator* during the fitting-out process.
Source: Bain Collection, The Library of Congress, Washington, DC.

the curiosity "of a large number of persons, not a few of whom will write to the company for an illustrated leaflet." These brochures and pamphlets "will be shown to dozens, and the pictured details of the accommodation will be discussed."[58] Robert Urie Jacob's *A Trip to the Orient*, which he published in 1907, begins with the author sitting at a table upon which lies an illustrated HAPAG brochure containing the prospectus of a Mediterranean cruise aboard the *Moltke*. He has been considering its contents for "some days" and has just decided to book a cabin.[59]

The most elaborate publicity material that HAPAG prepared for the *Imperator* came in the form of a series of brochures aimed at cabin-class passengers. These were published in Hamburg and New York and included *Dampfer Imperator: Das Grösste Schiff der Welt*; *Turbinen-Schnelldampfer Imperator*; and *Imperator: The World's Largest Ship, Embodying Maximum Comfort and Safety for All*.[60] The choice of liner for steerage passengers was often governed by the desire to find the most economical fare. But clientele of means seeking the most comfortable, leisurely, and safest crossing were more susceptible to the literal and figurative image of a particular liner, along with the impression created by an entire shipping company.[61] R.A. Fletcher believed publicity illustrations were also particularly important to third-class passengers, stating that "they form their conclusions by the illustrations supplied them."[62]

In *Dampfer Imperator*, the liner is described as a "richly developed artwork" and HAPAG's brochures were clearly intended to be worthy of the product they were promoting; they decoratively match the style and luxury that was being sold in the form of the vessel.[63] These brochures are small but attractive, even sophisticated publications. It is clear that considerable thought was given not only to their content but also to their format, design, and typeface. Very finely designed, printed, and produced, they are important examples of German graphic art and typography from the period and deserve to be studied as outstanding examples of publication design. Some take their aesthetic from the machine-nature of the *Imperator* and serve to present it as a work of modern engineering. The look of the fonts and graphics employed in *Turbinenschnelldampfer Imperator*, for example, is modern; one might even say they represent an Art Deco aesthetic a decade before its time.

The German publications are formatted like books with a table of contents and, in the case of *Turbinen-Schnelldampfer Imperator*, chapter divisions and an appendix providing a host of facts and figures. The brochure is divided into chapters as follows: "The Fortified Ship" emphasized the details of the liner's construction and spoke especially of its safety; "The Comfortable Ship" focused on its first-class cabins while "The Hospitable Ship" treated its dining facilities; "The Sociable Ship" described the first-class lounge and library and the "The Healthful Ship" emphasized the possibilities for recreation offered by its promenade decks, gyms, and swimming pool; "The Helpful Ship" spoke about the healthcare facilities provided on board, as well as measures for fire protection and the vessel's life boats; finally, "The Serving Ship" provided details about its crew, kitchens, and the vast amount of provisions carried on every voyage. The text is detailed and can make for dry reading for anyone without an interest in the subject. Yet the prose is confident, even boastful at times, and is occasionally animated by a metaphor or literary flourish. In one instance, the *Imperator* is described as similar to a heavily armoured knight.[64] And the text of the German brochures is more extensive, denser, and focuses more on engineering and technical details than that of the English-language brochure, *Imperator: The World's Largest Ship*. The latter's format is larger, as are the impressive photographs and artists' impressions of the liner's cabin-class interiors to which much of it is devoted. Concentrating on the indicators of comfort, including spaciousness and sophisticated appointments, these images engender an atmosphere of elegance and luxury.

Yet all of HAPAG's brochures offer a very strong visual appeal, and it is the images that first attract the eye when perusing them. Their pages are full of photographs, line drawings, artists' impressions and, in some cases, cross-section diagrams of the *Imperator*. The company even published a postcard-size brochure devoted solely to photographs. Most of these depict the liner's interiors and are accompanied by captions in German and English.[65] It is worth noting that the vast majority of images depicting the interior of the vessel is devoted to its first-class cabins and public rooms. While the reader cannot be other than impressed by the photographs in these publications, it is the artists' impressions and line drawings that lend them a sophisticated, even artistic flair that raises them above merely informative brochures. They are, in fact, small books, luxury items in their own right, that are worth preserving and that, in their sophistication, anticipate the experience of sailing aboard the *Imperator*.

We must be careful, however, when viewing any images of the liner produced prior to the time it entered service. HAPAG was anxious to put pictures of the *Imperator* before the eyes of the public. But this sometimes resulted in inaccurate representations. For example, several photographs were taken of the vessel being pulled by tugs from its berth in the Kaiser Wilhelm Hafen on 31 May 1913. These were sold to the public in the form of postcards on the occasion of its maiden voyage shortly thereafter. But as the *Imperator* was not completed when the photographs were taken, they had to be retouched: the absent third funnel was added, crooked and out of place, and the eagle figurehead and flags were sketched in. In addition, the liner was missing key features: there were no lifeboats attached to its davits, nor was the bridge painted white. These photographs, which also found their way into the press, amounted to what Arnold Kludas has described as a veritable caricature of the vessel.[66]

Nonetheless, readers of HAPAG's brochures were provided with a reasonably accurate depiction of the *Imperator*'s exterior appearance. In keeping with passenger steamers of the time, and in contrast to contemporary ocean liners like Cunard's *Queen Mary II*, the large hull was surmounted by a low superstructure. Towering above this were three funnels. The third was a dummy and housed ventilator shafts for the engine room. At eighty-two feet, the *Imperator*'s funnels were the tallest of their day and, before they were cut down during its first annual overhaul, gave the liner a somewhat imbalanced appearance. Three funnels also meant a departure from the standard profile of the day; it was common for the largest transatlantic liners to be equipped with four. As *The Daily Telegraph* indicated at the time of its launch, having only three funnels made the *Imperator* look smaller than liners with four, such as White Star's *Olympic*.[67] And this may have made some emigrant passengers believe it less safe than its British rivals. In 1913, R.A. Fletcher recounted an instance in which a group of Central European emigrants, upon finding that the liner on which they had booked passage in 1911 possessed only two funnels, questioned whether it was as safe as one with three.[68]

A light schooner rig of two masts supported the wireless telegraph antennae, bore the *Imperator*'s flags and marker lighting, and carried the crow's nest. The prow was decorated with its eagle figurehead and the liner's name appeared on the bow in gold lettering. The prow of the *Vaterland* would bear the arms of the Empire in white and gold. The *Imperator* was constructed with a traditional counter stern with the rudder projecting above the water line. The stern was also decorated with the vessel's name and "Hamburg," its port of registry, surrounded by gilded scrollwork. Before it entered service, the liner was pictured in various colour schemes in advertising and on postcards published by HAPAG. But when it finally took to sea, its hull was black, its superstructure white, and its funnels buff-coloured.

If readers of promotional brochures were not convinced by the images alone, at least one described the *Imperator* as having proportions that are "harmonious and uplifting" and that lend it a graceful appearance in the water.[69] It was common for HAPAG to promote its vessels in this manner. For instance, it described the *Kaiserin Auguste Victoria* as having "beautiful lines" and resting "so gracefully" upon the water that it was difficult for spectators to appreciate its immense size.[70] Some commentators agreed with such descriptions, one even extolling the *Imperator*'s lines as constituting "a model of beauty."[71] Yet there is something in Douglas Burgess's contention that the *Imperator* had less of the yacht-like grace of previous liners, its more rigid geometry giving it something of a workmanlike, functional appearance.[72] The *Vaterland* and *Bismarck* had more refined forward superstructures with pillars and windows, and with their bridges stained in a mahogany hue. And it was more common for the *Vaterland*'s lines to be described as beautiful and graceful, be it by the *Morning Post* in London, *The Washington Post*, or the *San Francisco Chronicle*.[73] This may be the result of its adoption of a cruiser stern, or one similar to that of a navy cruiser. With is rudder entirely beneath the water line, this was a departure from the design of passenger liners and resulted in increased stability. It also permitted the building of higher superstructures than was previously feasible.

In addition to their images, the text of HAPAG's brochures provided a wealth of particular information designed to impress and assure potential passengers about the liner's safety, reliability, and stability, and promote it as a floating, luxury hotel. The size and power of the *Imperator* were usually the first issues to be addressed. The liner displaced 52,117 gross tons and was 908 feet in length. While the hull's lines were unremarkable, it was of unprecedented proportions, and this was a recurring theme in HAPAG advertising. It described the liner as "a veritable skyscraper afloat" and, in one of its brochures, provided an illustration of it standing on its stern towering above the Woolworth Building, the world's tallest structure at the time.[74] This was a comparison that was often made in English and American professional journals and newspapers.[75] No British liner of the period equalled the size of the *Imperator*. But while large for its time, the vessel was relatively small, at least in terms of tonnage, when compared to ocean liners commissioned in recent years. Cunard's *Queen Mary II* measures 1,132 feet in length and weighs 149,215 tons. Modern cruise ships are built on an even larger scale. The *Harmony of the Seas*, operated by Royal Caribbean International and launched in 2015, is the largest passenger ship in the world. It boasts a gross tonnage of 226,963 and a length of 1,181 feet. While not significantly longer than the *Imperator*, it is more than four times larger in terms of total volumetric capacity.

Nonetheless, readers of HAPAG advertising could only have been impressed by the *Imperator*. Its hull was built of the largest forgings and castings yet produced for a steamer of the German merchant marine. Construction required 520,000 hundredweight of sheet steel, bar, and angle iron; 28,000 hundredweight of rivets and screws; 12,000 hundredweight of cast and forged iron of various types; and 6,000 cubic metres of various species of wood. A double bottom extended for most of the hull's length. A double skin, or inner hull, reaching above the waterline, ran aft from the collision bulkhead to the forward-most boiler room. The space between this outer and inner shell was bunkered with coal amidships. Describing this double hull as an "invulnerable skin," the *Kansas City Star* was confident that it would prevent disaster.[76]

The hull's length was compartmentalized by a series of watertight bulkheads that rose above the waterline. These were fitted with twenty-three bulkhead doors that were situated under the waterline and could be hydraulically closed from the bridge. In the event the *Imperator*'s hull was pierced in a collision, this arrangement would prevent the flooding of the entire vessel. Five steel decks ran the length of the hull with four more above the main deck. All decks exposed to the weather were sheathed with Oregon pine. And to improve stability, the *Imperator* was fitted with Frahm anti-rolling tanks amidships. These shifted 500,000 litres of water between the port and starboard sides of the vessel in order to provide balance and reduce roll. Given the concern surrounding seasickness, the stability of a vessel was an important consideration.[77]

In addition to details about the structure of its hull, readers were provided information about the *Imperator*'s propulsion machinery. The liner was Germany's first turbine-driven, quadruple-screw vessel. Its steam turbines could generate 62,000 horsepower and were capable of an average speed of 22.5 knots. This made it possible to reach London and Paris on the sixth day and Hamburg on the seventh day of sailing from New York. The *Imperator*'s bunkers carried 8,500 tons of coal to fire forty-six boilers, and the vessel was steered by a giant rudder cast by Friedrich Krupp AG.

HAPAG advertising placed special emphasis on the safety of its liners long before the sinking of the *Titanic*.[78] Consequently, this aspect of its publicity campaign did not change substantially in the wake of the tragedy. And it should be noted that the *Imperator*'s double bottom was standard for the time and not added as the result of the sinking of the White Star liner. Nonetheless, a considerable effort was made to assure the public of the safety of HAPAG's newest vessel. It was common for an emphasis on the *Imperator*'s size to be employed as a means of assuring potential passengers of its safety. For example, the brochure *Dampfer Imperator* insisted that only a liner of its size and cost could be fitted with the latest, expensive security features and technology.[79] And company advertising expressly enumerated the various advances made in building materials; in the construction of watertight bulkheads; in navigational instrumentation and technology; and in on-board fire and safety equipment, all of which had been incorporated in the *Imperator*'s construction and outfitting.

Company literature emphasized that the liner was equipped with eighty-three lifeboats and that a fully loaded boat could be launched in fifty seconds or less. This was achieved by electrical winches. As the vessel was outfitted with a reserve generator above the waterline, these could function even if the engine rooms were flooded.[80] Should the rudder break, the fitting of four propellers ensured the liner's ability to navigate without it. In addition, both the *Imperator* and the *Vaterland* were equipped with the most advanced navigation equipment including gyroscopic compasses and wireless telegraphy. The *Imperator*'s wireless had a range of 1,500 nautical miles while the *Vaterland* was the first liner equipped with long-distance wireless telephones. It was claimed that wireless telegraphy reduced the need for speedy crossings as passengers could conduct their business via the wireless in mid-ocean.[81] Furthermore, *Dampfer Imperator* asked readers to remember that HAPAG's concern for passenger safety was as high as the value of the liner itself; it urged them to consider the "feeling of moral responsibility" that guided the company.[82] In fact, the text emphasized that advances in maritime engineering had made what was once a perilous journey into something that resembled more of a pleasure cruise.

Having introduced the *Imperator* as a powerful, safe, and reliable marvel of modern engineering and technology, advertising then enumerated the arrangements made for its passengers. The journal *Hansa* suggested that the liner was so large that those going aboard for the first time experienced unease as to whether they would be able to find their way around the vessel and not simply wander aimlessly from deck to deck. One feels embarrassed, it explained, not to know which direction was fore or aft and which side port or starboard.[83] But for those who took the time, company literature apprised its readers of the *Imperator*'s configuration in detail. This was done in textual description but also through the use of photographs and diagrams.

The boat deck, or A deck, was the uppermost and located nine decks above the waterline. In addition to the bridge and officers' quarters, it was fitted with the first-class smoking room, gymnasium, and photographic darkroom. Much of it was devoted to promenade decks, and it was here that many of the liner's lifeboats were stowed. These could be swung outboard in fair weather to provide more space for the deck to be used for the recreation of first-class passengers. First-class public rooms occupied B deck, or the upper promenade deck, almost entirely. The ladies' drawing room, the library, and the writing room were located forward of the first funnel. Aft of this funnel was the main lounge, or what was referred to as the social hall in German, along with the winter garden or palm court. The Ritz-Carlton restaurant was located between the second and third funnels while the grill room and veranda café were situated at the aft-end of the deck. By this time it was usual for first-class cabins and public rooms to be situated amidships. Before the 1880s, it was the aft section of a liner that was reserved for first-class accommodation. But during that decade it became more common to relocate the first-class lounge amidships, forward of the engines, so that affluent passengers would be less disturbed by the vessel's pitch and emissions from its funnels.

The *Imperator*'s lower promenade deck, or C deck, was home to first-class cabins as well as two so-called Imperial suites, one on the port and one on the starboard side. These suites consisted of two bedrooms, a breakfast room, a sitting room with private veranda deck (the first to be installed on shipboard), a pantry, two baths with toilets, and a luggage room. There was also accommodation for servants. The second-class promenade was located at the aft end of this deck. D deck was also occupied principally by first-class cabins with the second- and third-class lounges and smoking rooms and the second-class gymnasium situated aft. First- and second-class cabins comprised E deck which was punctuated by the gallery of the first-class dining room, the first floor of which was located amidships on F deck. This was large enough to serve all first-class passengers in one sitting. A second-floor gallery wound around it and provided additional seating. F deck also housed the second-class dining room, the steerage dining hall in the ship's bow, and third-class cabins aft.

The swimming pool, or Pompeiian bath, was located on G deck and rose two stories such that the gallery that surrounded it was situated on F deck. This was for the use of first-class passengers. Modelled on the swimming pool in the Royal Automobile Club in London, it was somewhat smaller in scale. The basin itself measured thirty-nine feet long by twenty-one feet wide and boasted a maximum depth of nine feet. The hall's bronze and glass ceiling was supported by fluted Doric columns, and the pool deck was accented with a fountain and marble benches. A double staircase at one end gave access to the gallery. The entire bathing complex included a Turkish bath, mineral bath, electric bath, and foot bath. G deck also housed second- and third-class accommodation aft with steerage passengers accommodated in the bow as they were on H and I decks. The decks below the water line housed the *Imperator*'s machinery and storage for provisions, luggage, freight, and mail. And prospective passengers were assured that none of HAPAG's passenger liners carried cattle, pigs, or sheep in their cargo holds.[84]

One of the most attractive features of the *Imperator*'s first-class public rooms, and something that was repeatedly emphasized in advertising, was their spaciousness. Yet in keeping with the practice of the time, the dining room and lounge were constructed between the uptakes that ran from the boilers to the funnels. As a result, they were connected by corridors running along the sides of the vessel. This arrangement served to disconnect the rooms and break up the flow of space that could be achieved in palatial architecture. One of the major differences between the *Imperator* and its successors, the *Vaterland* and *Bismarck*, was the manner in which this situation was altered aboard the latter two liners. The uptakes of their funnels did not pass through the centre of the decks, as aboard the *Imperator*. Instead, they were split and rose along their port and starboard sides. Consequently, cabins and public rooms did not have to be built around large funnel casings. Open planning with no intrusive vertical casings to break up space, along with axial interior layouts, created a real and perceived roominess with interior vistas the like of which had never been seen aboard an ocean liner. First-class public rooms could now be connected with grand entrances running along an uninterrupted centre line. In this respect, the *Vaterland* and *Bismarck* set a precedent for liners launched following the First World War.

Figure 2.3 The *Imperator*'s swimming pool.
Source: German Maritime Museum, Bremerhaven.

Apprised of the *Imperator*'s technological sophistication and its impressive interior layout and spaces, readers of HAPAG advertising were also assured that an expert and disciplined crew would care for the well-being and safety of all on board. German crews, it was claimed, had the best reputation for competence, devotion to duty, and discipline. The *Imperator* was sailed and serviced by a crew of 1,180 people. Commanded by a commodore, this included four captains, seven officers, one chief engineer, three first engineers, twenty-five engineers and electricians, and three telegraphers. The engine rooms were manned by 422 men. In addition, there was a large staff of personnel serving the *Imperator*'s cabin-class passengers in both staterooms and public spaces. A chief steward oversaw hospitality in each class. In first-class accommodation, he was aided by ten assistants and oversaw 271 stewards including a female housekeeper and fourteen stewardesses. A system of electric bells was said to ensure prompt service to first-class cabins, and HAPAG ensured readers that stewards would be neither seen nor heard.

The *Imperator* offered libraries for first-, second-, and third-class passengers and a bookshop selling recent publications to those travelling in first-class. Pianos were available to passengers of all classes, except those in steerage,

Figure 2.4 Commodore Ruser and the *Imperator*'s captains.
Source: Bain Collection, The Library of Congress, Washington, D.C.

along with a collection of scores featuring classical and modern music. In November 1913, *The Washington Post* reported that an experiment aboard the *Imperator* in the previous month had led to a decision to make film showings a regular occurrence aboard all HAPAG liners.[85] The *Imperator* also featured two telephone operators, four barbers, one hairdresser, three printers, one carpenter, a tailor, and a gardener.[86] In addition to a flower shop and confectionery, a photographic darkroom was made available on the boat deck for first-class passengers. The liner also boasted a hospital with sixty-two beds and an operating room for passengers of all classes staffed by three doctors, two assistants, and a nurse. There was also a pharmacy.

Importantly, advertising also assured prospective passengers that they would be well fed aboard the *Imperator*.[87] For the one-way crossing to New York, the liner was loaded with provisions for both passengers and crew including 45,000 pounds of fresh meat; 8,500 pounds of game and poultry; 8,000 pounds of fresh fish, lobster, crayfish, and oysters; 15,000 pounds of bread; 48,000 eggs; 25,000 pounds of fresh vegetables; 12,000 pounds of fruit; 150 crates of lemons and oranges; and 1,500 containers of ice cream. Other foodstuffs were loaded to provide for both the westward crossing and the return to Hamburg including 100,000 pounds of potatoes; 4,000 pounds of onions; 24,000 pounds of salted and canned meat for the crew and steerage passengers; 8,300 pounds of ham, sausage, tongue, and bacon; 25 metric tons of herring; 5,500 pounds of cheese; 6,500 litres of milk and cream; 5,000 pounds of butter and 5,500 of margarine; 1,200 pounds of dried vegetables; 5,000 pounds of sauerkraut and salted beans; 600 pounds of nuts and almonds; 6,500 pounds of dried fruit; 10,000 pounds of sugar, syrup, and honey; 5,100 pounds of coffee; 350 pounds of tea; 5,000 bottles of white wine and 4,500 bottles of red; 3,000 bottles of French champagne and 2,100 bottles of German; 2,200 bottles of liqueurs and cognacs; and at least 15,000 litres of beer.

It is no wonder that the *Imperator*-class liners were commonly referred to as "entire cities."[88] The metaphor of a swimming city can be traced to the 1850s.[89] It was used by shipping companies in a positive sense and without any of the negative connotations of a congested urban space. And HAPAG advertising did more than suggest passengers would enjoy a reasonable semblance of the comforts and conveniences they had access to ashore; the mass of details it provided potential passengers about on-board facilities and conveniences gave the distinct impression that the *Imperator* was indeed a floating city in miniature. One company brochure stated that the liner was outfitted with "what the self-aware, modern individual considers the most important requirements for a comfortable existence."[90] More than that, the message to cabin-class passengers was that they would find a better urban environment aboard ship than on land as they exchanged "the world of everyday existence for a man-made environment that reflected an idealized, prosperous, harmonious, and technologically advanced society."[91]

In addition to appearing in advertising, the metaphor of a floating city was also widely employed in the press. Writing of the *Imperator* in the *Hamburgischer Correspondent*, the author Carl Müller-Rastatt described the modern technology embodied in the liner as a "poet" able to transport "an entire city" from one continent to another over stormy seas as was only previously possible in the imagination of an artist.[92] The *Hamburger Fremdenblatt* claimed that no "city on dry land can bare comparison with what this swimming city bears within its hull, in terms of its furnishings and sanitary arrangements, its cultural richness and the possibilities it affords for a stimulating and comfortable experience."[93] In 1908, *The Washington Post* reported that Ballin was behind an idea that would enable passengers to have the latest London and Paris fashions made to order aboard HAPAG's next liner which it identified as the "Europa." The paper explained that the vessel would feature a London tailor, one or two from America, and a French dressmaker selected from one of the leading Parisian fashion houses. It suggested that there may also be an exhibition and sales room of one of the best known New York jewellers aboard ship.[94] Another article speculated that competition for ever more spectacular shipboard luxury might prompt HAPAG to install an equestrian track aboard the *Imperator* along with stables and an elevator for horses.[95] Caustically, *The Wall Street Journal* suggested that the liner "only needs a board of tax wasters and a street car strike to be a city."[96]

IV

The *Imperator* was launched at a time when transatlantic liners were habitually construed as mechanical and technological wonders of a new age. As Douglas R. Burgess explains, "the image of a steamship's hull waiting to be launched became the most recognizable symbol of both technological and societal progress in the nineteenth century."[97] And yet one of the most interesting issues raised by the journalist quoted at the beginning of this chapter is the notion that established modes of description were not adequate to the task of representing such an astounding piece of technology as the *Imperator*. We are told that "our language lacks a name." Yet given the amount of text devoted by HAPAG and the international press to promoting and discussing the *Imperator*, this sentiment was not universal.

Company advertising and press reporting on both sides of the Atlantic repeatedly discussed the technological sophistication of the *Imperator*-class liners, be it in their design and construction, their propulsion machinery, or their navigation and communication equipment. To many commentators, these vessels were monuments to the technical and scientific progress of the western world. And the tone of this reporting ranged from sober and detailed enumeration of fact to expressions of astonishment. For example, *The New York Times* described the *Imperator* as "a magnificent specimen of the marine engineering skill of the twentieth century."[98] Among many other things, the press in that city was intrigued by how easily a vehicle of such enormous size could be handled and docked.[99] *The Washington Post* marvelled at the fact that, although the combined weight of the *Imperator*'s rudder and stock was 200 tons, the vessel could "be moved at the delicate touch of a wheel on the bridge nearly a sixth of a mile away."[100] It described the liner as "a perfect work of human art and applied science."[101] *The New York Times* also spoke of the *Vaterland* as "the wonder ship."[102] The paper emphasized that it was not the size of the liner that was "the wonder" as much as "the perfection of the ship."[103] John A. Sleicher of *Leslie's* described his visit to the *Vaterland*'s bridge as a rare treat and wrote an enthusiastic account of the "multitude of devices" he saw there.[104] At least one German newspaper published a list of the world's seven modern wonders that included the *Imperator*.[105] The others were wireless telegraphy, the Panama Canal, the dirigible airship, the flying machine, radium, and the cinematograph.

The press also demonstrated considerable interest in ever speedier crossings of the Atlantic and the compression of time and space facilitated by steamships. In fact, mechanized speed preoccupied the imagination of the Atlantic world.[106] Many commentators "viewed the new speed favourably as a symbol of vitality, a magnification of the possibilities of experience, or an antidote to provincialism."[107] Scholarly discussion of its role in transforming western European and North American society has often focused on railroads.[108] And yet, *as The Washington Post* stated in 1913, public interest in transatlantic liners "has always been directed first of all to the matter of speed."[109] Speed was a requisite of success for shipping companies, especially in the United States.

A survivor of the *Titanic*'s sinking "commented that the public demanded more speed every year and refused to patronize the slower liners."[110] In many minds, it meant increased safety on the seas.[111] But it also engendered, and was necessary to satisfy, what *Harper's Weekly* described in 1901 as the present "craze ... to rush across the Atlantic as fast as steam and powerful engines can carry you."[112]

When the *Imperator* entered service, the terms "ocean greyhound" and "trans-Atlantic greyhound" were commonly used to describe the newest and fastest liners.[113] Newspaper reports sometimes discussed the speed of crossings in considerable detail with respect to time, average speeds, daily runs, number of screw revolutions per minute, and the condition of the seas. The North Atlantic was commonly referred to as a highway and even as "the ocean race track."[114] Special attention was given record-breakers like NDL's *Kaiser Wilhelm der Große* which entered service in 1897 and went on to take the Blue Riband from the Cunard Line in 1898.[115] HAPAG's *Deutschland* attracted similar interest when it captured the same prize in 1900 and held it, with one interruption, until 1907.[116] The American press depicted the two ships as rivals and their voyages as "a marvelous contest of speed ... to get the American mails to Europe first."[117] The simultaneous crossing of two liners was often presented as a "race" across the Atlantic.[118] Competition between British and German vessels, in particular, was interpreted as a national contest. Press rhetoric sometimes turned to hyperbole, for example when *The Washington Post* described the rivalry between the two nations for the speediest crossing as a "titanic struggle," called the *Lusitania* "epoch-making," and described it as "flying" across the ocean.[119] The paper also reported keen interest by the German public in the maiden voyage of the *Lusitania*, and great relief when it did not capture the Blue Riband from the *Deutschland* in September 1907.[120]

By the time of the *Imperator*'s launch, prospective passengers were informed that travel time from New York to London was six days and that Hamburg could be reached in seven. And there was speculation that the speed of Atlantic crossings would dramatically increase in the near future. Reporting on the invention of new turbine gearing, *The Wall Street Journal* speculated in 1909 that transatlantic travel would be reduced to three days in the near future.[121] Albert Ballin was of the belief that "startling as have been the developments in the past, the future will be even more surprising" and "in twenty years' time the people will laugh at our existing ideas of speed."[122]

HAPAG advertising routinely promoted the speed of its newest liners and sometimes reproduced excerpts from the New York press announcing the latest record-breaking voyage of one of its vessels.[123] One of its promotional brochures included thirty-three excerpts from several New York papers announcing swift Atlantic crossings by company steamers and records established as a result.[124] Of course, the company explicitly denied that the *Imperator*-class liners were built for speed. And yet, given the fascination with the subject, there was speculation that they would attempt to capture the Blue Riband.[125] For example, the press in London and New York reported public expectation that the *Vaterland* would attempt to break the record set by the *Mauretania* in 1909. It was said that "heavy wagers" were laid on the liner in Germany.[126]

Ultimately, even if it was not an "ocean greyhound," the *Imperator* contributed to a sense that the world was not only accelerating but also shrinking, as a revolution in speed embodied in steamships, railways, automobiles, trams, and telegraphy altered patterns of experience. Commentators gave expression to a sense that distance was being greatly reduced as lived space expanded. This impression was especially strong among the European and American middle-classes. Commenting in 1900 on HAPAG's plan to take passengers on a cruise around the world aboard the *Prinzessin Victoria Luise, The Washington Post* wrote that "excursions that would have been considered impossible are planned in the most matter-of-fact manner. Tourists plan to depart for South African war fields before the bullets have ceased from flying."[127] A map published by the *New York Herald* charting the progress of the *Vaterland* on its maiden voyage to New York made the distance between Europe and America seem quite short.[128]

While their technological sophistication and speed were subjects of extensive promotion and interest, what struck many commentators first and foremost upon encountering the *Imperator* and *Vaterland* at Hamburg, Cuxhaven, Southampton, and New York was their size. The enormous proportions of the liners were a common topic, especially in the popular press in Germany, Britain, and America; in fact, press reporting often began with commentary on their size. Expressions of awe and even unease, like those by the Swiss journalist quoted at the beginning of this chapter, were usual responses to the *Imperator* during its construction, at the time of its launch, and during its career. Many observers seem to have experienced a sense of being almost overwhelmed in the towering presence of a vehicle that appeared too large to have been created by human hands.[129] *The New York World* described the *Imperator* as a "marine mountain" and published a photograph looking up at the vessel from the water line that very effectively reinforces the metaphor.[130] Emphasizing that the liner was "one of the largest objects ever constructed," the *New York Herald* stated that it was difficult to comprehend the size of the vessel even by means of a comparison with the world's largest buildings.[131] In fact, many commentators attest to the difficulty of finding adequate points of comparison from which to properly appreciate what was described by the *San Francisco Chronicle* as "the most colossal piece of mechanism ever constructed by the hand of man."[132] This fascination with the *Imperator*'s size also extended to the unprecedented scale of individual components such as its rudder.[133]

A transatlantic liner's bulk was often discussed in terms of the greatness of the nation that launched it. This was especially the case from the 1880s in England and Germany. But the *Imperator* was also a major new attraction in an international culture of large constructions prevalent at the time.[134] In this culture, enormous size and technological sophistication were not seen as distinct from one another. In fact, colossal proportions were often taken as an indication of engineering prowess. As Darcy Grimaldo Grigsby has emphasized, giant constructions like the Eiffel Tower and Panama Canal were regarded as emblems of a new cultural and industrial epoch.[135] They were monuments to progress at a time when size was equated with technological advance and bigger meant better.

Many different formulations were employed to describe and illustrate the ever-increasing proportions of passenger liners in the early years of the twentieth century. In advertising and the press in Europe and America, it was common to draw dramatic comparisons with the nautical past that emphasized the degree of change occurring in the modern era. For example, *The Washington Post* published an article entitled "Growth of Sea-Going Craft. From 200 Tons in 1492 to 50,000 Ton Monster in 1912."[136] The paper employed an illustration similar to those used in HAPAG advertising, and proportionally far larger than the accompanying text. This bore the caption "A Vision of Christopher Columbus's Flagship and the Liner Imperator." In it, a non-specific image of a giant ocean liner, bearing the name *Imperator* on its bow, fills almost the entire picture plane as it plows towards the viewer. The image is formatted to emphasize the massive bulk of the vessel: set against a dark background of sky, only its forward section is in view, as the hull breaks the bounds of the image frame and disappears beyond its borders. The viewer looks up at its towering prow while the hull's dramatic, diagonal recession-in-depth emphasizes the speed, power, and steadiness with which it cuts unstoppably through a stormy sea. In short, the liner is monumentalized and overpowers both the frame and the viewer. In the immediate foreground, the darkened hull of Columbus's tiny vessel appears the plaything of the ocean waves as it narrowly escapes being plowed under by the knife-edge of steel that is the *Imperator*'s prow. The accompanying text suggests that the only disadvantage pertaining to the exceptional size of such vessels was the danger of suction posed to smaller craft in their vicinity. This way of depicting the *Imperator* was often repeated in the media and advertising.

Reference to the past was a way of emphasizing the size and sophistication of the latest transatlantic liners. But this past was not limited to the nautical. One image of the *Imperator* depicted it standing on its stern next to, and towering over, Cologne Cathedral. It was common for all major shipping lines to make such comparisons. Cunard's *Mauretania*, for example, was pictured standing beside the Great Pyramid at Giza. An article in *The Observer* was accompanied by a diagram in which the *Imperator*'s length was shown to be more than twice the height of St. Paul's Cathedral.[137] *The World*, published in New York, referred to the *Imperator* as "the new pyramid of the Atlantic," suggesting that modern western civilization had surpassed that of ancient Egypt.[138] But portraying transatlantic liners beside the greatest human creations of the past was not simply a way to emphasize their proportions; it invested them with cultural prestige. This was also achieved by commentary that sought points of comparison in the contemporary world with a metaphor like "sky-scrapers of the seas."[139] The *Kansas City Times* referred to

Figure 2.5 Poster with an image by A.F. Bishop depicting the *Imperator* and *Borussia*: 1913–1914.

Source: Hapag-Lloyd AG, Hamburg.

passenger liners as "modern floating skyscrapers."[140] The German journalist and author Eugen Zabel compared the impression of first seeing the *Imperator* to that of encountering the Flat Iron Building in New York. He was astounded by its size, saying the liner was not a floating palace but like a city.[141]

It was common to communicate facts and figures about the *Imperator*-class liners in astonished, even hyperbolic tones. Evocative turns of phrase often drew upon literary tropes to describe transatlantic liners and sometimes speak of them in the vocabulary of the sublime.[142] This language seems to have been frequently employed for sensational effect. The popular illustrated journal *Über Land und Meer* described the *Imperator* as a "50,000-ton monster," a "Goliath of the Ocean," and as one of several "steamship leviathans."[143] The term "colossus" was often used in the German press to describe it and the *Vaterland*.[144] In New York, *The World* announced the arrival of the second of HAPAG's new trio with the following headline: "$6,000,000 Sea Monster *Vaterland* to Move Majestically into This Harbor Today."[145]

Yet this type of language was not unusual even in sober reporting that sought to transmit a sense of the liners' size. *The Nautical Gazette*, for example, which was published in New York and devoted to shipbuilding and marine engineering, reported on the *Imperator*-class liners in astonished tones. It spoke of the "monster proportions" of the *Imperator's* floor plates, of the giant rivets used to construct its hull, and of the "immense engines" of the "recently launched leviathan."[146] The American journal *"Shipping" Illustrated* described the liner as a "behemoth."[147] This type of biblical language was not uncommon in representations of transatlantic liners. This is also seen, for instance, in the following comment on their increasing size from *The Washington Post*: "Great leviathan of metal, who shall draw thee out with a hook?"[148]

Contrasting impressions were sometimes combined in a single report as in the latter paper's description of the *Imperator* as the "new Queen of the Ocean" and a "monster."[149] Bigger may have meant better, but the many descriptions of the *Imperator* as a giant, unnatural, living creature, suggest that its sheer size, and that of new technology in general, was greeted with a certain amount of uncertainty. As Bernhard Rieger has suggested, commentators faced the size and sophistication of much new technology with a mixture of admiration and anxiety. The rhetoric of "modern wonder" did not prevent a sense of ambivalence; innovations "elated observers *and* sent shivers down their spines." They were "intellectually and emotionally confusing" and contributed to a "pervasive sense of dislocation."[150] Furthermore, then as now, many critics interpreted technology as dangerous to the independence of humanity. Ultimately, however, "welcoming sentiments outweighed skepticism about technological innovations as commentators underlined technology's scientific foundations as well as its historical role in promoting progress."[151]

Yet facts, figures, and textual description, even if presented in hyperbolic tones, could only go so far. As previously noted, press reporting was explicit about the difficulties of representing the large size of transatlantic liners, and the language it employed often suggests disorientation. *The Washington Post* claimed it was impossible to convey an adequate impression of the size of the *Imperator* by means of photographs and drawings because of the difficulty of finding points of reference.[152] "Atlantic liners are now so large," it explained, "that it is difficult to gain an adequate conception of their magnitude because there is little with which we can actually compare them."[153] In Britain, *The Marine Engineer and Naval Architect* claimed that it was impossible to give a correct impression of the vessel and that it must be seen to be appreciated.[154] Speaking of the *Vaterland, The Daily Telegraph* explained that "mere figures give little idea of her size."[155] This sentiment extended to the liners' interiors. Also in Britain, *The Syren and Shipping Illustrated* stated that, while descriptions of the *Imperator's* interiors occupied "an inordinate amount of space" in newspaper and journal articles, "they convey very little to the mind of the reader, unless he be an expert in the art of decoration."[156]

As a result, images were extensively employed to promote and report upon HAPAG's new liners. As we have noted, company advertising was replete with imagery. In the early years of HAPAG's existence, the company advertised principally in newspapers, often publishing small notices with essential information and, if at all, tiny, non-specific profile images of ships. But from the middle of the 1860s, German shipping lines began to represent themselves through the developing medium of posters. Examples from the 1870s, although often colourful, are devoted mostly to text and employ relatively small images. Most common are distant, broadside, or profile views of a vessel at sea, steaming through the waves with its sails billowing and smoke pouring from its funnels. By the 1880s, the relation between text and image on posters began to change as shipping lines realized that more could be said with pictures than with words. Greater emphasis was placed on the attraction of the ships themselves with text evermore reduced to essentials and pushed to the upper and lower margins. These posters were more eye-catching and more graphically attractive. At the same time, the images they bore became more dynamic. Now situated in the foreground with their stacks billowing smoke, steamers were often depicted obliquely from the bow on a diagonal line that created a sharp recession into the picture space. This compositional format generates a sense of energy and directional movement as the large vessel steams inexorably through the waves towards the viewer. As David Klemm describes it, the viewer's gaze is pulled towards the vessel as if by a type of suction or undertow created by its rapid movement through the water. By suggesting that natural forces posed no opposition or danger to a liner on its voyage across the Atlantic, this type of image promoted the safety of a line's vessels and services.[157]

Posters could be seen on the premises of the many agents that represented HAPAG where potential passengers could also obtain image-rich brochures and sailing schedules. The display windows of travel bureaus often exhibited not only images but even models of the new liners.[158] An overlooked facet of HAPAG advertising are the colour and monochrome art postcards, as well as the photographic cards published by the company. Offering a bolder representation than a tinted photograph, art postcards representing new liners were often issued before they entered service. Yet much of the imagery depicting the *Imperator*-class liners, which appeared on posters, postcards, and sailing schedules, was in marked contrast to the manner in which passenger liners were depicted even into the first decade of the twentieth century. The imagery employed on posters published by shipping lines often replicated the conventions of marine painting. In fact, HAPAG employed marine artists like Hans Bohrdt (1857–1945), Felix Schwormstädt (1870–1938), and Willy Stöwer (1864–1931) and reproduced their painted images on posters. This often meant that a naturalistic, detailed, and seemingly accurate rendition of a vessel was set into foaming seas and against a backdrop of large cloudbanks. From the 1890s, some posters demonstrate a *Jugendstil* influence especially in framing devices, ornament, and lettering. And it was not unusual for posters from this period to employ allegorical figures. One published by HAPAG in 1897 to advertise its services to New York includes female figures representing America and Hammonia.[159]

Figure 2.6 Poster with an image by Hans Bohrdt depicting the *Deutschland*: 1902–1903.
Source: The Mariners' Museum, Newport News, VA.

A similar type of imagery is found in HAPAG brochures. One example is that published in New York in the 1890s to promote the express steamers *Augusta Victoria, Columbia, Fürst Bismarck,* and *Normannia.*[160] In its pages, artists' impressions depict the vessels at sea. Filling the picture frame, these are often represented broadside, at a distance from the viewer, and contained within their own space. The images are framed by decorative surrounds composed of Rococo-inspired scrollwork. This is animated by floral motifs and incorporates vignettes and motifs including Neptune, a mermaid, birds, and even a putto. Giant vessels of steel are thus presented to the reader in an artful manner that downplays their machine-like qualities and emphasizes the fact that they are also works of art, welcoming environments, and luxury items to be consumed by their passengers. As the brochure emphasizes, "the best European artists" were "retained to design, decorate, and furnish" these vessels.[161]

By the time the *Imperator* came into service, advertising images were simpler, less cluttered, and bolder, while compositional formats were more concentrated and based on simple geometry. Many images of the *Imperator*-class liners, such as the one in which it towers over Columbus's vessel, are constructed in such a way as to emphasize how their monumental proportions and enormous power dwarf humanity; they appear as mountains of steel. As Bernhard Rieger has suggested, the size of liners "stretched established frames" and advertising testifies "to the difficulties of representing liners in coherent or complete images." More generally, it demonstrates the problems of representing monumental technology using established formulas.[162] HAPAG began representing its liners in this way before the launch of the *Imperator.* One example is the artist's impression on the cover of the May edition of the *Hamburg-American Gazette* for 1910, published in New York.[163] The viewer is not confronted with a ship at sea but with a wall of steel and machinery that nearly obliterates both ocean and sky and is so large that the cover can capture only a partial view of it. The anonymous vessel bursts out of the picture space, steaming headlong, and billowing smoke, into the space of the viewer. Artists' impressions of anonymous vessels on the covers of sailing schedules issued by HAPAG in 1911 and 1912 offered similar images of giant hulls.[164] Set in the immediate foreground, towering over tiny tugboats, but with minimal picture space devoted to setting or context, the liners are depicted from low vantage points and from their bows. These giant vessels, or what is visible of them, often steam out of the picture frame in the reader's direction, overwhelming them with their enormous bulk in a way that mimicked the overwhelming and disorienting experience of seeing such a vessel at close hand.

While the posters published by shipping lines during the Belle Époque have attracted popular interest, it is perhaps by means of postcards that images of the *Imperator*-class liners were most widely disseminated on both sides of the Atlantic. The two decades before the First World War are considered the golden age of the postcard in the western world, and there was an enormous market for them. While a means of communication, they were also given as gifts and collected as souvenirs. Postcards depicting the *Imperator, Vaterland,* and

Bismarck feature images in which their giant hulls dominate the picture space and everything in it. Some bear photographs or artists' impressions depicting the liners at a distance and portraying their entire length. Art postcards permitted more dramatic representations such as a bow view of a liner rapidly bearing down on the observer who seems to be at water level, floating on the waves. In either case, the vessels are monumentalized, and their size and power emphasized. While scenes are animated by the colour of water and sky, the liners are not part of their environment nor simply at ease in it; they dominate it. They are giant machines, their funnels towering into the sky. Much smaller craft, often sailing ships, are sometimes posed in the background or foreground. Many of these appear to be from another age and serve to emphasize not only the size of the *Imperator*-class liners but also the technological and engineering progress they embodied. The caption "World's Largest Ship" or some variation of it as well as statistics including the vessel's length and tonnage are occasionally included in the image itself. Passenger directories for the *Imperator* and *Vaterland* also employ these type of low-angle bow views in which the vessels tower over smaller ones and recess dramatically into the background.[165]

One of the most striking images of the *Imperator* was designed by the prominent graphic designer and artist Lucian Bernhard (1883–1972). This featured in an advertisement for the sparkling-wine manufacturer Henkell & Co., which reminded readers that the world's largest ship had been christened with its product.[166] Bernhard played an influential role in the development of what is known in Germany as *Plakatstil*, an early form of poster art. He and other artists turned from the often intricate compositions and sinuous forms of Art-Nouveau-inspired design to a style of representation grounded in the geometric clarity, even austerity of much avant-garde art of the period. His image of the *Imperator* embodies the defining hallmarks of this style: bold geometric forms; an uncomplicated composition focused on a single dominant object; minimal spatial construction; bold and flat colouring; and pronounced, simple lettering. In Bernhard's image the great, hulking, black mass of the *Imperator* lying on its stocks occupies almost the entire picture plane which, once again, appears too small to contain it. A crowd of tiny spectators in the foreground is completely overwhelmed by the vessel and serves to emphasize its enormity. This is an image of mechanical might and technological power designed to overwhelm the viewer even in its small format. It is an image of disorienting immensity.

In addition to the images found in HAPAG advertising, the press and numerous publications attempted to provide a sense of the *Imperator*'s enormous dimensions through the medium of photographs. *The Washington Post* suggested a solution to the problem of accurately representing the size of the liner by claiming that the best way to do this was to dissect the ship and present details in comparison with smaller and more familiar objects. It published a photograph of one of the *Imperator*'s funnels and emphasized that it was large enough for a locomotive and its train to pass through. The

Figure 2.7 Postcard depicting the *Imperator*. 1912–1914.
Source: The Hoboken Historical Museum.

photograph's low point of view, the fact that the funnel fills almost the entire picture plane, and the inclusion of a human figure dwarfed by its bulk all lend themselves to the impression of monumental size.[167] Also focusing on the *Imperator*'s rudder, the article stated that even when individual pieces of the liner are compared to the stature of a man, "the effect is startling." A large photo of the rudder post, rising to a height of fifty-three feet and weighing 100 tons, depicted a man standing underneath it, dwarfed by the giant casting. The photograph is out of proportion to the block of text and the impact of the piece is more visual than textual.

Yet numerous published photographs sought to represent the *Imperator*-class liners in their entirety. While these were taken at various stages of their careers, those taken of the *Imperator* while under construction are especially interesting. Many such photographs were published by the *Zeitschrift des Vereines Deutscher Ingenieure* and are particularly impressive.[168] These may have been shot by the Hamburg photographer Johann Hamann. First commissioned by HAPAG in 1899 to photograph its express steamers and their captains, Hamann was also engaged to photograph the *Imperator* on its stocks. Some images were taken from a low angle to emphasize the impression of the liner's height. Others adopt a bird's-eye perspective to provide the viewer with an indication of the extent of the undertaking. Still others were taken from within the building site and place the viewer in the midst of what seems a cathedral of steel and wood. Photographs like these appeared in advertising, the press, and professional journals in Germany, Britain, and America.

The cult of technology in this era celebrated human ingenuity and shipyard workers occasionally appear in these images. There are even some close-up shots of men involved in tasks such as hammering rivets. And yet, in the majority of photographs they appear not as agents of construction but only as staffage, dwarfed by the giant objects on which they work. Most often, these men are not working at all but pose for the camera; they are employed to provide the viewer with a reference point for envisioning the massive size of the vessel and serve to emphasize its enormity. The focus is overwhelmingly on machine, not man. In fact, it is as if the *Imperator* rises of its own volition without human agency.

A fascination with the technological sophistication, speed, and size of HAPAG's new liners was part and parcel of their elevation to international monuments. Pitted against the forces of nature, steamships became "the favorite vehicle for ideas about progress" in general.[169] Unsurprisingly, this was accompanied by speculation about future innovation in transatlantic transportation. Central to the international culture of modernity was a belief in the conquest of nature by technology and faith in open-ended innovation. In the case of ocean liners, just how open-ended and rapid this innovation was perceived to be is captured by the title of an article published by *The Baltimore Sun*: "Imperator – The Ocean's Newest Giant May Be Midget Tomorrow."[170] In 1913, R.A. Fletcher claimed there was no other branch of industry where there had been such rapid progress.[171] There is a breathless, excited feel to the prose

Figure 2.8 The *Imperator*'s rudder.
Source: Bain Collection, The Library of Congress, Washington, D.C.

of his book *Travelling Palaces* that creates the sense that there is no foreseeable end to innovation in shipbuilding. When the White Star Line announced plans in 1908 to build two vessels of 1,000 feet in length, one author asked whether these "new leviathans" would have "trolleys or moving sidewalks to carry passengers up and down their far-reaching decks?"[172] By the time of the *Bismarck*'s launch, the *Kansas City Times* predicted that the large liner of the future would feature a "motor car speedway."[173] The *Hamburger Fremdenblatt* began its account of the *Imperator*'s launch by stating that it was difficult to appreciate what a wonder the liner was because the current age of rapid technological development produced daily "surprises" on land, in and under the water, and in the air.[174]

In the popular press and advertising, the modernity embodied and symbolized by the *Imperator* and other transatlantic liners was often explicitly construed as a dramatic rupture with the past. To be sure, this was not always nor exclusively the case. The innovations of modern shipbuilding were often presented as issuing from decades of development. Articles about the latest advances embodied in the most recent transatlantic liners were frequently accompanied by historical overviews charting "the triumphant march of the steamship."[175] This was also the case with much of HAPAG advertising.[176]

Yet time and again commentators pointed to the rapidity of change in shipbuilding, emphasized dramatic breaks made with its recent past, and highlighted the way in which it was offering possibilities considered remote only a short time before. *The Christian Science Monitor* told its readers in 1912 that the number of passengers who travelled to New York in 1911 – nearly one million in the ships of twenty-five steamship companies – required fleets of ocean liners that only the "world's dreamers" could have imagined only a few years ago.[177] Emphasis was often put on the way in which perceived limits in size and motive power embodied in the newest "last word" in shipbuilding were so quickly exceeded. In 1908, *The Washington Post* reported that the public had not ceased to wonder at the "immensity of length and tremendous power" of Cunard's *Lusitania* and *Mauretania* before the White Star Line publicized plans to build a steamer 1,000 feet in length.[178] In 1911, the paper stated that present realities in shipbuilding would have been considered "utopian and chimerical" from the perspective of 1900.[179] Looking ahead, it saw "sensational possibilities" in both size and luxury.

Soon after the *Vaterland* first called at New York, *The Wall Street Journal* questioned whether there was a practical limit to the size of passenger liners.[180] It reported that the shipping industry believed only the inadequate port facilities on both sides of the Atlantic were preventing the construction of larger vessels. In his interview with *The New York Times*, Dr. Ernst Foerster of HAPAG explained that, apart from the cost of constructing giant liners, the limits of shipbuilding had been reached only because of shallow waters at the entrance to American and European ports.[181] "There is no last word in shipbuilding," he insisted, "since the possibilities are so extensive."[182] In England, *The Observer* quoted expert opinion stating that, if adequate docking facilities and navigable channels allowed, ocean-going ships would be fifty percent larger by 1970.[183]

The very nature and tone of reporting on transatlantic liners served to augment the impression of rapid change. Press interest in the latest vessels was usually fleeting. For most, "the headlines flared briefly – beginning with the launch continuing through the fitting-out, and culminating in the maiden voyage – then dissipated ... and the press moved on to other stories until the next challenger arose from the stocks."[184] A poem published in *The New York Times* at the time of the *Imperator*'s maiden voyage to New York gives humorous expression to a sense of rapid and seemingly limitless progress. Penned by the American satirical poet and journalist W.J. Lampton, the text reads as follows:

> Imperator, Imperator!/Thou mightiest monster of the sea,/That hath the megatherium skinned/By thy leviathanity,/We gaze upon thy bulging bulk,/Upon thy width and length,/Likewise upon thy height and depth/And thy gigantic strength,/And gasp, amazed to realize/That man is able to/Combine his mind with matter and/Compose a thing like you!/Nevertheless,/Imperator! Imperator!/We hasten to advise/That you Imperate all you can/At present, for your size/Will not protect you, and eftsoon/Some ship will be afloat/To make the grand Imperator/Look like a motor boat./Next![185]

Moreover, the taste expressed by the press for the rivalry between shipping companies to build the biggest and fastest liners was often impatient to the extent that it did not wait for the launch and commissioning of new vessels. The media in Britain and America anticipated the appearance of larger and faster liners by announcing that German companies had placed orders for new vessels, as yet unnamed, and providing estimates of the size and speed they would attain.[186]

Given the character and frequency of reporting on transatlantic liners, some commentators wondered about the nature of its impact on readers. There were those who believed that superlatives were being overused. The *Hamburger Nachrichten* claimed that the public's senses had been so deadened by the frequent use of hyperbole that calling the *Imperator* the greatest steamship ever constructed seemed nothing out of the ordinary.[187] The paper was certain that any records achieved by the vessel would sooner or later be superseded by another. While marvelling at the enormity and complexity of the *Imperator*, the British journal *The Syren and Shipping Illustrated* believed that the public had grown so accustomed to large liners that the building of a steamship half a mile in length "would probably have no more effect than that of causing them to look a little bit surprised."[188]

No matter the effects on readers, advances in the size, speed, and technology of transatlantic liners were generally seen as positive by most commentators. The celebration of technological progress and the narrative of technological triumphalism were often cast as a struggle against the forces of nature, and there was a sense that the sea had become humanity's servant. HAPAG publicity spoke of the *Imperator* as a conqueror of the seas construed as hostile to humanity and even "enemy territory."[189] The author and journalist Philipp Berges said that the old gods of the sea would flee before the *Imperator* as humanity won another victory over the forces of nature.[190] But positive assessment was not ubiquitous. After the *Vaterland* had difficulty docking in Hoboken upon completion of its maiden voyage, some questioned whether it was practical to construct such "marine mammoths." They were, as *The*

Baltimore Sun put it "Too Big for Convenience." The challenges of providing adequate docking facilities would only increase for giant liners that were like "Gullivers among Lilliputians and threaten destruction to everything around them."[191] More significantly, reporting on the *Imperator*-class liners expressed serious concerns about humanity's technological hubris. Albert Ballin believed that "the size, speed and other qualities of the unfortunate *Titanic* had nothing to do with her loss."[192] And, as the *Berliner Tageblatt* stated in April 1912 following the sinking of the White Star liner, "we will stand paralyzed many a time, watching how nature cruelly humiliates human pride in human works; despite this, our battlecry [sic] must be: forward!"[193]

Yet such determination was sometimes tempered by concern that humanity was overstepping long-standing boundaries too quickly. The possibility of bridging great distance in unprecedented time provoked negative reactions to what was perceived as an over-hasty age.[194] In the wake of the *Titanic*'s sinking, Joseph Conrad predicted "more irresponsibility in the future when steamships could plow across the ocean in all weather at forty knots."[195] In an article entitled "The Next Great Disaster," the *Chicago Record Herald* said it was only a matter of time before "the mania for building bigger ships" would result in another tragedy at sea.[196] Boasting of the *Titanic*'s invulnerability had not prevented its sinking. And now, the author continued, the *Imperator* had caught fire, while lying at dock in Hoboken, and burned for nearly five hours. Was this "a gentle hint to man that he should not press too far in his folly?" The English maritime author Edward Keble Chatterton questioned whether modern shipbuilding was not "flying in the face of Nature, and asking for trouble?" In what he described as "the fight between Man and Nature," human ingenuity might "fool her [nature] very well in many ways" but could not do this indefinitely.[197]

While many commentators mused about a perilous future, others responded to rapid progress in transatlantic travel with nostalgia for the era of sail, the charm and adventure of a sea voyage, and a time when humanity was closer to nature. Generally speaking, thinking about the past in the early twentieth century was often coloured by a touch of regret for the end of an era and a world that was more slow-paced and secure; it was often motivated by a search "for stability in the face of rapid technological, cultural, and social change."[198] Some feared speed would kill a contemplative engagement with the world. Reflecting on his experience aboard NDL's *Spree* while crossing the Atlantic in 1892, the German ophthalmologist and medical historian Julius Hirschberg mused that the "larger the ship, the more the poetry of the sea voyage fades." In a cabin high above the waterline, he could see nothing of the vessel's machinery and could hear and feel little of the working of its engine. Nor could he observe what he described as the "colorfully eventful life of the steerage passengers."[199] Writing about passenger steamers in 1893, Mark Twain remarked that "one thing is gone, to return no more forever – the romance of the sea."[200]

HAPAG advertising often compared the present state of shipbuilding with that of the past. Unsurprisingly, the company insisted that the romance of sea travel had not been lost with the advent of giant passenger liners and modern technology; it was simply experienced in a different manner.[201] Or, as the *Hamburg-American Gazette* put it, "romance may indeed be waning, but magic has taken its place."[202] And not all commentators agreed that vessels like the *Imperator* marked the inevitable loss of the romance of sea travel. Keble Chatterton, for example, wrote that the sea

> is tyrannical in her strength, untamable, dominant; and when you launch into her bosom heavy masses of iron and steel, and deceive yourself with high-sounding names – call them *Great Easterns*, *Majestics*, *Indomitables*, *Titanics*, and all the rest – the Sea only laughs at you, for she knows perfectly well that a blow or two from her mighty arm will end their days and settle their fate for all time.[203]

Yet dissatisfaction with what the size and technological sophistication of vessels such as the *Imperator*-class liners had done to the nature of sea travel can often be found in press reporting. In 1913, for example, *The Washington Post* opined that the destruction

> of that thrilling romance of the sea, which comes of its uncertainties, the sense of the unknown, of the marvelous, of possible hardship and strange experiences, of the unexpected that may at any time come to pass, robs the voyage of that which from time immemorial has given the keenest tingle to sea life.[204]

Life aboard liners like the *Imperator* now offered the same "humdrum and commonplace pleasure and immunities of the land" and "banished all the higher pleasures of the occult and the strange." The article claimed, however, that "the great majority" of travellers will continue to be gratified by longer voyages

> on ships not quite so splendidly equipped for safety and luxury ... where the horizon of thought has a little more appeal to the imagination, where the every-day surroundings are a little more provocative of genuine sea-wonder, and the sophistries of existence a little less pronounced.

A liner like the *Imperator* would remain the preserve of the rich and "the much greater majority ... will continue to travel in the older-fashioned steamers" where there will "be enough opportunity for all sorts of sea experience."

V

While the *Imperator* was widely construed as a wonder of modern engineering and technology, HAPAG emphasized that, during the process of outfitting the vessel, "culture and elegance will find its place in the monster."[205] To be sure, the liner was more than just an impressive work of maritime engineering. It was a means of transportation designed to carry passengers from all social classes: 908 in first class; 606 in second class; 962 in third class; and 1,772 in steerage or what was known as fourth class aboard the vessel. With a crew of 1,180, the *Imperator* could accommodate 5,428 persons. In fact, the combined passenger capacity of the *Imperator*-class liners was almost equal to that of the company's entire North Atlantic fleet.[206]

The nature and experience of Atlantic travel changed considerably in the second half of the nineteenth century and German shipping lines contributed significantly to this. In contrast to Charles Dickens' description of his voyage aboard Cunard's *Britannia* in 1842, Mark Twain's account of his experience crossing the Atlantic on NDL's *Havel* in 1893 is a celebration of the advances made in on-board accommodation. Twain explained that he was surprised by what he found aboard the 7,000-ton vessel. In times past, he pointed out, "the inside of a ship was the plainest and barrenest thing, and the most dismal and uncomfortable that ingenuity could devise." But what he discovered on the *Havel* was that "the modern ship is a marvel of rich and costly decoration and sumptuous appointment, and is equipped with every comfort and convenience that money can buy."[207] He claimed that passengers aboard the vessel were more comfortable than in the best hotels in Europe. The food was good, the cabins steam-heated, and the bathrooms as well equipped as in any private house in America.[208] Twain described Cunard's *Batavia*, aboard which he had travelled from Liverpool in November 1872, as poorly lit by candles and lamps, and seating passengers in its dining saloon on long benches. In contrast, the *Havel* was equipped with electric lighting and swivel chairs with cushion backs.

Accommodating travellers in surroundings that approximated those they were familiar with ashore "was to offer them the most effective bromide against fear, anguish and sea-sickness."[209] HAPAG repeatedly stressed that it was determined, since its very inception, to offer passengers more comfortable accommodation than could be found aboard the ships of other lines.[210] And, in addition to actual shipboard improvements, the company made considerable efforts to counter the image of sea travel as dangerous and unsanitary. It did this with campaigns that "turned the common understanding of ocean travel on its head."[211] Of course, doing so meant confronting a "powerful, long-standing cultural tradition that emphasized the dangers of the sea."[212] As late as 1912, the sinking of the *Titanic* and the *Empress of Ireland* "provided powerful reminders of the ongoing risks involved in maritime voyages."[213] In January 1914, HAPAG's *Fürst Bismarck* was caught in a storm as it sailed for Boston and "was pounded by the seas until it was feared she would be overwhelmed." All aboard were "panic stricken" and the steerage passengers "were huddled below, many of them praying for deliverance."[214]

But there was something that shipping companies could do little about: seasickness. Interviews conducted with immigrants who entered the United States "on the most advanced vessels" between 1907 and 1929 indicate the widespread nature of this problem.[215] HAPAG insisted that the *Imperator*'s great bulk, along with its system of Frahm anti-rolling tanks, would "counteract the motion of the most violent sea, assuring even the 'poorest sailors' of a pleasant crossing."[216] And in fact, newspaper reports often related that passengers were pleased with the stability of the vessel and the smoothness of the voyage. It was even reported that a HAPAG physician had discovered a cure for seasickness in "a simple electric vibration chair" that did away with symptoms by eliminating nervous excitement. Apparently, the company intended to place these chairs on all its liners.[217] And yet the problem of seasickness was not solved. For the first two days after departing Cherbourg in September 1913, the *Imperator* encountered a heavy sea in which it pitched such that many passengers were ill.[218]

In spite of the persistent dangers and ailments of transatlantic travel, HAPAG claimed that, 400 years after Columbus, what was once a heroic deed had become a pleasant voyage. And it took to promoting its liners as destinations to be enjoyed in their own right. Just as the bourgeois home was conceived as a refuge from daily life, shipping companies presented their premier transatlantic liners as palaces of illusion separated from the real world.[219] Or, as the German art critic and journalist Max Osborn noted in 1912, the intention was to provide passengers with the sensation of being in a grand hotel, not at sea.[220] HAPAG took up this strategy especially from 1906 when it presented the *Kaiserin Auguste Victoria* not as offering a speedy Atlantic crossing, but as affording the opportunity for relaxation and recreation.[221] One publication from that year describes the experience of a first-class passenger as he

> rises from in front of the huge fireplace in the grand Elizabethan smoking-room, ascends under the oaken rafters to the second story or balcony of this beautiful retreat, and saunters out on an upper deck for a glance at the immensity and grandeur of the ocean. From here he wanders to the lively streets and squares of the deck promenades, and mingles with a gay crowd on an Atlantic Pall Mall or Rialto. He lingers to get the latest stock reports, and news of important events occurring on land that morning, as told by the wireless, then moves on to his spacious apartments, carrying a fresh bunch of roses to Miladi, with whom he next consults as to the advisability of giving a dinner party that night at the Ritz Café. The telephone is resorted to, a table engaged, and a choice of menu built up. More telephoning and the invitations are given and accepted. At the conclusion of the dinner, coffee is taken in the superb palm room, amid palms and fresh flowers, while listening to the strains of beautiful music.[222]

Quite beyond its promotion as safe and comfortable, travel aboard HAPAG's liners was presented to cabin-class passengers as engendering well-being and offering freedom from obligation.[223] It was an occasion "for pleasure and recuperation."[224]

It was elite consumption and leisure that were prioritized in HAPAG advertising. And a large proportion of the interiors of the *Imperator*-class liners were devoted to the leisure and rituals of the upper-middle classes. In a long and richly illustrated article published in 1913, the *Boston Herald* employed the headline "Craze For Luxury Makes The *Imperator* Possible."[225] But not all commentators agreed on who drove this craze. One English writer accredited the luxury of first-class accommodation to the rise of German prosperity and its corollary: "an instant desire to spend money in all sorts of self-indulgence."[226] Others, however, identified the influential role of the American travelling public in the development of the interior design of passenger vessels launched by European companies. *The New York Times* reported that William James Pirrie, chairman of the Belfast shipbuilding firm Harland & Wolff from 1895 to 1924, travelled to the United States "to get ideas as to the kind of ships the American public demanded for transatlantic travel." An American traveller, the paper claimed "who can afford to pay the price, desires all the luxuries of a first-class hotel aboard a steamer."[227]

The German journalist Max Osborn explained that it was especially wealthy Americans who were being sold European luxury, "Old World" elegance, and a taste of aristocratic life as they stepped aboard German liners in New York. In as much as HAPAG appealed to this taste, it was often aided by reporting in the American press. *The Washington Post*, for example, reported that the chairs of the main dining saloon aboard HAPAG's *Amerika* were upholstered in the same pattern of tapestry used by Marie Antoinette in the Petit Trianon. It also claimed that the liner's silverware was from the same service as that wrought for the Kaiser when he undertook his Mediterranean cruise on the *Hamburg*.[228] Speaking of the possible reproduction of rooms from famous British country houses on future liners, Frederick A. Talbot wryly noted that "the tourist then will be spared the round of visits through these islands – he will become familiarized with our historic architectural treasures while crossing the ocean by rambling through his temporary floating home."[229]

The *Imperator*-class liners were singular attempts to meet American and European social fantasies with respect to prosperity, well-being, and luxury consumption; they were "the logical response to the expectations of a powerful plutocracy and to the aspirations of the *haute bourgeois* traveling public."[230] Cabin-class clientele were sold a sense of exclusivity, entitlement, and privilege in engineered spaces that "turned dream-like visions of luxury consumption into material reality."[231] Giant manifestations of the growth of consumerism and commodity culture on both sides of the Atlantic, the *Imperator, Vaterland*, and *Bismarck* were ocean-going expressions of an expanding market for luxury goods and services that included hotels, spas, and exclusive retail outlets.[232] Advertising even transformed them into artworks.[233] HAPAG emphasized that "the best European artists" were retained to design, decorate, and furnish the cabin-class interiors of its liners.[234] *The Baltimore Sun* informed its readers that the "leading decorators of Europe" had designed and furnished the *Vaterland*'s "sumptuous cabins" each of which was a "masterpiece."[235]

Press reporting and popular commentary in Europe and America revelled in the luxury of modern transatlantic liners in general, claiming they surpassed "the fabled Golden House of the Caesars." One author believed that an accurate description of them "would have taxed the imagination of Baron Münchausen and exhausted the credulity of the sultan who believed all the tales of Scheherazade save one."[236] Frederick A. Talbot stated that at the time of Charles Dickens "the passenger paid his money to be transported across the ocean" and not, as was the case in 1912, "to be entertained like an Oriental potentate."[237] In 1911, *The Washington Post* predicted that the future would witness the construction of "ocean palaces" reserved for the "super-rich, who demand sybaritic comforts at sea."[238]

We should note, however, that HAPAG advertising was addressed not only to the habitué of transatlantic crossings but to those not used to travelling regularly, nor grandly. For example, in 1907, the *Hamburg-American Gazette* described the experiences of the fictional John Jones "going to Europe for the first time" aboard one of its steamers.[239] He and his family would be met by "willing porters" on the pier and conducted to their state room replete with "brass beds, with mahogany furniture in rich designs, with silk and damask draperies, and with velvet carpets." Their accommodation would be furnished with "every convenience which taste even more refined than that of the Joneses could expect." The family would dine on the choicest foodstuffs from America, London, Paris, and Vienna served on "silver or rare china." They would enjoy music performed by an orchestra and, while Mr. Jones might meet friends and acquaintances in the smoking room, he could also work off his energy in the gymnasium or "massage emporium."[240]

The textual descriptions in HAPAG's advertising brochures create the impression of elegant sociability and present a transatlantic crossing as a social affair that involved eating, drinking, relaxing, and flirting. The empty ocean, the weather, the monotony, and the cold are written out of the experience. Potential passengers were sold the prospect of comfort, luxury, conviviality, glamour, and romance through enticing descriptions and in language that is sometimes distinctly literary. It was said of the *Imperator*'s first-class dining room that a "shimmer of magical elegance radiates from the room and its guests when the dinner hour has begun and the pleasures of the table, conversation, and music awake the rhythm of enraptured joie de vivre."[241] The allure of first-class conviviality aboard the *Vaterland* was cast in equally evocative terms: when, during dinner, "enchanting fragrances ooze from greenhouse flowers on slim stems ... when conversation in all languages gushes like the champagne in shining glasses and soft, playful tunes blend with the laughter of beautiful, elegant women, the illusion" of not actually traversing the ocean "is perfect."[242]

Long before the *Imperator* entered service, HAPAG employed short stories as a vehicle for promoting the merits of their liners, stories in which much of the dialogue includes unsubtle discussion of a vessel's fittings and services. These also highlight the prospect of ocean travel as romantic and offering the possibility of sexual adventure. One of the company's brochures, published in New York, included a short story entitled "On Summer Seas. A Romance of an Ocean Voyage."[243] The drama takes place aboard the *Deutschland*. The lonely protagonist, Edward Burroughs, is returning to

England after a year in the United States. In the first-class dining room with its "perfect appointments," "perfect service," and "a menu of the daintiest excellence," he meets a young woman, Eleanor Gray. She is travelling as a tourist to Europe, accompanied by her father. The couple promenade on the deck in a romantic flood of moonlight, discussing their experiences in the United States. "Six days of companionship," the brochure explained, "even without such a bond as existed between Eleanor and Burroughs, will do much to mature an incipient love affair."[244] On the last day of the voyage, Burroughs proposes marriage and promises to engage passage on the *Deutschland* for a Mediterranean cruise in January to fulfil Eleanor's desire to travel there. "Let it be the initiatory cruise," he entreats her, "to that long and happy voyage of Life, which, please God, we will make together."[245] Eleanor accepts his proposal of marriage.

In addition to a place where one might find love, HAPAG's "moving marine mansions" and "temples of travel" were also "ocean playgrounds" aboard which passengers enjoyed a variety of entertainments, sports, and games.[246] First-class passengers aboard the *Imperator* could take exercise in the first-class gymnasium. This was fitted with three riding horses, two rowing machines, horizontal and parallel bars, as well as bar bells. For the very first time, second-class passengers were also provided a gymnasium of their own. And, of course, there was the Pompeian Bath. *The Baltimore Sun* stated that the swimming pool aboard the *Vaterland* lent the liner "the attraction of a great spa or bathing resort."[247] When Charles Dickens crossed the Atlantic in 1842, he enjoyed a foot bath while seated in his stateroom with his feet in the passageway.

It is no wonder that advertising and the press likened the *Imperator* to a spa, and its first-class passengers to *Kurgäste*.[248] This was something HAPAG commonly did to market its leisure cruises. The vessels aboard which these excursions were undertaken were described as analogous to seaside resorts and advertising even encouraged passengers to consider travel from a medical standpoint. Furthermore, publicity suggested that the company had made cruising so comfortable and convenient that it was easier than staying at home, as "life in our modern cities is not free from complexity."[249] Promoting cruises aboard the *Cleveland*, *Kaiserin Auguste Victoria*, *Blücher*, and *Victoria Luise* in 1911 and 1912, HAPAG brochures described the experience in the following terms:

> Rare enjoyment is not merely ahead of the tourist as he presses on to distant havens; his enjoyment begins the moment he steps on board the vessels, which are built and furnished on such a lavish and generous scale that they yield their own rich enjoyment, aside altogether from the places on the itineraries.[250]

HAPAG and the press often likened its transatlantic liners to palaces and aristocratic houses. The metaphor of a floating palace was used as early as the 1820s and was well established by 1860. In 1905, the *Hamburg-American Gazette* published an article describing its "moving marine mansions" and "temples of travel" as "the most attractive and popular of imaginable playgrounds."[251] *The Washington Post* described the *Imperator* as "the last word in floating palaces."[252] It was said that the "charms of the most perfect hotel, of the most exclusive club, of the highly organized private household, are united" aboard the liner "to invite Croesus and his family."[253] The German author and journalist Philipp Berges stated that the dream of travelling in a royal palace had become a reality aboard the *Imperator*.[254]

But perhaps the most common description of the liner, in advertising and the press, was as a "vast moving hotel."[255] This comparison was commonly employed to lend transatlantic liners an aura of exclusivity that disassociated them from images of emigrants, discomfort, and disease.[256] One of the passengers on the *Imperator*'s maiden voyage expressed the opinion that the comfort and richness of its interiors "beats any hotel in New York city."[257] The popular journal *Über Land und Meer* even claimed that the description "floating hotel" was, in fact, "far short of the truth" when applied to the *Imperator*. There is no hotel in the world, it emphasized, that could accommodate 5,000 people, or the population of a small city.[258] Shortly before the *Imperator*'s launch, *The Washington Post* stated that passenger liners could no longer be referred to as "floating hotels." This was because "the new boats offer many more attractive and novel features than have yet been attempted by any builder of hotels."[259]

The tradition of comparing transatlantic liners to hotels can be traced back to the 1860s.[260] But it was in the mid-1880s that first-class accommodation aboard these vessels began to mimic that of luxury hotels. Before then, concessions to comfort and hospitality at sea were minimal. As Philip Dawson explains, passengers lived aboard ship "virtually as supernumeraries, with no ship's duties to perform."[261] Yet especially from the 1890s, the interior decoration of passenger liners was increasingly influenced by retail and hospitality architecture.[262] And German shipping lines played an important role in the development of "modern hospitality architecture at sea."[263] First-class passengers had increasing experience with luxury hotels in Europe and the United States and, in an effort to attract their custom, steamship companies began to entrust the interior design of their liners to architects with experience in hotel construction. From this time, cabin-class interiors were executed in a hotelier aesthetic or what might be described as the French-inspired aesthetic of the European hospitality industry. Companies also introduced on-board service comparable to that of establishments such as the Waldorf Astoria in New York (1897), the Paris Ritz (1898), and the Berlin Adlon (1907).

The *Imperator* "marked the definitive shift towards 'grand hotel' design with regard to internal arrangements."[264] But while the design of its interior architecture sought to deny its nautical function, HAPAG advertising stressed the comfort and luxury of first-class accommodation, not their aesthetics. In fact, as we will see in chapter four, it seems passengers took little interest in the particular style in which a liner's interiors were decorated. The important consideration was that they were comfortable and elegant. Luxury, comfort, service, and good food were more important than the style of the rooms in which they were offered.

The *Imperator*'s first-class public spaces – its lounge and dining room, for example – received considerable attention in advertising and the German and foreign press. But it appears to have been individual cabins that mattered most to the travelling public. Diaries, letters, and private travel reports from the period indicate that it was the impression made by cabins that was decisive in determining a passenger's opinion of the entire liner.[265] Most first-class passengers travelled in single staterooms and advertising for the *Imperator* enticed them with a host of details about their accommodation. A feature that was repeatedly stressed was the size of first-class cabins. In fact, HAPAG made much of the fact that the *Imperator*'s interior spaces, with respect to accommodation for all classes, were characterized by a degree of spaciousness previously unseen in maritime construction. These were conceived with a concern for passenger comfort and not simply in accordance with the constraints imposed by the form and dimensions of the vessel's hull. To a certain extent, it is true that all three liners were designed "from the inside out" with the intention to "create hotel environments with ships wrapped around, rather than designing ships and only later working out how to fit hotels inside them."[266] The important point is that spaciousness was equated with luxury and comfort and constituted an important appeal.

As R.A. Fletcher explained in 1913, greater space and more luxury meant higher prices and a larger clientele tempted to pay them.[267] During the high season of 1914, the most expensive first-class cabins for two adults crossing the Atlantic to or from Hamburg were located on the *Imperator*'s B deck and cost either $750.00 or $850.00 in American funds. For the same voyages, one of the liner's twelve first-class suites, accommodating one to three adults and consisting of a bedroom, parlour, bath, toilet, and trunk room, were priced at $1,600.00. One of the two Imperial suites for one to six adults, and one to four servants, and consisting of two bedrooms, parlour, dining room, private veranda, two baths with toilets, two trunk rooms, and two rooms for servants, cost $5,000.00.[268] Second-class cabins to or from Hamburg were considerably less expensive, with the most costly priced at $77.50.[269]

Roomier first-class cabins meant they were outfitted with more comfortable furniture including easy chairs, sofas, armoires, and tables. By the time of the *Imperator*'s commissioning, bunk beds had been abandoned for free-standing metal ones. Fold-down wash basins, once common in first-class cabins, had been replaced by marble washstands with hot and cold running water.[270] There were 229 tub and shower-baths in first-class, all of porcelain. The *Imperator* imitated the sanitary facilities that became more common in luxury hotels and wealthy private homes from the third quarter of the nineteenth century. First-class cabins were described as well ventilated (dampness and stale air being a problem at sea) and equipped with electric light as well as both steam and electric heating. Passengers who enjoyed electricity in their homes would also do so aboard the *Imperator* where it was employed in a variety of functions. The liner was lit by approximately 10,000 electric lamps; there were 380 lights in the first-class lounge and seven in a first-class cabin. In fact, a report on the vessel prepared for Cunard in 1921, just prior to the date on which the British company took possession of it, described "the electric lighting all over the ship" as "absolutely extravagant" and warned that it "takes a good deal of power" from the engines.[271] Electric bells in all cabins ensured prompt service from stewards and electricity also powered five passenger elevators, three in first class and one in second class, all travelling between the second deck and the boat deck. Intercommunicating telephones connected all first-class cabins.

While the facts and figures are striking in themselves, advertising brochures offered numerous photographs of the *Imperator*'s first-class interiors. As with those of the vessel under construction, they are often impressive. This is even the case with images published in small format. A sense of roominess, clear lighting, and airiness immediately strike the viewer. Photographs taken from a low angle, or those that look down on their subject, enhance the impression of spaciousness. So does the fact that most of the images published in company advertising are without people. This may have been intended to enable prospective passengers to imagine themselves inhabiting these spaces. One brochure published in New York was devoted entirely to photographs of the *Imperator*'s first-class cabins.[272] On its opening pages are images of one of the Imperial suites. Given their spaciousness, furnishings, and the un-crowded arrangement of the latter, and although their ceilings are low, it is easy to mistake them for rooms in a luxury hotel or stately home. The less expensive first-class accommodation depicted in the remaining photographs are more clearly shipboard cabins. And yet, in both cases – and even in the small format of the brochure – the photographs strike the viewer with the luxury and comfort of the cabins and the absence of any nautical functionalism.

In case these particular photographs did not "speak" clearly enough, the brochure's short introduction directed readers how to see them. "The unusual size and homelike appearance of the cabins," it indicated, "will at once be observed."[273] The text also emphasized that although the first-class public rooms – which were not pictured in the brochure – were "unusually large," the *Imperator* would carry only a few more passengers than steamers half its size "in order to assure the maximum comfort for all."[274] Clearly, space was an important requisite of luxury, and this point was continually emphasized in company advertising.

In addition to cabins, much advertising was devoted to the *Imperator*'s first-class public rooms. It offered very large, high-ceilinged spaces for a transatlantic liner. The main staircase rose to a height of seventeen metres. The first-class dining saloon spanned the entire thirty-metre width of the hull, rose to a height of 8.5 metres, included a gallery, and was capped by a glass dome. The impression of light and airiness in the main staircase and dining saloon is heightened by the fact that their wall surfaces were finished in white lacquer. This was in keeping with the style in which the dining saloon was decorated, that of Louis XVI. But in terms of spaciousness, the first-class lounge was perhaps the most impressive innovation in the *Imperator*'s interior: it was 22.5 metres in length, seventeen metres wide, six metres high, and was

Figure 2.9 Detail of a first-class cabin aboard the *Imperator*.
Source: German Maritime Museum, Bremerhaven.

constructed without supporting columns to interrupt the space. Its impression of roominess was increased by the fact that it was well lit by arched windows standing four metres high on both the port and starboard sides. Furthermore, it was capped by expansive skylights. The latter were also used to light the Ritz-

Figure 2.10 The *Imperator*'s first-class lounge.
Source: German Maritime Museum, Bremerhaven.

Carlton restaurant, winter garden, smoking room, and the main staircase. HAPAG advertising described the lounge as "an unprecedented sight for every seasoned sea traveler."[275]

In addition to being spacious, the *Imperator*'s cabin-class public rooms were elegantly decorated in an array of historical-revival styles similar to those found in the best hotels in Europe and America. These were the "period styles of upmarket commercial hospitality" that were also adopted by NDL and the Cunard and White Star Lines.[276] Examining photographs of these spaces, one is struck by the elegant restraint of their decoration. Gone is the extravagance of the Neo-Baroque, the intricacy of the Rococo, and the heavy, dark Neo-Renaissance aesthetic often employed on earlier transatlantic liners. Most of the first-class public rooms aboard the *Imperator* were designed and decorated according to the Neo-Classical taste of eighteenth-century France. The dining saloon imitated the style of Louis XVI, while the Ritz-Carlton restaurant and winter garden were executed in the Directoire style. While the former aesthetic is notable for its pale hues, the latter is somewhat heavier and more colourful. The ladies' drawing room was decorated in the white-lacquered Adam style of eighteenth-century England. All these styles are characterized by straight lines, geometric shapes, and restrained, classically inspired detailing and ornament, some of it in gold colouring.

Figure 2.11 The *Imperator*'s winter garden and Ritz-Carlton restaurant.
Source: German Maritime Museum, Bremerhaven.

Some rooms were designed to have a more solemn ambiance. The first-class lounge, was decorated in the style of Louis XIV and panelled in light oak. But even here the sculptural detailing is restrained. And with its large windows, along with glass doors and a giant skylight, much of its wall surface was given over to glass. Boasting eighteen exterior windows and a skylight, the smoking room was decorated in an English Tudor style with wooden columns, timber-framed walls, light oak panelling, a red-tiled floor, and a heavy stone fireplace. With its walls decorated with weapons and hunting trophies, the smoking room leant "a pensive solemnity to after-dinner drinks in friendly company."[277] The grill room imitated an interior from seventeenth-century Schleswig or Friesland with a heavy-beamed ceiling and dark panelling. And, of course, these spaces were furnished to match. While the wing chairs, armchairs, and bergères of the first-class lounge were heavily upholstered and imitated early- and mid-eighteenth century styles, those of the dining saloon, Ritz-Carlton restaurant, and winter garden were lighter and imitated late-eighteenth-century Neo-Classical taste.

The second-class public rooms were also smartly decorated in historical revival styles. Like its first-class equivalent, the second-class dining room was decorated in the Louis XVI style but was much less grand. In the public rooms of third-class, it

Figure 2.12 The *Imperator*'s smoking room.
Source: German Maritime Museum, Bremerhaven.

was clear that one was aboard ship. In these quarters, historical revival styles were abandoned, and functionalism with much less embellishment prevailed. In the third-class dining saloon, passengers dined at long, narrow communal tables seated on fixed swivel chairs. In steerage quarters, there was no attempt to disguise nautical functionalism.

It is interesting to note that while the *Imperator*'s engineering and technology were often defined as masculine and the liner construed as an expression of male strength, its interiors mostly conformed to well-bred feminine taste, apart from obvious exceptions like the smoking room. As the German journalist Hans Ossig explained, the liner was decorated with "the softest cushions and the daintiest things of exquisite feminine boudoirs."[278] And as Bernhard Rieger points out, shipping companies "resorted to a feminized imagery of elite consumption and leisure for promotional purposes because this iconography was unlikely to spark criticism of excessive 'materialism' on board."[279] The pursuit of leisure and material consumption came to be seen as respectable female activities before the First World War and shipping companies promoted their liners as places where upper-class ladies could enact these roles. As we will see in chapter four, Ilse Dernburg (1880–1965), a German interior designer, provided designs for some of the suites aboard the *Imperator*, apparently the only woman to do so.[280]

Clearly, HAPAG advertising sought to assure the line's more affluent clientele that there would be no change to the patterns and pleasures of their lifestyle aboard such a floating hotel, even in the mid-Atlantic. Thus, in addition to a host of details about staterooms and public spaces, the company stressed the improved dining arrangements aboard their latest liners and emphasized that passengers "could maintain their usual habits of consumptive individualism on board."[281] Long before the launch of the *Imperator*, HAPAG developed a reputation with the travelling public for the quality of its cuisine and the elaborate meals served in first-class dining rooms. The dinner served aboard the *Fürst Bismarck* on 19 February 1902 was comprised of soup à la Flamande; red mullet; leg of mutton à la India; ragout of tongue with olives; farced squabs; cauliflower à la Lyonnaise; Columbia ice cream; and Viennese pastry.[282]

Advertising for the *Imperator* assured first-class passengers that they would have a variety of dining options. As one American newspaper described it, the appeal of different dining rooms aboard the liner was that passengers could indulge their individual tastes much as they could in any great city.[283] They could dine in the first-class dining room, the winter garden, or the grill room. Alternatively, passengers could choose to purchase their dinner, at extra cost, in the Ritz-Carlton Restaurant much as they would in "a distinguished hotel in the city."[284] Two head chefs supervised a staff of 116 people preparing meals for the latter, as well as for the first-class dining room. While 124 stewards waited on table, a staff of twenty-one was employed as dishwashers and silver polishers. Each class aboard the *Imperator* was served by its own kitchen with one devoted to the preparation of kosher meals. The latter were available on all HAPAG liners travelling to America from 1904.[285] Publicity photographs of all the *Imperator*'s kitchens emphasized well-ordered cleanliness. There were also two bakeries aboard ship and a large butchery equipped with refrigerated storage.

If HAPAG was at pains to emphasize that cabin-class passengers would experience no change to the patterns and pleasures of their lifestyle aboard the *Imperator*, the liner was credited with facilitating change in shipboard habits. In keeping with "gender conventions prevalent in the best circles," it provided lounges to which women and men could retire separately.[286] But in 1913, one commentator claimed that the *Imperator*'s first-class lounge marked a "change of ideas and habits among passengers" with respect to the mixing of the sexes. In the lounge, "both sexes can chat, read, write, and smoke, and in the evening, when the removal of the splendid pink carpet reveals the parquet floor, they can dance."[287] In Britain, *The Times* also noted this change aboard the *Imperator* and claimed that "the smoke room has lost its great importance." "The latter," it suggested

> like the ladies' room, is the resort of extremists, men who wish to get away
> from the ladies, as members of the opposite sex go to the ladies' room
> when they want to be entirely free from tobacco smoke. The popular resort
> is the lounge.[288]

In the 1915 edition of her *Encyclopedia of Etiquette*, Emily Holt advised that, on German steamers, it was not a breach of etiquette for a woman to enjoy coffee in the smoking room with a male relative or friend. But this custom was not, she said, "in vogue" on American, British, and French liners.[289]

As with the grand hotels and spas of Europe and America, the *Imperator* was a meeting place for a cosmopolitan elite. Travel accounts from the period often describe a mix of passengers from different nations aboard transatlantic liners. The music programs aboard HAPAG vessels were international in character, and orchestras performed popular German and English songs, marches, and overtures. Souvenir brochures published by the company included the lyrics of "God Save the Queen," "America," and "The Star Spangled Banner." They also provided a list of useful sentences and phrases in English, French, and German.[290] The *Imperator*'s libraries stocked titles in the three languages.

But if liners were sites of international interaction and exchange, they were also a theatre for international tensions. In 1907, an American passenger aboard HAPAG's *Oceana* assaulted a German traveller who had behaved "indecorously in the presence of his wife in the dining saloon."[291] The captain was reported as saying that "a great deal of ill feeling existed between the English and American passengers on one side and the German passengers on the other. The former accused the Germans of gross bad manners." When the American passenger was ordered to leave the vessel, it was said the English and American passengers "are very indignant over the whole incident."

Some passengers seem to have been attracted to HAPAG's liners for reasons other than the opportunity they afforded to cross the Atlantic in comfort and luxury. It was not unusual for card sharps to book passage, despite precautions taken by the company. In August 1907, a group of such cheats aboard the *Kaiserin Auguste Victoria* "were prepared to fleece such of the male passengers as they could get into a crooked game." This provoked a series of physical conflicts, and two American men were said to have "fought all over the deck" with the result that one was carried badly injured from the ship at Plymouth and the other was placed in irons.[292] A similar event occurred aboard the *Vaterland* in June 1914 and detectives were sent on board when it docked in New York to question gamblers who had been using marked cards.[293] In 1910, an American passenger aboard the *Amerika* was said to have been robbed of $40,000 in jewels.[294] The Hamburg police believed the thieves belonged to an international gang that worked aboard transatlantic liners.

For those who never travelled aboard the *Imperator*-class liners, press reporting often apprised them of the more spectacular social events aboard the vessels. In September 1913, for example, the *Chicago Daily Tribune* reported that probably "the most remarkable 'revelry by night' ever held on the high seas was that which crowned the last voyage of the steamer *Imperator*."[295] On the evening prior to the vessel's arrival in New York, approximately 500 Americans participated in a ball in the first-class lounge. This was a gathering "remarkable for [the] wealth of the people." Naming several eminent businessmen and wealthy women – including Louis C. Tiffany and Mrs. W.K.

Vanderbilt – the *Tribune* stated that their combined fortunes were estimated at \$1,000,000,000. Although "they tangoed briskly," the paper emphasized that this was done in a modest manner and that no "standards of propriety were set at defiance." When the *Vaterland* arrived in America on its first crossing, the *New York Herald* announced in a headline: "Trip Across Ocean Delightful; Gayeties Fill the Hours."[296]

Interest in transatlantic liners, then and now, has often focused on their cabin-class interiors, services, and passengers. But it must be remembered that they were intended to carry a cross-section of American, and especially European society from its wealthiest magnates in first-class accommodation to its poorest emigrants in steerage quarters. As we have seen, the *Imperator* and *Vaterland* were promoted as seductive spaces "that set the scene for conventional forms of sociability devoid of threatening overtones."[297] But the reality was more complicated; these vessels hosted a social microcosm of great disparity and were monumental symbols of class inequality. Ultimately, HAPAG's liners were more varied and complex social spaces, and the site of more dynamic social intercourse, than is often described. They were not simply ocean palaces for wealthy clientele.

VI

On its maiden voyage to New York the *Imperator* reached quarantine shortly before midnight on 18 June. It came up the bay on the following morning with high tide. Before docking at Hoboken, liners had to be inspected at the New York State Quarantine Station in the lower bay on two artificial islands, Swinburne and Hoffman. Immigrants suspected of having contagious diseases were removed to the quarantine hospital and refused permission to enter the United States until deemed fit to do so. Healthy immigrants were unloaded in the lower reaches of the harbour and taken by ferries and tenders to Ellis Island. Only first- and second-class passengers were permitted to continue to the Hoboken docks.

Different classes of passenger were organized in tiers aboard ship, and in a variety of accommodation arrangements that represented the social hierarchy. Cross-section diagrams appeared in the advertising of shipping companies demonstrating the physical and social stratification aboard their vessels. In no other spaces did the extremely rich and extremely poor coexist in such close proximity. In the words of Johannes Merck: "in a confined space, social opposites run up hard against one another as nowhere else in the world. Exaggerated display here, wretchedness there, sometimes without air and daylight."[298] Contact between social opposites in these relatively compact spaces could sometimes be very close. In 1907, *The Washington Post* reported that the volume of first-class passengers returning to America from Europe was so large that "in several cases the wealthiest people have travelled in the steerage because they were unable to wait three weeks for better accommodations."[299]

Between the extremes of first-class and steerage passengers were those of moderate means who could be sensitive about their situation aboard a liner. Some HAPAG advertising makes an obvious attempt to assuage second-class fears of being associated with steerage passengers, cleverly appealing to their social ambitions by describing their accommodation as nearly as good as first-class.[300] In a sophisticated brochure published in New York in 1914, and directed specifically at second-class passengers, the company claimed its second-class cabins compared favourably with first-class accommodation found aboard steamers a decade ago.[301] This was a general axiom at the time.[302] Readers of *Turbinen-Schnelldampfer Imperator* were informed that the liner's second-class cabins accommodated two, three, or four persons. They were assured that passengers would no longer be required to share accommodation with strangers, as the vessel also featured cabins for married couples and people travelling alone. And, for the first time, those in second-class cabins were provided with a drawing room and lounge for female travellers. HAPAG emphasized the care it took to keep second-class accommodation scrupulously clean and noted that the plumbing, sanitary equipment, and bedding were identical to that found in first-class. Furthermore, only food of the best quality was prepared in the kitchens and served in dining rooms that are "tastefully decorated, light and airy."[303] The English journal *Shipbuilding and Shipping Record* described second-class accommodation aboard the *Vaterland* as "hardly inferior" to that of first class.[304]

It was aboard the *Amerika* and *Kaiserin Auguste Victoria*, both launched in 1905, that HAPAG introduced third-class accommodation. This separated "the more well-bred element of steerage passengers from the crowds of south-eastern European emigrants, accommodated them in cabins, and provided them with special food."[305] HAPAG even prepared advertising directed specifically at this class of clientele. Aboard the *Imperator*, third-class passengers were housed in cabins of two, three, four, or six berths. A report on the vessel prepared for Cunard in 1913 found these arrangements to be "very excellent."[306] The third-class dining room was panelled and treated more decoratively than was usual. There was also a smoking room and drawing room, and it was said at the time that third-class passengers "are catered for in a manner quite out of the ordinary."[307] HAPAG publicity ensured third-class passengers that they would not come into contact with those in steerage. It appealed to their desire to travel well and inexpensively and assured them that, if simple, third-class accommodation was "excellently" furnished.[308]

Passengers travelling in steerage quarters, or what was known as fourth class, comprised the largest number of people aboard the *Imperator*-class liners. Discussion of this accommodation is not often found in HAPAG advertising and press reporting. Travel writing from the period also usually ignores these passengers, except as curiosities. When they are spoken of, mostly by commentators accommodated in cabin-class, they are often transformed into caricatures. In 1912, the Hungarian author Arthur Holitscher published an account of crossing the Atlantic aboard NDL's *Kaiser Wilhelm der Große*. The text provides an insight into the anxiety, but also the curiosity that must have animated the thoughts of many cabin-class passengers with respect to those travelling in steerage. It also offers a glimpse into the physical situation of the different classes aboard a transatlantic liner. Literally looking down on them from the promenade deck, the author was both fascinated and repelled by what he described as a "throng."[309] To Holitscher, the emigrant passengers were an exotic "Other," the spectacle of their colourful costumes, accordion music, and singing appreciated with an air of anthropological curiosity. But they also constituted a kind of alien and potentially dangerous organism that one might observe through a microscope and that should be kept at a distance. From his condescending perspective, those in steerage were lucky to have a week aboard ship that they could have nowhere else, except perhaps in prison; a week in which they could eat and sleep well, use decent bathing facilities, and not have to struggle to make ends meet.[310] But he recalled how there was a sign attached to the railing that enclosed the promenade deck instructing cabin-class passengers not to throw money or fruit to steerage passengers on the decks below.[311] While describing the hygienic facilities in steerage as "first-rate," Holitscher also expressed the fear that contagious disease could spread with "disastrous speed" through their quarters.[312]

As R.A. Fletcher explained in 1913, most British lines "will not carry emigrants from Central Europe because of their dirty habits." He pointed to the "disgusting condition of some of the men and women who come from that part of the Continent," saying one would be surprised that they were even allowed aboard the trains that carried them to the seaports.[313] And yet steerage passengers generated large amounts of revenue for HAPAG; as noted in the previous chapter, Ballin believed that, without them, the company would quickly go bankrupt. Many vessels carrying European emigrants were infamous for overcrowding in steerage as well as for the poor sanitary and dietary provisions they offered these passengers. In his book *In Steerage*, published in Berlin in 1909, Johannes Gaulke was critical of the conditions faced by emigrant passengers including dirt, bad air, and the condescending treatment of stewards and crew members. He also spoke of a shared sense of anger among those in steerage directed at the more privileged passengers.[314]

Despite these facts, competition between shipping lines improved the quality of steerage accommodation as companies sought to attract passengers by offering better facilities than their rivals. And HAPAG placed a priority on offering comfortable accommodation for those travelling in steerage. These passengers were lodged in cabins of two, four, and eight persons, not in barrack-style halls. Dining and toilet facilities were communal but, from 1896, HAPAG provided steerage passengers with eating utensils and bedding at no extra cost.[315] Management's rationale was that the comfortably accommodated emigrant would be more likely to recommend HAPAG to family and friends who were yet to make the journey to America. While extremely basic, this accommodation was an improvement upon that found aboard most liners prior to this time. Even before the launch of the *Imperator*, one commentator said that he found none of the reports of squalid steerage conditions to be true aboard HAPAG vessels. Furthermore, he added that "the difference between the home life of these people and the comforts and cleanliness which they enjoy on shipboard is tremendous."[316] Theodore Roosevelt, who returned to America from Europe aboard the *Imperator* in June 1914, wrote to Albert Ballin saying that he was particularly impressed by the "excellent" accommodation provided to steerage passengers, those in third class, as well as the crew, stokers, and firemen. He stated that it was almost "unbelievable" how much this had improved in the forty-five years since he had first crossed the Atlantic.[317]

Nonetheless, the *Imperator*'s steerage quarters were cramped and bare, with exposed steel bulkheads, floors, and ceilings. The dining area, with its long benches and rows of tightly spaced tables, was located in the forward section of the hull and was affected by the movement of the vessel much more than the first-class dining room situated amidships. Furthermore, the open deck space allocated to steerage passengers was limited to the liner's bow beneath the forward mast. These conditions provoked the criticisms of the German art historian and critic, Karl Scheffler, who was particularly disturbed by the disparity between the space allotted to first-class and steerage passengers respectively. "One is forced to think," he suggested,

> of the contrast between the front of a great house with a palace façade and proletarian tenements, and it is difficult to comprehend why there are not specially built transport ships for immigrants and luxury ships for those on pleasure cruises.[318]

Even Johannes Merck commented that while first-class passengers enjoyed incredible luxury, and second- and third-class passengers were much better accommodated than previously, "steerage was hardly different from the old manner of transporting emigrants like livestock of fifty years previously."[319]

At the bottom of the class structure of a liner's crew were the trimmers and firemen who handled the coal and fuelled its engines.[320] In English, these men were known as the "black gang." They worked in hot, dark, dirty, cramped, dangerous, and suffocating conditions. The British merchant sea captain James Bisset recalled that, at the end of their four-hour watch of "killing work," they came up on deck for fresh air "like demons out of hell."[321] They looked like "inhuman underground creatures, zombies barely alive, dressed in filthy dungarees, flannel shirts, hobnailed boots, and drenched sweat rags around their necks."[322] Bisset described how their faces "streaked with sweat, had a dulled, animal-like look, and they seldom smiled."[323] Writing about conditions aboard the *Vaterland*, Egon Erwin Kisch described its firemen and trimmers as feeding the glowing mouths of a hungry monster in something resembling a "region of Hell." Only when the red light of the fire fell upon their faces could one make out that they were human beings.[324] Trimmers made between seventy and eighty-three marks per month, while firemen earned ninety-eight marks.[325] Johannes Merck claimed that the quality of the crew's quarters was reduced aboard the *Imperator* and that several of HAPAG's directors were outraged by the fact.[326] As we will see in chapter three, discontent among crews sometimes boiled over. And, occasionally, firemen and trimmers committed suicide by jumping overboard.[327]

Given such conditions and spatial proximity, shipping companies including HAPAG drew attention to "measures that enforced social hierarchies and prevented conflict on board."[328] Advertising intended for cabin-class passengers made it clear that travellers from different social classes were isolated from one another. In particular, brochures often emphasized strict supervision of emigrants in steerage during a transatlantic crossing. Attempts to allay anxieties sometimes extended to casting the steerage-class experience in benign and even romantic terms. During a fictitious tour of a transatlantic liner, a passenger "happened upon"

> a lively scene such as one finds only in the character and surroundings of large emigration ships. Couples were twirling to the captivating sound of an accordion in one of the stirring dances that suit the children from the country of the Magyars so well ... One could watch the international society of steerage passengers for hours, one could undertake ethnographic studies.[329]

It is true that HAPAG advertising compared the amenities offered aboard the *Imperator* to those found in a modern city.[330] But as Bernhard Rieger has demonstrated, advertising also often avoided using metaphors of urban life to describe passenger liners because urbanity was associated with social and political volatility.[331] Transatlantic vessels "replicated the public-health hazards of the most infamous urban rookeries that concerned social reformers on both sides of the Atlantic in the second half of the nineteenth century."[332]

Yet measures taken to prevent conflict aboard ship did not always succeed. For example, in July 1907, the captain of HAPAG's *President Lincoln* arranged a dinner for first-class passengers in honour of the friendly relations between Germany and the United States. But when those travelling in second class heard of their exclusion from the celebration, "they began clamoring for admission to the festivities." The "excited throng" threatened to force its way into the first-class dining room, and it was only with "great difficulty" that the crew succeeded "in quelling an incipient riot." In consequence, "it was necessary to place a guard upon the second cabin reservation and keep it there for the remainder of the voyage."[333]

VII

The *Imperator*'s brief career as a German liner suggests it was not as great a marvel as the Swiss journalist quoted at the beginning of this chapter believed it to be. The liner left Hamburg for trials in the North Sea on 22 April 1913 only to run aground on a sandbank in the Elbe River at Altona, just a few hundred metres from its berth. Lifted after thirteen hours by the next tide, and pulled without damage off the sandbank by tugs, it proceeded to Cuxhaven and into the North Sea. In trials, the vessel proved satisfactory except in two respects. Two bearings in one of its turbines overheated. But more seriously, the *Imperator* proved top-heavy and prone to rolling and listing on the open sea. During final preparations at Cuxhaven before HAPAG took possession of the vessel, a flash fire in one of its compartments killed five men and another two died when one of its boilers exploded. As a result, a cruise on the North Sea intended for the Kaiser, and even the maiden voyage, planned for 24 May, had to be postponed.

On 10 June 1913, the *Imperator* finally sailed from Cuxhaven on its maiden voyage to New York via Southampton and Cherbourg. A large crowd gathered to see the ship off in the afternoon, and it made its way into a heavy sea. On board were 3,290 passengers: 550 in first class; 290 in second class; 800 in third class; and 1,650 in steerage.[334] HAPAG's senior management was represented aboard the liner by Directors Huldermann, Storm, and Warnholtz.[335] Seventy-five representatives of the German and English press also travelled in first-class accommodation to Southampton where the vessel arrived on 12 June. After a stopover in Cherbourg, the *Imperator* took to the open seas completing the 3,153 miles to New York in six days, five hours, and fourteen minutes at an average speed of 21.13 knots. In that city, *The Sun* reported that the liner ran into a strong gale and a heavy rolling sea. But it claimed that it did not roll appreciably and that passengers continued to dance in the first-class lounge. One of the headlines it employed was "Dance Goes On in Storm."[336] As the *Imperator* made its way up New York harbour to its Hoboken Pier on 19 June, it was greeted by an enthusiastic reception.

During its first sojourn in New York, a fire broke out in the aft end of the vessel and fireboats were employed to assist in extinguishing the blaze. A large volume of water was poured into its hull, pulling the *Imperator* over onto its starboard side to which it was already listing. Fortunately, the fireboats stopped pumping water before the vessel capsized, something that was not uncommon in such a situation. The damage was not serious enough to postpone its return voyage to Europe which began on 25 June with approximately 2,300 passengers aboard.

Just prior to its second voyage to New York in July 1913, the Kaiser took an eighteen-hour cruise aboard the liner in the North Sea. He distributed decorations to HAPAG directors including the "Crown Order of the Red Eagle of the Fourth Class" to Commodore Ruser. He was also treated to a picture show consisting of scenes aboard the vessel during its maiden voyage.[337] Commodore Ruser claimed that the

> Emperor was simply charmed with the *Imperator*. In the two days he was with us [8–9 July] he left no part of the ship un-explored. He roamed about the ship at will, inspecting the quarters of the various classes of passengers, the living apartments set aside for the crew, the engine rooms, in fact, every inch of her.[338]

But not everyone shared the Kaiser's enthusiasm. In fact, the British journal *Shipbuilding and Shipping Record* reported in October 1914 that even Ballin referred to the *Imperator* as a "first-rate hotel but a third-rate ship."[339] Johannes Merck believed HAPAG had been too involved in matters specifically related to the vessel's construction, matters that should have been left to Vulcan. According to Merck, his company bore a large part of the responsibility for its several faults.[340] And rumours concerning the *Imperator*'s "constructional shortcomings" seem to have been circulating even before the vessel was completely outfitted.[341] The turbines were unreliable and its draught too great for the Elbe; this necessitated the construction of docking facilities in Cuxhaven. It also lacked stability, was top-heavy, and listed both to port and starboard. Most early photographs show the vessel with a pronounced list, and New York pilots are said to have dubbed it the *Limperator*.[342] The liner also rolled significantly, even in calm seas, despite being outfitted with Frahm anti-rolling tanks. In fact, it was not until the addition of stabilizers to liner hulls in the 1950s that the problem of rolling was properly addressed. During its first annual overhaul, which was undertaken in Hamburg between November 1913 and March 1914, attempts to rectify these problems involved shortening its three funnels; replacing heavy marble and wood panelling on the upper-decks with panelling in lighter materials; and removing much of the wooden furniture in the public rooms and fitting them with wicker chairs and tables. The grill room at the aft end of B deck was removed to be replaced by a veranda café and, most dramatically, 2,000 tons of cement were poured along the *Imperator*'s bottom.

Yet the liner's problems were never completely solved and HAPAG was often on the defensive, especially in the American press, against what it claimed were malicious reports aimed at damaging the vessel's reputation. *The Washington Post* published a cable from Berlin stating that the *Imperator* had to be "partially rebuilt to be profitable." It claimed that its deficient boilers were to be reconstructed; it would be equipped for oil fuel; and its unprofitable Imperial suites would be converted into smaller state rooms.[343] Similar reports appeared in "all daily papers" in Boston and in *The Times* in London.[344] But Ballin and HAPAG were quick to issue statements to the American and English press that denied these claims. *The Wall Street Journal* published such a statement in which the managing director insisted that any assertion that the *Imperator*'s "present boiler equipment has been found insufficient" was "founded on malicious and entirely false rumors."[345] And when it was suggested that HAPAG had brought, or was about to bring suit against Vulcan for installing faulty boilers, Ballin denied this.[346] The company also denied that the *Imperator* was altered to rectify the problem of top-heaviness. Quoted *in The New York Times*, a company official explained that its stacks had been cut down to improve its appearance and that the refitting of some of its interiors was intended to provide better quarters for the engineers and steerage passengers.[347] Ballin maintained that only the *Imperator*'s refrigeration facilities required reconstruction.[348]

Despite its difficulties, the *Imperator* proved successful in attracting the travelling public of all classes. It carried its highest number of passengers – 3,646 – on its third voyage to New York. But events beyond HAPAG's control ensured that not everything was smooth sailing for the liner. Early in the morning of 28 August 1913, another fire broke out in one of the *Imperator*'s provision holds while it was docked at Hoboken. The blaze burned for four hours before being extinguished by the crew with the aid of the Hoboken fire department and two fireboats from Manhattan. Unfortunately, the second officer, Karl Gobrecht, described by HAPAG as "one of the most promising officers in our service," was killed fighting the fire.[349] At the time it broke out, only first- and second-class passengers had been disembarked and the press reported a "stampede of steerage passengers" onto the pier after the alarm was raised around 4 a.m.[350] Numbering almost 1,850 people, and including passengers in third-class, none of these individuals had been inspected by customs or health authorities. As a result, they were surrounded by armed guards and transported to Ellis Island later that day.

Press photographs show the liner listing to starboard at its moorings after having an estimated 2,000,000 gallons of water pumped into its hull.[351] Cleaners and painters quickly went to work on the vessel, it was re-provisioned, and company officials claimed that not a single reservation was cancelled. The *Imperator* departed New York as scheduled.[352] And HAPAG was quick to alert the public that the fire could not have happened at sea. It even turned the tragedy to its advantage, saying that the event proved the liner was as fire-proof as it could possibly be and that it demonstrated the ability of the on-board fire-fighting equipment to deal with such emergencies.[353]

Yet almost a month later, a photograph of the *Imperator* listing at its Hoboken moorings appeared in the window of one of NDL's Stuttgart agents. Attached was a card explaining that the liner was awaiting repairs at that dock. NDL claimed the photograph was exhibited by a junior clerk without the knowledge of the agency nor that of NDL. It insisted that it was not its intention to "do injury" to HAPAG. Nonetheless, the latter was concerned that an image showing the *Imperator* in a "most unfavourable position" would prejudice potential passengers against travelling aboard it or might "give them the impression she was laid up for repairs and so prevent them from attempting to book for her." In a claim for damages made by HAPAG against NDL, the former emphasized that the fire did not delay the sailing of the *Imperator* from New York.[354]

On 13 March 1914, during the first crossing of the season, the *Imperator* encountered a heavy gale and lost four lifeboats and the wings of the eagle that was perched on its prow. The liner's commander, Captain Thomas Kier, said that "I was glad that we did not lose the gold crown from the eagle's head, because the sailors would have looked upon it as an ill omen to happen on the thirteenth."[355] The eagle was removed and replaced by gilt scrollwork similar to that on the stern and featuring an armorial shield with an imperial crown.

Ballin insisted that the *Imperator* was a financial success beyond HAPAG's expectations.[356] But although the liner proved very popular with American travellers, Johannes Merck claimed it was too large and too expensive to generate positive earnings.[357] In fact, given necessary overhauls, time spent lying up, as well as depreciation, the *Imperator* suffered a loss of 103,000 marks during its first season of service.[358] A particular problem highlighted by Merck was that of continually attracting sufficient numbers of passengers to three liners of such enormous size. *The New York Times* reported that only a third of the available 750 first-class berths aboard the *Vaterland* were filled for its maiden voyage westward, but that the vessel was booked to capacity for its return to Europe.[359] Merck argued that booking all berths on every voyage undertaken by the new trio would have meant letting HAPAG's other liners sail empty. "I must reproach Ballin and Storm, the director of our passenger department, in the strongest terms," he wrote, "for not reckoning on this in their earlier calculations."[360] Merck also claimed that, in order to make the financial failings of the *Imperator*-class liners less conspicuous, HAPAG agents were directed to sell berths aboard them at discounted rates without consideration for the profitability of the company's other liners. And he suggested that Ballin realized, even while the *Imperator* was under construction, that his project would turn out badly. This, he claimed, is why the managing director insisted on the building of evermore first-class cabins on board the vessel to the detriment of the crew's accommodation.[361]

Merck also asserted that, upon realizing that first-class passengers alone would not make the *Imperator*-class liners profitable, Ballin endeavoured to increase the number of steerage berths.[362] But the number of emigrant passengers HAPAG could carry was regulated by international agreement and Ballin was forced to approach NDL with a proposal that his company's percentage be increased. When the latter refused to comply, Ballin terminated HAPAG's involvement with the Atlantic Conference in April 1913. As Merck explained, "Ballin achieved his intentions, but in the meantime competition over cheap fares for steerage-class passengers damaged not only the interests of other lines, but also very seriously damaged our own earnings."[363] When asked in early 1914 if a slump in trade and shipping had anything to do with the recent enormous increase in shipbuilding, Ballin dismissed the suggestion in *The Manchester Guardian* saying the duty of the shipping companies was "to make hay while the sun shines."[364]

It was not only HAPAG's senior management that was aware of the unprofitability of the *Imperator* and *Vaterland*. The financial viability of the liners was also questioned in the German and foreign press.[365] The English journal *Shipbuilding and Shipping Record* suggested that the financial difficulties arising from the construction of such large vessels could be avoided if the same energy was devoted to building smaller ships from components that could almost be mass produced.[366] *The Washington Post* even stated in 1913 that the "day of gigantic liners is declared to be over, and the companies are adopting a policy of moderate sized boats."[367] Looking back from 1940, Jack Lawrence, a shipping news reporter for New York's *Evening Mail*, wrote that the *Kaiserin Auguste Victoria* was a paying investment for her owners and it would seem that they would have been wise to plan more ships of the same type. But the trend toward giant liners, begun with the *Olympic* and *Titanic*, caused the Hamburg-American Line to embark on a shipbuilding program that was to prove to be ruinous folly.[368]

The *Imperator* and *Vaterland*, Lawrence claimed,

> were to represent a total loss so far as the Hamburg-American Line was concerned. Whether the company could have succeeded in making them popular and profitable seems very doubtful. After the war, under other flags, the two ships were operated at a loss.[369]

VIII

The *Imperator* made a total of six round-trip voyages to New York in 1914. It set out from Cuxhaven on its last westward crossing on 8 July and started back to Europe ten days later, passing the *Vaterland* in mid-Atlantic. It would never again sail into New York harbour under the HAPAG or the German flag. By this point, the spotlight of public attention on both sides of the Atlantic had passed to the *Vaterland*. Its keel was laid down in September 1911 by Blohm & Voss as hull number 212. Launched on 3 April 1913, the liner completed its trials in the North Sea in early May 1914. These proved more satisfactory than those of the *Imperator*: the vessel attained a speed of twenty-six knots running with the wind, lacked vibration, did not share the *Imperator*'s problem of top heaviness, and rolled only gently. HAPAG reported that the *Vaterland* "behaved magnificently."[370]

The liner departed Cuxhaven on its maiden voyage to New York on 14 May 1914. On board were 274 passenger in first-class, 114 in second, 348 in third, and 909 in steerage.[371] It completed the crossing in five days and seventeen hours. Arriving in New York harbour on 21 May, it enjoyed an enthusiastic reception and was met at Quarantine by a flotilla of twenty-five tugs. But a strong ebb tide made it very difficult to manoeuvre and dock even with their assistance. While attempting to reach its berth at pier four in Hoboken, the *Vaterland* was swept broadside downstream for more than a mile, almost drifting ashore on the west side of the Hudson.[372] Holding up river traffic for more than an hour, it finally gained the pier on its fourth attempt. But while backing out of its Hoboken slip on the homeward leg of its maiden voyage, the liner spanned the Hudson and narrowly missed striking the Manhattan piers. The suction created by the churning of its screws in reverse tore two freight steamers, one of 4,605 and the other of 5,000 tons, from their Manhattan moorings, crashing them into their pier and damaging both. The volume of water sent aft as the vessel then proceeded ahead swamped a barge carrying 1,700 tons of coal.[373]

The *Vaterland* made only three round-trip voyages to New York. It began the fourth on 22 July 1914 and arrived in New York on the 30th. While preparing for its homeward journey, the liner received a communication from Germany warning of British and French cruisers waiting to seize the vessel.[374] With the outbreak of the First World War, the *Vaterland* was interned at its Hoboken pier and, when America entered the conflict in April 1917, it was seized and converted into a troop transport. The keel of the *Bismarck* was laid down by Blohm &Voss in April 1913 as hull number 214. Very similar to the *Vaterland*, it was launched on 20 June of the following year and would remain the largest ocean liner in the world for two decades. But construction on the vessel was stopped in August 1914 and its hull lay uncompleted in Hamburg for the duration of the conflict. It would never sail under the German flag.

With its decision to build the *Imperator*-class liners, HAPAG's primary concern was to capture an ever greater share of transatlantic travellers with vessels that would sustain the company's position in the first rank of shipping lines and produce significant profits. Given the fascination with premier passenger steamships at the time, it was inevitable that they would become international sensations in the Atlantic world in the manner described in the preceding pages. Yet the company's aim was not to create national monuments. However, as we will see, HAPAG played an important role in their construction as such. Yet it was especially in the wider sphere of Germany's popular media that the *Imperator* and its sisters became vessels loaded with national symbolism. Referring to the *Bismarck*, the *Hamburger Nachrichten* described it as embodying a "towering monumentality" that would be a symbol of German achievements in engineering, technology, and commerce.[375] As revealed in the following chapters, the construction and reception of the *Imperator*-class liners as national monuments occurred not only in Germany but across the English Channel and on the other side of the Atlantic Ocean.

Notes

1 Quoted in Susanne Wiborg and Klaus Wiborg, *1847–1997: Unser Feld ist die Welt: 150 Jahre Hapag-Lloyd* (Hamburg, 1997), 179.
2 Bernhard Rieger, *Technology and the Culture of Modernity in Britain and Germany, 1890–1945* (Cambridge, 2005), 23.
3 Rieger, *Technology*, 224.
4 Quoted in Peter Zerbe, *Die Grossen Deutschen Passagierschiffe: Imperator, Vaterland, Bismarck* (Hamburg, 1999), 40.
5 "New Eastward Record for the Liner Kaiser Wilhelm", *Scientific American* 77 (16 October 1897), 243.
6 W.H. Beehler, "Germany as a Sea Power", *The Century Magazine* 84 (July 1912), 407.
7 "The Sumptuousness of Modern Travel", *Current Opinion* 56 (June 1914), 480.
8 See Rieger, *Technology*.
9 Stephen Kern, *The Culture of Time and Space 1880–1918* (Cambridge, MA, 1983), 100 and 90.
10 This is also stressed in Rieger, *Technology*.

11 Dagmar Bellmann, *Von Höllengefährten zu schwimmenden Palästen. Die Passagierschiffahrt auf dem Atlantik (1840–1930)* (Frankfurt and New York, 2015).
12 Gerhard A. Ritter, "The Kaiser and His Ship-Owner: Albert Ballin, the HAPAG Shipping Company, and the Relationship between Industry and Politics in Imperial Germany and the Early Weimar Republic", in Hartmut Berghoff, Jürgen Kocka, and Dieter Ziegler, eds., *Business in the Age of Extremes: Essays in Modern German and Austrian Economic History* (Washington and Cambridge, 2013), 26.
13 "Atlantic Shipping", *Manchester Guardian*, 20 December 1913.
14 See Frank Broeze, "Albert Ballin, the Hamburg-Bremen Rivalry and the Dynamics of the Conference System", *International Journal of Maritime History* 3 (1991), 23.
15 Broeze, "Albert Ballin", 19–20.
16 Staatsarchiv der Freien und Hansestadt Hamburg (hereafter St. A.H.) 621-1/95. HAPAG – Reederei 2656 Band 3. Verträge und Vereinbarungen zuSchiffsneubauten Band 3: D "Imperator" 1910–1914. MUG 128A 04 05; see also "Steamship Competition", *The Wall Street Journal* (New York), 10 March 1909.
17 As reported in "Atlantic Rate War", *Manchester Guardian*, 28 January 1914.
18 St. A.H. 621-1. HAPAG – Reederei 2656 Band 3. Verträge und Vereinbarungen zu Schiffsneubauten Band 3: D "Imperator" 1910–1914. MUG 128A 04 05 A – Bau-Offerte und Bauvertrag.
19 Lamar Cecil, *Albert Ballin: Business and Politics in Imperial Germany, 1888–1918* (Princeton, NJ, 1967), 219.
20 HAPAG, *Die Hamburg-Amerika Linie: Im Sechsten Jahrzehnt Ihrer Entwicklung 1897–1907* (Berlin, 1907), 70.
21 "Die Handelsmarine im Jahre 1913", *Jahrbuch für Deutschlands Seeinteressen* 16 (1914), 385.
22 "Designer of Vaterland's Hull Describes Biggest Ship", *The New York Times*, 24 May 1914.
23 "The Thousand-Foot Ship", *The Washington Post*, 27 April 1913.
24 Johannes Merck, "Meine Erinnerungen an die Hamburg-Amerika Linie und an Albert Ballin, 1896–1918" (1920). St. A.H. 622-1/62. Merck II 8 Konv. 2b., 106.
25 Merck, "Meine Erinnerungen", 99.
26 Merck, "Meine Erinnerungen", 105.
27 Merck, "Meine Erinnerungen", 106.
28 Merck's criticism is briefly discussed in Gerhard Ahrens and Renate Hauschild-Thiessen, *Die Reeder: Laeisz, Ballin.* (Hamburg, 1989), 57.
29 Merck, "Meine Erinnerungen", 109.
30 Cecil, *Albert Ballin*, 359.
31 "The Imperator", *The Times* (London), 12 June 1913.
32 "50,000-Ton Liners", *The Observer* (London), 14 April 1912; "Greater than the 'Titanic'", *The Nautical Gazette* 82 (24 July 1912), 5.
33 "More 'Last Words' in Ocean Steamship Marvels", *The Washington Post*, 11 June 1911.
34 "Imperator-The Ocean's Newest Giant May Be Midget Tomorrow", *The Baltimore Sun*, 22 June 1913.
35 "To Name Liner for Buelow", *The New York Times*, 17 July 1909.
36 See for example "A New Ocean Giant", *The Washington Post*, 1 January 1911.
37 See Arnold Kludas, *Die Geschichte der Hapag-Schiffe* (Bremen, 2008), vol. 2, 160.
38 Les Streater, *Berengaria: Cunard's "Happy Ship"* (Charleston, SC, 2001), 6.
39 William H. Miller, *The First Great Ocean Liners in Photographs* (New York, 1984), 39.
40 "Hamburg-American's Big Ship", *The Wall Street Journal* (New York), 25 June 1910.
41 Merck, "Meine Erinnerungen", 110.

42 Merck, "Meine Erinnerungen", 110.
43 HAPAG, *Turbinen-Schnelldampfer Imperator* (Hamburg, n.d.), 13.
44 "Three Big Ships for Hamburg Line", *The New York Times*, 24 November 1912; "Plans for Three Big Liners", *Chicago Daily Tribune*, 24 November 1912.
45 "Forthcoming Launch of the Third 'Imperator'", *The Times* (London), 27 May 1914.
46 "Second Liner of the 'Imperator' Class", *"Shipping" Illustrated* 43 (12 April 1913), 37.
47 "Aus anderen Blättern", *Hamburgischer Correspondent*, 22 June 1914.
48 St. A.H. 621–1. HAPAG – Reederei 2656 Band 3. Verträge und Vereinbarungen zu Schiffsneubauten Band 3: D "Imperator" 1910–1914 MUG. 128A 04 05 A – Bau-Offerte und Bauvertrag.
49 Streater, *Berengaria*, 6.
50 Melvin Maddocks, *The Great Liners* (Alexandria, 1978), 51.
51 "Ein moderner Riese", *Hamburger Echo*, 4 April 1913.
52 "Launch of the 'Imperator'", *"Shipping" Illustrated* 38/39 (1 June 1912), 220.
53 "Der neue Riesendampfer der Hamburg-Amerika Linie", *Hamburger Fremdenblatt*, 2 April 1911.
54 Quoted in Matthew Jeffries, *Hamburg: A Cultural History* (Northampton, 2011), 69f.
55 See Zerbe, *Die Grossen Deutschen Passagierschiffe*.
56 "Vom Bau des Imperator", *Hamburger Nachrichten*, 19 August 1912.
57 R.A. Fletcher, *Travelling Palaces: Luxury in Passenger Steamships* (London, 1913), 92.
58 Fletcher, *Travelling Palaces*, 93.
59 Robert Urie Jacob, *A Trip to the Orient* (Philadelphia, PA, 1907), 1.
60 HAPAG, *Turbinen-Schnelldampfer Imperator* (Hamburg, n.d.); HAPAG, *Dampfer Imperator: Das Größte Schiff Der Welt* (Hamburg, n.d.); HAPAG, *Imperator: The World's Largest Ship, Embodying Maximum Comfort and Safety for All* (New York, n.d.); HAPAG, *Vaterland* (Hamburg, n.d.).
61 Susanne Wiborg, *Albert Ballin* (Hamburg, 2000), 31.
62 Fletcher, *Travelling Palaces*, 94.
63 HAPAG, *Dampfer Imperator*, 14.
64 HAPAG, *Turbinen-Schnelldampfer Imperator*, 8.
65 HAPAG, *Imperator* (Siegburg bei Köln, n.d.).
66 Kludas, *Die Geschichte der Hapag-Schiffe*, vol. 2, 164.
67 "The Imperator. World's Largest Liner. Her Maiden Voyage", *The Daily Telegraph* (London), 13 June 1913.
68 Fletcher, *Travelling Palaces*, 95.
69 HAPAG, *Imperator*, 14.
70 HAPAG, *The New Twin-Screw Express Steamers of the Hamburg-American Packet Company* (New York, n.d.), 4.
71 "The Latest Marine Behemoth", *"Shipping" Illustrated* 43 (21 June 1913), 276.
72 Douglas R. Burgess, *Seize the Trident: The Race for Superliner Supremacy and How it Altered the Great War* (New York, 2005), 173f.
73 "The Vaterland. Maiden Voyage to New York", *Morning Post* (London), 16 May 1914; "Largest Ship and Statue", *The Washington Post*, 17 May 1914; "Vaterland to Sail Next Week", *San Francisco Chronicle*, 5 May 1914.
74 See for example HAPAG, *Imperator*.
75 See "The Ship of the Year. The Imperator", *The Syren and Shipping Illustrated* 66 (8 January 1913), 97.
76 Article from the *Kansas City Star* reproduced in "Guards against Risk of Collision", *The Washington Post*, 11 May 1913.

77   Bellmann, *Von Höllengefährten*, 209.
78   See for example HAPAG, *The New Twin-Screw Express Steamers*, 4–8.
79   HAPAG, *Dampfer Imperator.*
80   HAPAG, *Turbinen-Schnelldampfer Imperator*, 33.
81   "50,000-Ton Liners", *The Observer* (London), 14 April 1912.
82   HAPAG, *Dampfer Imperator*, 6.
83   "Auf der ersten Reise des 'Imperator'", *Hansa: Deutsche nautische Zeitschrift* 50 (21 June 1913), 525.
84   HAPAG, *Across the Atlantic* (New York, n.d.), 22.
85   "Photoplay News", *The Washington Post*, 9 November 1913.
86   HAPAG, *Turbinen-Schnelldampfer Imperator.*
87   See HAPAG, *Turbinen-Schnelldampfer Imperator*, 49f.
88   "Eine moderne Arche Noah", *Illustrirte Zeitung* (Leipzig) 142 (28 May 1914), 1185f.
89   Bellmann, *Von Höllengefährten*, 119ff.
90   HAPAG, *Imperator Auf See: Gedenkblätter an die erste Ausfahrt des Dampfers am 11. Juni 1913* (Hamburg, 1913), 49.
91   Rieger, *Technology*, 160.
92   "Die erste Fahrt des Imperator", *Hamburgischer Correspondent*, 15 June 1913.
93   Quoted in Zerbe, *Die Grossen Deutschen Passagierschiffe*, 40.
94   "To Make Clothes on Liner", *The Washington Post*, 8 January 1908.
95   "More 'Last Words' in Ocean Steamship Marvels", *The Washington Post*, 11 June 1911.
96   "By the Way –", *The Wall Street Journal* (New York), 20 September 1913.
97   Douglas R. Burgess, *Engines of Empire. Steamships and the Victorian Imagination* (Stanford, CA, 2016), 13.
98   "Imperator, Biggest of Liners, in Port", *The New York Times*, 19 June 1913.
99   "Imperator Minds Helm Like a Yacht", *The New York Times*, 20 June 1913; "The Imperator, Greatest Steamship Afloat, Ends Half of Her Maiden Voyage Amid Ovation of Sister Craft", *New York Herald*, 20 June 1913.
100 "Smokestack of Ocean Liner", *The Washington Post*, 20 April 1913.
101 "Drawbacks of Sea-Going Luxury", *The Washington Post*, 6 July 1913.
102 "Vaterland on Way across Atlantic", *The New York Times*, 16 May 1914.
103 "The Vaterland", *The New York Times*, 22 May 1914.
104 "On the Bridge of a Liner", *The Washington Post*, 21 June 1914.
105 See "Seven Wonders of World", *The Washington Post*, 27 February 1914.
106 On this subject see John Tomlinson, *The Culture of Speed. The Coming of Immediacy* (Los Angeles, CA, 2007).
107 Kern, *The Culture of Time*, 128.
108 See for example Wolfgang Schivelbusch, *The Railway Journey: The Industrialization of Time and Space in the Nineteenth Century* (Los Angeles, CA, 1987); Michael J. Freeman, *Railways and the Victorian Imagination* (New Haven, CT, 1999); John R. Stilgoe, *Train Time: Railroads and the Imminent Reshaping of the United States Landscape* (Charlottesville, VA, 2009).
109 "Racing for Ocean Supremacy", *The Washington Post*, 12 January 1913.
110 Kern, *The Culture of Time*, 110.
111 "Demands of Ocean Travel", *The New York Times*, 2 October 1897.
112 George E. Walsh, "New Giant Steamers", *Harper's Weekly* 8 (1901), 807.
113 See for example "A New Ocean Greyhound", *The New York Times*, 23 September 1901.
114 "Eastward Record Broken", *The New York Times*, 7 October 1897.
115 See for example "New Ocean Speed Record", *The New York Times*, 27 September 1897; "New Queen of the Seas", *The New York Times*, 3 October 1897;

"Eastward Record Broken", *The New York Times*, 7 October 1897; "The Kaiser's Rough Trip", *The New York Times*, 20 October 1897; "Kaiser Wilhelm der Große", *The New York Times*, 17 November 1897.

116 See for example "Ocean Record Broken", *The New York Times*, 15 August 1900; "An Atlantic Record Beaten", *The New York Times*, 20 June 1901.

117 "Ocean Greyhounds to Race", *The Washington Post*, 2 August 1900; "Race of Ocean Liners", *The New York Times*, 4 September 1900.

118 See for example "Raced across the Ocean", *The Washington Post*, 30 March 1906.

119 "Flying across Ocean", *The Washington Post*, 11 September 1907.

120 "Germany Is Relieved", *The Washington Post*, 14 September 1907.

121 "New Turbine Gearing", *The Wall Street Journal* (New York), 20 October 1909.

122 "Germany 'Stands Pat'", *The Washington Post*, 24 November 1907.

123 HAPAG, *The New Twin-Screw Express Steamers*, 18–20.

124 HAPAG, *The Hamburg-American Packet Co.* (New York, n.d.), 18–20.

125 "Special Cable to The New York Times", *The New York Times*, 15 May 1914. The same paper had earlier stated in relation to the *Imperator*-class liners that "there is plainly no intention to compete for the Blue Ribbon of the Atlantic"; see "Three Big Ships for Hamburg Line", *The New York Times*, 24 November 1912.

126 "For Atlantic Blue Ribbon", *The New York Times*, 2 May 1914.

127 "Cruise Around the World", *The Washington Post*, 20 May 1900.

128 "The Vaterland to Get Royal Welcome When She Arrives in Port to-Day", *New York Herald*, 21 May 1914.

129 See for example "Die erste Fahrt der Vaterland", *Hamburger Nachrichten*, 17 May 1914.

130 "Marine Mountain Goes to Her Pier as Easy as a Child", *The New York World*, 20 June 1913.

131 "New Sea Giantess, the Imperator, Is Launched", *New York Herald*, 24 May 1912.

132 "World's Largest Liner", *San Francisco Chronicle*, 17 June 1913.

133 See for example, "Der Rudersteven des 'Imperator'" *Die Gartenlaube* 23 (13 June 1912), 495f.

134 See Darcy Grimaldo Grigsby, *Colossal: Engineering the Suez Canal, Statue of Liberty, Eiffel Tower, and Panama Canal* (Pittsburgh, PA, 2012).

135 Grigsby, *Colossal*.

136 "Growth of Sea-Going Craft", *The Washington Post*, 12 May 1912.

137 "50,000-Ton Liners", *The Observer* (London), 14 April 1912.

138 "Greatest of All Ocean Giants Is Nearing Us on Maiden Trip", *The World* (New York), 18 June 1913.

139 "Greatest Atlantic Liner on Fire at the Pier", *The Washington Post*, 30 August 1913.

140 "Great Progress in Shipbuilding" republished in *The Washington Post*, 5 July 1914.

141 HAPAG, *Imperator Auf See*, 54f.

142 Bellmann, *Von Höllengefährten*, 97.

143 Reproduced in "Largest Steamer in the World", *The Washington Post*, 17 March 1912.

144 See for example "Zum Stapellauf des 'Imperator'", *Tägliche Rundschau* (Berlin), 24 May 1912; "Stapellauf des Riesendampfers 'Imperator'", *Berliner Tageblatt*, 23 May 1912; "Der Stapellauf des 'Vaterland'", *Berliner Tageblatt*, 4 April 1913.

145 "$6,000,000 Sea Monster Vaterland to Move Majestically into This Harbor to-Day", *The World* (New York), 21 May 1914.

146 "Greater than the 'Titanic'", *The Nautical Gazette* 82 (24 July 1912), 4.

147 "Marine Monsters", *The Washington Post*, 5 March 1905; see also "New Ship a Monster", *The Washington Post*, 1 October 1905; "Monster of Sea in Port", *The*

Washington Post, 20 May 1906; "The Latest Marine Behemoth", *"Shipping" Illustrated* 43 (21 June 1913), 276.

148   "More 'Last Words' in Ocean Steamship Marvels", *The Washington Post*, 11 June 1911.

149   "New Queen of the Ocean Arrives on Maiden Voyage", *The Washington Post*, 21 June 1913.

150   Rieger, *Technology*, 2.

151   Rieger, *Technology*, 49.

152   "Smokestack of Ocean Liner", *The Washington Post*, 20 April 1913.

153   "Rudder Post of Imperator", *The Washington Post*, 23 June 1912.

154   "The Quadruple Turbine Liner 'Imperator'", *The Marine Engineer and Naval Architect* 35 (July 1913), 469.

155   "World's Biggest Liner", *The Daily Telegraph* (London), 16 May 1914.

156   "The Ship of the Year. The Imperator", *The Syren and Shipping Illustrated* 66 (8 January 1913), 97.

157   David Klemm, "Das Schiffahrtsplakat im Wandel der Zeiten", in Olaf Matthes and Carsten Prange, eds., *Hamburg und die HAPAG: Seefahrt im Plakat* (Hamburg, 2000), 42f; see also Gisela Schütte, "Plakatkunst der Passagierschiffahrt", in Volker Plagemann, ed., *Übersee. Seefahrt und Seemacht im deutschen Kaiserreich* (Munich, 1988), 330–7.

158   See Zerbe *Die Grossen Deutschen Passagierschiffe*, 8 for a photograph of such a display.

159   See Matthes and Prange, eds., *Hamburg*, catalogue no. 5.

160   HAPAG, *Across the Atlantic*.

161   HAPAG, *Across the Atlantic*, 12.

162   Rieger, *Technology*, 26.

163   HAPAG, *Hamburg-American Gazette* 19 (May 1910).

164   HAPAG, "Across the Atlantic" (22 March 1911); "Sailings across the Atlantic" (20 November 1911); "Sailings across the Atlantic" (20 March 1912).

165   Deutsches Schiffahrtsmuseum I. 1458/77; III.95-27.

166   See for example *Vossische Zeitung* (Berlin), 24 May 1912.

167   "Smokestack of Ocean Liner", *The Washington Post*, 20 April 1913.

168   L. Wachtel, "Der Vierschrauben-Turbinen-Schnelldampfer 'Imperator'", *Zeitschrift des Vereines Deutscher Ingenieure* 58 (20 June 1914), 993-106.

169   Bellmann, *Von Höllengefährten*, 112.

170   "Imperator – The Ocean's Newest Giant May Be Midget Tomorrow", *The Baltimore Sun*, 22 June 1913.

171   Fletcher, *Travelling Palaces*.

172   "Two Steamships 1,000 Feet Long to Be Built for Atlantic Traffic", *The Washington Post*, 15 March 1908.

173   "Great Progress in Shipbuilding" republished in *The Washington Post*, 5 July 1914.

174   "Der Stapellauf des 'Imperator'", *Hamburger Fremdenblatt*, 24 May 1912.

175   See for example "Racing for Ocean Supremacy", *The Washington Post*, 12 January 1913.

176   See for example HAPAG, *Europe: First Class Cabin Rates* (New York, 1914).

177   "Transoceanic Ship Lines Are Advancing", *Christian Science Monitor* (Boston), 29 May 1912.

178   "Two Steamships 1,000 Feet Long to Be Built for Atlantic Traffic", *The Washington Post*, 15 March 1908.

179   "More 'Last Words' in Ocean Steamship Marvels", *The Washington Post*, 11 June 1911.

180   "Increasing Size of Ocean Vessels in Last 20 Years", *The Wall Street Journal* (New York), 13 June 1914.

181 "Designer of Vaterland's Hull Describes Biggest Ship", *The New York Times*, 24 May 1914.
182 "Designer of Vaterland's Hull Describes Biggest Ship", *The New York Times*, 24 May 1914.
183 "Big Ship Era", *The Observer* (London), 6 April 1913.
184 Burgess, *Seize*, 142.
185 W.J. Lampton, "To the Imperator", *The New York Times*, 24 June 1913.
186 "To Break Ocean Records", *The New York Times*, 2 May 1900.
187 "Der Stapellauf des Imperator", *Hamburger Nachrichten*, 23 May 1912.
188 "The Ship of the Year. The Imperator", *The Syren and Shipping Illustrated* 66 (8 January 1913), 97.
189 HAPAG, *Dampfer Imperator*, 9.
190 Philipp Berges, "Eine schwimmende Insel – das größte Schiff der Welt", *Hamburger Fremdenblatt*, 19 March 1911.
191 "Too Big for Convenience", *The Baltimore Sun*, 28 May 1914.
192 "Ballin Deeply Impressed", *The New York Times*, 17 April 1912; "Designer Carlisle Explains", *The Washington Post*, 17 April 1912.
193 Quoted in Rieger, *Technology*, 75f.
194 Sebastian Conrad, *Globalization and the Nation in Imperial Germany* (Cambridge, 2010), 53.
195 Kern, *The Culture of Time*, 110.
196 "The Next Great Disaster" republished in *The Washington Post*, 14 September 1913.
197 Edward Keble Chatterton, *Steamships and Their Story* (London and New York, 1910), 213.
198 Kern, *The Culture of Time*, 36.
199 Julius Hirschberg, *Um die Erde* (Leipzig, 1894), 4.
200 Samuel Clemens (Mark Twain), "About All Kinds of Ships. The Modern Steamer and the Obsolete Steamer" (1893) in Charles Neider, ed., *The Complete Humorous Sketches and Tales of Mark Twain* (New York, 1961), 55.
201 HAPAG, *Imperator auf See*, 18f.
202 Lawrence Perry, "Luxury of the Modern Liner", *Hamburg-American Gazette* 12 (March 1907), 7.
203 Quoted in John Malcolm Brinnin, *The Sway of the Grand Saloon*, 2nd edn. (London, 1986), 385.
204 "Drawbacks of Sea-Going Luxury", *The Washington Post*, 6 July 1913.
205 HAPAG, *Dampfer Imperator*, 14.
206 Merck, "Meine Erinnerungen", 106.
207 Clemens, "About All Kinds", 544.
208 Clemens, "About All Kinds", 543.
209 Philip Dawson, *The Liner: Retrospective and Renaissance* (New York and London, 2005), 57.
210 See for example HAPAG, *Turbinen-Schnelldampfer Imperator*; HAPAG, *Dampfer Imperator*; HAPAG, *Sixty Years of Ocean Navigation and the Half Century Anniversary of the Establishment of the First Line of Steamships Flying a German Flag* (New York, 1906), 9.
211 Rieger, *Technology*, 162.
212 Rieger, *Technology*, 161.
213 Rieger, *Technology*, 161.
214 "Fuerst Bismarck Battered", *The New York Times*, 18 January 1914.
215 Rieger, *Technology*, 162.
216 HAPAG, *Europe*.
217 "Cure for Seasickness", *The Washington Post*, 5 February 1906.

218 "Imperator Here with Record Crowd", *The New York Times*, 18 September 1913.
219 Anne Wealleans, *Designing Liners. A History of Interior Design Afloat* (London, 2006), 36.
220 Max Osborn, "Über Zweck, Form und Schmuck. Bemerkungen zu Ilse Dernburgs 'Imperator' Kabinen", *Innen-Dekoration: Die Gesamte Wohnungskunst in Bild und Wort* 24 (December 1913), 477.
221 Bellmann, *Von Höllengefährten*, 178.
222 HAPAG, *Sixty Years*, 51.
223 Bellmann, *Von Höllengefährten*, 214.
224 HAPAG, *Across the Atlantic*, 2.
225 "Craze for Luxury Makes the Imperator Possible", *Boston Herald*, 22 June 1913.
226 Quoted in Brinnin, *The Sway*, 318.
227 "Demands of Ocean Travel", *The New York Times*, 2 October 1897.
228 "New Ship a Monster", *The Washington Post*, 1 October 1905.
229 Frederick A. Talbot, *Steamship Conquest of the World* (London, 1912), 78.
230 Philip Dawson and Bruce Peter, *Ship Style: Modernism and Modernity at Sea in the 20th Century* (London, 2010), 31.
231 Rieger, *Technology*, 183.
232 Rieger, *Technology*, 165.
233 Rieger, *Technology*, 176.
234 HAPAG, *Across the Atlantic*, 12.
235 "World's Largest Ship", *The Baltimore Sun*, 5 April 1914.
236 "The Sumptuousness of Modern Travel", *Current Opinion* 56 (June 1914), 478f.
237 Talbot, *Steamship*, 72.
238 "More 'Last Words' in Ocean Steamship Marvels", *The Washington Post*, 11 June 1911.
239 Perry, "Luxury of the Modern Liner", 7.
240 HAPAG, *Große Orient- und Indienfahrt 1914* (Magdeburg, 1913), 10.
241 HAPAG, *Turbinen-Schnelldampfer Imperator*, 120.
242 HAPAG, *Turbinenschnelldampfer Vaterland* (Hamburg, 1914), 21.
243 HAPAG, *Across the Atlantic: Photographic Reproductions of the Company's Various Types of Steamers Comprised in the Transatlantic Passenger Services* (New York, 1905).
244 HAPAG, *Across the Atlantic*, 12.
245 HAPAG, *Across the Atlantic*, 13.
246 HAPAG, *Hamburg-American Line Gazette* (New York, 1905), 4.
247 "World's Largest Ship", *The Baltimore Sun*, 5 April 1914.
248 HAPAG, *Turbinen-Schnelldampfer Imperator*.
249 HAPAG, *Have You Seen the World?* (New York, n.d.), u.p.
250 HAPAG, *Have You Seen?*
251 "On an Ocean Playground", *Hamburg-American Gazette* 9 (July 1905), 4.
252 "Chats of Visitors to the Capital", *The Washington Post*, 27 June 1913.
253 "Drawbacks of Sea-Going Luxury", *The Washington Post*, 6 July 1913.
254 Philipp Berges "Eine schwimmende Insel – das größte Schiff der Welt", *Hamburger Fremdenblatt,* 19 March 1911.
255 "Imperator on Fire", *The Times* (London), 29 August 1913.
256 Rieger, *Technology*, 167f.
257 "Interviews with Capital's Visitors", *The Washington Post*, 28 June 1913.
258 Reproduced in "Largest Steamer in the World", *The Washington Post*, 17 March 1912.
259 "A New Ocean Giant", *The Washington Post*, 1 January 1911.
260 Bellmann, *Von Höllengefährten*, 119ff.

261 Dawson, *The Liner*, 52.
262 This point is especially emphasized in Dawson and Peter, *Ship Style*.
263 Dawson and Peter, *Ship Style*, 23.
264 Dawson and Peter, *Ship Style*, 31.
265 See Bellmann, *Von Höllengefährten*.
266 Dawson and Peter, *Ship Style*, 32.
267 Fletcher, *Travelling Palaces*, 246.
268 HAPAG, *Europe. First Class Cabins* (New York, 1914), 4. High season eastbound lasted from 1 May to 31 July and westbound from 1August to 15 October.
269 HAPAG, *Europe: Second Cabin Rates* (New York, 1914), 10.
270 HAPAG, *Sixty Years*, 25.
271 Cunard Archive. D42/C1/2/215. Chairman's Correspondence. "Imperator."
272 HAPAG, *Hamburg American Line. S.S. Imperator* (New York, n.d.).
273 HAPAG, *Hamburg American Line. S.S. Imperator*, 2.
274 HAPAG, *Hamburg American Line. S.S. Imperator*, 2.
275 HAPAG, *Turbinen-Schnelldampfer Imperator*, 25.
276 Dawson and Peter, *Ship Style*, 30.
277 HAPAG, *Turbinen-Schnelldampfer Imperator*, 121.
278 HAPAG, *Imperator Auf See*, 39.
279 Rieger, *Technology*, 167.
280 F.R., "Die Inneneinrichtung des 'Imperators'", *Hamburger Fremdenblatt*, 10 June 1913.
281 Rieger, *Technology*, 166.
282 Menu from the *Fürst Bismarck*, 19 February 1902.
283 "Craze for Luxury Makes the Imperator Possible", *The Sunday Herald* (New York), 22 June 1913.
284 HAPAG, *Turbinen-Schnelldampfer Imperator*, 121; see also Britta Heitman, "Spitzengastronomie auf hoher See: Ritz-Carlton Restaurants auf HAPAG-Dampfern", *Schiff et Zeit* 70 (2009), 28–36.
285 Kludas, *Die Geschichte der deutschen Passagierschiffahrt*, vol. 3, 67.
286 Rieger, *Technology*, 166.
287 "New Hamburg-American Liner", *The Marine Review* 43 (July 1913), 246.
288 "The Imperator", *The Times* (London), 12 June 1913.
289 Emily Holt, *Encyclopedia of Etiquette* (Garden City and New York, 1915), 443.
290 See for example John H. Gould, *Over the Ocean: An Illustrated Souvenir of the Hamburg-American Line* (New York, 1895).
291 "Ordered from Liner", *The Washington Post*, 3 August 1907.
292 "Fight in Liner Cabin", *The Washington Post*, 27 August 1907.
293 "Vaterland Docks in Hour and a Half", *The New York Times*, 14 June 1914.
294 "Big Theft on Ship Alleged", *The Washington Post*, 23 July 1910.
295 "Guests at Ball Own a Billion", *Chicago Daily Tribune*, 21 September 1913.
296 "The Vaterland, New Queen of the Atlantic, Arrives", *New York Herald*, 22 May 1914.
297 Rieger, *Technology*, 167.
298 Merck, "Meine Erinnerungen", 111.
299 "Rich Folk in Steerage", *The Washington Post*, 15 September 1907.
300 Burgess, *Engines*, 159.
301 HAPAG, *Europe: Second Cabin Rates*, 1.
302 Dawson, *The Liner*, 57.
303 HAPAG, *Europe: Second Cabin Rates*, 1.
304 "The Hamburg-Amerika Liner 'Vaterland'", *Shipbuilding and Shipping Record* 3 (7 May 1914), 560.
305 HAPAG, *Die Hamburg-Amerika Linie*, 76.

306 Cunard Archive. D42/C1/2/215. Chairman's Correspondence. "Imperator".
307 "The Quadruple Turbine Liner 'Imperator'", *The Marine Engineer and Naval Architect* 35 (July 1913), 468.
308 Zerbe, *Die Grossen Deutschen Passagierschiffe*, 204.
309 Arthur Holitscher, *Amerika, Heute und Morgen. Reiseerlebnisse* (Berlin, 1912), 12.
310 Holitscher, *Amerika*, 15.
311 Holitscher, *Amerika*, 16.
312 Holitscher, *Amerika*, 13.
313 Fletcher, *Travelling Palaces*, 275.
314 Johannes Gaulke, *Im Zwischendeck. Ein Kulturbild aus dem Auswandererleben* (Berlin, 1909); see Bellmann, *Von Höllengefährten*, 188ff.
315 Kludas, *Die Geschichte der deutschen Passagierschiffahrt*, vol. 2, 10.
316 Clarence Richard Lindner quoted in "Steerage Myths", *The Washington Post*, 30 January 1910.
317 As reported in "Wohnungseinrichtungen auf 'Imperator'", *Hansa: Deutsche nautische Zeitschrift* 51 (25 July 1914), 708.
318 Karl Scheffler, "'Imperator': Ein Offener Brief an den Generaldirektor der Hamburg-Amerika-Linie", *Kunst und Künstler* 12 (1913), 85.
319 Merck, "Meine Erinnerungen", 109.
320 See Jürgen Rath, "Heizer und Trimmer", in Plagemann, ed., *Übersee*, 265–7.
321 Quoted in Fox, *Transatlantic*, 322.
322 Fox, *Transatlantic*, 322.
323 Quoted in Fox, *Transatlantic*, 322.
324 Wiborg and Wiborg, *1847–1997*, 161f.
325 Wiborg and Wiborg, *1847–1997*, 162.
326 Merck, "Meine Erinnerungen", 109.
327 See Egon Erwin Kisch, *Reportagen von der Seefahrt 1914–1924* (Oldenburg, 1979), 63–7.
328 Rieger, *Technology*, 169.
329 Quoted in Rieger, *Technology*, 170.
330 HAPAG, *Turbinen-Schnelldampfer Imperator*, 16.
331 Rieger, *Technology*, 164.
332 Rieger, *Technology*, 161.
333 "Revolt on Ocean Liner", *The Washington Post*, 27 July 1907.
334 *Zeitschrift der Hamburg-Amerika Linie* 12 (20 June 1913), 84.
335 "Imperator Sails in North Sea Gale", *The New York Times*, 12 June 1913.
336 "Great Imperator Glides into Port", *The Sun* (New York), 19 June 1913.
337 "Kaiser's Imperator Cruise Is Ended", *The New York Times*, 10 July 1913.
338 "Imperator Arrives with 2,500 Aboard", *The New York Times*, 17 July 1913.
339 "The Imperator", *Shipbuilding and Shipping Record* 4 (1914), 351.
340 Merck, "Meine Erinnerungen", 107f.
341 "Public Views Imperator", *The New York Times*, 29 May 1913.
342 Nils Schwerdtner, *German Luxury Ocean Liners. From Kaiser Wilhelm der Grosse to AIDAstella* (Stroud, 2011), 53.
343 "Many Changes on Imperator", *The Washington Post*, 10 September 1913.
344 These reports were noted in "The Big Imperator", *The Wall Street Journal* (New York), 12 September 1913.
345 "Hamburg-American", *The Wall Street Journal* (New York), 12 September 1913. The reports were also denied by Director Meyer in "Imperator to Make Regular Trips", *The Washington Post*, 11 September 1913.
346 "Hamburg-American Line", *The Wall Street Journal* (New York), 15 November 1913.
347 "The Imperator in New Trim", *The New York Times*, 10 March 1914.
348 "The Big Imperator", *The Wall Street Journal* (New York), 12 September 1913.

349 Quoted in "Big Liner Afire; Ship's Hero Dies", *Chicago Daily Tribune*, 29 August 1913.
350 "Fire in Biggest Liner", *The Washington Post*, 29 August 1913.
351 See "Greatest Atlantic Liner on Fire at the Pier", *The Washington Post*, 30 August 1913.
352 See "Big Liner Afire; Ship's Hero Dies", *Chicago Daily Tribune*, 29 August 1913.
353 "One Life Lost in Imperator Fire", *Boston Daily Globe*, 29 August 1913.
354 Cunard Archive. D42/C1/2/102. Chairman's Correspondence. "Claim by Hamburg-Amerika Linie against the Norddeutscher Lloyd for Damages and for Dismissal of an Agent at Stuttgart."
355 "Imperator Arrives, Battered by Storm", *The New York Times*, 20 March 1914.
356 "The Big Imperator", *The Wall Street Journal* (New York), 12 September 1913.
357 Merck, "Meine Erinnerungen".
358 Broeze, "Albert Ballin", 25.
359 "Vaterland on Way across Atlantic", *The New York Times*, 16 May 1914.
360 Merck, "Meine Erinnerungen", 111.
361 Merck, "Meine Erinnerungen", 109.
362 Merck, "Meine Erinnerungen", 111.
363 Merck, "Meine Erinnerungen", 112.
364 "German Trade Handicap", *The Manchester Guardian*, 17 April 1914.
365 See for example "Wirtschaftliche Rundshau", *Hansa: Deutsche nautische Zeitschrift* 49 (1 June 1912), 453f.
366 "The Rise of German Shipbuilding", *Shipbuilding and Shipping Record* 4 (7 January 1914), 18.
367 "Many Changes on Imperator", *The Washington Post*, 10 September 1913.
368 Jack Lawrence, *When the Ships Came in* (New York, 1940), 215.
369 Lawrence, *When the Ships*, 224f.
370 "The Vaterland", *The Marine Engineer and Naval Architect* 36 (June 1914), 429.
371 "Probefahrt und Ausreise des Dampfers Vaterland", *Zeitschrift der Hamburg-Amerika Linie* 13 (20 May 1914), 127.
372 "Biggest Ship Balks in Docking", *Boston Daily Globe*, 22 May 1914.
373 "The Giant Vaterland", *The Times* (London), 27 May 1914.
374 Milton H. Watson, *Flagships of the Line: A Celebration of the World's Three-Funnel Liners* (Wellingborough, 1988), 115.
375 "Der Stapellauf des Riesendampfers Bismarck", *Hamburger Nachrichten*, 20 June 1914.

3 Picturing the *Imperator*

Making and debating seagoing monuments in Germany's popular culture

I

The morning of the *Imperator*'s launch – 23 May 1912 – dawned grey and wet in Hamburg. Yet this had little effect on the mood of expectant excitement coursing through the city. Large crowds made their way to the harbour early in the morning, arriving on foot, in carriages, and in automobiles. The Helgoländer Allee, running from the Reeperbahn to the Landungsbrücken in St. Pauli, was clogged with traffic shortly after 7:00 a.m. In the harbour, small steamers and pleasure boats adorned with flags, and loaded with thousands of curious spectators, maneuvered for the best vantage point from which to see the liner slip down the ways. In the city centre, a large crowd gathered outside the Dammtorbahnhof eagerly anticipating the Kaiser's arrival by train at 8:20 a.m. Rumours that he would not attend the ceremony had appeared in the preceding days. King Frederick VIII of Denmark died suddenly on 14 May, and the Imperial court was in mourning. Wilhelm's decision to travel to Hamburg is indicative of the degree to which he took a personal interest in the *Imperator*. More importantly, his presence demonstrates the extent to which the liner, and this particular event, was seen as symbolically momentous. And the Kaiser was coming not just to witness the launch of HAPAG's new liner but to christen it. In so doing, he was undertaking a role traditionally assigned to women.

Stepping off the train in his admiral's uniform, Wilhelm and his entourage were received by a group of Hamburg and Imperial dignitaries including Mayor Johann Heinrich Burchard, Mayor Carl August Schröder, and Admiral Alfred von Tirpitz. From the station, the party was driven to the Landungsbrücken where it boarded Hamburg's *Staatsdampfer*, the *Johannes Dalmann*, to be transported to the Vulcan shipyards where tens of thousands of people gathered closely around the hulking mass of the liner. Eyewitness accounts speak of being overwhelmed by the sheer size of the hull, some comparing it to a mountain or giant rock face. While these spectators waited excitedly in the vessel's shadow, shipyard workers were busy knocking away the timbers that supported it.

A wooden, roofed platform (*Taufkanzel*) had been constructed at the *Imperator*'s bow. Resembling a garden gazebo perched on stilts, it was reached by a long flight of stairs decorated with drapery and festoons. Only a small number of dignitaries, including Mayor Burchard and Albert Balllin, accompanied the Kaiser to the top of the platform. There was a small commotion when a block of wood – a piece of scaffolding or ill-secured gangplank – fell from above and narrowly missed Wilhelm. The mishap attracted attention as far away as the United States: *The Detroit News* devoted a small article to the incident with the title "Death Comes Close to the German Emperor."[1] *The Sun*, published in New York, also included the event in its headline: "Imperator Launched; Kaiser Escapes Peril."[2] This may account for the reason why the banker Max Warburg, while describing the ceremony to his brother Aby as "extremely interesting and uplifting," also noted that the Kaiser seemed "drawn and nervous."[3]

The centrepiece of the launch ceremony was the christening address given by Mayor Burchard. As we will see, this gave expression to the variety of interwoven symbolic meanings with which the *Imperator* had already been

Figure 3.1 The Kaiser leaving the stand after christening the *Imperator*.
Source: Bain Collection, The Library of Congress, Washington, D.C.

loaded in the German print media. The Kaiser's only words were "I christen you *Imperator*." These were followed by the breaking of a bottle of champagne on the liner's bow by a mechanical device. But the vessel did not budge. Before release from its berth, the Kaiser boarded the *Johannes Dalmann* once again and was ferried to the *Ablaufpavillon* from where dignitaries viewed the launch. The pavilion was situated on the Ellerholzhöft, on the shore opposite the Vulcan yard, and "allowed for an interlude between the naming of the ship and its launching, which created suspense and space for further ceremonial."[4] Finally, at 9:36 a.m., the Kaiser gave the signal for the launch to begin. The last supports were removed and, at 9:43 a.m., after several minutes of suspense, the *Imperator* began to slip from its berth accompanied by the cheers of those in the shipyard, along the shore, and in the harbour.

It took an entire minute for the *Imperator* to be fully afloat. Once it was, drag chains brought the liner to a rapid halt to prevent it running aground on the opposite river bank. The port and starboard anchors were also deployed to break the vessel. But as the former had not been secured to the hull, it disappeared into the water with the entirety of its chain. Once afloat, the liner was escorted by tugs to its fitting-out berth where, over a period of almost a year, its engines, superstructure, funnels, and interiors were installed. As with the spectators gathered around the vessel on that May morning, many Germans came into direct contact with the *Imperator*. Apart from its launch, there were numerous opportunities to see it docked in Hamburg or at Cuxhaven. And, of course, many travelled aboard it. But it was the launch ceremony, in particular, that orchestrated patriotic enthusiasm in connection with the vessel. It physically gathered Germans around a symbol of national power to celebrate national creativity, especially in the form of the Empire's economic, technological, and engineering prowess. In fact, the launch of all three *Imperator*-class liners was in keeping with the inauguration of monumental statues and works of architecture across Germany in the years prior to 1914. These events were stages for symbolic nation building designed for both a national and international audience.

Part of this chapter is devoted to analysing the *Imperator*'s launch. Of particular interest is the most recoverable and most important part of the ceremony: the address given by Mayor Burchard. In order to enrich an understanding of its content, the chapter dissects the speeches made at the launch of all three *Imperator*-class liners. What these reveal is their capacity to function as symbolic vessels capable of bearing a variety of interpretations. In them, we discover an understanding of Germanness that was neither singular, nor uniform, but constructed and coloured by a variety of differing perceptions. These were rooted in specific social, cultural, and political contexts. Consequently, we might say that the *Imperator* featured in the "struggle to appropriate custodianship of the symbols of nationhood" that characterized Imperial Germany.[5] But at the same time, and especially when concentrated in one expression, what we find is that these perceptions were not mutually exclusive and that they could be employed in an integrated image of Germany's nature and achievements.

Figure 3.2 The launch of the *Vaterland*.
Source: German Maritime Museum, Bremerhaven.

The chapter, however, does not begin with the *Imperator*'s launch. Instead, it starts by establishing a context in which to interpret and understand it. Long before it was afloat, the liner was elevated from its role as the new flagship of HAPAG to its status as flagship of the German Empire. To be sure, the argument that the integration of Germany's merchant shipping into the "symbolism of national greatness" was due to popular enthusiasm for the Imperial Navy is not incorrect.[6] But what needs to be stressed, and what the *Imperator*-class liners demonstrate, is that popular enthusiasm for Germany's premier passenger vessels was also a self-generated and self-sustained phenomenon.

Of course, while many Germans had a first-hand encounter with the liners, the vast majority did not. Nor did they see the Empire's other national monuments with their own eyes. Instead, Germans encountered the statues and structures that decorated their cities and adorned their landscape in a variety of widely circulated texts and images, especially in the numerous articles and photographs published in newspapers and popular magazines. These representations functioned as an important medium for imagining the German nation; they kept national monuments in the public eye such that they became "virtual monuments" to the characteristics and achievements of the Empire and "mental pictures of the nation."[7] In fact, as Kirsten Belgum has shown, many national monuments took on the status of commodities in the pages of popular publications; giant constructions of stone and metal ended up vying for space with advertisements for household wares and health products.[8]

This was the case with HAPAG's newest vessels and monumental status was achieved, in part, simply by widespread diffusion in popular media. In addition to appearing in advertising, newspapers, and popular magazines, the *Imperator*-class liners were represented time and again in books and travel guides, and on posters and postcards. Travelling aboard the *Vaterland* on the occasion of its maiden voyage, one of its passengers admitted that an endless amount of praise could be heaped upon the vessel. Moreover, the experience had impressed him with the truth of Goethe's words: in the face of the "truly great," it is best to avoid petty commentary and abandon oneself to "pure admiration."[9] Yet representation and discussion of all three liners took a variety of forms. These ranged from detailed, often tedious technical descriptions to poetic adulation.

To a certain extent, it was not difficult to make national monuments of steamships that presented themselves as such. Their very names announced this pretension and Imperial symbolism decorated their hulls and cabin-class interiors. In addition to the eagle mounted on the *Imperator*'s prow, the Kaiser presided over two of the most important public spaces aboard the liner. Dominating the main staircase was a full-length portrait of Wilhelm II in his admiral's uniform painted by Hans Olde, Director of the Royal Academy of Art in Kassel. The Kaiser also presided over the first-class lounge in the form of a large marble bust sculpted by Walter Schott that stood 1.2 metres tall.

Yet in addition to the deliberate symbolism borne by the vessels, various tropes, metaphors, and compositional strategies were employed in text and image to implicitly and explicitly present them as emblematic of the characteristics and achievements of the German Empire. This chapter closely analyses several of these representations to show how the *Imperator*-class liners were transformed into national symbols through a range of ephemeral material directed at a mostly middle-class audience who bought newspapers, consumed popular media, and were motivated by patriotic sentiment. It reveals their role in a "national optics" that provided Germans with material for collective identification and contributed to what may be described as a sense of Germanness.

What becomes clear is that HAPAG's liners functioned as complex signs that reveal the multi-faceted, multi-layered nature of German national identity at the time. This is hardly surprising given that – especially in the case of the press – they were represented across Germany in a variety of different fora defined by divergent perspectives and agendas. In the case of the *Imperator*, the vessel was celebrated in Hamburg as an embodiment of all that HAPAG had achieved. It was also promoted as a bold new symbol of the historic port city. Here, and elsewhere in Germany, the liner was construed as an emblem of a nation defined by an enterprising, modern, future-oriented middle class focused on economic growth and international cooperation and exchange. Yet it was also seen as representative of a Germany defined by the Imperial government and

Figure 3.3 The *Imperator*'s main staircase.
Source: German Maritime Museum, Bremerhaven.

a Kaiser who played a role in forging a strong nation, encouraged its maritime development, and fostered its modernization.

Yet there were many Germans who felt the *Imperator*, *Vaterland*, and *Bismarck* were not worthy of the status of national monuments or, if they were, that their symbolism was negative, not positive. Among the aristocracy and middle classes, there were those who thought the *Imperator* was the embodiment of all the evils wrought by political, social, and cultural transformation.[10] Others felt it "appeared as a typical manifestation of the new Germany, with its huckstering, and obtrusive manners, more a snobbism than a symbol of German competence."[11] But it was among the working classes that enthusiasm for the *Imperator*-class liners was most clearly absent. This chapter reconstructs how the symbolism with which the vessels were loaded ran up against the social reality of those who actually built and operated them. In the case of the *Imperator*, many of these people felt it represented much of what was wrong with their society. These contradictory and even antagonistic responses to the celebration of HAPAG's liners as national monuments are hardly surprising. In fact, they serve to highlight the significance that the vessels assumed in popular culture and clearly demonstrate that they were widely perceived as monuments to the nation.

There are, however, two important points to keep in mind. First, not all passenger liners launched by German shipping companies received the same attention, nor were they elevated to the same status. Many were largely devoid of the overt national symbolism with which the *Imperator*-class liners were loaded and made no pretensions to monumental stature. Even the names with which they were christened reveal that the companies that commissioned them had other priorities. Liners such as NDL's *George Washington* or HAPAG's *Cleveland, Cincinnati, President Lincoln,* and *President Grant* were so named partly to attract emigrants on their way to becoming new Americans. William Miller suggests that this plan succeeded to some extent, as many immigrants "selected these ships, assuming that their entry process and naturalization would be better achieved."[12]

Second, we must not overgeneralize about the representation of the *Imperator, Vaterland,* and *Bismarck.* Considering the publicity campaigns conducted by shipping lines in Germany and Britain, Bernard Rieger has noted that it was common to promote passenger liners as illustrating the "competitiveness and dynamism of the national economies capable of creating these maritime wonders." In this respect, "commercial public-relations drives and national enthusiasm reinforced each other."[13] Rieger is right to make this point. But close analysis of HAPAG advertising reveals that much of it did not explicitly construe and promote the *Imperator*-class liners as emblematic of Germany. Nor were they always and obviously presented as such in newspapers, popular magazines, on postcards, and posters. In fact, as we will see, popular representations of ocean-going steamships also provided Germans with material to think about the world beyond their borders. And yet this does not diminish the portrait that emerges in the following pages of steam-powered, ocean-going monuments to the German Empire as ubiquitous, complex, and contested as the many others built of brick, bronze, and stone.

II

The stage was set for the celebration of the *Imperator, Vaterland,* and *Bismarck* as national monuments long before they were launched. By the beginning of the twentieth century, "the orientation to the coasts, to sea travel, and to the world beyond the seas" had developed in Germany to a degree unimaginable at the beginning of the nineteenth century.[14] Popular awareness of, and interest in the merchant marine was part and parcel of this phenomenon. Even a cursory review of the popular media of Imperial Germany demonstrates this. Interest in merchant and passenger shipping extended well beyond the major port cities of Hamburg and Bremen and was more prevalent than historians have generally recognized. As part of this phenomenon, German steamship companies became popular objects of national pride. Describing NDL in 1905, the industrialist Philipp Harjes praised the company as a "splendid monument" to what the "magnificent entrepreneurial spirit, tireless energy, unceasing industry, and self-sacrificing disposition" of Germans could achieve.[15]

One incident, in particular, demonstrates the extent to which the sentiments expressed by Harjes were shared by other Germans. This was the challenge posed to German shipping by the International Mercantile Marine Company. Formed in the early twentieth century, the IMM was a shipping conglomerate that was bankrolled and led by the American financier J.P. Morgan. It was popularly known as the Morgan Trust. The conglomerate succeeded in purchasing several British shipping lines, most of them small. But its amalgamation of the White Star Line, a prestige British company, caused a sensation in the United Kingdom in 1902. In fact, the takeover resulted in government subsidies to the Cunard Line to ensure that it remained in British hands and to facilitate the construction of the *Lusitania* and *Mauretania*.

Not content with acquiring British lines, the Morgan Trust also set its sights on HAPAG and NDL. Bernhard Huldermann has argued that the conglomerate posed no real danger to German companies. On the contrary, he claimed that competition mounted by one large rival was easier to manage than the unregulated competition between numerous small shipping lines.[16] Yet one important danger posed by the Morgan Trust was that, through the purchase of shares in HAPAG and NDL, it was possible American interests would come to control them. Another lay in the conceivable amalgamation of American railway interests with the shipping lines owned by IMM. American railways carried goods to the nation's ports where they were consigned to foreign vessels for transport across the Atlantic. But if the Morgan Trust succeeded in combining American shipping and railway interests, German vessels would be cut off from approximately seventy percent of the goods they transported.[17]

Given its gravity, this situation attracted international attention. In the United States, *The Washington Post* reported that German newspapers were publishing dispatches from New York "giving the view that the combination has thrown into American hands the mastery of the trans-Atlantic traffic."[18] It also reported on fears expressed in the German press that, if the Morgan Trust controlled ocean navigation, not even protective tariffs could prevent the flooding of the German market with American iron and steel.[19]

In response to these challenges, HAPAG and NDL altered their statutes to prevent the possibility of American control. In addition, the union of railways and shipping lines in the United States was prevented by federal law. And, in February 1902, a profit-sharing partnership was signed between the Morgan Trust and the German shipping lines. And yet, what needs to be emphasized as especially revealing is the considerable attention these events attracted in Germany. On the one hand, the Kaiser became personally involved in the affair, scrutinizing the agreement arranged between the German companies and the IMM. On the other hand, the German press seems to have been particularly animated by these events. HAPAG described the popular response as follows:

> Suddenly a panic took hold of the German public: the immensely rich American [Morgan] had extended his irresistible hands also to the German shipping companies, to the Hamburg-Amerika Line and the North German

Lloyd; there was the danger that Germany's mighty national shipping companies, Germany's pride, would become an American dependency. So great was the months-long excitement in the entire German press, that few level-headed elements could escape the general terror.[20]

It must be emphasized that, before the details of the agreement with the Morgan Trust were made public, German newspapers expressed differing opinions concerning its effect on the Empire. The *National Zeitung* believed that cooperation with the American conglomerate was not only necessary but also that the terms offered to the German shipping lines would be favourable.[21] And yet it seems the overwhelming response in the press was negative. The *Frankfurter Zeitung* feared an agreement would advantage the Morgan Trust more than the German lines. The *Berliner Tageblatt* argued that "steps must be taken at once to protect these lines from Americanization."[22] But no matter the diversity of opinion, the response of the German press is one indication of the extent to which national sentiment was bound up with the Empire's merchant marine.

How did this come about? HAPAG believed Germans were comparatively slow to recognize their nation's achievements in all aspects of merchant shipping. Discussing the liners it employed as cruise ships, a company publication from 1907 suggested that Americans had long admired HAPAG's vessels while Germans were only "slowly beginning to become aware of this estimable feature of their global shipping."[23] And yet no matter the speed at which it occurred, popular interest in passenger shipping was only partly generated and transmitted as a component of widespread enthusiasm for the Imperial Navy. As Volker Plagemann has indicated, there were a variety of ways in which Germans were brought into direct contact with the products and achievements of their merchant marine.[24] By the time of the *Imperator*'s launch, the Empire's premier transatlantic passenger liners were the subject of widespread popular interest in their own right.

Public awareness of Germany's merchant marine grew as the result of a variety of events, initiatives, and the workings of several institutions. It was fostered by the expansion of professional training in shipbuilding under Wilhelm II and the founding of schools such as the *Königlich Preußische Technische Hochschule* in Berlin. It was spread through the work of institutions such as the *Berliner Institut für Meereskunde*, founded in 1900 as part of the University of Berlin, and the associated museum that opened in 1906. The annual Kiel Week Regatta also served to generate awareness and interest in the merchant marine. This became especially popular in the 1890s and HAPAG vessels participated as floating hotels from 1902. Events such as the German Shipbuilding Exhibition mounted in Berlin in 1908 also played a role. So too did the work and publications of institutions and associations devoted to trade, commerce, and German colonial endeavours in which merchant shipping played an integral role.

Of course, many Germans came into direct contact with their nation's principal shipping lines through the presence they maintained in its major cities. By 1897, HAPAG operated offices in Dresden, Frankfurt a.M., Hanover,

Leipzig, and Munich. In 1906, it purchased property on Unter den Linden in Berlin to accommodate tourist and passenger bureaus. Knowledge of German endeavours on the North Atlantic was also disseminated through popular books devoted to steamships and their history. Several were published in Germany in the decades before the First World War and some focused specifically on the development of the modern passenger liner.[25] Literature, and travel writing in particular, often provided accounts of crossing the Atlantic aboard a German liner. Travelling to New York aboard NDL's express steamer *Spree* in 1892, the ophthalmologist and medical historian Julius Hirschberg took a keen interest in the vessel. He explored the engine room and the bridge and provided his readers with several pages of technical detail concerning the liner's machinery and on-board technology.[26]

Many of these publications featured illustrations and we must remember that maritime subjects formed a prominent part of Imperial Germany's visual culture. In fact, they were the focus of several painters. Some – including Hans Bohrdt (1857–1945), Christopher Rave (1881–1933), and Willy Stöwer (1864–1931) – were famous in their day as specialists in the field. Much of their work focused on the Imperial Navy and Bohrdt and Stöwer were favourites of the Kaiser. The former, who supported the building of a German battle fleet, acknowledged that "literature and art have put themselves, consciously or unconsciously, in the service of the Fatherland and through their works produce an understanding for maritime matters in the people."[27] Both Bohrdt and Stöwer depicted vessels of the merchant marine, and both completed watercolour studies of the *Imperator* at the time of its launch. Bohrdt also painted an official portrait of the liner for HAPAG shortly thereafter.[28] Most Germans would not have seen these images in their original form in galleries or in the offices of the shipping lines that commissioned them. Yet they reached a wide audience when reproduced, as they often were, in the advertising published by HAPAG and other companies. This was especially the case with the postcards examined in greater detail in the subsequent section.

Measured in terms of volume alone, it was daily newspapers that brought Germany's merchant marine to its widest audience. This was increasingly the case with the advent of modern shipbuilding in Germany and the expansion of the merchant fleet from the 1880s. A patriotic note was not explicitly struck in all instances in which commercial shipping featured in the popular press. Nonetheless, this facet of the Empire's maritime power appeared not only in reports devoted specifically to it but also, to varying degrees, in the wide range of articles on economics, trade, and commerce that were published in daily newspapers across Germany. As managing director of HAPAG, Albert Ballin's views on the state of German merchant shipping were often sought and published in the German press, especially in Hamburg. We will examine newspaper reporting on the *Imperator*-class liners in greater detail in the subsequent pages. Before doing so, it is worth noting other means by which the merchant marine was put before the German public.

There were, of course, professional journals such as *Hansa* and *Schiffbau*, founded in 1864 and 1900 respectively, that addressed shipbuilding and a variety of matters related to the industry. So did the *Zeitschrift des Vereines Deutscher Ingenieure*. These publications spoke primarily to a professional audience. A much broader reading public was offered popularized accounts of scientific and technological innovations – including those in the shipping industry – in popular illustrated magazines such as *Die Gartenlaube*, the *Illustrirte Zeitung*, and *Über Land und Meer*. As the premier organ of Germany's middle classes and liberal values in popular culture, *Die Gartenlaube* was a particularly important publication.[29] It was the nation's most successful middle-class family magazine and reached a large audience in all regions of the Empire.[30] In formulating "an attractive model of what Germany should become," *Die Gartenlaube* supported industrialization, the nation's mercantile ambitions, an expansionist foreign policy, and endorsed the development of a navy seen as a symbol of German unity and progress.[31] It played an important role in disseminating "mental pictures of the nation," and published articles on the development of the German merchant marine.[32] *Die Gartenlaube* reported on technological developments as they applied to merchant shipping and the construction and launch of premier passenger liners provided especially rich material for similar publications.[33]

In both newspapers and popular magazines, there was a long history of reporting on transatlantic passenger shipping in particular. The *Helena Sloman*, Germany's first transatlantic, iron-hulled steamship – built in Britain and operated by the Hamburg-based Sloman Line – attracted media attention when it made its maiden voyage to New York in 1850. Published in Leipzig, the *Illustrirte Zeitung* reported on the event with a focus on issues and themes that became staples in press coverage of transatlantic liners down to the time of the *Imperator*.[34] The magazine spoke of the *Helena Sloman* as a marvellous realization of modern engineering and ever-increasing technological sophistication, claiming that it represented the developed state of human progress. It praised the use of the most modern materials in its construction and took particular note of its safety. But the author was especially impressed by the way in which "the comfort, convenience and convivial social life of dry land" was maintained in a floating hotel that matched the functional with the "graceful and beautiful." Over sixty years later, the *Illustrirte Zeitung* would greet the *Imperator* in similar fashion as the latest wonder of the modern age and, more specifically, as a powerful symbol of Germany's achievements in industry, engineering, and technology.

Unsurprisingly, the most concerted and consistent effort to raise public awareness of Germany's merchant marine was conducted in the sophisticated publicity and public-relations campaigns that were a major investment for all steamship companies. As William Miller explains, the success of passenger liners "was determined to a great extent by early public-relations men."[35] Britain's Cunard Line, for example, spent £54,000 on advertising for its Atlantic trade in 1913.[36] HAPAG was particularly skilled in the art of self-promotion and it has often been said that Ballin possessed a flair and genius for advertising.[37] The company boasted publishing divisions that managed the production of posters, brochures, and literature. It understood the power of images and ensured that the material it published, such as the booklets examined in chapter two, were richly illustrated. To achieve the best results, HAPAG employed professional photographers such as Oswald Lübeck. He worked for the company from 1904 to 1914 documenting its vessels and photographing life aboard its transatlantic liners and on its many cruises.[38] HAPAG also established a bureau to manage communication with the press and business community.[39]

In some of this material, the company explicitly construed, not simply its premier passenger liners, but its entire enterprise as central to Germany's status as a maritime and world power. In essence, the firm promoted itself as a type of national monument. One important example is the official history published by HAPAG in 1907. In its pages, the company stated that it stood at the centre of Germany's maritime development. It explained that "historical scholarship finds in the history of the Hamburg-America Line a true mirror image of modern German maritime history in general."[40] But it did much more than that: the author described HAPAG's founding as a patriotic act and its development as intimately bound up with the state and the welfare of the entire nation:

> National endeavours certainly played a definitive role in the founding of the company sixty years ago. At that time, it was the interests of Hamburg that mattered, as today it is those of the entire German Empire. The larger the company became, the larger became its significance for the popular welfare and that of the state. The well-understood interests of the company coincided evermore frequently with those of the economic whole.[41]

HAPAG insisted that it was much more than a shipping line; it emphasized that it had made major contributions to German industry, trade, and commerce. Ultimately, it described itself as "an important national force" undertaking "national tasks" for the good of Germany.[42] The very same self-perception was repeated in an official history published in 1922. In this, Kurt Himer explained that HAPAG was not only part of German economic history but also constituted "part of German history as such." Its development and success, he claimed, "was shared with pride by the whole German nation and was regarded as an emanation of all the productive forces of the German economy."[43] This vision and patriotic rhetoric is very similar to that used to extol the role and importance of HAPAG at the launch of the *Imperator*-class liners.

We may be inclined to question the extent to which the national sentiment expressed in company advertising was intended, first and foremost, to enhance its public profile and maintain good relations with the state. Put simply, did HAPAG exploit nationalist sentiment for its own gain? In the specific case of the *Imperator*-class liners, there is no doubt that the company was motivated by a mixture of sound business sense that sometimes involved promoting the vessels as national monuments. But it would seem this was mixed with genuine pride in what HAPAG had achieved as a German enterprise. As Bernard Huldermann explained:

> Ballin often remarked that such huge concerns as the Hamburg Amerika Line were no longer private ventures purely and simply. The ties that bind them to the whole economic life of the nation are so close and so manifold that it would be disastrous to ignore or sever them. (HAPAG's) hundreds of thousands of passengers and immigrants, and the huge volume of German made products and manufactured articles carried on board its vessels, spread the German name and German fame throughout the civilized world. Hence, to Albert Ballin, the national flag and that of HAPAG were two symbols expressive of but one idea.[44]

Of course, the *Imperator* flew both flags. But the question concerning HAPAG's intentions is to a large extent irrelevant. What is more important is the fact that any nationalist sentiment expressed by the company in relation to the liner was also taken up, multiplied, and widely disseminated by various organs of the German media.

Also important is the fact that, while promoting itself as a type of national monument, HAPAG presented its history and successes as intimately bound up with international politics, trade, and economic development. Explicitly and implicitly, the company created its self-portrait as a German enterprise operating on the global stage. This was achieved in a variety of forms in advertising that often included explanations of how HAPAG's business was directly affected by economic developments in East Asia or America; information on the lines and services it offered to ports around the world; itineraries of its cruises; and posters that often incorporated an image of the globe to emphasize the company's international reach.

In creating this image of itself, HAPAG reflected a liberal vision of the German Empire – also disseminated through popular novels, journals, and travel accounts – that saw securing markets and materials necessary for economic development as integral to establishing Germany as a world power. Concurrently, the company emphasized that it played an important role in connecting Germans to the world.[45] The history published in 1907 explicitly celebrated these achievements:

> It can be asserted without exaggeration, that by means of the cruises it has offered during the last decade, the Hamburg-America Line has contributed much to the development of German enterprise, German knowledge of the world, and joie de vivre. The sea is no longer a desert to those living in the German hinterlands, but the giver of powerful health and the pilot to great wonders of the earth. But ocean cruises have also brought a deeper under-standing of the achievements and requirements of ocean shipping to the people that certainly can only have a beneficial influence on shipping and transportation in general.[46]

HAPAG was as an agent of world travel "upon which hangs a large portion of the intellectual culture of our people, its commercial spirit, knowledge of the world, and joie de vivre."[47]

Clearly, what needs to be kept in mind is that, as much as HAPAG promoted itself as symbolic of Germany and intimately bound up with its history, its self-presentation also emphasized that the new nation was oriented towards, and embedded in the world. As we saw in chapter two, the many posters published by the company to advertise its cruises in the Mediterranean, to Scandinavia, the Far East, and around the globe, brought the world into the lives of Germans in unrealistic but alluring and evocative images prepared with considerable artistic skill. The liners employed on these cruises often appear only in the background of these poster images – sometimes in the far distance – leaving the foreground and most of the picture plane to an evocative representation of the destination. Motifs including famous historical monuments, stereotypically construed figures, and representative flora and fauna were presented in bold colours and designs in a way that must have helped confirm the preconceived ideas and images of many who saw them. For example, posters advertising cruises to Egypt pictured the pyramids, the Sphinx, or a giant statue of an Egyptian pharaoh.[48] On one such poster, pith-helmeted tourists ride camels past an ancient temple.[49] As with the several economic, social, and cultural forces at work in the German Empire and discussed in chapter one, this type of self-promotion fostered an awareness of the increasingly globalized nature of the world.

At the same time, these images and, in fact, the phenomenon of cruising itself served the workings of nationalism in as much as they allowed Germans to define themselves against other cultures. Scholars writing about the processes of globalization in the decades before the First World War are careful to emphasize that nation states were not undermined as a result. Indeed, as large empires declined, the world became increasingly defined by nations that fixed their boundaries with tighter border controls; passed laws on nationality such as the Reich Citizenship Law of 1913; issued passports; celebrated their cultural particularity; erected monuments celebrating the nation; and wrote their histories in national terms.[50] And, of course, the radicalization of nationalism in Germany from the 1880s, and its establishment as a popular phenomenon accompanying increased political participation, is a well-studied phenomenon.

In sum, it is not surprising that the German press responded as it did to the supposed threat posed to the Empire's merchant shipping by the International Mercantile Marine in 1902.[51] Long before the *Imperator*'s launch, the business, products, achievements, and importance of Germany's merchant marine were put before the German public in a variety of forms and instances. This encouraged a response to companies such as HAPAG and NDL as objects of national pride. And even if most German transatlantic liners were not explicitly construed as national monuments in and of themselves, the celebration of the *Imperator*, *Vaterland*, and *Bismarck* as such was in keeping with an increasing appreciation of the role and importance of Germany's merchant marine. This celebration began in the early days of their construction.

Figure 3.4 An American poster with the type of imagery found on many German
          examples. 1909–1914.

Source: Hapag-Lloyd AG, Hamburg.

III

HAPAG promoted its passenger liners and, in particular, those of the *Imperator*-class
in a variety of forms. One particularly direct and impressive way was to employ
models. A model of the *Imperator*, featuring electrical illumination of its interior,
was installed in the display window of the company's offices on Unter den Linden.[52]
A larger model, measuring six metres in length, was exhibited at the International
Hygiene Exhibition in Dresden in 1911. A podium erected at its stern allowed
visitors to look down along the entire length of the vessel.[53]

The use of such models was common; photographs of HAPAG's New York
offices clearly show them installed in wooden and glass display cases. And
evidence suggests that this was an effective means of advertising. A report in
the journal *Hansa* claimed that even as a model the *Imperator* made a powerful
impression. Writing about the one exhibited at the International Hygiene
Exhibition in Dresden, the author marvelled at the amount of deck space and
consequent freedom of movement afforded its passengers.[54] Anyone who has

seen the model of the *Imperator* still displayed in the headquarters of Hapag-Lloyd in Hamburg can attest to the powerful effect and fascination created by this direct and tangible means of advertising.

The liner was also commemorated and promoted in other tangible, if smaller forms. These included a bronze medallion measuring 59 mm in diameter and cast by C. Kuhl. This was commissioned by HAPAG and presented to passengers who sailed aboard it on its maiden voyage.[55] The obverse bears a profile of the Kaiser in uniform accompanied by the inscription "Wilhelm II. Imperator. Rex." On the reverse is an image of the vessel from the port bow with the inscription "Turbinen Schnell Dampfer Imperator. 1913, Hamburg-Amerika-Linie."[56] Brought into direct conjunction with the Kaiser, this is a striking example of the liner's elevation to a national symbol. But its dissemination was limited. Souvenir spoons and pocket knives, decorated with an image of the vessel, were also sold to the public.[57]

But it was on paper that the *Imperator* was most commonly depicted and its image most widely circulated. As previously noted, HAPAG also produced a wide range of printed advertising material to promote its liners and services, and the *Imperator*-class vessels were the subjects of sophisticated publicity campaigns in Germany and the United States. Advertisements were placed in newspapers and various popular forums such as the *Fliegende Blätter* and the almanac *Lahrer Hinkenden Bote*.[58] In addition, the company offered a range of merchandise such as travel guides, calendars, and travel diaries. Much of this material could also be purchased aboard ship.[59] One of the decorative calendars published by the company in 1912 featured an image of the *Imperator* by Willy Stöwer.[60] Even promotional stickers resembling postage stamps were used to advertise the company's cruises from 1909. Although small, they were printed with sophisticated designs that included not only text but also images of liners, company insignia, and terrestrial globes.[61] Furthermore, between 1901 and 1934, HAPAG published the *Zeitschrift der Hamburg-Amerika Linie*, which featured articles about its services, vessels, cruises, and ocean-going travel.

It has been argued that much of the publicity produced by German and British shipping lines construed their largest and most luxurious vessels as national monuments. Writing of Cunard's *Mauretania* in 1912, Frederick A. Talbot described it as "British in style, treatment and workmanship, solid and durable, so that it fulfils national traditions."[62] As we will see, there is at least one striking instance in which HAPAG explicitly promoted the *Imperator* in the very same way. And it often used images to present the liner as a national monument in striking and memorable fashion. As noted in chapter two, picturing transatlantic liners next to iconic buildings – to dramatically demonstrate their size, invest them with cultural prestige, and celebrate the advances of modern technology – was a common publicity strategy. It was also employed to load the vessels with local and national symbolism. A postcard published by HAPAG in 1905 depicted the *Kaiserin Auguste Victoria* standing on its stern and towering over Hamburg's city hall.[63] Another advertising image pictured the *Amerika* in the same position rising over Cologne Cathedral.[64]

To help its readers gain a graspable perspective on the *Imperator*'s size, *Über Land und Meer* explained that the height of Cologne Cathedral would rise only to the second funnel of the liner if it was stood upright on its stern.[65] The *Imperator* was also pictured standing in this position next to, and towering over, the cathedral. This comparison elevated the vessel to the status of a national monument simply by bringing it into association with a structure widely recognized as one. But it also emphasized that the *Imperator* was larger than the historic structure and, in this way, invited reflection on the achievements of modern Germany vis-à-vis its medieval incarnation. Furthermore, by contrasting the engineering aesthetic of the liner's design with that of the Gothic edifice, the image emphasized that the *Imperator* was an appropriate symbol for a modern nation. By extension, it also contrasted the liner's modernism with the historicism of many monuments erected in the later years of the German Empire. And yet HAPAG's liners were also construed as modern monuments by bringing them into direct connection with iconic contemporary structures. *Über Land und Meer* stated that the Tietz department store on Berlin's Alexanderplatz would fit within the *Imperator*'s hull and provided an image, often reproduced in advertising and the print media, depicting an elephant striding easily through one of the vessel's funnels laid on the ground.[66] And there was a tradition of comparing HAPAG liners to contemporaneous American structures. For example, the *Amerika* was depicted straddling Madison Square Garden and standing upright on its stern in the middle of Manhattan, towering over its "skyscrapers."[67] Likewise, as we will see in chapter six, the *Imperator* was compared to New York's Woolworth Building.

But what needs to be emphasized is that nationalist sentiment and posturing was not explicitly present in much of HAPAG advertising. As described in chapter two, publicity material was designed, first and foremost, to appeal to an international clientele. And in fact, as chapter four will demonstrate, when it came to the interior decoration of the *Imperator* HAPAG was criticized for pandering to the tastes of wealthy American travellers and ignoring progressive trends in German art and design. Understandably, the company's priority was to impress prospective clientele with the size, safety, technological sophistication, luxury, and comfort of the liner. And yet, in so doing, advertising contributed to the transformation of it, on the most fundamental level, into a ubiquitous symbol of German capability, achievement, and ambition in engineering, technology, transportation, and mastery of the seas. Advertising leant itself to the merging of technology and patriotism and the idea that national self-assertion was bound up with technological innovation and achievement.[68] And, as Bernhard Rieger has emphasized, many Germans viewed products of engineering "as tools to transform the international environment that stifled their political ambitions."[69]

Postcards played an important role in feeding German society's fascination with technology. They also served to combine patriotism and technology in the form of steamships. Many were published by HAPAG itself and we may take them as an example of the type of visual imagery that appeared in much of its advertising. Given the numbers in which postcards were produced and circulated, it is reasonable to assume that, along with reporting in daily newspapers, they did the most to popularize the *Imperator*-class liners. Postcards were extremely popular in Europe and America in the two decades before the First World War. Although many were posted, the majority were purchased for collections and never used for correspondence. This appears to have also been the case with German postcards depicting passenger steamers. Gerhard Kaufmann has estimated that up to eighty percent were never mailed. Most of those that were bear messages that have nothing to do with the ship or voyage per se.[70] Thus, it is difficult to know how the people who sent and received these cards responded to the images they bore. Nonetheless, German cards depicting passenger steamers are representative of many European and American postcards from the period in as much as they "show a fascination with the new environment, its technology, its crowdedness and its engineering grandeur."[71]

Postcards portraying German passenger liners proliferated in the 1890s; they were produced by various publishers often in collaboration with shipping lines.[72] Many were also published in the United States and entire series were offered for sale featuring reproductions of artworks by painters such as Bohrdt, Rave, and Stöwer.[73] These mostly represented the vessels at sea and less commonly at dock. Most followed the traditional compositional formats of maritime painting by depicting a total view of the vessel from the port or starboard side, or obliquely from the bow.[74] From the time the *Augusta Victoria* appeared on a postcard in 1889, a variety of HAPAG liners were represented on numerous examples.

The *Imperator* was pictured on several postcards even before its maiden voyage. Many reproduced black and white photographs while others were printed with colourful chromolithographs of tinted photographs or artists' impressions. The latter pictured the vessel in various colour schemes and often took liberties by enlarging the eagle mounted on its prow, or by extending its stacks. Postcards sometimes depicted the *Vaterland* with a similar eagle figurehead. The majority of postcard images match the format of those found on posters and in the brochures discussed in chapter two: depicted from a low vantage point, the *Imperator* appears as an enormous mass of steel. And although the postcard format is small, the fact that the liner almost fills the entire picture plane creates an impression of its massive size that is nonetheless striking. This impression is enhanced by depicting a much smaller craft, such as a tug or yacht, alongside it. A view from the bow is frequently employed to create a dramatic recession in depth, and the *Imperator* is sometimes shown plowing through a stormy sea, its stacks billowing smoke.

Thus, although small, postcard images and those reproduced in newspaper advertisements, brochures, travel guides, calendars, and travel diaries create a powerful impression of a formidable piece of German engineering and technology. And these small pieces of ephemera were often elaborate. On postcards depicting the *Imperator*, close-up vignettes of the eagle figurehead or Commodore Ruser were often included in the image field. So too were the "arms" of HAPAG – a scalloped shield mounted on an anchor and bearing the

Turbinen-Schnelldampfer (HAPAG)
„Imperator"
Länge 268 m,   Breite 29,5 m
Höhe 19,5 m,
Rauminhalt 5o,ooo Tons,
Platz für 4ooo Passagiere,
Besatzung 12oo Mann,
Schornstein 21 m hoch, 5 ¹/₂m Durchm.

Figure 3.5 Postcard depicting the *Imperator*. 1912–1914.
Source: Author's collection.

company's monogram – along with decoration in the form of maritime motifs including anchors and compasses. Moreover, a great deal of information was communicated through the medium of postcards. Text often appeared not only on the reverse but was also incorporated into the image on the front. This almost always declared that the *Imperator* was the largest ship in the world. Data about the vessel's length and tonnage was sometimes provided to support this claim. Postcards depicting the *Imperator*'s first-class interiors were also published but were less common. Others depicted significant events in the liner's career, including its launch. In sum, if they did not engage in expressly promoting the *Imperator* as a national monument, these ephemeral items catered and contributed to the self-definition of Germany's nationalistic middle classes. This depended, in large part, not only on the consumption of art and history, but involved "the love of technology, consumption and material advance."[75]

This love was more fully indulged in the booklets that HAPAG published in Germany prior to the commissioning of the *Imperator*. As we saw in chapter two, publications such as *Dampfer Imperator* constitute the most elaborate and sophisticated form of publicity devoted to the vessel. And, as we might expect, advertising published in Germany sometimes struck an explicitly patriotic note that was absent in publicity produced for the American market. For instance, *Dampfer Imperator* described the vessel as a new symbol of Hamburg.[76] It also told its readers that the liner was "a new, powerful advance in the history of our very short, success-filled history of shipping."[77] The booklet even claimed that the *Imperator* carried the advances and achievements of German culture onto the seas.[78] Such patriotic sentiment was exclusive neither to HAPAG nor to other German shipping lines, and was also common in Britain and France.[79]

But again, it must be stressed that an overtly patriotic note was not often struck in this advertising. Yet there is one example, published after the *Imperator*'s launch, that does so stridently and repeatedly. In 1913, HAPAG's literary bureau produced a small, but elaborate commemorative album entitled *Imperator Auf See: Gedenkblätter an die erste Ausfahrt des Dampfers am 11. Juni 1913*. Its pages featured a collection of impressions and poems by "authors and representatives of leading newspapers," all of whom sailed aboard the liner on its maiden voyage to Britain. As part of HAPAG's publicity campaign, journalists were offered free passage to Southampton along with a complimentary two-day stay in London. Newspaper men from Berlin, Cologne, Hamburg, Munich, and Stuttgart were joined by English and American colleagues.

HAPAG claimed that the album's contents gave expression to the nation-wide fascination with the vessel. To the present-day reader, the tone, imagery, and abundance of superlatives employed in the text may seem ridiculous. Alongside descriptions of the *Imperator*'s luxurious interiors, its smooth running, and the absence of sea sickness among its passengers, near poetic accounts announced its triumph over the ocean and the natural elements of wind and waves in the North Sea and English Channel. J. Landau contributed a poem entitled "Seasickness" in which he celebrated the end of this affliction and cast Albert Ballin as the doctor, the Vulcan shipyard as the pharmacist, and the *Imperator* as the medicine.

Yet there are more serious contributions that warrant close attention. Some contributors, such as Dr. Wilhelm Doerkes-Boppard, struck a universal tone when he wrote that all ocean-going nations shared an equal part in the *Imperator* as a triumph of transatlantic travel. He also described the ship as a bearer of German culture and the entrepreneurial spirit of the Hanseatic cities. K.F. Kurz pictured the liner as one of the greatest "marvels" produced by humankind, while W. Fred described the moment in which the vessel got underway in Cuxhaven as a "highpoint of human existence." The *Imperator* provoked Paul R. Krause to speculate on the limits of human ingenuity; at what point, he wondered, would the exhaustion of the world's coal resources force technology to pursue new directions, or would a surrogate for coal be found? Others emphasized what they believed was the ambassadorial role of the *Imperator*. Hubert Henoch claimed that the highpoint of the maiden voyage was achieved when the liner flew the German flag between Portsmouth and the Isle of Wight while sailing among English warships. He praised HAPAG for forging a link between Germany and England with such a vessel. Carl Müller expressed the wish that the *Imperator* would be "an agent of peaceful convictions" among the different peoples who found themselves crossing the ocean together on its decks. He hoped it would be a vessel for mutual understanding, representing the knowledge that "enduring

peace forms the surest stronghold of the welfare of all developed nations."
Hans Ossig claimed that the *Imperator* pointed to a future in which the world
would be one economic unit, undivided by oceans; a world in which travel
would permit individuals to establish themselves wherever the best
possibilities for development were to be found. All of these texts are
examples of the way in which HAPAG advertising often prompted Germans
to think as much about the world beyond their borders as about themselves.

Yet many contributions to *Imperator Auf See* explicitly addressed the liner
as a distinctly national monument. Rudolf Denzel's poem, "Des Imperators
erster Tag," claimed that German hearts were filled with pride by this
expression of national power. For some authors, this was due to the fact that
the ship embodied the practical achievements of German industry and
technology, while for others it represented a triumph of *Kultur*. While
Dr. Ernst Schultze saw the *Imperator* as a symbol of Germany's creative
aptitude and competence, Demetrius Hornicke described it as a "powerful
prophet" preaching confidence in the "mission of German power" that
triumphs over the "seamy side of the everyday" and over "timidity, weakly
self-denial and bourgeois dullness." The *Imperator* was a triumph that
reaches those "clear heights from where the ideals of power and beauty shine
over land and sea." Max Leser claimed the liner was no ordinary vessel but
represented a highpoint of German will and gave form to a national
"yearning." He described the *Imperator* as *volkstümlich* in a manner similar
to Cologne Cathedral, Bismarck, Sanssouci, and the dramatist and novelist
Gerhart Hauptmann.

The *Imperator* was also construed as a symbol and actualization of German
unity. Bernhard Reuter's poem, "Imperator," claimed the vessel was an
indication that Germans had forgotten their cultural and political divisions. As
a product of German spirit and power, the liner proclaimed German unity.
"From the shores of the sea to the summit of the Alps; German men raise their
hands in an oath: 'May the German eagle go forth in all the world; with God,
for Kaiser and for Fatherland.'" Reporting for the *Neue Hamburger Zeitung*,
Hans Ossig described the way in which all Germans felt at home aboard the
vessel during its maiden voyage: Berliners felt themselves to be on the
Kurfürstendamm; residents of Munich did not have long to look for a "good
mug of beer"; and Hamburgers felt themselves to be among friends in
Harvestehude.[80]

Imperator Auf See is something of an exception. Nowhere in HAPAG
advertising is the liner so blatantly and insistently construed as a national
monument as in its pages. To be sure, the booklet gave expression to the voices
of many who did not work for the company. And many of these voices belonged
to enthusiastic journalists who wrote about the liner in daily newspapers. In fact,
while HAPAG conducted extensive and sophisticated publicity campaigns, it is
outside of company advertising that the celebration of the *Imperator* as a national
monument was most obvious, consistent, and widespread.

IV

Those Germans who were most well-informed about the *Imperator*-class liners were probably those who read professional publications. Unsurprisingly, the trio attracted the attention of journals devoted to shipbuilding, engineering, and maritime affairs. Some of the coverage of the *Imperator*, in journals such as *Schiffbau* and *Hansa*, took the form of short reports on the principal stages of its development including its construction, launch, maiden voyage, and refitting.[81] There were also articles, for example in the *Jahrbuch der Schiffbautechnischen Gesellschaft*, focused on very particular aspects of its technology such as its wireless telegraphy.[82] And there were comprehensive and detailed overviews of its construction, technology, and outfitting that were often richly illustrated.[83] Perhaps the most complete reporting on the *Imperator* was published in the *Zeitschrift des Vereines Deutscher Ingenieure*. Short articles, printed while the liner was under construction and at the time of its launch, were followed, in June 1914, by an extended and comprehensive feature that addressed everything from the *Imperator*'s engines to the decoration of its interiors in great detail.[84] This was accompanied by numerous detailed plans, diagrams, and photographs that documented the vessel under construction along with various aspects of its technology. Several photographs also depicted the accommodation and public rooms provided all classes of passenger. The article published by the *Zeitschrift des Vereines Deutscher Ingenieure* was, and still is, one of the best sources of information on the *Imperator*.

Yet the number of people who the read the journal, in addition to other professional publications that reported on the *Imperator* such as *Schiffbau*, must have been relatively small in comparison to those who encountered the liner in newspapers, popular journals, and company advertising.[85] And, as with HAPAG advertising, professional publications did not explicitly construe the *Imperator* as a national monument. Written mostly in a detached, technical voice, their articles offered a host of facts and figures that strike the reader with, among other things, a sense of the incredible amount of thorough planning that preceded the construction of such a vessel. But it is worth noting that many authors could not help expressing enthusiasm for, and pride in the *Imperator* and its sisters. They occasionally employed descriptors such as "powerful" and "extraordinary," or commented that it was naturally the case that their interior decoration and outfitting outdid anything previously seen on the Atlantic.[86] The *Jahrbuch für Deutschlands Seeinteressen* described the building of the *Imperator* as "a praiseworthy example of German entrepreneurial spirit and boldness."[87] In the opening line of one of its articles, *Hansa* described it as a "mighty ship, a miracle of technical skill, and a magnificent expression of intelligence, deliberation, and labour."[88] Underlying the mass of technical detail, trade publications gave voice to an admiration for what German shipbuilding had achieved.

The nature of reporting in these journals raises, once more, an important point about the manner in which the *Imperator*-class liners were construed as national monuments. In the minds of HAPAG and most commentators, it was neither the vessels' names, nor their pictorial and sculptural embellishment that elevated the liners to this status. Instead, it was the fact – repeatedly emphasized in media of all types – that they constituted a marvel of German entrepreneurial spirit, shipbuilding, engineering, technology, and applied art. Again, it is well known that many middle-class Germans demonstrated "a passionate fascination for technology."[89] Information about new developments was disseminated in a variety of media from books and newspaper articles to advertising and postcards. As we saw in chapter two, technological innovation was often greeted with ambivalence and sometimes with trepidation. But on the whole, positive sentiments outweighed concern and scepticism. In fact, the celebration of technology and the promotion of its advance was part of a middle-class strategy for strengthening political liberalism in Imperial Germany and for cultivating bourgeois sensibilities and mindsets. Maiken Umbach has argued that middle-class hegemony was performed through public architecture and a material culture that foregrounded commerce, industry, and technology.[90] She describes the German middle class as finding new places, times, and subjectivities through the performative use of technology and as looking forward to technological utopias of human engineering and the mastery of nature. The point to be made is that, even when not explicitly construed as national monuments, the *Imperator*-class liners signalled, in impressive fashion, Germany's achievements in modern engineering and technology. Given the extent of interest in the latter, no explicit elucidation was required, whether in advertising or press reporting, for the vessels to function as symbols of national endeavour and accomplishment. The merging of technology and national pride did not require specific instruction.

Popular magazines demonstrated patriotic enthusiasm for the *Imperator*-class liners in more explicit form. *Über Land und Meer* described the *Imperator* as a "50,000-ton monster," a "Goliath of the Ocean," and as one of several "steamship leviathans."[91] The language employed even adopted a quasi-biblical tone when it described the liner as "such a vessel as hitherto man's eye has not beheld." The *Berliner Illustrirte Zeitung* and the *Illustrirte Zeitung* presented HAPAG's new vessels to the public through the publication of large photographic montages with minimal text. It is principally through the nature of the images, formatted to emphasize the gigantic size of the vessels, along with the amount of space devoted to their reproduction, that one senses the enthusiasm and pride of the publishers. In fact, these montages seem to be a case in which the authors heeded Goethe's words and, in the face of the "truly great," eschewed petty commentary and abandoned themselves to "pure admiration."[92]

On 2 June 1912, the cover of the *Berliner Illustrirte Zeitung* was devoted to the launch of the *Imperator*. It reproduced a large photograph of the vessel's bow. Portrayed from a low vantage point, the liner seems not so much a ship as a giant, metal sculpture in the style of geometric abstraction.[93] The magazine would later publish images emphasizing the luxury of the first-class interiors of the *Imperator* and *Vaterland*. These included photographs of passengers dancing in the former's first-class lounge and disporting themselves in its swimming pool.[94] The *Illustrirte Zeitung* also published an impressive photographic collage on the occasion of the *Imperator*'s launch. The five large images, accompanied by minimal text, depicted both the Kaiser and the liner with the photographs of the latter formatted to emphasize its size.[95] The magazine also covered – principally through photographic essays – the maiden voyage of the *Imperator* and the launch of the *Vaterland*.[96] To mark the maiden voyage of the latter, it published an article by Else Grüttel entitled "A modern Noah's Ark." This was accompanied by an impressive photographic montage of the liner's interiors including full-page images of the first-class lounge and winter garden.[97] The short text emphasized that the world's largest ship was built on the world's largest stocks, with the world's largest crane and the world's largest floating dock; it was a German ship, built in a German shipyard for a German shipping company. In a direct and emphatic conjunction of technology and national pride, Grüttel announced that a "new epoch has begun for the German merchant marine."

The illustrations published by magazines such as the *Illustrirte Zeitung* are very effective in creating a sense of the monumental size and luxury of the *Imperator*-class liners. Much of the reporting in such fora relied heavily on the wordless immediacy and impact of the visual to translate its message to their readers. This was also the case with the daily newspapers that reported on the *Imperator*, *Vaterland*, and *Bismarck* across Germany. And it was in the popular press that the trio received their most widespread and sustained presentation to the German public as national monuments.

Unsurprisingly, the most extensive, persistent, and enthusiastic reporting occurred in Hamburg. Conservative and liberal newspapers including the *Hamburgischer Correspondent*, *Hamburger Nachrichten*, *Hamburger Fremdenblatt*, and the *Neue Hamburger Zeitung* covered all stages in the development of HAPAG's new liners. Consistent reporting on the *Imperator* began in the early days of its construction with some papers publishing photographs of the vessel in the Vulcan yard.[98] In fact, the liner was treated as a sensation more than a year before it was launched and before much certain information was available.[99] With palpable anticipation, the *Hamburgischer Correspondent* claimed that something great was being constructed in the Vulcan yards, something much larger than the *Deutschland*, something that would be "a new sensation in terms of safety and comfort at sea."[100] More dramatically, what was rising on the banks of the Elbe would announce a new epoch in shipbuilding.[101] Reporting on the *Imperator* in March 1911, the author and journalist Philipp Berges offered one of the most breathless accounts. While providing details pertaining to the luxury and spaciousness of its planned interiors, Berges described the vessel that Vulcan was constructing as a swimming island, a royal palace, and a cosmopolitan city.[102]

It is worth noting that the enthusiasm demonstrated by the Hamburg press for the *Imperator* went beyond reporting. In June 1912, the *Hamburger Fremdenblatt* organized an exhibition of photographs and other images depicting the construction, launch, and interior decoration of the vessel. Mounted in the newspaper's offices, HAPAG loaned a large model of the liner to the exhibition which, it was reported, attracted a substantial number of enthusiastic visitors.[103]

Consistent coverage in Hamburg continued through the liner's construction, to its launch, sea trials, maiden voyage, and all the major events in its career down to July 1914. Reporting addressed all aspects of the *Imperator* from its machinery to its interiors; commentary returned over and over again to the vessel's technological sophistication, the elegance, luxury, and comfort of its first-class public spaces, as well as the recreational facilities available to passengers, and especially the swimming pool. Newspaper articles were also fascinated by the volume of provisions with which the *Imperator* was stocked. To be sure, much of the commentary on all three liners was technical in nature. In fact, many accounts simply overwhelm the reader with a barrage of details about all aspects of the vessels. For example, two of the many articles on the *Vaterland* published by the *Hamburger Fremdenblatt* amounted simply to the enumeration of technical details organized according to keywords.[104] While dry, the facts and figures are impressive and conjure the image of a monumental undertaking.

But if technical, newspaper articles were often enlivened by photographs, artists' impressions, and diagrams. For example, in June 1913, the *Hamburger Fremdenblatt* published an impressive photo spread of the *Imperator*'s first-class interiors. While the accompanying text emphasized their comfort and the "exceptionally harmonious" nature of their designs, this is almost superfluous to the power of the images themselves.[105] Furthermore, on many occasions a wealth of detail was accompanied by clearly stated admiration in the manner of Philipp Berges's account for the *Hamburger Fremdenblatt* in March 1911. Hamburg's newspapers lavished praise on the *Imperator* as a "wonder," a "colossus," and a "swimming city."[106] Just as in the HAPAG brochure entitled *Dampfer Imperator*, it was not unusual for language to turn almost poetic and for journalists to reference classical culture and literature as they addressed the educated middle-class public that read the Hamburg dailies.

Unsurprisingly, HAPAG received its share of congratulation and praise and was described as "our great world line."[107] The *Hamburger Nachrichten* emphasized that it was the company, first and foremost, that was to be thanked for building the *Imperator* and claimed it was principally a monument to its achievements.[108] Concurrently, the liner was celebrated by the Hamburg press as a symbol of their city. Describing it as a "richly developed artwork," the *Hamburger Fremdenblatt* claimed that the *Imperator* had risen on its stocks as a new symbol of Hamburg.[109] The *Hamburgischer Correspondent* construed its commissioning as marking a new stage in the relationship between the Kaiser and the city.[110] In so doing, it provided a particular interpretation of the liner's name, arguing that it symbolized the middle-class contribution to the modern German nation and the liberal and democratic values embodied by this class. The title *Imperator*, it explained, was not simply connected with dictatorial power and military deeds. "The Roman statesman who, for the first time, permanently combined civic and military power in his own hands referred to the people and senate as Imperator. It is this meaning of the word that has come down to our age." In the opinion of this liberal Hamburg broadsheet, the *Imperator* embodied an understanding of German history that conceived of Kaiser and burghers working together to achieve Germany's national destiny. The "triumph" that the paper wished the vessel – over Germany's competitors at sea and over the elements themselves – would be the combined triumph of the Kaiser and all Germans. This interpretation was in keeping with the iconographical programs of many monumental artworks commissioned by local authorities and private associations in German cities after 1871. Clearly, in its construction as a national monument, the *Imperator* could be, and was presented as a complicated sign.

The Hamburg press also repeatedly, and often stridently, construed the liner as a symbol of the entire German nation. This involved considerable mirror gazing and self-congratulation. The *Hamburger Fremdenblatt* described HAPAG's new trio as "factors in national life" that compelled Germans to respect their own achievements.[111] It reminded its readers that the *Imperator* was not simply a swimming city but a swimming "German city."[112] In particular, the liner was celebrated as a symbol of the Empire's engineering and technological prowess and as an embodiment of the advances made by the nation in trade and commerce. The *Hamburger Nachrichten* described the 23rd of May as "a glorious day both for the boldness of Germany's farsighted commercial spirit and for the capability of German industry." The *Imperator* was "proof of the leading position that Germany is taking in international trade and among the industrial nations of the world."[113] In addition, the vessel was touted as both a symbol and an actualization of German unity. The view of Hans Ossig that all Germans felt at home aboard the *Imperator* was also printed in the *Neue Hamburger Zeitung*.[114]

Given its name, it was easier for the *Vaterland* to be explicitly described as a symbol of the German Empire by the Hamburg press. In fact, reporting on it was often accompanied by reflection on the nation's history and unification, reflection that presented all three HAPAG liners as the outcome of Gemany's ineluctable and positive historical trajectory.[115] For some, the name *Vaterland* indicated that the vessel was literally a piece of Germany.[116] The *Bismarck* was treated in similar fashion. It clearly memorialized the Empire's first chancellor who, following his death in 1898, grew to mythic proportions in the nation's collective memory. Transformed by numerous writers and artists into a symbol of Germany, the commemoration of Bismarck, especially among the middle classes, reached the proportions of a national cult around 1900. As the *Hamburgischer Correspondent* claimed, "all the longing and desire of the German people, all its power and enthusiasm is embodied in the name of Bismarck."[117] The last liner of HAPAG's trio was understood as a commemoration of the Iron Chancellor; an expression of all that he had come to symbolize in terms of national self-definition and the German character; and as a physical manifestation of everything Germany had achieved since he had forged its unification.[118]

The *Hamburger Nachrichten*, for example, claimed that the *Bismarck* represented the energy, industry, and "consciousness of their own strength" that had awakened in the German people in the wake of their political unification.[119] The article it published on 20 June 1914 contains a marked tone of national pride that verges on the belligerent. The text inserted the liner into a narrative of growing German influence and strength as a world power under the guidance of powerful leaders, and through the means of armed struggle. It emphasized that the excellence of German shipbuilders had made Germany free from foreign influence in that respect; in fact, it was thankful to those who had so fully developed "the capabilities" inherent in the "power of our people." In contradiction to the view of the *Hamburgischer Correspondent*, the conservative *Nachrichten* claimed it was proper that the first of the *Imperator*-class liners was named in honour of the Kaiser who stood at the head of the Empire. It was equally fitting that the second should bear the name *Vaterland* and be a symbol of the fact that "all that we are, have, and accomplish is only possible in a united, strong German fatherland." And it was correct that the third liner be christened in honour of Bismarck, as his "creation was the greatest and most estimable in the entire two-thousand-year-old German history" and made possible all that the Empire had achieved in the last four decades.

An important aspect of the self-congratulation in which the Hamburg press engaged was praise of the role played by the *Imperator*-class liners in representing Germany to the world. Prosaically speaking, all three were of great economic importance, each a "swimming exhibition" that presented the products of German ship building, mechanical engineering, and applied art to foreign nations. More profoundly, they were ambassadors of German industry, skill, and discipline providing non-Germans with a "true image of our nature."[120] Writing of the *Imperator* in the *Hamburgischer Correspondent*, the author Carl Müller-Rastatt was proud of the fact that it would carry the German flag over the ocean as a "masterpiece" of German technology, industry, and trade.[121] In Hamburg, and in the German press generally, such celebration was often accompanied by assertions of how amity between nations would be fostered through increased and more efficient communication.

Yet writing on the *Imperator* as a national symbol also promoted it as a challenge posed to other maritime nations, principally Britain. The *Hamburger Nachrichten* stated that, in building the liner, Germany had taken "a new giant step forward in the undoubtedly peaceful yet nonetheless fierce competition between nations."[122] It was occasionally and erroneously claimed that the *Imperator* would challenge Cunard for the speediest crossing of the Atlantic and that it would regain the Blue Riband for Germany.[123] As for America, the vessel was proudly compared to its skyscrapers in an attempt to create a powerful impression of its length and the height to which its superstructure was raised above the waterline.[124] Most reporting, however, saw the challenge to other nations that the *Imperator* embodied as much more substantial and related to matters of technological innovation, economics, and global influence. As we will see in chapter five, this is precisely the way many organs of the English press interpreted it. And this was encouraged by the fact that reporting in Hamburg on all three liners could tend towards the belligerent. Writing about the *Vaterland*, the *Hamburger Fremdenblatt* described it as an announcement to foreign nations: "here is a product of German labour, German industry! Could you deliver better or even merely as good?"[125] Strangely, this boasting ignores a fact examined in the following chapter: that HAPAG's new liners were the products of international cooperation and that much of the outfitting and decoration of their interiors was executed by foreign firms.

Of course, press reporting on the *Imperator*-class liners was not restricted to Hamburg. And, as Bernhard Rieger has argued, many newspapers "wrote about the new passenger liners in exactly the same terms as public-relations departments," and journalists respected them as national symbols.[126] While true, this conclusion needs to be qualified. Looking to the prominent publishing centres of Berlin, Cologne, Frankfurt, and Munich, we find much less press interest in HAPAG's vessels. Many newspapers published only cursory accounts of the launch and maiden voyages of the *Imperator* and *Vaterland*. In fact, much of what appeared in the press outside Hamburg amounted to little more than an enumeration of technical details and the expression of astonishment at the size and luxury of the vessels. Many newspapers, including the *Frankfurter Zeitung*, the *Münchner Neueste Nachrichten*, and the *Neue Preußische Zeitung* published nothing on the launch of the liners or printed only cursory reports with mundane accounts.

Furthermore, much of the reporting that occurred in German newspapers focused on the HAPAG vessels as the latest wonders in transatlantic travel. While this shared the enthusiasm of the Hamburg press, much of it did not explicitly treat the liners as emblematic of the Empire. There was great interest in the luxury of the *Imperator*'s first-class interiors. Writing in the *Berliner Tageblatt*, Oscar Bongard described travelling aboard the liner in glowing and evocative terms similar to those found in HAPAG advertising. He described the winter garden, for example, as like the garden of the Grand Oriental Hotel on the "paradise island" of Ceylon.[127] Similar "dreams," he told his readers, were to be found throughout the vessel. Comparing the *Imperator* to a luxury hotel and spa, and claiming passengers could easily forget they were at sea, he marvelled at the quality of the cuisine and its various leisure facilities. The *Kölnische Zeitung* was particularly fascinated by the enormity of the *Vaterland* and provided details about its technology, interiors, and provisions for safety. It told its readers that "technically and aesthetically" the vessel "so exceeded all previous conceptions" of what a transatlantic liner could be that one could hardly imagine further improvement in shipbuilding.[128] The paper stated that the vessel was a "wonder ship of our gigantically striding age."[129] But as was often the case in German newspapers, it did not strike an explicitly patriotic tone.

Yet this is not to diminish the role many newspapers played in putting the *Imperator*-class liners before the German public as national monuments. They were described as awesome symbols of Germany's industrial might and technological achievements, its dynamic economy, and its world-power status. The *Berliner Tageblatt* described the launch of the *Imperator* as opening "a new epoch in the history of German merchant shipping."[130] It stated that, with its launch, "we are now marching at the head of all nations."[131] The *Allgemeine Zeitung* described the same event as a "momentous symbol of the enormous progress of German trade and industry."[132] Claiming the vessel was a triumph of German shipbuilding, it also emphasized that it was a symbol of the nation's position of strength on all the world's oceans, a position that had been won by its "robust power" and "indefatigable diligence." "The heart of every German," it proclaimed, "must beat faster in the knowledge of this fact." This enthusiasm was extended to all three liners. The *Tägliche Rundschau* stated that the trio symbolized "the strong roots of our power" as it resided in "our German Emperor, the elemental forces of our German people, and in the spirit and legacy of Bismarck."[133]

HAPAG was so pleased with the nature and extent of positive reporting in the German press that it reproduced some of it in large-format handouts preserved in the company's archive and perhaps intended as advertising.[134] These were prepared by the literary bureau to mark milestones in each liner's development, especially launches and maiden voyages. They are simply, but handsomely designed and feature large photographs that are some of the best-quality images of the *Imperator, Vaterland,* and *Bismarck* ever produced. These may have been taken by Johann Hamann or Oswald Lübeck.[135] Yet nothing could equal the experience of seeing the giant new liners with one's own eyes. And it was the launch of each vessel that provided the public with perhaps the most exciting and elaborate visual and rhetorical spectacles in their careers.

V

The launch of the *Imperator* was the event that attracted the greatest concentration of press reporting in Hamburg and across Germany. On the occasion, the *Daily Chronicle* told its British audience that the German newspapers "surpass themselves in patriotic outbursts at Germany having built the largest ship afloat."[136] Of course, in Hamburg, coverage was front-page and extensive and often involved impressive photographic montages.[137] And we should note that photographs were not the only visual images of the event. A twelve-minute film entitled *Der Stapellauf des größten Ozean-Shiffes der Welt "Imperator,"* that included images of the liner under construction, was produced by Fricke and Witte of Hamburg and first projected on 31 May 1912.

In other German cities, the launch was sometimes front-page news, but often it was not. In either case, journalists spoke of the festive atmosphere in Hamburg and recounted the events that constituted the ceremony. They also described the contents of Mayor Burchard's speech, sometimes publishing it verbatim and in its entirety. In fact, in some instances, newspaper articles amounted to little more than a printing of the christening address.[138] But many journalists contributed to the nationalist sentiment of the speech through their commentary. The *Tägliche Rundschau*, for example, spoke of the launch of the *Imperator* as an important contribution to Germany's call to "mastery of the world's oceans."[139] Germans also encountered the *Imperator*'s launch in some of the advertising that appeared in German newspapers. The sparkling-wine manufacturer Henkell & Co., for example, did not miss the opportunity to appropriate the *Imperator* to its purposes. As we saw in chapter two, the company paid for newspaper advertisements comprised of an image by Lucian Bernhard that depicted the *Imperator* on its stocks just prior to launch. The text reminded readers that the world's largest ship had been christened with a bottle of Henkell Trocken.[140] And the rhetoric, pageantry, and symbolism of this occasion was borne across the seas to Britain and America where several newspapers reported on the event.[141]

As Jan Rüger has emphasized, the 1890s saw the emergence of the "naval theatre" in both Britain and Germany and the launch of warships became an important means by which the navy was put onto the public stage. Designed and stage-managed by political and naval authorities – but also influenced by the forces of popular media, consumerism, leisure, and entertainment – the launch of a battleship became an elaborate event to be consumed by tens of thousands of spectators.[142] These events were also reproduced and restaged for larger audiences in newspapers, popular journals and, from 1897, on film.[143] In Germany, the Kaiser was instrumental in turning the launch of warships into major imperial pageants in which, as in Britain, "tradition, power and claims to the sea were demonstrated to both domestic and foreign audiences."[144] In effect, the launch of a naval vessel amounted to its celebration as a national monument. The very same can be said of the launch of the *Imperator*-class liners.

And yet, faced with concern in Britain about the rate at which Germany was building battleships, the Imperial Navy wished to avoid too much "naval muscle-flexing" in order to prevent "a further acceleration of British naval building."[145] This opinion was shared by Albert Ballin who felt the launch of warships should be made less extravagant affairs. In July 1908, Chancellor Bernhard von Bülow reported to the Kaiser that Ballin felt:

> we should do everything to avoid drawing attention to them [naval vessels] as is the case with ostentatious launch ceremonies accompanied by speeches. The English are not like the Germans who form their impressions from books and tables (if not from the depths of their soul). John Bull is impressed by what he sees in front of him.[146]

And yet it appears Ballin did not feel the same way about the launch of passenger liners, especially those built by HAPAG.

As demonstrated at the beginning of this chapter, the launch of the *Imperator*-class liners were large, lavish, and carefully stage-managed pieces of public theatre. They physically gathered tens of thousands of Germans around giant symbols of national achievement and ambition; it is estimated that 40,000 people attended the launch of the *Vaterland*.[147] The *Hamburger Nachrichten* claimed the launch of any transatlantic liner was a "premiere" like no other; not even the performance of a work by one of Germany's greatest authors could compare.[148] The paper stated that the "magnificent spectacle" of the *Bismarck*'s launch attracted "thousands and thousands" of viewers. Everyone in Hamburg, it opined, felt that their personal interests were represented in the event, be they involved in shipbuilding, the shipping industry, commerce, or whether they intended to travel aboard the vessel. The use of the term "spectacle" was not unusual in reporting on the launch of the *Imperator*-class liners. These events were designed to appeal to the public desire for sensation and, as with the launch of battleships, first-hand accounts "convey a strong sense of visual fascination."[149] Much of what was visually compelling about the launch of the *Imperator* was its sheer size and one can easily understand why reporters spoke of being overwhelmed by the vessel. This sensation was almost inevitable given the situation of those in attendance. Photographs taken at the launch of the *Imperator* portray the great mass of the hull or the Kaiser and his entourage; few represent the crowds gathered to participate in the event. But those that do show large groups of people gathered close around the liner. They are either seated in specially built stands or assembled on foot beneath its bow and are dramatically dwarfed by a giant mass of steel.

The ceremonies that marked the launch of all three liners borrowed the customs and rituals that accompanied the launch of a capital warship. At the launch of the *Imperator*, the Kaiser was the central human actor in the drama; dignitaries from Hamburg and Berlin watched the event from a specially constructed *Ablaufpavillon*; male and female spectators were divided into separate tribunes; military societies were in attendance; and decorations were awarded as part of the celebration. As we will see, the influence of naval custom also extended to the content of the speeches delivered on these occasions. And several other events surrounded the launch ceremony. A silver model of the *Imperator*, weighing just over nine kilograms, was presented by Vulcan to the Kaiser who then gave it to Ballin.[150] Telegrams were received from dignitaries at home and abroad. Chancellor Bethmann-Hollweg sent one to HAPAG congratulating the company and expressing his wish that "the proud ship" would be "a symbol" of "German entrepreneurial spirit."[151] The text was published in several German newspapers.[152] Best wishes also arrived from NDL and Cunard.

The launch patrons for the *Imperator*, *Vaterland*, and *Bismarck* were, respectively, the Kaiser, Prince Rupprecht of Bavaria, and Countess Hannah von Bismarck, granddaughter of the Iron Chancellor. This, in itself, is indicative of the symbolic importance with which the liners were weighted. In Imperial Germany, warships were mostly christened by men and merchant ships predominantly by women.[153] The christening of HAPAG's new liners took place from a platform (*Taufkanzel*) constructed at the bow of each vessel and was preceded by a short address, usually the only speech made on these occasions. These were given by the Mayor of Hamburg, respectively Johann Heinrich Burchard, Carl August Schröder, and Max Predohl. While each speech was different, the following pages deal with them thematically, not individually, in order to emphasize the consistency of particular themes that ranged across all three.

There was consistency in the very language that the speeches employed.[154] As Rüger has emphasized with respect to the addresses given at the christening of warships, "they charged the ship with metaphors in which technology, masculinity and heroism merged with ideas of tradition and identity."[155] The same can be said of the speeches that preceded the christening of the *Imperator*-class liners. It may have been common to speak of them as sisters, but Hamburg's mayors characterized the vessels as "massive," "giant," "colossal," "mighty," and even as having "a fighting spirit." At the launch of the *Imperator*, Mayor Burchard employed phrases commonly used at the launch of a warship and "ranked the *Imperator* alongside the capital battleships of the Imperial Navy, all under the command and foresight of the Kaiser."[156] Rüger feels that "the extent to which the Vulcan yard, which had built the liner, and the HAPAG line, which had ordered it, allowed military language and display to dominate the launch of a commercial passenger liner was remarkable."[157] To be sure, not all contemporaneous commentators heard the speeches in the same way. For example, in Britain, the *Daily Chronicle* reported that Burchard's address was "couched in the usual flowery language employed in Germany on such occasions" and described the Mayor as "poetical."[158] But it is true that Mayor Schröder's description of the *Vaterland* as "beautiful," and his mention of "the beauty of its lines" are atypical. Instead, the speeches commended HAPAG and the German Empire for their vigour, power, might, and fearlessness as they struggled to realize and develop themselves in the face of international challenges and competition. The celebration of these traits was closely tied to the theme of tradition and an elaboration of German identity. But what tradition and which identity were being celebrated?

On one level, all of the christening addresses were celebrations of HAPAG and its history. At the launch of the *Imperator*, Mayor Burchard recalled how the launch of the *Hamburg*, at Stettin in 1899, signified the beginning of an auspicious course for the company.[159] Always open to new ideas, eager to innovate, future-oriented, and prepared to make bold decisions, HAPAG had built passenger steamers that met the highest standards for comfort and luxury. The company now competed successfully on the global stage with the shipping lines of other nations. Burchard emphasized that HAPAG's steamers now sailed to all major American ports, Arabia, Persia, East India, China, Japan, and to West- and East Africa. At the launch of the *Vaterland*, Mayor Schröder even provided statistics that emphasized the growth of the company since 1847; he asserted that, with sixteen million kilometres logged by its vessels in 1912, the line certainly now had the right to claim as its motto "My field is the World." He also made the point that the ship would carry the fame of its builder, Blohm & Voss, around the globe.

Celebrating HAPAG also meant celebrating the urban, commercial, and industrial identity of Hamburg and its historic role in Germany's maritime development. The self-congratulatory aspect of the christening speeches might be described in terms of what several studies have shown: that it was easier for Germans "to assume a national identity mediated by the connection to their own *Heimat* or homeland."[160] This was especially the case for Hamburg; although its history after 1871 was one of political and economic harmonization with the Empire, the Free and Hanseatic City of Hamburg – that had existed as a republic for several centuries prior to 1871 – remained especially proud of its unique political, economic, and cultural identity. As with the building of the city's Bismarck memorial, HAPAG's new steamers provided important opportunities for civic self-representation.[161]

It hardly needs reiterating that the city's prosperity was heavily dependent on shipbuilding and international commerce and that this formed an important part of civic iconography. The decoration of the city hall's *Großer Saal*, which was restored specifically for the opening of the Kaiser-Wilhelm-Kanal in 1895, is an especially important example. Furthermore, the building of the German navy found considerable resonance in Hamburg from the 1890s. More generally, support for the navy was central to middle-class, liberal thinking; a battle fleet was seen as crucial to establishing Germany as a world power and, in particular, to securing markets and products necessary for national economic development.[162] Thus, as Rüger has noted, civic self-representation became central to the launch of warships in Hamburg's shipyards: "festivities and functions, receptions and speeches, balls and dinners, visits and excursions ... were organized and financed by local society."[163] The city acquired special privileges at the launch of naval vessels including the construction of a tribune solely for Hamburg senators.[164] In similar fashion, local civic, middle-class, and commercial interests and culture ensured that the launch of the *Imperator*-class liners were celebrations of the important role played by Hamburg's urban and industrial elite in the Empire's development.

As Mayor Burchard declared, the bold, innovative, forward-looking vision of HAPAG was also "the Hamburg and Hanseatic way." Mayor Schröder recalled that the first HAPAG steamers to enter service in 1856 – the *Hammonia* and *Borussia* – displaced just over 2,000 tons apiece and had to be built in Britain. But in 1913, Hamburg now built ships twenty-five times as large, and with 200 times as much hold space as the vessels commanded by Christopher Columbus. It may have been, as Mayor Predohl envisioned at the launch of the *Bismarck*, that "the power of the Reich ... swells the proud, tradition-true, hanseatic sail." But there was no doubting the sense of satisfaction expressed by Hamburg's mayors in what the city itself had achieved. In this respect, the day of a launch belonged not just to HAPAG, but to Hamburg.

And yet if the *Imperator*-class liners were proud products of HAPAG and Hamburg, they were also touted as the pride of all Germany and modern symbols of nationhood. It was usual for christening addresses to set a major vessel into the context of German maritime achievements. Indeed, *The Washington Post* described Mayor Burchard's address at the launch of the *Imperator* precisely as a speech on recent developments in German shipbuilding.[165] But new vessels were also set into the wider context of national unification and the subsequent political, economic, social, and foreign policy successes of the Empire. This was the case, for example, at the launch of HAPAG's *Deutschland* at the Vulcan shipyards in Stettin on 10 January 1900. On this occasion, Bernhard von Bülow – then German Foreign Secretary – gave a speech in which he "argued that progress in marine engineering underlay both the nation's economic rise and its new bids in colonial and world politics."[166] Bülow spoke in the presence of the Kaiser, Admiral Tirpitz, and thousands of German spectators. In addition, Secretary Jackson of the American Embassy, the naval attachés of the United States and several other nations, as well as the entire Chinese Embassy were in attendance. Members of the foreign press were also present and a summary of Bülow's speech, with translated excerpts, was published in New York and Washington on the very next day.[167]

In similar fashion, the *Imperator*-class liners were construed as national monuments; they were described as symbolic of what Germany had accomplished in concert and as "embodiments of German strength," as Mayor Predohl explained at the launch of the *Bismarck*. Their names, he said, "move the heart of the friend of the Fatherland." Described as triumphs of German shipbuilding and technology, the liners were also presented as testaments to the future-oriented vision of the nation. As Predohl insisted, "their construction and success symbolizes a national act, decided and brought to fruition by brilliant far-sightedness and energy." The progress that facilitated the building of the *Bismarck* "was only possible on the solid foundation of the power of Kaiser and Reich, in a unified Fatherland." As with the many monuments built after 1871 by the German state, local governments, and various private associations, HAPAG's steamers were presented as emblematic of a shared German identity; they were used to project an image of political consensus, social harmony, and shared mission to Germans and the Atlantic world.

As was often the case with monuments built of stone, this image of a nation unified and dynamic in the present, and oriented to the future, was bound up with an equally sure vision of the German past. This was most explicitly in evidence at the launch of the *Vaterland* when Mayor Schröder portrayed Germany's expansion on the seas as the logical continuation of unification achieved on the battlefield. Given the vessel's name and the year of its launch – 1913 – Schröder felt compelled to relate the history – mythologized as it was – of Germany's struggle for nationhood. Looking back to 1813, he told of how "tired of long, onerous bondage, the Prussian people rose up; a king called and all, all came." A desire for the existence of a German Fatherland was awakened beyond the borders of Prussia and "the unified onslaught of the German people broke the French yoke." Half a century later – when another "Napoleon threatened the borders of our Fatherland" – north and south joined in "a mighty defense" to achieve the unity that "our fathers once sought in vain." Schröder hoped that the *Vaterland* would "be worthy of your heritage, be worthy of your storm-tossed homeland, be worthy of your beautiful name that is deeply engraved in our hearts." After having recounted the history of a nation forged in war, Schröder immediately emphasized that the *Vaterland* would serve the cause of international peace. But the point to be made is that the rhetoric, tone, and content of Schröder's address were germane to the dedication of many of the monuments built to celebrate German unification after 1871.

The greatest of these was the *Völkerschlachtdenkmal* commemorating the Battle of Leipzig in which Prussia and its allies defeated Napoleon in October 1813. The monument was dedicated in that city in the same year as the *Vaterland*'s launch. And yet, as Jason Tebbe has emphasized, the *Völkerschlachtdenkmal* did not pay tribute to the role of the Hohenzollern dynasty in the creation of the German nation; instead, it celebrated the *Volk* and espoused a more popular, non-dynastic nationalism. In so doing, it contradicted the message of monuments that made the Hohenzollerns the focal point of national loyalty and, as a result, received a "frosty reception" from Wilhelm II.[168] The *Völkerschlachtdenkmal* is indicative of the fact that competing interpretations of the Empire's nature and history received various forms of expression in the decades preceding the First World War. Indeed, the history of the markedly bourgeois culture that sought to stamp Germany with its values, and represent the democratic-republican aspect of the Empire's heritage, is well known.[169] In light of this, we need to look more closely at the political, social, and cultural image of Germany projected by Hamburg's mayors through the medium of the *Imperator*-class steamers.

Mayor Schröder's speech at the launch of the *Vaterland* presented an image of Germany united by tradition and experience. We recall that, in reference to the campaign against Napoleon in 1813, he used the expression "a king called and all, all came." Yet, like the *Völkerschlachtdenkmal*, the speeches made by Hamburg's mayors paid little attention to the Hohenzollerns; instead, they emphasized the middle-class contribution to the nation. This was in keeping with numerous occasions, such as the inauguration of the Kaiser-Wilhelm-Kanal in 1895, upon which the navy "appeared less as a monarchical symbol and more as the expression of the key role played by the middle classes and the urban and industrial elite."[170] At the launch of the *Imperator*, Mayor Burchard claimed the ship represented, "above all … the product of a flourishing, self-conscious German bourgeoisie." In fact, all three christening addresses were, in large measure, celebrations of these middle classes, be it in the plaudits given to HAPAG; the tribute paid to Hamburg's entrepreneurial spirit; the celebration of German shipbuilding, technology, industry, and commercial enterprise; the recognition of the Empire's future-oriented vision; and, as we will see, the positive assessment of the way in which the new steamers would facilitate international trade and global economic growth.

We must also consider the fact that, at the launch of the *Bismarck*, Mayor Predohl described the vessel as a new monument to the Iron Chancellor. Erected all across Germany from the late 1890s, Bismarck memorials are seen by historians as counteracting official monuments celebrating the imperial monarchy. Tebbe explains that

> for the middle classes, those most responsible for these monuments on the local level, he [Bismarck] better represented the nation than the monarchy. The preference of Bismarck over Wilhelm thus reflected the clashing priorities of nationalism and the state in commemoration.[171]

In 1906, Hamburg had unveiled the largest and probably best known Bismarck memorial, and Mayor Predohl brought HAPAG's liner into dialogue with the giant granite image that "looks down on us here as the once legendary Roland in the service of his imperial lord." Like Hamburg's memorial, the *Bismarck* would be an expression of "eternal thanks" to the man "whose spirit and deeds prepared the first ground" for the developments that led to the construction of such a ship. It would complement the city's monument by carrying "the name Bismarck over the seas."

As Mayor Predohl saw it, the names of all three HAPAG steamers expressed the fact that "imperial power, love of the Fatherland, and the counsel and deeds of the first chancellor" were necessary prerequisites for the practical and applied energies that gave birth to achievements like the *Bismarck*. He emphasized that Germany's first chancellor provided not only a model for statesmanship, but also for German business, a fact to which the very building of the *Bismarck* attested. Predohl spoke of the characteristics that made Bismarck great: realism; tenacity; clear understanding of the demands of the present; innovative thinking; confident action; and careful exploitation of success. Predohl's understanding of Bismarck was not simply that of a Prussian Junker defending Germany's pre-industrial elite, nor the Roland of Hamburg's memorial serving his emperor by preventing the development of a liberal, constitutional state; he was a forward-looking statesman who presided over the unification of Germany and its bureaucratic, legal, industrial, financial, and economic modernization. Indeed, one could be forgiven for thinking Predohl was describing not Bismarck, but Albert Ballin.

Thus, on the one hand, the launch of the *Imperator*-class liners reveal at least ambivalence towards dynastic rule in Germany; they give expression to a more popular, middle-class understanding of the Empire's socio-economic constitution and history. And yet the vessels bore the symbolism of imperial power, most obviously in the name *Imperator* meaning, as Mayor Burchard explained, that the ship was "inseparably bound with the Kaiser's majesty." Wilhelm II was the launch patron of the *Imperator* and was present at the launch of the *Bismarck*, while the *Vaterland* was launched by Prince Rupprecht of Bavaria. The speeches made by Hamburg's mayors were explicitly addressed to the Kaiser and Prince Rupprecht, and ended with salutes to, and cheers for the royal guests. Press coverage of the *Imperator*'s launch treated the Kaiser as the principal human actor in the drama. Furthermore, Hamburg's mayors heaped praise upon the Kaiser: while Mayor Burchard wished that the *Imperator*'s voyages would "be as sunny and successful as our Kaiser's blessed life," Mayor Predohl hoped that "halcyon days" would be granted all three ships just as they had been granted to Germany "under the beneficent leadership of your majesty."

But more particularly, each christening address acknowledged the important role played by imperial power and the Emperor in forging a strong nation, encouraging its maritime development, and fostering its modernization. As Mayor Burchard explained, the coming-of-age of the German middle classes happened "under the protection of the Kaiser." Wilhlem's critical role in promoting the Empire's maritime development was particularly emphasized at the launch of the *Imperator* and the *Bismarck*. Burchard believed the Emperor would receive the praise of history for having "wedded all German people to the sea." For all the attention that Mayor Predohl's address gave to Bismarck, it also recognized the Kaiser's involvement in, and importance for the growth of German industry and shipbuilding. Recalling the young Prince Wilhelm's insistence in 1887 that HAPAG break with convention by building one of its new express steamers in a German – and not a British – shipyard, Predohl described the move as "groundbreaking for the improvement of German shipbuilding."

Ultimately, the speeches made by Hamburg's mayors projected a complex image of the German Empire. In so doing, they mirrored a sense of Germanness that was not singular, nor uniform, but constructed and coloured by a variety of differing perceptions rooted in specific social, cultural, and political contexts. What is particularly interesting is that so many different facets of, and perspectives on German identity are combined in these addresses. But while they offered a multi-faceted portrait of the German Empire, they also projected an image of social consensus and the picture of a society with a shared sense of history and mission. Local history and identity was set within the context of national history and identity; the imperial monarchy and middle classes were described as working together to found, develop, and modernize the nation. We might enumerate several reasons for this. First, this is exactly what many monuments did, especially the many murals painted in city halls across Germany after 1871.[172] Second, we are not dealing with monuments conceived as such and intended to promote a partisan vision of the nation. Instead, the *Imperator*-class liners were the products of private enterprise and a commercial venture with ties to the Kaiser. Furthermore, we must consider the fact that the launch of HAPAG's vessels was staged, not only for domestic, but also for foreign consumption. This influenced the image of the Empire that the ceremonies projected.

At the launch of the *Vaterland*, Mayor Schröder recalled a national history marked by the struggle for self-realization. "On France's blood-soaked fields," he said, "a newly-united German Empire arose, that now powerfully protects its borders, and secures a position that demands respect for our Fatherland among the council of nations." Schröder may have cast Germany as justified in throwing off the French yoke, and defending the Fatherland, but his account of national unity was unavoidably coloured by aggression. And yet an important note struck in each christening address was that of the peaceful intentions of the German Empire and the productive role it played on the world stage.

This was a common theme at the launch of HAPAG's premier passenger steamers. On the occasion of the *Deutschland*'s launch in 1900, Bernhard von Bülow spoke of the "great Emperor and his immortal advisors;" praised the spirit of sacrifice and patriotism demonstrated by "all races and classes of the German people;" and described Germany's determination to "overcome obstacles on the path marked out for us by destiny."[173] But in addition to this expression of satisfaction in a singularly national project, Bülow added an emphasis on the importance of the Empire's participation in transatlantic trade and cooperation. In particular, he called upon God to protect the friendship and commerce that existed between Germany and the United States. The correspondent for *The New York Times* reported that when Bülow "expressed the wish that the friendship of Germany with America would continue to grow, hearty applause emphasized the feeling of his hearers." Similarly, when the HAPAG passenger steamer *Cleveland* was launched in Hamburg in 1908, speeches were made by Mayor Burchard and Count Goetzen, the Prussian representative in the city, that "dwelt upon the intimate relations between the United States and Germany."[174]

At the launch of the *Imperator*, Mayor Burchard was at pains to emphasize that while HAPAG expanded it services around the globe, it did not wish to displace the shipping lines of other nations. On the contrary, it worked with them in a coordinated effort to increase the volume of trade and more effectively apply the power of capital, thereby serving "the course of our vigorous age." He claimed that the *Imperator* was "the creation of a highly-cultivated age of peace" and emphasized that the "peaceful might of the German Empire" was embodied in it. Mayor Schröder made the same point at the launch of the *Vaterland* even as he characterized the vessel – in relation to the challenges posed by the stormy waters of the North Atlantic – as "strong and with a fighting spirit" and claimed that while Germany had only thought of peace, it remained armed for war. The *Vaterland*, he proclaimed, would enter "into peaceful competition with the other nations … serve peaceful trade on the wide sea and more securely and closely bind the bonds of friendship between the peoples of the earth." Yet special attention was paid to the manner in which HAPAG's new trio would foster relations between the United States and Germany. At the launch of the *Vaterland*, Prince Rupprecht gave a short speech in which he pointed to the high purpose of a ship that was dedicated to bind Europe and America in peaceful endeavour. The *Imperator*, Mayor Burchard claimed, would also "bring two powerful continents closer together … facilitate the trade of two great nations," and "serve the peaceful development of civilization."

Yet if this characterization of the Empire seems explicitly intended for foreign powers, it was also, inevitably, a mirror held up to Germans. The speeches provided them not only with a sense that "Germany's standing abroad is tremendously elevated by these three ships and their success," as Mayor Predohl claimed. They also offered a vision of the way in which their nation was embedded in the world and how it participated in the various processes of globalization. Mayor Burchard claimed that the *Imperator* signified German enthusiasm for travel beyond the borders of the Empire. But while relatively few Germans enjoyed this privilege, the addresses made at the launch of the *Imperator*-class liners at least helped feed what was a "lively imagination of the world beyond the nation."[175]

VI

The ceremonies and speeches that marked the launch of the *Imperator*, *Vaterland*, and *Bismarck* staged social harmony and political consensus just as did those made at the launch of warships. Furthermore, reporting in the liberal and conservative press sometimes spoke of unanimous enthusiasm for the *Imperator*-class liners. It seems reasonable to assume that the various constituencies to which Hamburg's mayors addressed their remarks – HAPAG, Hamburg's commercial middle classes, the German bourgeoisie, and the Imperial monarchy – could look favourably on the speeches, and the vessels themselves, as reflecting their role and achievements in the German Empire. And yet, just as Germany was socially fractured, so enthusiasm for the *Imperator*-class liners was far from unanimous. As Corey Ross has emphasized, what Germans heard in public addresses, or read in the popular media, was mediated by class, locality, gender, and cultural milieu.[176] It should be no surprise that this extended to the *Imperator*.

Some critics were embarrassed by the outpouring of nationalist rhetoric that surrounded the liner. As we saw in chapter two, the *Imperator* ran aground in the Elbe on 22 April 1913 while on route to its sea trials. Perturbed by the excitement this caused, the German naval officer and journalist Count Ernst von Reventlow spoke of "the absurd tendency to make of the launch of the Imperator a national triumph." In his opinion, boasting about the liner before its sea trials was "unwise" and undignified.[177] Other criticism was more profound and questioned what it was that the *Imperator* actually symbolized. Lamar Cecil has argued that, to the Prussian aristocracy, HAPAG's liners were "only the effete and sensuous emblems of a decaying empire."[178] To be sure, there were those among the aristocracy and middle classes who thought that the *Imperator* was the embodiment of all the evils wrought by political, social, and cultural transformation.[179] Others felt it "appeared as a typical manifestation of the new Germany, with its huckstering, and obtrusive manners, more a snobbism than a symbol of German competence."[180] In chapter four, we will analyse the opinions of a group of middle-class intellectuals who thought the *Imperator*'s interior decoration was disappointingly unrepresentative of the advanced state of modern German art and design.[181]

More challenging to reconstruct are the opinions that circulated among the social constituency that was conspicuously absent from the speeches made at the launch of all three liners: the working classes and, more specifically, that "army of semi-skilled manual workers housed in the poorly plumbed, under-heated 'rent-barracks' of Hamburg's proletarian quarters."[182] In photographs taken of the vessels while under construction, the men whose hands actually built them are often absent. As noted in the previous chapter, many of these images are eerily devoid of any indication of physical labour and even any human presence; the *Imperator*-class liners seem to rise on the stocks of their own accord and without human agency. When workers appear, they often seem to be employed by the photographer as staffage for the purpose of emphasizing the enormity of the vessel on which they labour. As Darcy Grimaldo Grigsby has shown, the rhetoric of progress – seen here in photographs and also found in textual descriptions – hid social and economic realities.[183] Discussion of engineering projects that focused on scale overlooked the political and commercial motives that drove them, while engineering was promoted as altruistic and not exploitative. In a word, shipyard workers were written out of the history of the *Imperator*.

Unsurprisingly, they are mostly absent from photographs taken at the launch of the *Imperator*-class liners. There is, however, a particularly revealing picture that was taken at the launch of NDL's *Kronprinzessin Cecilie* on 1 December 1906. The image depicts the Kaiser and his entourage proceeding to the launch platform. Although the photograph is black and white, the crowd of well-dressed participants to the left is animated by the grey and white tones of their costume, hats, and waving handkerchiefs. They seem to be in motion, to be energized and excited by the event, with many stretching to get a glimpse of the Kaiser. The animation of these people is such that one can almost hear their voices. But looking more closely at the picture's background, the viewer discerns a group of workers, presumably employees of Vulcan, standing on scaffolding erected under the liner's bow. Their forms are obscured by their dark and presumably dirty clothing such that they seem to meld with the bow of the vessel their labour has built. And their reaction to the event is very different from that of the enthusiastic crowd gathered on the left: they stand solemnly, arms at their sides, seemingly unmoved by what they are witnessing. Moreover, they are visibly silent.[184]

It is using the example of shipyard workers that Jan Rüger demonstrates how spectators participated in the launch of a warship in complex and contradictory ways. In particular, he emphasizes that popular participation in these events did not mean popular enthusiasm for militarism and naval expansion. The photograph taken at the launch of the *Kronprinzessin Cecilie* suggests that something similar can be said of the launch of passenger liners. Our question is as follows: how did members of the working-classes respond to the launch of the *Imperator* and the symbolism of the vessel?

It was probably the case that a complement of shipyard workers was obliged by Vulcan to attend the launch. Yet their presence may also have been motivated by a variety of reasons born of genuine enthusiasm and interest. As we have seen, the launch of the *Imperator*-class liners was an important form of civic self-representation for the citizens and residents of Hamburg. Consequently, many of the workers in attendance may have been drawn by a sense of local pride. The mass media and the entertainment industry – "the new forces of media, leisure and entertainment" – played an important role in generating enthusiasm for the launch of warships.[185] Similarly – and especially given the large and enthusiastic volume of press coverage devoted to the *Imperator*-class liners, as well as the imposing physical and media presence of HAPAG in Hamburg – many working-class spectators may have attended the launches out of sheer curiosity. No matter what was said by Hamburg's mayors, a large number of these spectators must simply have been fascinated by the technological and visual spectacle of committing the largest vehicles ever built to their element.

At the same time, it seems to be among the working classes that enthusiasm for HAPAG's new liners was most clearly absent. Again with reference to the launch of warships, Rüger notes that, for whatever reason they attended these events, many workers agitated against naval enthusiasm.[186] Some are recorded as regarding naval pomp and ceremony as a waste of money; many were made redundant after a vessel's launch and saw these events as marking the loss of their employment.[187] Some of this discontent was acted out at launch ceremonies. When the battleship *Kaiser Karl der Große* was launched in Hamburg on 18 October 1899 in the presence of the Kaiser and Mayor Johann Georg Mönckeberg, Blohm & Voss employees threw sandwiches at the company's director.[188] What seems to be the case is that the launch of a warship could actually be "a site for the enactment of a 'counter public' or *Gegenöffentlichkeit*."[189]

Evidence suggests this was also the case at the launch of passenger liners. *The Manchester Guardian* reported that the Kaiser was enthusiastically cheered everywhere at the *Imperator*'s launch.[190] Yet this was definitely not the case. In fact, a "quiet, but effective, show of opposition" to Wilhelm marked the event; police reports recorded that the "workers of the Vulcan shipyard did not lift their hats nor did they cheer when his majesty passed."[191] Considerable circumstantial evidence suggests that many workers who attended the launch of the *Imperator* would not have responded enthusiastically to the rhetoric of the christening address. The construction of a "counter public" was underway long before, and apart from, the launch ceremony and must have conditioned the response of those members of the working classes who attended it.

The context in which HAPAG commissioned the *Imperator*-class liners was one of vibrant and combative industrial relations. The Social Democratic Party and the trade-union movement developed a significant presence in Hamburg in the late nineteenth century and articulated strident demands for social and political reform. By 1890, there were eighty-four trade unions in the city with approximately 40,000 members. These represented a variety of skilled and semi-skilled labor.[192] In the particular case of the merchant marine, industrial relations became a serious issue during the 1870s and various efforts were made to organize sailors, firemen, and trimmers during the strikes of 1888–1890.[193] These initiatives led to the founding of the *Verein der Heizer und Trimmer von Hamburg*, the *Seemanns-Verein zu Hamburg*, and the *Hamburger Werftarbeiterverband*. In 1898, these local unions combined to form the *Seemannsverband in Deutschland*. This soon boasted 3,000 members and, with the support of the Social Democratic Party, sought to improve the working conditions of those in the maritime trade.[194] Its organ was the newspaper *Der Seemann*, which was founded in 1897 and published editions of 4,000 copies at its height in 1902.[195] The *Seemannsverband* was integrated into the *Deutscher Transportarbeiter-Verband* in 1910.

The organization of maritime labour and the efforts made to improve its situation had a real impact. In 1893, the nautical journal *Hansa* claimed that the men employed in the engine rooms of Germany's merchant fleet had spread "social-democratic poison" among seamen.[196] Ten years later, the sociologist Ferdinand Tönnies argued that, among engine-room workers, a proletarian class consciousness was replacing the more corporate identity found among traditional seamen.[197] Hamburg police reports from the period are full of notes taken on conversations between workers voicing dissatisfaction with low pay and poor working conditions in shipyards, particularly those of Blohm & Voss, the builders of the *Vaterland* and *Bismarck*. In the opinion of one worker, the conditions at the company were "just like the army, but the treatment and the whole system is much worse."[198] And with increased class consciousness came action that expressed itself in the major strike of dock workers in Hamburg that began in November 1896. Further strikes followed in 1906 and 1907 and spread to New York City where 1,000 longshoremen employed by HAPAG joined the work stoppage.[199] This reached the point where several thousand foreign workers were brought in and were lodged, and provided for, on company vessels and in its warehouses. A strike also broke out in the Vulcan shipyard on 30 April 1912 when management threatened to lock out all those who stopped work on May Day.[200]

HAPAG took a strong stand against labour organization and was central to the coordination of a response to it. It was a member of the Association of Hamburg Shipping Companies that was formed to offer protection against organized labour's demands. The company also provided the stimulus for the foundation of the Central Association of German Shipping Companies in 1906. In addition, a *Hafenbetriebsverein* was organized to provide for the protection of the general interests of shipping firms and stevedores. During the strike of 1896–1897, HAPAG attempted to resolve the dispute by offering limited wage increases. But these were refused and, after weeks off the job, workers settled with the company for circumscribed gains.[201]

In July 1901, Ballin became chairman of the Association of Hamburg Shipping Companies. In this role, he took a hard line against the Social Democratic Party and labour unions, sharply condemning strikes by sailors and dockworkers. During the strike of 1906–1907, he moved against strikers who ultimately capitulated and agreed to a settlement that met only part of their demands.[202] Ballin also opposed attempts to organize made by HAPAG captains and engineers. *Seefahrt*, the magazine of the *Verein der Kapitäne und Offiziere der Handelsmarine in Hamburg*, stated that many in its circle saw Ballin as "an opponent of our endeavours to improve our social situation."[203] In short, due to effective organization, and in cooperation with other steamship lines, HAPAG was able to overcome the challenge of labour agitation without lasting disruption of its business.

Der Seemann published continual criticism of the Association of Hamburg Shipping Companies and once referred to Ballin as a "capitalist beast."[204] It has been argued, however, that during the strikes of 1896–1897 and 1906–1907, Ballin's attitude was less rigid than that of other shipping magnates. While trade unions may have been "a thorn in the eye" for HAPAG's managing director, he was willing to negotiate with his company's employees.[205] Thus it would seem that, while an adversary of organized labour, Ballin was not an intractable enemy of the working classes per se. In fact, one might even expect him to be sympathetic to their demands given his own humble beginnings. In a history of HAPAG published in 1911, Adolph Goetz stated that Ballin made sincere efforts to improve the well-being of his employees and that the latter acknowledged this. The author claimed that the managing director often came face to face with workers during strikes but "never encountered an unfriendly word."[206]

All the same, HAPAG did much to hide the nature of industrial relations and the manner in which they affected the company. On the one hand, it made an effort to keep the reality of labour conditions, especially in the engine rooms of its steamships, from becoming public knowledge. But this posed a particular problem for HAPAG. As Bernhard Rieger notes, the depiction of engine rooms proved a challenge for company advertising.[207] While publicity emphasized the size and power of the machinery that drove the *Imperator* and *Vaterland*, it said almost nothing about the workforce that operated this equipment.[208] As with photographs of the liners under construction, stokers and trimmers are either absent from images of their engines and boilers or they are present only as staffage emphasizing their enormity. These images provide no explicit indication of the hot, dirty, exhausting work that operating this technology demanded. As Rieger has argued, this amounted to the deliberate production of ignorance about steamship labour.[209]

On the other hand, HAPAG represented itself as a fair and equitable employer. Along with Ballin's opposition to labour organization went a "paternalist attitude" and a commitment to providing social benefits to the company's employees.[210] In fact, HAPAG claimed that it provided for the welfare of its workers more thoroughly than did many other shipping lines. It emphasized that they benefited from health insurance, as well as the accident, disability, and old-age insurance provided by the state. And HAPAG was proud of its pension fund for ships' officers, machinists, and administrative staff. A company history published in 1907 explained that the "disability-, widows-, and orphans-pension fund" that it founded in 1888 was so well endowed "that it has not been necessary to draw upon the contributions of the members for all pension payments until today."[211] Speaking of industrial relations and its workforce, the company explained that:

> the agitation of the leaders has incessantly endeavoured to prevent this important group of colleagues from feeling themselves as aids and allies in a common enterprise. Relations with dockworkers, longshoremen and ships' crews have become evermore difficult in the last ten years. At the same time, wages, working conditions and provisions for welfare have steadily and considerably improved with the growth of the entire enterprise and as the result of the company's own initiative.[212]

Efforts in aid of company employees included the fund-raising ball held aboard the *Imperator* on its crossing to New York in September 1913. This raised $4,798 for the relief of destitute families of German seamen. It seems, however, a small sum given press reports that many people of "exceptional wealth" were in attendance whose combined fortunes amounted to $850,000,000.[213]

Ultimately, the point to be made is that, given the state of industrial relations, it is hardly surprising that the response of working-class participants at the launch of the *Imperator* was subdued. The same was true of the Social Democratic press. Social Democrats often criticized Hamburg's shipyards and shipping companies as harsh employers. In 1910, a Social Democratic member of the Reichstag "castigated shipping companies for their disregard of workers' security in the face of frequent deaths and mutilations."[214] But when it came to passenger liners themselves, Social Democratic newspapers often remained silent. This tactic "allowed them to escape accusations of national betrayal and lack of patriotism without compromising their commitment to social-reform programs."[215] *Vorwärts*, Essen's *Arbeiter Zeitung*, and the *Leipziger Volkszeitung* did not report on the launch of the *Imperator* and *Vaterland*.

The *Hamburger Echo*, however, was an exception. In keeping with other Hamburg newspapers, the *Echo* published articles that related details about the building and launch of the *Imperator*-class liners. It did so, however, with less frequency and less enthusiasm.[216] It also resented the attempt made at the launch of the *Imperator* to orchestrate observers as willing subjects of the Empire and to distract Germans from significant political and social problems.[217] Yet what really characterizes the *Echo*'s coverage as distinct is that it viewed the building of the liner through the prism of workers' rights and labour relations.[218] In contrast to the praise for the vessel in the liberal and conservative press, the paper denounced it as an expression of class inequality. It emphasized that the construction of the *Imperator* had advanced so rapidly because of "unprecedented exertions" by the shipyard workers and "senseless haste." The latter, in particular, had resulted in the death of ten men and injury to 100 others; "death has reaped a rich harvest amongst the workers."[219] This tragedy, the paper asserted, should make the directors of Vulcan aware of the fact that much is still to be done to protect the health and welfare of its workers. Only when steps were taken to do so, would there really be cause for pride in the construction of such a vessel. But all of this, the paper claimed, meant nothing to HAPAG and the Kaiser who was eager to christen the liner. Of course, the *Echo* pointed out, while praising the Kaiser whose only act was to break a bottle of champagne on the liner's bow, Mayor Burchard made no mention of those who actually built the ship and those who lost their lives doing so. The reward of the latter was not honour and decorations but "broken bones."

The *Echo* also questioned whether the provisions HAPAG had made for the crew, who were essential to the *Imperator*'s operation, were sufficient for their well-being in terms of accommodation and working conditions. Here, it is interesting to note that labour discontent and unrest extended to life aboard the *Imperator* and *Vaterland*. While company advertising claimed all Germans felt at home aboard the *Imperator*, this was not the case for many of its stewards, engineers, machinists, stokers, and trimmers. Those members of the crew who worked in the engine rooms laboured in dangerous conditions and were often injured on the job.[220] In fact, their workplace environment was so horrendous that some committed suicide by jumping overboard in mid-ocean.[221] But suicide was not restricted to those who toiled in the bowels of a transatlantic liner. *The New York Times*, for example, reported that a stewardess aboard NDL's *Kaiser Wilhelm der Große* jumped to her death during the liner's maiden voyage in 1897. It did not, however, speculate as to her motivations.[222]

The press in Britain and the United States reported that some of the crew members aboard the *Imperator*, dissatisfied with their working conditions, had committed acts of "irreparable damage" to its furnishings and water system before the vessel departed on its maiden voyage.[223] *The New York Times*, for example, claimed that carpets, pictures, and other furnishings "have been wantonly cut and slashed to such an extent as utterly to ruin them, and that liquid cement has been poured into the water pipes and allowed to harden rendering the water system useless." It was also suggested that labourers at work on the liner had taken revenge on it because, being accommodated on a comparatively desolate part of the coast near Cuxhaven, they were "cut off from their ordinary pleasures." In addition, the paper noted that there were complaints about inadequate and unsanitary quarters for the crew.[224]

In response, HAPAG released a statement that all such claims of sabotage aboard the *Imperator* were false.[225] In England, *The Times* and *The Manchester Guardian* published a telegram from the company stating that both it and Vulcan were "anxious in the interests of the working classes emphatically to state that nothing of the kind has occurred and that all the rumours are pure inventions."[226] As for complaints with respect to working and living conditions aboard the *Imperator*, it was reported that HAPAG would investigate the situation but that the company believed the crew's accommodation was as fine as on any transatlantic liner. Ultimately, the company claimed there was no merit in charges made by crew members that their quarters were inadequate and unsanitary.[227] And, as always, HAPAG claimed that negative reporting about the liner in the foreign press was intentionally designed to damage its image.[228]

Yet this did not alter the situation. In Canada, *The Globe* reported that, upon the liner's first arrival in New York, 1,000 crew members held a meeting in Hoboken and adopted a resolution that was presented to Commodore Ruser. This denounced working conditions aboard the vessel and demanded "better food, better sleeping accommodation and a nine-hour day." Speakers at the meeting claimed that crew members were "treated like pigs"; they were poorly fed, overworked, and their quarters overcrowded.[229] "Sixteen hours work a day," the statement claimed, "was not unusual, and the sanitary equipment inadequate." Those supporting the resolution included stewards, pastry cooks, coal trimmers, and firemen.

The *New-York Tribune* reported on rumours of dissatisfaction among stewards aboard the *Vaterland* with respect to wages, food, and accommodation.[230] It was claimed that Commodore Ruser had made it clear that any refusal to work, or any departure from the liner, would be considered desertion and dealt with accordingly by the German government.[231] Nonetheless, the *Vaterland* experienced a series of strikes and protests during May 1914 in which the Syndicalist Industrial Association of Hamburg and Vicinity played a role. These lasted until the outbreak of war in August but were neither supported by the Social Democratic Association of Transport Workers nor the *Hamburger Echo*.[232]

Labour unrest in and around the *Imperator* and *Vaterland*, along with contradictory and even antagonistic responses to their symbolic function, are hardly surprising. And they do nothing to diminish the importance of the liners' presence and role in Germany's popular culture. On the contrary, such reactions only serve to highlight the significance that they assumed in the eyes of many Germans. While emphasizing that the vessels were widely perceived as national monuments of some sort, they accentuate their composite and complex symbolic working in the discourses of national identity and the debate over the symbols of nationhood that characterized Imperial Germany.

VII

The extensive publicity and media coverage that surrounded the construction and launch of the *Imperator*-class liners inspired many Germans to see them with their own eyes once they were afloat. Large crowds turned out on the occasion of the *Imperator*'s first docking in Hamburg. This occurred following completion of its outfitting and preceding its sea trials in April 1913. As one journalist described the scene, on what would otherwise have been a quiet Sunday in the Kuhwärder Harbour, numerous small craft jostled for position on the water so that photographers could get their best shots of the "spectacle."[233] As with the vessel's launch, commentators referred to this event in these terms and explicitly described it as "theatre." Photographs show that large crowds also turned out to watch the *Imperator* depart Hamburg for its sea trials.[234] And, on 28 May 1913, just prior to its maiden voyage, the liner was opened to public inspection at Cuxhaven and was visited by 3,000 people.[235]

In a similar scene, thousands of spectators cheered the *Vaterland* as it was towed out of Hamburg on the afternoon of 25 April 1914 for its sea trials.[236] In fact, it was reported that so many people made their way to the banks of the Elbe that trams and trains could barely cope with their numbers.[237] The *Hamburger Nachrichten* described a scene of excited festivity in which postcard vendors did a brisk business as did the sellers of "*Vaterland* chocolates."[238] One wonders if music such as the Ragtime tune entitled the *Imperator Marsch*, composed by Bruno Kohlmetz in 1912 and dedicated to Albert Ballin, entertained those who participated in these events.[239]

In addition to attracting the interest of the general public, dignitaries from Hamburg and the Imperial government continued to play a role in the major events that marked the careers of the new liners up until and including their maiden voyages. Here again, the vessels were surrounded with rhetoric that construed them as national monuments. For example, in early May 1914, HAPAG invited the members of the Reichstag and Bundesrat to visit the *Vaterland*. While the Social Democratic representatives declined the invitation, 140 members from both houses were conveyed by a special train from Hamburg to Cuxhaven on 3 May. There they spent the better part of two days aboard the liner and were accommodated in first-class cabins. The party toured the vessel and ate in the first-class dining room. They also heard a speech from Max Schinckel, chair of HAPAG's board of directors, in which he described the *Vaterland* as "an agent of cultural connections between its homeland and the wider world." The liner, he explained, was but one part of a merchant marine sailing the world's oceans, calling at its ports, and demonstrating that "in the areas of industry, trade, and commerce, as also in the realm of national culture, Germany took second place to no other nation."[240] The Secretary of the Interior, Clemens von Delbrück, responded to Schinckel's address saying that the

Reichstag and Bundesrat were proud that the liner carried "a part of Germany" over the Atlantic Ocean. The members of both houses believed that it bore testimony to "German skill and volition" and "the power and greatness of our Fatherland."[241]

The *Vaterland*'s third and final sea trial took place on 10 and 11 May with approximately 120 distinguished guests on board. These included Crown Prince Franz of Bavaria, several military officials, members of Hamburg's senate and citizens' assembly, and representatives of the city's chamber of commerce. The party was hosted by Albert Ballin. Central to the festivities was a speech by Crown Prince Franz in which he claimed that, while he had read and heard much praise for the *Vaterland*, "all his expectations were surpassed." He hoped the liner would "proclaim the glory of the German name abroad."[242]

Just a few days later, on 14 May, "an enormous concourse of spectators lined the new 'America' quays at Cuxhaven to wave good-bye" as the *Vaterland* departed on its maiden voyage to New York.[243] There, as we will see in chapter six, it was greeted with great enthusiasm, just as the *Imperator* had been. *The New York Times* stated that "she fairly represents the genius of the German people, their enterprise and thrift, their determination to do in the best way possible whatever is worth doing."[244] This is precisely the message with which Germans were presented from the early days of the *Vaterland*'s construction. Now they heard its echo from across the Atlantic as German newspapers, especially in Hamburg, summarized the glowing reports that appeared in the American press. These included the often-expressed opinion that the *Imperator* and *Vaterland* symbolized the incredible achievements of German shipbuilding, engineering, industry, trade, and commerce.[245]

And yet this news came as a partial disappointment to a small, but influential group of Germans who took a special interest in the *Imperator*-class liners. This included the architect and designer Bruno Paul; the art historian and critic Karl Scheffler; the architect Fritz Schumacher; and the pioneering art and cultural historian Aby Warburg. In opposition to much popular enthusiasm, these intellectuals and artists saw the *Imperator*, in particular, as the embodiment of a failed cultural politics. In their eyes, a literally monumental opportunity to showcase contemporary German art and interior design to an international public had been lost. More importantly, the *Imperator* failed to present a true image of Germany to the Atlantic world. The story of this group's criticism of the liner, along with the way they "pictured" or imagined its possible transformation, serves to accentuate the importance it assumed as a national monument. It also introduces the principal theme explored in chapters five and six: the complex ways in which German national identity was constructed, interpreted, and contested in an international context.

Notes

1 "Death Comes Close to German Emperor", *The Detroit News*, 23 May 1912.
2 "Imperator Launched; Kaiser Escapes Peril", *The Sun* (New York), 24 May 1912.
3 Warburg Institute Archive. General Correspondence. Max Warburg to Warburg, 25 May 1912.
4 Jan Rüger, *The Great Naval Game: Britain and Germany in the Age of Empire* (Cambridge, 2007), 37.

5 James Retallack, "Looking Forward", in James Retallack, ed., *Imperial Germany 1871–1918* (Oxford, 2008), 268.

6 Heide Gerstenberger and Ulrich Welke, *Vom Wind zum Dampf: Sozialgeschichte der deutschen Handelsschiffahrt im Zeitalter der Industrialisierung* (Münster, 1996), 260.

7 Rudy Koshar, *From Monuments to Traces: Artifacts of German Memory, 1870–1990* (Berkeley, CA, Los Angeles, CA, and London, 2000), 48f.

8 Kirsten Belgum, *Popularizing the Nation: Audience, Representation, and the Production of Identity in Die Gartenlaube, 1853–1900* (Lincoln, NE, 1998).

9 G.R., "Die erste Fahrt der Vaterland", *Hamburger Nachrichten*, 17 May 1914.

10 See the opinions of Gorch Fock in Jörgen Bracker, "Dampfer Imperator; das reisige Friedenschiff", in Volker Plagemann, ed., *Industriekultur in Hamburg: des Deutschen Reiches Tor zur Welt* (Munich, 1984), 64.

11 Hugo Freiherr von Freytag-Loringhoven quoted in Lamar Cecil, *Albert Ballin: Business and Politics in Imperial Germany, 1888–1918* (Princeton, NJ, 1967), 110.

12 William H. Miller, *The First Great Ocean Liners in Photographs* (New York, 1984), 39.

13 Bernhard Rieger, *Technology and the Culture of Modernity in Britain and Germany, 1890–1945* (Cambridge, 2005), 163.

14 Volker Plagemann, "Kultur, Wissenschaft, Ideologie", in Volker Plagemann, ed., *Übersee. Seefahrt und Seemacht im deutschen Kaiserreich* (Munich, 1988), 308.

15 Philipp Harjes, *Eine Reise nach dem Lande wo die Arbeit adelt* (Gotha, 1905).

16 Bernhard Huldermann, *Albert Ballin* (Oldenburg and Berlin, 1922), 73.

17 Huldermann, *Albert Ballin*, 73.

18 "Reassuring the Germans", *The Washington Post*, 27 April 1902.

19 "German Lines Cautious", *The Washington Post*, 26 January 1902.

20 HAPAG, *Die Hamburg-Amerika Linie: Im Sechsten Jahrzehnt Ihrer Entwicklung 1897–1907* (Berlin, 1907), 85f.

21 See "Reassuring the Germans", *The Washington Post*, 27 April 1902.

22 See "Reassuring the Germans"; "Viéws of Herr Ballin", *The New York Times*, 12 November 1901.

23 HAPAG, *Die Hamburg-Amerika Linie*, 117.

24 Plagemann, "Kultur", 299–308.

25 NDL, *Die Fortschritte des Deutschen Schiffbaus* (Berlin, 1909).

26 Julius Hirschberg, *Um die Erde* (Leipzig, 1894), 3–26.

27 Quoted in Plagemann, "Kultur", 302.

28 See Helmut R. Leppien, "Marinemalerei zu Kaisers Zeiten", in Plagemann, ed., *Übersee*, 342ff.

29 Matthew Fitzpatrick, "Narrating Empire: *Die Gartenlaube* and Germany's Nineteenth-Century Liberal Expansionism", *German Studies Review* 30 (February 2007), 97–120; see also Belgum, *Popularizing*.

30 See Belgum, *Popularizing*.

31 Belgum, *Popularizing*, 98.

32 Koshar, *From Monuments*, 48f.

33 See for example Max Buchwald, "Die Entwicklung der Welthandelsflotte", *Illustrirte Zeitung* (Leipzig) 142 (7 May 1914), 1007; "Feuerschutz auf Riesendampfern", *Arena: Oktav-Ausgabe von Über Land und Meer* 30 (May 1914), 1631–4; the latter featured a photograph of the fire protection equipment installed on the bridge of the *Imperator*.

34 See Arnold Kludas, *Die Geschichte der deutschen Passagierschiffahrt* (Hamburg, 1986), vol. 1, 14ff.

35 Miller, *The First Great Ocean Liners*, 14.

36 Rieger, *Technology*, 163.

37 Eduard Rosenbaum, "Albert Ballin: A Note on the Style of His Economic and Political Activities", *Leo Baeck Institute Yearbook* 3 (London, 1958), 262.
38 See Jens Bove, ed., *Oswald Lübeck: Bord- und Reisefotografie 1909–1914* (Dresden, 2011).
39 HAPAG, *Die Hamburg-Amerika Linie*, 134f.
40 HAPAG, *Die Hamburg-Amerika Linie*, 7.
41 HAPAG, *Die Hamburg-Amerika Linie*, 146.
42 HAPAG, *Die Hamburg-Amerika Linie*, 144.
43 Quoted in Rosenbaum, "Albert Ballin", 271.
44 Huldermann, *Albert Ballin*, 291.
45 HAPAG, *Die Hamburg-Amerika Linie*, 7.
46 HAPAG, *Die Hamburg-Amerika Linie*, 118.
47 HAPAG, *Die Hamburg-Amerika Linie*, 7.
48 For examples see Olaf Matthes and Carsten Prange, eds., *Hamburg und die HAPAG: Seefahrt im Plakat* (Hamburg, 2000).
49 See Matthes and Prange, eds., *Hamburg*.
50 Sebastian Conrad, *Globalization and the Nation in Imperial Germany* (Cambridge, 2010), 67; see also Sebastian Conrad, "Wilhelmine Nationalism in Global Contexts. Mobility, Race, and Global Consciousness", in Sven Oliver Müller and Cornelius Torp, eds., *Imperial Germany Revisited: Continuing Debates and New Perspectives* (New York and Oxford, 2011), 281–96.
51 Harjes, *Eine Reise*.
52 "Ein zweites Modell des Vierschraubenschnelldampfers Imperator", *Zeitschrift der Hamburg-Amerika Linie* 10 (5 September 1911), 85.
53 See "Ein Riesenmodell des 'Imperator'", *Hansa: Deutsche nautische Zeitschrift* 48 (10 June 1911), 431f.
54 "Ein Riesenmodell", 431f.
55 "Imperator-Medaille", *Zeitschrift der Hamburg-Amerika Linie* 12 (5 July 1913), 98.
56 Royal Museums Greenwich. Coins and Medals. MEC2196.
57 Les Streater, *Berengaria: Cunard's "Happy Ship"* (Charleston, SC, 2001), 13.
58 See Arnold Kludas, *Die Geschichte der Hapag-Schiffe* (Bremen, 2007), vol. 1, 95 and 128.
59 For a discussion of advertising, see Dagmar Bellmann, *Von Höllengefährten zu schwimmenden Palästen. Die Passagierschiffahrt auf dem Atlantik (1840–1930)* (Frankfurt and New York, 2015), 157–83.
60 See Kludas, *Die Geschichte der Hapag-Schiffe* (Bremen, 2008), vol. 2, 160.
61 See Kludas, *Die Geschichte der Hapag-Schiffe*, vol. 1, 98.
62 Frederick A. Talbot, *Steamship Conquest of the World* (London, 1912), 79.
63 Arnold Kludas, "Die Passagierschiffahrt", in Plagemann, ed., *Übersee*, 162.
64 HAPAG, *Marine Monsters* (New York, n.d.), u.p.
65 Reproduced in "Largest Steamer in the World", *The Washington Post*, 17 March 1912.
66 Reproduced in "Largest Steamer in the World", *The Washington Post*, 17 March 1912.
67 HAPAG, *Marine Monsters*, u.p.
68 See Rieger, *Technology*.
69 Rieger, *Technology*, 18.
70 See Gerhard Kaufmann, "Postkarten von Überseedampfern", in Plagemann, ed., *Übersee*, 328.
71 Christiane Harzig, "Gender, Transatlantic Space, and the Presence of German-Speaking People in North America", in Thomas Adam and Ruth Gross, eds., *Traveling between Worlds: German-American Encounters* (College Station, TX, 2006), 168.
72 See Kaufmann, "Postkarten", 325–9.

73 See Kaufmann, "Postkarten".
74 See Kaufmann, "Postkarten", 326.
75 Rudy Koshar, *German Travel Cultures* (Oxford and New York, 2000), 48.
76 HAPAG, *Dampfer Imperator: Das Grösste Schiff der Welt* (Hamburg, n.d.), 9.
77 HAPAG, *Dampfer Imperator*, 5.
78 HAPAG, *Dampfer Imperator*, 6.
79 Bellmann, *Von Höllengefährten*, 176.
80 Hans Ossig, "Die erste Imperatorfahrt – II", *Neue Hamburger Zeitung*, 16 June 1913.
81 See for example "Nachrichten über Shciffe", *Schiffbau* 13 (12 June 1912), 703f; "Nachrichten über Shciffe", *Schiffbau* 14 (23 April 1913), 606f; "Der Stapellaufe des 'Imperator'", *Hansa: Deutsche nautische Zeitschrift* 49 (1 June 1912), 455f.
82 See for example H. Thurn, "Die funkentelegraphischen Einrichtungen des Dampfers 'Imperator'", *Schiffbau* 14 (26 November 1913); "Telefunken an Bord des 'Imperator'", *Jahrbuch der Schiffbautechnischen Gesellschaft* 15 (1914), 394–433.
83 See for example, R. Schmidt, "Imperator", *Schiffbau* 13 (10 July 1912), 755–64; "Der Turbinenschnelldampfer 'Imperator'", *Schiffbau* 14 (25 June 1913), 759–65.
84 L. Wachtel, "Der Vierschrauben-Turbinen-Schnelldampfer 'Imperator'", *Zeitschrift des Vereines Deutscher Ingenieure* (20 June 1914), 993–1006.
85 See "Imperator", *Schiffbau* 13 (10 July 1912); "Der Turbinenschnelldampfer 'Imperator'", *Schiffbau* 14 (25 June 1913).
86 See for example "Der Turbinenschnelldampfer 'Imperator' der Hamburg-Amerika-Linie", *Zeitschrift des Vereines Deutscher Ingenieure* 56 (1 June 1912), 889f; "Der Turbinenschnelldampfer 'Vaterland' der Hamburg-Amerika-Linie", *Zeitschrift des Vereines Deutscher Ingenieure* 58 (9 May 1914), 763f.
87 "Die deutsche Handelsmarine im Jahre 1911", *Jahrbuch für Deutschlands Seeinteressen* 14 (1912), 384.
88 "Auf der ersten Reise des 'Imperator'", *Hansa: Deutsche nautische Zeitschrift* 50 (21 June 1913), 525.
89 Rieger, *Technology*, 8.
90 Maiken Umbach, *German Cities and Bourgeois Modernism* (Oxford, 2009).
91 Reproduced in "Largest Steamer in the World", *The Washington Post*, 17 March 1912.
92 G.R., "Die erste Fahrt der Vaterland", *Hamburger Nachrichten*, 17 May 1914.
93 *Berliner Illustrirte Zeitung* 21 (2 June 1912).
94 See for example *Berliner Illustrirte Zeitung* 23 (19 July 1914), 554.
95 "Vom Stapellauf des auf der Vulkan-Werft in Hamburg für die Hamburg-Amerika-Linie erbauten 'Imperator', des größten Schiffes der Welt, am 23. Mai", *Illustrirte Zeitung* (Leipzig) 140 (30 May 1912), 1116.
96 "Die erste Fahrt des Riesendampfers 'Imperator'", *Illustrirte Zeitung* (Leipzig) 140 (1 May 1913), 1200; "Der Riesendampfer 'Vaterland'", *Illustrirte Zeitung* (Leipzig) 140 (10 April 1913), 923.
97 "Eine moderne Arche Noah", *Illustrirte Zeitung* (Leipzig) 142 (28 May 1914), 1185f.
98 See for example "Von Wachstum des Riesendampfers", *Hamburger Fremdenblatt*, 1 August 1912.
99 Philipp Berges, "Eine schwimmende Insel – das größte Schiff der Welt", *Hamburger Fremdenblatt*, 19 March 1911.
100 "Der kommende Riesendampfer der Hamburg-Amerika Linie", *Hamburgischer Correspondent*, 8 November 1910.
101 "Der neue Riesendampfer der Hamburg-Amerika Linie", *Hamburger Fremdenblatt*, 2 April 1911.
102 Berges, "Eine schwimmende Insel".

103 "Die 'Imperator' Aufstellung auf der Diele des 'Hamburger Fremdenblattes'", *Hamburger Fremdenblatt*, 8 June 1912.
104 "Kurze Angaben über den Dampfer 'Vaterland'", *Hamburger Fremdenblatt*, 8 and 9 May 1914.
105 F.R., "Die Inneneinrichtung des 'Imperators'", *Hamburger Fremdenblatt*, 10 June 1913.
106 See for example "Der Stapellauf des 'Imperator'", *Hamburger Fremdenblatt*, 24 May 1912.
107 "Imperator", *Hamburgischer Correspondent*, 23 March 1912.
108 "Zum Stapelleauf des Imperator", *Hamburger Nachrichten*, 23 May 1912.
109 "'Der Imperator': Zum Stapellauf des größten Schiffes der Welt", *Hamburger Fremdenblatt*, 23 May 1912.
110 "Imperator", *Hamburgischer Correspondent*, 23 March 1912.
111 "Von der Jungfernreise der 'Vaterland'", *Hamburger Fremdenblatt*, 19 May 1914.
112 "Der Stapellauf des 'Imperator'", *Hamburger Fremdenblatt*, 24 May 1912.
113 "Der Stapellauf des Imperator", *Hamburger Nachrichten*, 23 May 1912.
114 Hans Ossig, "Die erste Imperatorfahrt – II", *Neue Hamburger Zeitung*, 16 June 1913.
115 See for example "Vaterland", *Hamburger Nachrichten*, 4 April 1913.
116 "Von der Jungfernreise der 'Vaterland'", *Hamburger Fremdenblatt*, 19 May 1914.
117 "Auf Befehl Seiner Majestät des Kaisers taufe ich dich Bismarck", *Hamburgischer Correspondent*, 20 June 1914.
118 See "Der Stapellauf des Riesendampfers Bismarck", *Hamburger Nachrichten*, 20 June 1914.
119 "Der Stapellauf des Riesendampfers Bismarck", *Hamburger Nachrichten*, 20 June 1914.
120 "Von der Jungfernreise der 'Vaterland'", *Hamburger Fremdenblatt*, 19 May 1914.
121 "Die erste Fahrt des Imperator", *Hamburgischer Correspondent*, 15 June 1913.
122 "Der Stapellauf des Imperator", *Hamburger Nachrichten*, 23 May 1912.
123 See for example "Imperator", *Neue Hamburger Zeitung*, 23 May 1912.
124 See for example Berges, "Eine schwimmende Insel".
125 "Von der Jungfernreise der 'Vaterland'", *Hamburger Fremdenblatt*, 19 May 1914.
126 Rieger, *Technology*, 229 and 183–4.
127 Oscar Bongard, "Auf dem 'Imperator' nach Amerika", *Berliner Tageblatt*, 8 July 1913.
128 "Das neue deutsche Riesenschiff vor dem Stapellauf", *Kölnische Zeitung*, 3 April 1913.
129 "Das neue deutsche Riesenschiff vor dem Stapellauf", *Kölnische Zeitung*, 3 April 1913.
130 "Stapellauf des Riesendampfers 'Imperator'", *Berliner Tageblatt*, 23 May 1912.
131 "Der reisefertige 'Imperator'", *Berliner Tageblatt*, 11 June 1913.
132 "Der Stapellauf des Imperators", *Allgemeine Zeitung* (Mainz), 1 June 1912.
133 "Aus anderen Blättern", *Hamburgischer Correspondent*, 22 June 1914.
134 Hapag-Lloyd Archive: 1.5.14; 8.5.14; 12.4.13; 22.6.14; 25.6.14; 26.5.14.
135 See Jens Bove, *Oswald Lübeck: Bord-und Reisefotografien 1909–1914* (Dresden, 2011).
136 "The Imperator", *Daily Chronicle* (London), 24 May 1912.
137 See for example "Der Stapellauf des 'Imperator'", *Hamburger Fremdenblatt*, 24 May 1912.
138 See for example "Der Kaiser beim Stapellauf des Risendampfers 'Bismarck'", *Tägliche Rundschau* (Berlin), 20 June 1914.
139 "Zum Stapellauf des Imperator'", *Tägliche Rundschau* (Berlin), 24 May 1912.
140 See for example the *Vossische Zeitung* (Berlin), 24 May 1912.
141 "Giant Liner Is Launched", *The Washington Post*, 24 May 1912; "Kaiser at Launching of Greatest Liner", *The New York Times*, 24 May 1912.

142 Rüger, *The Great Naval Game*, 87.
143 Rüger, *The Great Naval Game*, 64.
144 Rüger, *The Great Naval Game*, 1.
145 Rüger, *The Great Naval Game*, 69f.
146 Peter Franz Stubmann, *Ballin: Leben und Werk eines deutschen Reeders* (Berlin-Grunewald, 1926), 250.
147 Miller, *The First Great Ocean Liners*, 73.
148 "Der Stapellauf des Riesendampfers Bismarck", *Hamburger Nachrichten*, 20 June 1914.
149 Rüger, *The Great Naval Game*, 110.
150 Miller, *The First Great Ocean Liners*, 63; see also Peter Zerbe, *Die Grossen Deutschen Passagierschiffe: Imperator, Vaterland, Bismarck* (Hamburg, 1999), 17.
151 "Der Stapellauf des Dampfers Imperator", *Zeitschrift der Hamburg-Amerika Linie* 11 (5 June 1912), 60.
152 See for example "Zum Stapellauf des 'Imperator'", *Tägliche Rundschau* (Berlin), 24 May 1912.
153 Clas Broder Hansen, "Schiffstaufen", in Plagemann, ed., *Übersee*, 142.
154 I have relied on the following sources for these speeches: "Der Stapellauf des Imperator", *Hamburger Nachrichten*, 23 May 1912; "Der Stapellauf des Imperator", *Hamburger Fremdenblatt*, 24 May 1912; "Stapellauf des Riesendampfers Vaterland", *Hamburger Fremdenblatt*, 4 April 1913; "Der Kaiser beim Stapellauf des Dampfers Bismarck", *Hamburger Fremdenblatt*, 21 June 1914.
155 Rüger, *The Great Naval Game*, 146.
156 Rüger, *The Great Naval Game*, 128.
157 Rüger, *The Great Naval Game*, 127.
158 "The Imperator", *Daily Chronicle* (London), 24 May 1912.
159 Burchard also gave the christening address at this launch.
160 Jason Tebbe, "Revision and 'Rebirth' Commemoration of the Battle of Nations in Leipzig", *German Studies Review* 33 (2010), 627; see also Celia Applegate, *A Nation of Provincials* (Berkeley, CA, 1990); Jennifer Jenkins, *Provincial Modernity. Local Cultural and Liberal Politics in Fin-de-Siècle Hamburg* (Ithaca, NY and London, 2003); Alon Confino, *Germany as a Culture of Remembrance* (Chapel Hill, NC, 2006).
161 Mark Russell, "The Building of Hamburg's Bismarck Memorial", *The Historical Journal* 43 (2000), 133–56.
162 See Matthew P. Fitzpatrick, *Liberal Imperialism in Germany: Expansion and Nationalism 1848–1884* (New York, 2008).
163 Rüger, *The Great Naval Game*, 99.
164 Rüger, *The Great Naval Game*, 101, nte. 39.
165 "Giant Liner Is Launched", *The Washington Post*, 24 May 1912.
166 Quoted in Rieger, *Technology*, 243.
167 "German Liner Launched", *The New York Times*, 11 January 1900; "Germany's Sea Power", *The Washington Post*, 11 January 1900.
168 Tebbe, "Revision", 630f.
169 For a summary of the subject of bourgeois reform, and bibliography, see Edward Ross Dickinson, "The bourgeoisie and reform", in James Retallack, ed., *Imperial Germany 1871–1918* (Oxford, 2008), 151–73.
170 Rüger, *The Great Naval Game*, 99.
171 Tebbe, "Revision", 627.
172 See Robin Lenman, *Artists and Society in Germany, 1850–1914* (Manchester and New York, 1997), 38f.
173 "German Liner Launched", *The New York Times*, 11 January 1900.
174 "New Liner Launched", *The Washington Post*, 28 September 1908.
175 Michael Geyer, "Where Germans Dwell: Transnationalism in Theory and Practice", *German Studies Association Newsletter* 31 (Winter 2006), 32.

176   Corey Ross, *Media and the Making of Modern Germany: Mass Communications, Society, and Politics from the Empire to the Third Reich* (Oxford, 2008).

177   "Expert Censures Imperator Talk", *Christian Science Monitor* (Boston), 24 May 1913; see also "German Interest in the Imperator", *The Manchester Guardian*, 6 May 1913.

178   Cecil, *Albert Ballin*, 110.

179   See the opinions of Gorch Fock in Jörgen Bracker, "Dampfer Imperator; das reisige Friedenschiff", in Plagemann, ed., *Industriekultur*, 64.

180   Hugo Freiherr von Freytag-Loringhoven quoted in Lamar Cecil, *Albert Ballin*, 110.

181   See Mark A. Russell, "Picturing the *Imperator*: Passenger Shipping as Art and National Symbol in the German Empire", *Central European History* 44 (2011), 227–56.

182   Niall Ferguson, *Paper and Iron: Hamburg Business and German Politics in the Era of Inflation, 1897–1927* (Cambridge, 1995), 31.

183   Darcy Grimaldo Grigsby, *Colossal: Engineering the Suez Canal, Statue of Liberty, Eiffel Tower, and Panama Canal* (Pittsburgh, PA, 2012).

184   See Kludas, *Die Geschichte der deutschen Passagierschiffahrt* (Hamburg, 1987), vol. 2, 170.

185   Rüger, *The Great Naval Game*, 87.

186   Rüger, *The Great Naval Game*, 122.

187   Rüger, *The Great Naval Game*, 107.

188   Rüger, *The Great Naval Game*, 108.

189   Rüger, *The Great Naval Game*, 109.

190   "Largest Liner Launched at Hamburg", *The Manchester Guardian*, 24 May 1912.

191   "Largest Liner Launched at Hamburg", *The Manchester Guardian*, 24 May 1912; see also Staatsarchiv der Freien und Hansestadt Hamburg. 331–3 (Politische Polizei), S18765: Bericht Szymanski, 24 May 1912, attachment.

192   Matthew Jefferies, *Hamburg: A Cultural and Literary History* (Oxford, 2011), 18.

193   See Michael Grüttner, *Arbeitswelt an der Wasserkante. Sozialgeschichte der Hamburger Hafenarbeiter 1886–1914* (Göttingen, 1984); Ulrich Bauche, "Arbeitsleben und Arbeitskampf", in Plagemann, ed., *Industriekultur*, 87–95; Johanna Meyer-Lenz, *Schiffbaukunst und Werftarbeit in Hamburg 1838–1896: Arbeit und Gewerkschaftsorganisation im industrialisierten Schiffbau des 19. Jahrhunderts* (Bern, 1995); Marina Cataruzza, "Gewerkschaftliche Organisationsprozesse der Werftarbeiter im Kaiserreich: eine komparative Studie" and "'Organisierter Konflikt' und 'Direkte Aktion': zwei formen des Arbeiterkampfes am Beispiel der Werftarbeiterstreiks in Hamburg und Triest (1880–1914)", in Sacha Zala, ed., *Die Moderne und ihre Krisen: Studien von Marina Cataruzza zur europäischen Geschichte des 19. und 20. Jahrhunderts* (Göttingen, 2012), 115–40 and 141–80.

194   Jürgen Rath, "Gewerkschaftliche Ansätze und der 'Seemannsverband'", in Plagemann, ed., *Übersee*, 269.

195   Rath, "Gewerkschaftliche Ansätze", 269.

196   Th. Lüning, "Unsere Matrosen. II. Theil.", *Hansa: Deutsche Nautische Zeitschrift* 30 (1893), 14.

197   Ferdinand Tönnies, "Die Ostseehäfen Flensburg, Kiel, Lübeck", *Schriften des Vereins für Sozialpolitik* 104 (1903), 512–614.

198   Quoted in Rüger, *The Great Naval Game*, 108.

199   "Battle on the Docks", *The Washington Post*, 8 May 1907.

200   "German Shipyard Strike", *The Manchester Guardian*, 1 May 1912.

201   Cecil, *Albert Ballin*, 32f.

202   Cecil, *Albert Ballin*, 33.

203   "Albert Ballin", *Seefahrt: Technische und kritische Zeitschrift für die Seeschiffahrt* 11 (15 June 1911), 277.

204   Susanne Wiborg, *Albert Ballin* (Hamburg, 2000), 52.

205 Gerhard Ahrens and Renate Hauschild-Thiessen, *Die Reeder: Laeisz, Ballin* (Hamburg, 1989), 46.
206 Adolph Goetz, *25 Jahre Hamburgische Seeschiffahrtspolitik* (Hamburg, 1911), 310.
207 Rieger, *Technology*, 172.
208 As Bernhard Rieger has noted, the engine and boiler rooms provided the greatest challenge for company advertising when it came to questions of image; see Rieger, *Technology*, 172.
209 Rieger, *Technology*, 171–5.
210 Gerhard A. Ritter, "The Kaiser and His Ship-Owner: Albert Ballin, the HAPAG Shipping Company, and the Relationship between Industry and Politics in Imperial Germany and the Early Weimar Republic", in Hartmut Berghoff, Jürgen Kocka, and Dieter Ziegler, eds., *Business in the Age of Extremes: Essays in Modern German and Austrian Economic History* (Washington, D.C. and Cambridge, 2013), 15–39.
211 HAPAG, *Die Hamburg-Amerika Linie*, 146.
212 HAPAG, *Die Hamburg-Amerika Linie*, 147f.
213 "Ship Dance Nets $4,798", *The Washington Post*, 18 September 1913.
214 Rieger, *Technology*, 32, nte. 43; see *Verhandlungen des Reichstags: Stenographische Berichte* (Berlin, 1910), vol. 260, 1656f.
215 Rieger, *Technology*, 184.
216 See for example "Ein moderner Riese", *Hamburger Echo*, 4 April 1913.
217 Rüger, *The Great Naval Game*, 94; "Zum Stapelauf des 'Imperator'", *Hamburger Echo*, 23 May 1912.
218 "Zum Stapellauf des 'Imperator'", *Hamburger Echo*, 23 May 1912.
219 "Der Stapellauf des 'Imperator'", *Hamburger Echo*, 24 May 1912.
220 See for example "Accident to the Liner Deutschland", *The New York Times*, 22 December 1902.
221 Rieger, *Technology*, 171.
222 "The Kaiser's Fast Trip", *The New York Times*, 28 September 1897.
223 See for example "The Imperator", *The Manchester Guardian*, 31 May 1913; "Vandalism on Imperator", *The New York Times*, 31 May 1913.
224 "Imperator Starts Return Trip to-Day", *The New York Times*, 25 June 1913.
225 "The Imperator", *The Times* (London), 3 June 1913; "Tales about Imperator", *The New York Times*, 3 June 1913.
226 "The Imperator", *The Times* (London), 3 January 1913; "The Imperator", *The Manchester Guardian*, 31 May 1913.
227 "Imperator Starts Return Trip to-Day", *The New York Times*, 25 June 1913.
228 See for example, "Vaterland to Sail without a Stike", *New-York Tribune*, 26 May 1914; "Tales about Imperator", *The New York Times*, 3 June 1913; "Imperator Starts Return Trip to-Day", *The New York Times*, 25 June 1913.
229 "Crew of Imperator Demands Better Food", *The Globe* (Toronto), 25 June 1913.
230 "Vaterland to Sail without a Strike", *New-York Tribune*, 26 May 1914.
231 "Vaterland to Sail without a Strike".
232 Folkert Mohrhof, *Der syndikalistische Streik auf dem Ozean-Dampfer "Vaterland" 1914* (Hamburg, 2008).
233 "Die erste Dockung des 'Imperator'", *Hamburger Fremdenblatt*, 1 April 1913.
234 See Zerbe, *Die Grossen Deutschen Passagierschiffe*, 154.
235 "Public Views Imperator", *The New York Times*, 29 May 1913.
236 "Vaterland Trial Trips", *The New York Times*, 26 April 1914.
237 "'Vaterland' vor der Abfahrt", *Hamburgischer Correspondent*, 25 April 1914.
238 "Die Ausfahrt des Vaterland", *Hamburger Nachrichten,* 25 April 1914.
239 Deutsches Schiffahrtsmuseum III.2.VI.2m.
240 "Bundesrat und Reichstag an Bord der Vaterland", *Zeitschrift der Hamburg-Amerika Linie* 13 (5 May 1914), 112f.

241 "Bundesrat und Reichstag an Bord der Vaterland", 115.

242 "Probefahrt und Ausreise des Dampfers Vaterland", *Zeitschrift der Hamburg-Amerika Linie* 13 (20 May 1914), 126.

243 "Special Cable to the New York Times", *The New York Times*, 15 May 1914.

244 "The Vaterland", *The New York Times*, 22 May 1914.

245 See for example "Der Dampfer 'Vaterland'", *Hamburger Fremdenblatt*, 23 May 1914.

4 Swimming symbols of German art and design?
Aby Warburg, Karl Scheffler, and German modernism at sea

I

In the early 1950s, the director of Hamburg's College of Fine Art gave a lecture to the city's rotary club entitled "The Interior Decoration of Ships."[1] Edgar Horstmann began by invoking the memory of a prominent figure from the city's past, Alfred Lichtwark, director of the Kunsthalle from 1886 to 1914. In particular, he recalled Lichtwark's ruminations on a cruise he had taken in the Baltic Sea in the summer of 1904 aboard the *Hamburg*. Launched by HAPAG in 1899 for its East Asia service, the vessel had been built in a British shipyard and was outfitted with all the "usual tastefulness" of that nation. As soon as he went aboard, Lichtwark had been struck by the ship's "special atmosphere." "Nowhere was there a trace of pomp and grandeur," he noted approvingly. "Nowhere was there an ornament or a furnishing with symbolic or elaborate embellishment." There had been no attempt to create a particular mood; instead, the industrial and technical nature of the vessel's design was allowed to speak for itself. Horstmann reminded his audience that these remarks had been made in 1904, a time when the interiors of most transatlantic liners were outfitted in historical revival styles in the manner of floating hotels.

Horstmann then recalled that, in 1912, as a child, he had witnessed the launch of the *Imperator*. In no way did that liner's interiors correspond to what Lichtwark had seen aboard the *Hamburg*. But it was an "interesting fact," he suggested, that at that time Albert Ballin had been in negotiation with the Belgian architect Henry van de Velde who worked in the Art Nouveau style. HAPAG's managing director hoped the architect would design the interior of a liner to be launched in the coming years. "I do not know why plans that were undoubtedly forward-looking did not come to fruition," Horstmann explained. But how different things might have been if, out of this collaboration of shipbuilder and architect, "a kind of prototype of a German ship had been born!"

Now, in the years following the Second World War, nations such as Italy and the United States had taken the lead with respect to the interior design of passenger liners. This was evident, for example, in the fact that the outfitting of American vessels was informed by their technical and industrial nature. In their use of metal, waterproof textiles, fireproof table tops, and wall-mounted and collapsible furnishings, these interiors were, simply put, ship's interiors; the intention was not to imitate luxury hotels. If Germany was to compete with these achievements, Horstmann believed, it had to take account of the fact that "the time has certainly passed when one might decorate an automobile in the manner of a stagecoach; one should find the courage to build something in keeping with its characteristics, and not fear the consequences." If we give ourselves over to the "feeling for material," he explained, "then we will have 'beautiful ships' once more," ships in the style demanded by progressive forces. Horstmann concluded his lecture by stating that this was the task he had set himself as director of the College of Fine Art. Furthermore, he knew that many of his students were prepared to assist him in this endeavour.

Speaking forty years after the launch of the *Imperator*, Horstmann's remarks reveal an aspect of the liner's history that has not been examined in significant detail. In his mind, HAPAG had missed the opportunity to build a vessel that abandoned historical-revival interiors for spaces designed and constructed according to a modernist aesthetic, spaces that would mark it as specifically and proudly German. Horstmann mentions Lichtwark's impression of the *Hamburg* along with Ballin's passing interest in hiring van de Velde to design the interiors of one of the company's liners. But what his brief account neglects is the extent to which the interior decoration of German passenger liners was discussed, debated, and contested in the years before the First World War. And it provides no indication of the way in which the *Imperator* featured as part of this phenomenon.

As we have seen, facts and figures about its size, power, and technological sophistication featured prominently in the construction of the liner as a national monument. But the perspective of many commentators was from the outside and focused on its exterior aspect. This chapter turns to the *Imperator*'s interior decoration and opinions as to how its first-class interiors should be designed and decorated. In 1912, the art critic and journalist Max Osborn claimed that the vessel was so "enchanting" and "magnificent" that "every critical voice was silent."[2] Yet this was definitely not the case. Nor did every observer believe the liner was "a masterpiece 'made in Germany'" as Susanne Wiborg has described it.[3] In fact, several influential German commentators expressed incisive and sometimes impassioned criticism of the way in which HAPAG executed its cabin-class public spaces. Some offered more than criticism and harboured hopes and visions of transforming the *Imperator* or, at least, influencing the interior design of future HAPAG liners.

This criticism and these hopes were aroused by a series of connected concerns. While the *Imperator* was celebrated as a monument to the spectacular strides Germany had made in shipbuilding, engineering, and technology, the task of overseeing the design and decoration of its cabin-class interiors was given to a French architect. The work was carried out, in part, by English and French firms. And the most important and symbolic public spaces aboard the liner were decorated mostly in French historical styles. Unsurprisingly, some commentators raised the objection that the *Imperator*'s interiors were not representative of German art, design, and culture. There was even talk that German prestige and identity had been compromised as the result of HAPAG's decisions.

This objection was sometimes combined with the more nuanced, yet incisive criticism that the liner's interiors presented a false impression of the true nature of modern German society. Of course, the explicit symbolism of the *Imperator* – from its name, to the imperial eagle on its prow, to the painted and sculpted portraits of the Kaiser that featured prominently in its first-class public spaces – was representative of the German Empire. But these prominent pieces of iconography clearly and exclusively embraced the symbolism of Imperial and aristocratic power. Furthermore, many of the paintings with which the cabin-class interiors of both the *Imperator* and *Vaterland* were hung focused on the "symbols, sites and ceremonies of bygone times." Their choice was motivated principally by the desire to satisfy American perceptions of the Old World; they appealed to what Christof Mauch has termed "the voyeurism of the New World."[4] These artworks sustained an image of Germany as "the land of the *Nibelungenlied* and of Grimm's Fairy Tales, of gnomes and giants, storks and turreted ring-walls, of Gothic houses in rows, and the glamour of medieval courtyards."[5] Unsurprisingly, in the opinion of several commentators, the *Imperator* failed to present an accurate image of the German Empire to the Atlantic world.

This chapter focuses on the most interesting, but mostly unknown cases in which this criticism of the liner was expressed. To provide context, it begins with a concise overview of the interior decoration of German transatlantic liners in the decades preceding its launch. It then turns to a discussion of the *Imperator*'s interior decoration before examining one of the least-known episodes in the liner's history: Aby Warburg's work for HAPAG as an advisor on the pictorial decoration of its first-class public spaces. Warburg (1866–1929) was the pioneering art and cultural historian who was born, and spent most of his career in Hamburg. His famous private library became the city's Kulturwissenschaftliche Bibliothek Warburg in 1926 and the Warburg Institute in the University of London in 1944. He saw, in the interior decoration of the *Imperator*, an opportunity to contribute to the reform of German art and to present this reform to the Atlantic world.

An account of Warburg's work on the *Imperator* is interesting in and of itself. It provides a unique insight into HAPAG's decisions regarding the artworks chosen to decorate the liner. But more importantly, it offers an introduction to a way of thinking about the vessel that was shared by other intellectuals and artists including the architect Fritz Schumacher (1869–1947); the architect and designer Bruno Paul (1874–1968); and the art historian and critic Karl Scheffler (1869–1951). These figures are well known to historians, but their interest in the *Imperator* is not. In contrast to the design of its interiors as conceived and executed by HAPAG, all "pictured" or imagined the manner in which the liner's first-class public spaces should have been constructed and decorated. In their eyes, the vessel offered a unique opportunity, not simply to showcase the achievements of German shipbuilding, engineering, and technology to Britain and America; it was also an important way of broadcasting the progressive nature and accomplishments of German art and design to an international audience. Yet the thinking of Warburg and others was informed by something more than a desire to attract a market for German manufactured goods. More profoundly, they believed the *Imperator* offered a distinctive means by which to present Germany as characterized by much more than its Imperial monarchy and aristocracy. The liner's interiors provided a special opportunity to disseminate the image of a thoroughly modern nation distinguished by a thriving urban, commercial, and industrial society and economy; an enterprising and assertive middle class; and a democratic-republican history and vision.

This way of thinking about the *Imperator* finds its clearest and most comprehensive expression in the criticisms mounted by Karl Scheffler and it is with these that the chapter concludes. Scheffler is well known to scholars as one of the most important German art critics of the first half of the twentieth century. His criticisms of the *Imperator* took the form of an open letter to Ballin that was published in the journal *Kunst und Künstler* in November 1913. This document has received little close attention in recent scholarly analysis of Scheffler's work.[6] While not a simple transcription of the opinions of others, the letter gives condensed expression to ideas scattered over, and implied within the writings of Warburg, Schumacher, and Paul. It is the clearest, most complete, and concentrated elaboration of the social, economic, and cultural perspectives that informed why and how these intellectuals and artists "pictured" the *Imperator* in the way that they did.

To be sure, this group was small and criticism of the liner's interiors in the German media was limited, especially outside Hamburg. Nonetheless, Scheffler's letter is important because, beyond the particular concerns of a handful of intellectuals, it gives expression to ideas about the form and role of art in modern Germany that were held by several progressive critics, artists, and organizations such as the *Deutsche Werkbund* (German Association of Craftsmen). Concerned with shaping German art and design in conformity with modern developments, reformers usually focused their attention on architecture, the applied arts, consumer goods, and industrial design.

There are numerous publications treating the social, political, and cultural dynamics of the German Empire through the medium of its art.[7] Architecture, painting, secession movements, artists' colonies, and national monuments have all received scholarly scrutiny. But there has been little discussion of passenger steamships as works of architecture and design that contribute to our understanding of the complexities of art – both German and foreign, modern and traditional – and its reception in Imperial Germany. There has also been considerable interest in the manner in which middle-class Germans organized themselves to shape and govern their society independent of formal political processes. This desire manifested itself in several ways including associations for lifestyle reform, the *Heimat* movement, the garden city movement, and the *Werkbund* and scholars are beginning to emphasize the democratic potential represented by these movements and to see them as a substantial "force for change" in Imperial Germany.[8] Yet there is no discussion of how merchant shipping featured as part of this phenomenon, nor any indication that transatlantic liners mattered to reformers such as Paul, Scheffler, and even Warburg.

Scheffler's letter deserves attention because it applies reform-minded thinking about the arts to an ocean-going steamship. It demonstrates that some influential figures, concerned with putting a modern face on the German Empire, regarded transatlantic passenger liners not only as major works of architecture and design that required critical attention, but also as important national symbols. The subsequent pages provide a concise exploration of an area of modern German art and culture yet to be fully investigated by historians; offer more proof that the *Imperator* was construed and greeted as a national monument; and analyse more incisively how it featured in the "struggle to appropriate custodianship of the symbols of nationhood" that characterized Imperial Germany.[9]

II

By the time of the *Imperator's* launch, transatlantic passenger liners had long been promoted and spoken of in Germany, not simply as the massive products of industrial, engineering, and technological prowess, but as carefully crafted cultural creations. What must be remembered is that these vessels were not constructed only by engineers working with modern materials and technology; their cabin-class interiors were built by highly skilled craftsmen, working by hand, and employing traditional materials such as wood and marble to recreate the most important styles of the European past. By highlighting their aesthetic qualities, company advertising and the popular press transformed transatlantic liners, not simply into luxury hotels as we saw in chapter two, but into works of art.[10] For example, HAPAG advertising described the first-class lounge of the *Fürst Bismarck* (1890) as "a masterpiece of modern German decorative art."[11] The same was true in other nations, especially Britain. In 1914, the Cunard Line described the *Aquitania* as the "Ship Beautiful" and praised it as an "epitome of Art in general and Anglo-Saxon art in particular."[12] Yet as Bernhard Rieger has noted, shipping companies had no high-minded agendas when adopting specific designs for their vessels; they promoted their liners as cultural icons for commercial reasons.[13]

The affect this type of promotion had in determining the choices of cabin-class passengers is unclear. Dagmar Bellmann indicates that, given what was written in diaries, letters, travel reports, and memoirs, the design and decoration of a liner's interiors was of no great concern to passengers. More important was the spaciousness of cabins and public rooms, the luxury and convenience of their outfitting, and the quality of a liner's service and cuisine. Put simply, passengers were concerned with comfort, not aesthetics.[14] As we saw in chapter two, HAPAG advertising and most press reporting on the *Imperator* did not focus on the style of its cabin-class interiors per se. Instead, attention was drawn to their spaciousness, sumptuousness, and the level of comfort they afforded no matter whether this was offered in an English Tudor or French Rococo style.

Creating floating versions of Belle Époque hotels was a means for HAPAG to secure the patronage of America's nouveau riche in particular. Writing in the *Neue Hamburger Zeitung* in 1913, Hans Ossig explained that "a shipping company must not ignore the taste of its public, and especially Americans, who particularly like paying for the most luxurious cabins with their dollars."[15] Business and leisure travellers from the United States accounted for the majority of first-class passengers aboard the company's transatlantic liners. In fact, it was often said at the time that the luxury of the *Imperator, Vaterland*, and *Bismarck* was especially intended to appeal to Americans and their desire to be surrounded by Old-World elegance as soon as they stepped aboard ship. As one commentator in *The Washington Post* noted in 1911, the "rapidly multiplying class of well-to-do Americans" expected "a splendor and costliness of surroundings from one hundred to five hundred percent above what they are satisfied with at home." This class of American traveller, the author explained, "is drifting away from democratic ideal simplicity and is becoming the chief factor in the calculations of the shipping companies."[16] The concession to the taste of wealthy Americans was also noticed in the foreign press. Yet German observers claimed that the development of floating hotels was attributable to the fact that their countrymen also wished to cross the Atlantic in style and comfort.[17] As the *Neue Hamburger Zeitung* suggested, Germany's *nouveau riche* preferred sumptuous, French-inspired interior decoration aboard ship just as much as their American counterparts.[18]

The architect Johann Georg Poppe (1837–1915) had perhaps the greatest influence on the development of the Neo-Rococo and Neo-Baroque aesthetic that became common in the cabin-class interiors of German passenger liners from the 1880s. As "the leading interpreter of the opulent bourgeois taste of Bremen's prosperous merchant families," Poppe built private villas, Bremen's public library and stock exchange, and NDL's headquarters.[19] NDL also employed him to design the interiors of several transatlantic liners. The first of these was the *Elbe*, built in Glasgow in 1881, and Poppe's mature style was to be found aboard the *Werra, Fulda, Eider*, and *Ems*, all of which entered service between 1882 and 1884. Some consider the first-class dining room of the *Lahn*, launched by NDL in 1887, to be the highpoint of the architect's work.[20] Poppe also designed interiors for the liners commissioned during the company's fleet expansion around 1900. These included the *Kaiser Wilhelm der Große, Kaiser Friedrich, Kronprinz Wilhelm*, and *Kaiser Wilhelm* II. Some of the first-class public rooms on these vessels, such as the dining saloon aboard the latter, were more opulent than similar spaces found in the best hotels of the period. HAPAG also engaged Poppe to design the first-class public spaces aboard the *Augusta Victoria*, which it launched in 1888.

Much of the popular literature on transatlantic liners adopts an admiring and nostalgic perspective on this Neo-Baroque and Neo-Rococo opulence. John Malcolm Brinnin, however, has described the interiors of German vessels as "grand galleries of an aspiration so Valkeyrian that only megalomaniacs might dally there in comfort or good conscience."[21] But what must be emphasized is that Poppe's creations also attracted criticism – albeit more considered and sober – from progressive architects and designers of the period. They decried the interiors he created for NDL for what was considered their anachronistic décor and furnishings.[22] Moreover, the German shipping industry itself found it necessary, at least to a limited extent, "to position itself *vis-à-vis* both aesthetic traditionalists and supporters of modernism."[23] Rieger has suggested that "in principle, shipping companies sided with reformers who believed that industrial products could reach high levels of stylistic sophistication."[24]

What can be said with certainty is that companies occasionally mounted challenges to the historical-revival aesthetic that dominated maritime architecture at the time. As noted above, Ballin considered hiring the architect Henry van de Velde in 1903 to design the first-class interiors aboard the *Amerika* and *Kaiserin Auguste Victoria*. Apparently, he changed his mind when objections were voiced by the Kaiser.[25] Yet literature published by HAPAG in 1907 demonstrates that it was aware of changing tastes in interior design and reveals a self-conscious attitude about the choices it had made. Commenting on the express steamers *Augusta Victoria*, *Columbia*, *Normannia*, and *Fürst Bismarck*, all of which were launched between 1889 and 1891, the company admitted that while the Rococo-style decoration of their first-class public rooms made "a strong impression," they could appear "cluttered and confusing" to "our modern taste."[26]

More successful efforts to bring progressive design aesthetics aboard transatlantic liners were undertaken by NDL. The company gave contracts to firms associated with the *Deutsche Werkbund*, to which we will turn our attention below, and these firms participated in the planning and execution of liner interiors.[27] Thus, while Poppe designed the first-class saloons aboard the *Kronprinzessin Cecilie*, which was launched in 1906, Bruno Paul, Joseph Olbrich (1867–1908), and Richard Riemerschmid (1868–1957) were employed by NDL to design the liner's first-class luxury suites in a *Jugendstil* aesthetic. All members of Munich's United Studios for Art in Craftwork, their work aboard the liner demonstrated the influence of Charles Rennie Mackintosh and Frank Lloyd Wright. And while none had experience designing cabins for passenger liners, their creations met with the approval of progressively minded artists and intellectuals.

In an article published in *Die Kunst* – accompanied by several large photographs depicting the completed cabins – the German art historian Karl Schaefer gave voice to themes and issues that would later inform discussion of the *Imperator*.[28] Schaefer described the work of Paul, Olbrich, and Riemerschmid as "the first large-scale attempt to put the best forces of our applied art at the service of furnishing a ship."[29] More substantially, he stated that modern engineering and progressive design aesthetics shared a strong relation and that they often took the same assumptions as their starting point. Considering the *Kronprinzessin Cecilie*'s architectonic, practical, but elegant cabins with their restrained ornamentation, Schaefer believed this relation was first successfully put to a rigorous test aboard the vessel. He also claimed that NDL was playing an important role in carrying the work of Germany's best artists beyond the borders of the Empire and across the Atlantic. Writing in 1906, Hermann Muthesius (1876–1950), the German architect, author, and promoter of architectural modernism expressed the importance of these developments and his understanding of the role of shipping companies in more general, but also more emphatic terms:

> one sees not only a positive sign of the new arts triumphing, but also a victory of incalculable significance. In fact, those people in international trade can accomplish a cultural worldwide mission for German production: the great German shipping companies carry international passengers who live during the voyage in enforced leisure and are easily influenced by the prevailing taste on board. We can observe how, compared with the pretentious and often deplorable taste exhibited until now on German ships, the new interior design created by the best artistic forces of German craftsmanship delights passengers ...

These developments, Muthesius believed, would "undoubtedly contribute towards the recognition of German art."[30]

As the *Kronprinzessin Cecilie* met with critical success, NDL continued to employ progressive designers to outfit its liners. The *Berlin*, which it launched in 1908, also featured interiors in a *Jugendstil* aesthetic and the company hired Bruno Paul, once again, to design the first-class lounge, smoking room, and reading room aboard the *George Washington*, which entered its service to New York in 1909. Plans for the liner's first-class dining room were drawn up by the Bremen architect Rudolph Alexander Schröder (1878–1962). As Philip Dawson and Bruce Peter explain, by "using only geometric lines and a variety of wood inlays, Paul devised comfortable spaces of austere elegance, and all without any applied historicist ornamentation whatsoever."[31] In fact, the *George Washington* "can justifiably be considered the first entirely modern ship, in the sense that all of the spaces, fixtures and fittings were planned in accordance with contemporary principles and without any reference to historical styles pre-dating the industrial age."[32]

In 1913, Gustav Pauli, then director of Bremen's Kunsthalle, praised the work that Olbrich, Paul, and Riemerschmid had undertaken for NDL in the journal *Kunst und Handwerk*.[33] He described Olbrich's work as elegant; said Paul's designs were informed by a feeling for architectonic relationships that emphasized the functionality of a liner; and claimed Riemerschmid was animated by a painter's sensibility for colour. That same year, the journal *Innen-Dekoration*, a promoter of modern German applied art and design, expressed the hope that recent styles and trends would eventually meet the travelling public's demand for comfort, refinement, and elegance and thus find their way aboard transatlantic liners.[34] And it is no wonder that photographs depicting the interiors of the *Kronprinzessin Cecilie* and *George Washington* were published in the *Deutsche Werkbund*'s yearbook for 1914, which showcased the best in progressive design as it was adapted to transportation.[35]

NDL's initiatives were also met with approval in the United States. *The International Studio*, a journal published in New York, admired the fact that the *Kronprinzessin Cecilie* and *George Washington* had been "fitted up with modern ideas" and saw the company's decision to do this as opening a new and important field for German art and design. Now, in addition to appearing at international exhibitions, Germany's "very best creations, bearing the impress of a strong individuality, are borne far and wide across the sea."[36] This positive response to innovation at NDL recalls the similar reaction that greeted the German contribution to the Saint Louis International Exhibition of 1904. In Germany, it was proudly reported that two-thirds of the nation's contribution to the exhibition had been sold.[37]

But while NDL's managing director, Heinrich Wiegand, took a keen interest in matters of art and design, he was also cognizant of the fact that there was danger in confronting the travelling public with architectural and artistic experimentation.[38] And HAPAG maintained a more conservative stance than NDL. According to the former, a transatlantic liner was a meeting place for travellers of all nations and especially Americans. As such, it was not the place to showcase German innovation in art and design. Nor should it be expected that passengers would "happily embrace the unfamiliar."[39] As Dawson and Peter indicate, liners operating on routes other than those to New York were often "more progressive in design because the means by which national identity was represented was less high a priority."[40] But aboard those commissioned for service to Manhattan, cabin-class interiors built according to progressive design aesthetics remained unique to a small number of German passenger liners. Modernism and consumerism aboard transatlantic vessels would be more definitely and widely linked in the wake of the First World War.

III

As of 25 September 1912, HAPAG had allotted 2,305,359 marks for the construction of the *Imperator*'s interiors.[41] Most of this money was used to decorate first-class cabins and public spaces characterized by a degree of spaciousness previously unseen in maritime construction and conceived, first and foremost, with a concern for passenger comfort instead of in accordance with the constraints imposed by the structure of the vessel's hull. The largest sums were budgeted for the swimming pool (366,136 marks); the winter garden (273,000 marks); the main staircase (270,000 marks); and the first-class dining room (230,000 marks).[42] The goal was to create an architectural unity between ship and shore.

HAPAG took particular care in designing the *Imperator*'s first-class public rooms because it understood that these would attract considerable attention in the domestic and foreign press and would serve as an advertisement for the liner. The French architect Charles Frédéric Mewès (1860–1914) was commissioned to direct the entire project. His work for HAPAG was handled through the firm of Mewès & Bischoff, founded with the Swiss architect Alphonse Bischoff, and headquartered in Cologne. The projects he concurrently undertook as a consulting architect for Cunard, including aboard the *Aquitania* which was launched in 1913, were managed from the offices of the firm Mewès & Davis. This was founded with the English architect Arthur Joseph Davis and headquartered in London. Mewès worked for César Ritz on his Paris hotel in the late 1890s and with Davis on the London Ritz which opened in 1906.[43] Ballin was impressed with the work of Mewès & Davis and hired them to design the cabin-class interiors of the *Amerika*, which was launched in 1905. Aboard the liner, Mewès created first-class public rooms that blended the styles of Louis XV and the Scottish Neo-Classical architect Robert Adam (1728–1792). These found considerable favour with the travelling public.

Contracts for the first-class public rooms aboard the *Imperator* were awarded to several firms, the majority of them German. These included J.D. Heymann of Hamburg for the first-class dining room; Schneider and Hanau of Frankfurt for the first-class lounge; A Bembé of Mainz for the main staircase; Fittje and Michahelles of Hamburg for the ladies' drawing room; and Bamberger Leroi & Co. of Frankfurt for the swimming pool. But contracts were also awarded to English and French concerns, principally A.G. Russell of London who designed the first-class smoking room, and P.H. Rémon of Paris who constructed the winter garden. All of these firms provided designs and samples to the offices of Mewès and Bishchoff in Cologne and Charles Mewès in Paris. And they occasionally exhibited plans and models of their projects in their offices and workshops before they were built aboard the vessel. In Hamburg, J.D. Heymann invited the public to view its designs for the first-class dining room and these were admired by the *Hamburgischer Correspondent*.[44] Many of the designers and firms that worked aboard the *Imperator* were also contracted to design the interiors of the *Vaterland* and *Bismarck*.

The decorative scheme designed by Mewès hid the structural and technological modernity of the *Imperator* under a variety of historical styles. The grand staircase – the site at which "the definitive statement" of a liner was traditionally made – was decorated in the style of Louis XVI.[45] Its matt-white walls were accented with detailing in wood. The same style was adopted for the first-class dining room and the winter garden. The first-class lounge, panelled in light oak carved with garlands, was completed in the style of Louis XIV. The Ritz-Carlton restaurant was designed in the French Empire style. The smoking room was constructed in English Tudor style and boasted oak panelling, a ceiling of oak beams, and a stone fireplace. The swimming pool was modelled on Mewès's creation at the Royal Automobile Club in London and has been described as "the most sensational facility of its kind ever to go to sea."[46] It was completed in what HAPAG referred to as "Pompeian" style and was often described as the Pompeian bath.[47]

The *Imperator*'s first-class interiors were conceived in keeping with developments in interior design that occurred during the first two decades of the twentieth century. Of course, these years witnessed the emergence of new styles and design ideas. But they were also characterized by the persistence of earlier period styles and their deliberate revival, with designers drawing inspiration from the Italian Renaissance, eighteenth-century France, the French Empire, as well as Georgian and Regency England.[48] Perusing photographs of the *Imperator*'s first-class interiors, what one notices is that they are much more sober than the Neo-Baroque and Neo-Rococo spaces aboard earlier vessels. Instead, what one finds is the "impressionism of classic style rendered in muted luxury."[49]

This restrained Neo-classicism is exemplified in the work of one of the presumably few women to work on the *Imperator*: the interior designer Ilse Dernburg (1880–1964/65). She designed two first-class cabins contracted to J.D. Heymann and Hermann Gerson, as well as the Imperial suites built by Fittje and Michahelles.[50] Dernburg also produced designs for first-class cabins constructed aboard the *Vaterland*. In 1913, the art critic and journalist Max Osborn devoted an article to her work aboard the *Imperator* in the journal *Innen-Dekoration*.[51] This is illustrated with no less than twenty-seven photographs of her completed cabins. In his text, Osborn described the *Imperator* as a "miracle" and acknowledged its important function as a symbol of Germany's entrepreneurial spirit and technological achievements. He also claimed that its "global significance" resided in the fact that it constituted a microcosm of all that was currently occurring in German applied art and interior design.[52] Osborn was critical of the use of historical styles in interior decoration, saying they had no correspondence with modern life. This was especially the case aboard transatlantic liners that were quintessential products of the modern age.[53] A salon in the style of Louis XVI was completely out of place in such a creation.

It is unfortunate, however, that Osborn turns his attention to Dernburg and her designs only briefly and at the end of his article. Here he describes her cabins as luxurious and, in that sense, similar to those found in a fine hotel. But it is also unfortunate that he speaks so vaguely about why he feels they are suited to a passenger liner. In a short article published in 1912, also in *Innen-Dekoration*, Osborn described Dernburg as part of a trend that understood the need for restraint in the applied arts. He said her designs for the *Imperator*'s cabins demonstrated a "functionality" and "simplicity." But he also described her as "no genius." Instead, she was an "adapter" and student of her husband, the architect Hermann Dernburg.[54] In Osborn's eyes, her real strength was her fine feminine feel for the decoration of a home. The one clear, positive point that Osborn made in the article of 1913 was that Dernburg's cabins adapted themselves to their shipboard environment; they made no attempt to deceive passengers that they were accommodated aboard an oceangoing vessel. The many photographs that accompany the text bear this out: Dernburg's designs employ simple forms, clean lines, uncluttered detailing, and restrained decoration along with the frequent use of silver-grey colouring for walls and furniture. The impression is that of a restrained Neo-classicism that elegantly hides, but is more in keeping with the nautical functionalism of the *Imperator* in a way that Baroque- and Rococo-inspired decoration was not.

Nonetheless, French historical styles were employed for the most important first-class public rooms aboard the *Imperator*. As we will see, they dominated the impression commentators had of the vessel. The object was to lend the liner's interiors a cosmopolitan feel; spaces designed in the French manner were bound to appeal to an international clientele. As Philip Dawson explains, first-class interiors that recreated historical styles "were never intended to be period revival schemes per se." Instead, they "emerged rather as a characteristic grand-luxe hotelier style." Interiors aboard the *Imperator* and other transatlantic liners were meant to appeal to a diverse public and intended to create a sense of elegance.[55] What guided Mewès was the "need to create an atmosphere of universal bon vivant in elegant surroundings that could be enjoyed and experienced within the guests' own terms of reference."[56] These guests included not only Americans but also wealthy Britons. The latter had long associated French interior design with aristocratic elegance and continued to decorate their grandest rooms "in the French classical styles, especially that of Louis Seize."[57] Consequently, transatlantic liners commissioned by the shipping companies of various nations were similarly decorated in historical-revival styles without significant differentiation. For example, the *France*, commissioned by the Compagnie Générale Transatlantique in 1912, boasted first-class public rooms decorated in Baroque and Rococo revival styles. In this sense, the interior decoration of transatlantic liners was international.[58] And choosing French historical styles to cater to an international public emphasizes the extent to which commercial interests took precedence, for HAPAG, over constructing a national monument.

Painting and sculpture completed the decoration of cabin-class accommodation aboard HAPAG liners. Compared to the sums spent on designing and building their interiors, the cost of the artworks that adorned these vessels was insignificant. But their symbolic role was important. The artwork aboard the liners commissioned by HAPAG and NDL often consisted of a mixture of imperial portraits, allegorical subjects, and romanticized depictions of the German landscape and its cities. As noted above, most of these images appealed to American visions of the Old World. For example, the first-class dining room aboard NDL's *Kaiser Wilhelm der Große*, which was launched in 1897, was hung with a large portrait of Wilhelm II. Its frame bore allegorical representations of Loyalty and Sagacity. Other paintings aboard the vessel depicted German castles and allegorical figures representing the trades, commerce, and shipping.[59] The paintings that decorated the first-class dining room aboard NDL's *Kronprinz Wilhelm*, launched in 1901, included portraits of the prince along with scenes from his boyhood and education. There were images depicting the Crown Prince's residence, and the cadet school in Plön where he was educated. The smaller dining rooms adjoining the main saloon were hung with landscape views of Potsdam, Sanssouci, Plön, and Bonn. The walls and ceiling of the library bore depictions of the muses, while the first-class lounge displayed a life-sized portrait of the Crown Prince along with pictures of Berlin, Breslau, Königsberg, Magdeburg, Hanover, Cologne, Frankfurt, and Stettin.[60]

Artworks were also chosen for the more general purpose of contributing to the air of exclusive luxury cultivated in first-class interiors. The dining room aboard HAPAG's *Amerika*, for example, was hung with copies of paintings by François Boucher (1703–1770) one of the most important proponents of the French Rococo style.[61] And the *Vaterland* provides an instructive example of how paintings were used to transform a liner's interiors into a pleasure palace for its privileged passengers. Of course, the liner was adorned with the usual imperial iconography. As aboard the *Imperator*, Walter Schott provided a bust of the Kaiser for the first-class lounge.[62] Ferdinand Wagner of Munich was chosen to paint the tympanum over the entrance to the latter with the image of a castle on the Rhine.[63] The forward staircase was hung with a portrait of Queen Luise and her two eldest sons, Friedrich Wilhelm IV and Kaiser Wilhelm I. Painted by Grete Ehrke of Hamburg, the image was a copy of the original work completed by Carl Steffeck in 1886.[64]

But apart from these works, the main staircase of the *Vaterland* was decorated with two large landscapes by the Venetian artist Giovanni Battista Pittoni (1690–1767). These measured more than two meters high and depicted idealized landscapes with allegorical motifs. In the auction catalogue published at the sale of the liner's interior appointments in 1938, one is described as depicting figures in a landscape with ruins. The other is described as a "large garden and terrace scene with distant mountains."[65] The *Vaterland*'s first-class lounge featured four large canvases by Gérard de Lairesse (1640–1711) in gilt frames each measuring approximately 144 by 132 inches. These depicted the myth of Pandora and were entitled "The Creation of Pandora"; "The Temptation of Pandora"; "Pandora Turns from Evil"; and "The Indignation of Pandora."[66] A painting by Waldemar Kolmsperger of Munich in the manner of Giovanni Battista Tiepolo (1696–1770) adorned the cupola of the first-class dining room and the lower portion of the vault was decorated with flowers, leaves, and birds. The ladies' drawing room was hung with a portrait of King Ludwig III of Bavaria by Peter Baumgartner, while the smoking room was decorated with two seascapes by Hugo Schnars-Alquist.[67] The swimming pool boasted a bronze copy of the Eros of Lysippos, the original of which is in the Vatican and dates to the fourth century BCE.[68] All of these artworks contributed to the elitist, and luxury-conscious ambiance of the *Vaterland*'s first-class public spaces.

Yet while the artworks in these spaces were intended to engender an Old-World, aristocratic elegance and sophistication, the images that decorated the *Vaterland*'s first-class cabins contributed to their hominess. The auction catalogue of 1938 contains a section entitled "Prints, Etchings and Engravings." Taken from first-class accommodation, these included old English scenes, views of Paris and New York, images of American topography, and French military subjects.[69] Although it is unclear as to whether the images listed in the catalogue were original to the liner, they are in keeping with the type of pictorial decoration that originally adorned these cabins. Such decoration could only serve to contribute to the comfort and familiarity of these spaces which, as we saw in chapter two, was also engendered by their size, furnishing, and the modernity of their sanitary facilities.

Figure 4.1 The *Vaterland*'s first-class lounge.
Source: German Maritime Museum, Bremerhaven.

IV

What prompted HAPAG to hire Aby Warburg in the summer of 1912 to provide advice with respect to artworks intended to adorn the *Imperator*'s first-class public spaces is unknown. It is not clear whether he sought this position or was approached by the company. He may have even been contacted by Albert Ballin himself through his brother Max. Max Warburg enjoyed a close business and personal relationship with Ballin. The former directed the family bank, M.M. Warburg & Co., and participated in several large loan operations for HAPAG.

No matter the circumstances of his hiring, Warburg made it clear to the company that, if there was to be a reform of German art, "then obviously the doors must be opened to competent modern artists" aboard the *Imperator*.[70] What he meant by a reform of German art was a decrease in the influence of stale academic norms and values for an increasing embrace of innovation. Warburg took an interest in avant-garde art, including the work of the German Expressionists and Italian Futurists. And yet, despite his desire to see the reform of German art, he made it clear to HAPAG that he did not think its liners were a suitable means of educating the public in the most modern styles. His aim, with respect to the *Imperator*, was to find a middle ground between the traditional and the modern.[71] At one point, he described his guiding principle as "Hamburg art without pathos."[72]

But what also motivated Warburg was the international attention he knew the liner would attract. He understood that, just as the label "Made in Germany" came to stand for the quality and reliability of a range of manufactured goods, the best German passenger vessels were admired by the Anglo-American travelling public for their technical sophistication, speed, luxurious interiors, and the quality of their food and service. Consequently, they were an ideal venue for exhibiting contemporary German art and design to the world.

Warburg was not alone in this conviction. In July 1913, the *Hamburgischer Correspondent* reported on the success of an art exhibition held aboard the French steamer *France* when crossing from Le Havre to New York.[73] It claimed that, in 1906, several German painters and artists associations had proposed the installation of similar exhibitions aboard German liners. The paper believed this was an excellent means for German art to reach an international audience. But the proposal had not been acted upon by the leading shipping companies. The *Correspondent* suggested that now was the time to act, especially as so many passengers travelling across the Atlantic preferred to do so aboard German vessels.

To be sure, some foreign observers were already complimenting German steamship companies for the extent to which they employed their liners to promote German art and design. In his book *Steamship Conquest of the World*, published in 1912, Frederick A. Talbot favourably compared what he found aboard German vessels to what he saw as the anonymity of artworks on British liners. In addition, he claimed that artworks aboard the latter were not executed by great living artists. The Germans, by contrast, "sought their foremost artists and offered them the mural decorations, mosaic, sculpture and plastic embellishment." The result, Talbot claimed, "is that every modern liner flying the German eagle constitutes a picture-gallery of famous native painters and craftsmen, and the work of the artist is acknowledged, so that all may admire – or deprecate."[74] Britain, he claimed, would do well to follow the German example.

When Warburg went aboard the *Imperator* in August 1912, he was enthralled. Describing it as "an awesome Cyclop's mill," he was disappointed that no artists were painting the ship while it was under construction.[75] But he was much less impressed by the artworks that typically adorned the first-class interiors of HAPAG liners. He had been aboard six of the company's largest steamers that summer and said he found pictures that had the effect of "a succession of servile compliments to bad taste." HAPAG, he wrote, "symbolizes German boldness and respectability, and that is why I wanted to contribute to the elimination of that laughable, incongruous style ... which pastes these proud, gigantic fish with mawkish postcards."[76] At least one of the company's directors was in agreement with Warburg. Writing about a portrait of the Kaiser that he saw in the ladies' drawing room aboard the *Amerika*, Johannes Merck said it "depicted him in the red uniform of the Garde du Corps in an unnatural stance with upturned moustache and arrogant expression." It was, he claimed, "the kitschy production of some obscure court painter, and in my opinion a highly unsuitable likeness for the American public."[77]

The *Imperator*'s first-class lounge was hung with two antique Gobelin tapestries representing Europe and Asia. A depiction of Sanssouci, the palace of Frederick the Great, decorated the winter garden. The company had also arranged for the work of contemporary artists that it deemed suitable to be hung aboard the liner. From the onset of his employment, Warburg insisted on the importance of decorating the *Imperator* with original artworks. He recognized that, in this respect, he would challenge the "egotistical interests" of the various designers at work on the vessel who were determined to relegate the paintings to mere accompaniments of their decorative schemes. "For them," Warburg wrote, "every surrogate is better than an original work."[78] To facilitate his task, he requested a list of all paintings commissioned by HAPAG for its transatlantic liners in the last five years.[79]

For the *Imperator*, Warburg's responsibilities included one of its most important and symbolic spaces: the main staircase was to be dominated by a painting, in a gilt frame, measuring 2.13 metres high by 1.54 metres wide. Chief Superintendent Sachse, who oversaw the liner's pictorial decoration, originally suggested a portrait of Frederick the Great or Frederick William, Elector of Brandenburg on horseback. He also considered an image of a sea battle depicting the *Kurbrandenburgischen* fleet.[80] Ultimately, the decision was made to hang a full-length portrait of the Kaiser in his admiral's uniform. Warburg was against a watered-down representation in the manner of the engravings of the eighteenth-century artist Daniel Chodowiecki.[81] He preferred a strong characterization of Wilhelm II, but one without pathos. It must not be forgotten that Warburg's taste was influenced by Hamburg's long-standing political, social, and cultural particularism. Until German unification in 1871, Hamburg had existed as a republic for several centuries and thought of itself as having a unique political and cultural identity within the German Empire. As a proud citizen of this merchant republic, Warburg was a critic of the official political aesthetic fostered by the Kaiser in Berlin; he labelled it "Berlin's sentimental Neo-Baroque style" and believed its products amounted to a "wax museum of patriotic spectacle."[82] Counteracting this aboard the *Imperator* would be one small step towards Warburg's vision of a reformed German art.

For the portrait of the Kaiser, Warburg recommended Hans Olde (1855–1917), director of the Royal Academy of Art in Kassel. Wilhelm admired the work of Olde and Warburg believed the artist's skill was demonstrated in the portraits of princes that he painted for the large lecture hall of the University of Jena.[83] He was pleased with Olde's preliminary studies and found the final product – a portrait of the Kaiser aboard the *Hohenzollern* – full of life and dignity, and devoid of bombastic rhetoric.[84] With Warburg's advice, HAPAG also hired Paul Kayser (1869–1942), Hermann Bruck (1873–1951), Friedrich Lissmann (1880–1915), and Hugo Schnars-Alquist (1855–1939) to paint seascapes, landscapes, and still-life scenes for the first-class dining room.[85] All were Hamburg artists who, to varying degrees, worked in a late-Impressionist style. Hiring local artists to paint pictures for transatlantic liners was not unusual. As Carsten Meyer-Tönnesmann explains, with the increase of shipbuilding in Hamburg towards the end of the nineteenth century, a new field of endeavour opened for local artists.[86] In October 1905, the art critic Heinrich Wallsee suggested in the *Hamburger Nachrichten* that the city's Art Association act as an agent to bring artists and ship owners together. He argued that this was preferable to letting this role be played by architects who lacked artistic sensibility.[87] Alfred Lichtwark, director of Hamburg's Kunsthalle, occasionally obtained such commissions for local artists.[88]

Warburg visited the artists to view sketches and made reports to Chief Superintendent Sachse and Ballin.[89] He told Ballin that Kayser had a very fine feeling for the Hamburg landscape; that Lissmann was an extremely talented artist; and that Bruck had already produced a powerful still life for the first-class dining room.[90] Writing to Sachse, Warburg described this as a "really delightful still life" that was neither too traditional, nor too modern.[91] He was also consulted regarding the sums to be paid for the artworks. Relative to the amount of money spent on designing and decorating the *Imperator*'s first-class interiors, this was paltry: Kayser received 6,000 marks for two landscapes for the dining room; Schnars-Alquist was paid 5,000 marks for the seascape that hung in the main staircase; Bruck was awarded 3,000 marks for his still life; and Lissmann was paid 1,500 marks for two small landscapes "with animals" for the ladies' drawing room. Professor Walter Schott earned 10,000 marks for his bust of the Kaiser and 1,300 marks for its plinth. By contrast, Bruno Kruse was paid over 20,000 marks for the eagle that adorned the liner's prow.[92]

Warburg considered his work on the *Imperator* finished by early November 1912. By that point, commissions had been granted to the artists he recommended to HAPAG. At the same time, he made it clear that he wanted nothing to do with the pictorial decoration of the *Vaterland*. This, he wrote, was solely the responsibility of the firms hired for that purpose.[93] He insisted that the painting of the cupola in the *Vaterland*'s first-class dining room was a matter for the architects. And yet he found it impossible not to involve himself in the matter. In fact, as he was advising on the pictorial decoration of the *Imperator*, he was also thinking about the *Vaterland*. Warburg requested the dimensions of the rooms aboard the latter for which paintings were intended and stated that the artworks should not slavishly conform to their design.[94] In June 1913, he informed HAPAG that the seascapes intended for the vessel were by an artist whom he did not value.[95] Warburg did not name the artist, but he requested the measurements of the cupola in the first-class dining room so that he could advise Friedrich Lissmann with respect to paintings for the space. He also concerned himself with a painting of Queen Luise and collected a number of reproductions of her portraits.[96] This time, the portrait of the Kaiser completed by Hans Olde did not meet with Warburg's approval; he did not consider it lively enough. Apparently, Ballin was also disappointed with Olde's work for the *Vaterland*.[97]

HAPAG's managing director seems to have appreciated the advice Warburg provided regarding the *Imperator* and thanked him for his "extremely valuable suggestions."[98] But ultimately, Warburg's plans for the pictorial decoration of the vessel were not to be realized. Things started to unravel in April 1913. Writing to Ballin early in that month, Warburg said he had heard from his brother Max that the managing director was not pleased with the pictures intended for the *Imperator*'s first-class dining room.[99] He had also heard of the removal of the paintings by Kayser and Bruck. As a result, he felt humiliated in the eyes of the artists he had engaged; "to myself, and in the eyes of the artists, I am now only a disavowed art agent" of HAPAG he wrote to Ballin. At the same time, he was distressed by what he regarded as the philistinism of the company's directorship, saying sometime later that art was a matter of "irresponsible play" for Ballin.[100]

Warburg had stated that he wanted nothing to do with the decoration of the *Imperator*'s first-class public rooms beyond the choice of pictures. Yet he expressed his dismay that HAPAG saw the paintings as nothing more than accompaniment to the interior's decorative schemes.[101] The real opposition to Warburg's choice of pictures came from Charles Mewès. The architect feared inconsistency between the design of the first-class interiors and the paintings; he protested that the works recommended by Warburg upset the architectonic form of his rooms.[102] Warburg described the style of the latter as *"Kellner-Eleganz"* (waiter chic) that was naturally "threatened in its dictatorship by every personal touch."[103] He asked Ballin for an opportunity to explain the pictures in the very spaces where they hung aboard the vessel. Ballin replied that they would discuss the matter aboard the *Imperator* and refused to hear any talk of Warburg resigning his position.[104]

Yet on 20 June 1913, Warburg wrote once again to HAPAG stating that he no longer considered himself engaged by the firm as its artistic advisor.[105] He explained that he took this decision after learning that one of the pictures he had recommended – the still life by Bruck – had been removed from the *Imperator*'s first-class dining room to be replaced by a work by Ascan Lutteroth (1842–1923). In his mind, he had undertaken the thankless task of artistic advisor to HAPAG to prevent inferior art like that produced by Lutteroth finding a place aboard the liner. Protesting against his treatment by the company, Warburg was angered that the replacement of the one artist's work by that of the other had happened without his knowledge. In the draft of a letter to HAPAG in his wife's hand, dated 30 June and marked "not sent," Warburg angrily exclaimed that Ballin and Sachse had promised that the paintings by Kayser and others would remain in place until he had the opportunity to explain his choices to the managing director aboard the vessel.

In the same letter, Warburg also stated that he had been surprised to read in the *Hamburger Woche*, on 17 April, that Ballin was so impressed by work produced by Fritz Schwinge for the second-class dining room that he commissioned the artist to paint two large landscapes for the first-class dining room. Warburg believed his efforts could not be more discredited than "through the ousting of a conscientious and intellectual artist such as Paul Kayser" and the replacement of his works with the "products" of Schwinge. According to Warburg, Schwinge's painting was superficial and represented artistic inferiority.[106] He would later complain to his friend, Gustav Pauli, that "he had tasted the anti-artistic philistine elements of HAPAG in their complete power."[107]

Ballin responded to Warburg's complaints in early July.[108] He insisted that no disrespect had been shown to his "honourary position," as he fully intended that the scholar would be paid for his work. In addition, he explained that Bruck's still life was removed not only because he personally thought it was unsuitable for the room, but also because all who saw it agreed with him. In fact, he had been told that Warburg was of the same opinion. The paintings, Ballin insisted, had to conform to the *Imperator*'s interior decoration and not vice versa. "Naturally, you take us for philistines," Ballin wrote.

> But you shouldn't forget that at least 90% of our passengers will be just as uneducated in these matters as we. Consequently, it is necessary either to hang paintings that are merely decorative and arouse no criticism, or to purchase works by Rembrandt.

Even if the company's directorship were not experts in the matter, Ballin insisted, they had the right to judge whether an artwork was beautiful or not. Personally, he favoured the work of Lutteroth and Scwhinge. In addition, he suggested that Bruck was welcome to paint another, more suitable work for the space. But Warburg considered this suggestion to be an insult both to the artist and to himself.[109] When he pleaded for a chance to contest the director's decision, Ballin consented and invited Warburg aboard the *Imperator*.[110] But when Warburg refused the invitation, his services were terminated.[111]

Warburg's correspondence pertaining to his work for HAPAG is largely uncoloured by explicitly nationalist sentiment. But there are traces of it. For example, he criticized Felix von Eckardt, editor of the *Hamburgischer Correspondent*, for not denouncing the French-style interiors of the *Imperator*.[112] On at least one occasion, he broadly described Mewès as having an antipathy to the German pictures.[113] And his wife Mary noted, erroneously, that Germans were dissatisfied that HAPAG failed to employ German painters.[114] But Warburg was principally concerned with the *Imperator*'s potential contribution to the reform of German art and its role in presenting this reform to the Atlantic world. He saw the liner as a potential contribution to a progressive cultural politics in Germany.

Other influential figures shared this vision. One was Hamburg's City Architect, Fritz Schumacher. Responding to criticism of the state of German design, Schumacher wrote an article for the *Hamburgischer Correspondent* praising the ability of his nation's artists to achieve superior results "without deliberate borrowing from other periods and foreign peoples." He also stated his belief that HAPAG's new passenger liners provided the Empire with the opportunity of "sending swimming symbols of German artistic skill as pioneers to foreign lands."[115] In February 1913, Schumacher wrote to Warburg recommending several artists and architects he thought suitable to design the *Imperator*'s interiors: Adelbert Niemeyer, Theodor Veil, and Wilhelm Bertsch in Munich; Peter Behrens, Hermann Muthesius, and Albert Gehmer in Berlin; Max Hans Rühne, Alex Hohrath, and Erwin Hempel in Dresden; Albin Müller in Darmstadt; and Friedrich Adler in Hamburg. He reminded Warburg that Ludwig Trost worked for NDL and stated his belief that the *Imperator*-class liners were the best means to promote Germany's position in what he described as the world market of taste.[116] Many of the artists Schumacher recommended were members of the *Deutsche Werkbund*, as was Warburg. Beyond membership, Warburg's practical involvement with the *Werkbund* was minimal.[117] But the point to be made is that he sympathized with the ambitions of those who sought a form of aesthetic expression that would more accurately reflect the rapidly changing social, economic, and cultural dimensions of German society.

The *Werkbund* was an alliance of industrialists, civil servants, academics, artists, designers, and architects that was founded in October 1907 with Schumacher as its first president.[118] Several firms became members between 1908 and 1910 including HAPAG and NDL. The association was an important manifestation of the phenomenon of cultural and social reform in Imperial Germany and offered "an alternative form of political engagement," a means for middle-class Germans "of shaping and governing their society independent of the formal political process."[119] The marginal impact of such groups on political decision-making – especially those with essentially cultural and artistic ambitions – has often led to negative assessments by historians. And yet they form an important chapter in the history of European modernism, have shaped scholarly understanding of the German bourgeoisie, and informed reassessments of the German Empire itself.

The express purpose of the *Werkbund* was to produce a unified German culture in tune with the realities of modern life. It was guided by the belief that a society based on industry and commerce could not rely on forms of expression developed by the aristocracy. In artistic terms, this meant rejecting "backward-looking handicraft romanticism" and recognizing the realities of industrialization and mechanization; it meant bridging the gap between art and industry to restore artistry to architecture, interior design, the applied arts, and commercial products through the employ of modern technology and design concepts.[120] As Matthew Jefferies explains, the best exhibitions of *Werkbund* ideas were the buildings constructed by its members throughout Germany. The most famous of these is the turbine factory in Berlin that Peter Behrens (1868–1940) completed for the Allgemeine Elektrizitäts-Gesellschaft (AEG) in 1909.[121] In the previous year, he had designed an AEG pavilion for the German Shipbuilding Exhibition in Berlin.[122] Members of the *Werkbund* also designed streetcars, motorboats, locomotives, and rail carriages, and the association's yearbook for 1914 was devoted to transportation.[123]

The *Werkbund* also sought to strengthen Germany's position in the international marketplace by promoting and selling quality consumer goods to the world. International expositions were one means of garnering recognition for German achievements in the applied arts, and this was certainly the case at the St. Louis World's Fair in 1904.[124] Proponents of modernism in German architecture and design did not experience the same level of official disapproval as their colleagues in the fine arts. In fact, the Standing Exhibition Commission for German Industry, established to coordinate German contributions to international exhibitions, was sympathetic to modern design.[125] The buildings and exhibition halls of the German delegation to St. Louis were designed by Erich Kleinhempel, Alfred Grenander, Paul Troost, Hermann Billing, and Bruno Möhring, all of whom later became members of the *Werkbund*. As a result, Germany was found to be at the forefront of new ideas and German and foreign commentators praised the nation's contribution to the fair as "a victory of the new aesthetic-ethical sensibility of the middle class."[126]

Albert Ballin understood the importance of these international exhibitions. When the German government decided that it would not participate in the Panama-Pacific International Exposition, which was mounted in San Francisco in 1915, HAPAG's managing director attempted to persuade it to organize an official delegation to the fair. When his efforts failed, he planned to mount an exhibition independent of the German government. *The New York Times* reported that, in conjunction with bankers, shipping magnates, manufacturers, and merchants, Ballin intended "to organize a German display which should be in every respect worthy of Germany."[127] It said he had "deliberately put himself at the head of a movement in open defiance of the action taken by the Kaiser's government."

Warburg and Schumacher felt the *Imperator* should fulfil the same role as German delegations to international exhibitions. As noted above, Hermann Muthesius also believed that transatlantic liners could play an important role in disseminating German art and design and be effective promoters of the firms that produced it. Writing in 1906, he stated that:

> Most to blame are our great shipping companies who constantly ignore the fact that here in Germany we have recently developed an art of interior decoration whose artistic value and essential purity has gradually been recognized throughout the world. These shipping companies could not only diffuse this worldwide, but would be the first to benefit from this new development. Instead, in the décor of their vessels the shipping companies cling to old and pretentious styles of imitation, only seeking approval from those who are uncultured and have bad taste, who feel at ease in Louis XIV-style surroundings, a style born, like its successors, to glorify the absolute figure of an absolute monarch, but antithetical to the simplicity of bourgeois sentiment and thought of our time.[128]

The architect and designer Bruno Paul shared this opinion and also felt that it was aboard Germany's passenger liners that *Werkbund* ideas were most wanting. Writing in the association's yearbook for 1914, Paul explained that the contrast between the high state of Germany's technological development, and the inadequacy of its achievements in the decorative arts, was nowhere as obvious as it was aboard its transatlantic steamers. He described their interiors as "grotesque peculiarities" and said their designers should learn a lesson from maritime engineers; that is, a lesson in the use of simple, unornamented forms. German liners, Paul believed, should exhibit the best of the nation's art and design in a harmonious blending of the work of artists and engineers.[129]

V

The paintings chosen to decorate the *Imperator* and *Vaterland* attracted commentary in the press, especially in Hamburg. Some reporting offered very specific detail. For example, in March 1913, the *Hamburger Fremdenblatt* described the painting by Hugo Schnars-Alquist that was originally intended to hang in the *Imperator*'s main staircase.[130] It provided a large reproduction of the image, the subject of which was the *Morian* and *Kürprinz von Brandenburg* at sea. The two frigates belonged to the navy of the March of Brandenburg before it merged with the Prussian Navy in 1701. The paper interpreted the painting as demonstrating the long history of Germany's ambition to be a great seafaring nation. The image also made it clear, according to the *Fremdenblatt*, that early German rulers understood that the development of a nation's trade necessitated the ability to defend it, just as the present Kaiser did.

The *Hamburger Nachrichten* described the choice of artworks to decorate the dining rooms and salons of the *Vaterland* as an important one.[131] It reported that the paintings were attuned to the particular atmosphere of the rooms that they decorated. Scenes of hunting, fishing, and fruit harvesting were brought into close coordination with the purpose of the first-class dining room. In the United States, the *Old Bay Line Magazine* approvingly described the *Vaterland* as decorated with "works by old Italian masters, as well as works of many notable contemporary artists."[132]

But it was the overall design and decoration of the *Imperator*'s first-class interiors that attracted the most press attention, and the vast majority of commentary was laudatory. The Hamburg press displayed the greatest interest. While construing the liner as a national monument, most commentators did not criticize the choice of French historical styles. And while reporting that foreign firms had participated in the project, press coverage was mostly uncritical of the fact.[133] On the contrary, newspapers sometimes expressed pride in the fact that much of the interior decoration had been executed by Hamburg firms, stating that this demonstrated the developed state of art and design in the city.[134] The *Hamburger Fremdenblatt* claimed that behind the city's lively interest in the *Imperator* was a feeling of pride that it was built in one of its shipyards, that so many local craftsman worked on its outfitting and interiors, and that it would make its maiden voyage, "surrounded by countless hopes" from a Hamburg pier.[135]

The liner's first-class interiors almost always received high praise for their grandeur, luxury, and comfort and the way in which they approximated similar spaces in the finest hotels. They were applauded for their "exceptionally harmonious" nature and for the fact that they made no concessions to the "typical character of a ship."[136] The "apology" offered by the *Hamburger Nachrichten* for the *Imperator*'s luxury on the occasion of its launch was unusual, but not really an apology.[137] This was neither for the *Imperator* per se, nor for the particular style in which its interiors were designed. Instead, it was motivated by the ever-increasing luxury to be found aboard transatlantic liners. The paper explained this was the result of what the travelling public demanded and that shipping lines had to meet public expectations if they were to remain competitive. Moreover, making transatlantic passage evermore comfortable was a worthy goal, it explained, and part of the project of facilitating communication between continents and peoples.

Enthusiastic reportage was reinforced, as it was in HAPAG advertising, by the illustrations that accompanied several articles. These mostly came in the form of photographs sometimes presented as a montage. But readers were also presented with artists' impressions of the liner's first-class interiors. All of these images generally made its spaces appear larger than they actually were.[138]

Yet not all press reporting was enthusiastic and complimentary. Some observers simply did not like what they saw. The most common complaint was that the mixture of styles employed in the *Imperator*'s first-class public rooms was not aesthetically pleasing. The *Hamburger Fremdenblatt* stated that the attempt to accommodate the taste of the travelling public of various nations could be disconcerting on first inspection. Passengers, it claimed, might be more struck by a sense of contradiction than by a feeling for the overall unity of the design.[139] Hans Ossig made a similar point when, writing in the *Neue Hamburger Zeitung*, he stated that there was "much that does not appeal [aboard the *Imperator*] and several contradictions between material and form, beauty and utility."[140]

Nor was the foreign press always complimentary with respect to both the *Imperator* and *Vaterland*. In England, *The Morning Post* admired the "extraordinary beauty" of the latter's lines and commented upon the "amazing effect of spaciousness" that its interiors impressed upon the viewer. But it had reservations about its "indescribable – though not always beautiful or congruous – luxury."[141] The paper described its "vast ball-room with panels by a respectable – though perhaps not very brilliant – artist of the Eighteenth Century." But the foreign press was not always well informed. For example, *The Daily Telegraph* described the first-class lounge of the *Imperator* as decorated in the style of Louis XV.[142]

Yet there was a trend of much more serious criticism that was mounted by commentators in the German press. As Bernhard Rieger has noted, entrusting a French architect with the interior decoration of a German national symbol "risked inviting charges of aesthetic high treason from nationally minded quarters of the press, and shipping lines consequently remained relatively silent about Méwès involvement."[143] Despite these precautions, there were German critics who complained about the foreign look of the *Imperator*'s cabin-class interiors and the fact that they had been built, in part, by foreign firms employing foreign labour. The *Hamburger Nachrichten* mounted its criticism within the context of a greater problem that it identified as the regrettable German weakness for foreign art. On a walk through the vessel, it explained, one feels transported to France. Germans, the author believed, should protest against the derision of their "Germanness." What would the Kaiser say if he discovered that the liner was partly the product of French and English labour?[144]

An anonymous article in *Der Kunstwart* – a journal with nationalist overtones – also complained about the French aesthetic of the *Imperator*'s interiors. This may have been written by the journal's editor Ferdinand Avenarius. It claimed that "Louis XVI appears to be the real emperor" aboard the liner. The vessel, it continued, should have promoted German industry and served as an exhibition to the world of modern German art and design. Why had HAPAG employed French and English firms? Were German talents not sufficient?[145] The criticisms published in *Der Kunstwart* were reproduced in the American and English press and *The New York Times* published a long excerpt:

> Where is there any manifestation of present-day German style, which typifies our progress and has made our industrial arts justly famed? …The company, of course, must cater to the international public, especially Americans. It is possible that the only way to attract such customers is to offer them superlative luxury in a riot of different styles. The general interest of the German public, however, demands that leviathans like the Imperator … shall make a propaganda of Germanism and not of internationalism. They should, in a certain sense, be floating expositions of German industry of the day.[146]

In London, *The Observer* also quoted at length from the German article under the title "Is the Imperator a German Ship?"[147]

Writing in *Kunst und Künstler*, Germany's leading art periodical from 1906, the art historian and journalist Otto Grautoff took direct aim at Ballin when he said that a man "in such a responsible position, should possess enough national sentiment that he would consider it an honour to have his ships – which circle the globe – built by the best and most German of architects." He insisted that the manner in which Ballin had shown up the shortcomings of German art was "a betrayal of Germanness."[148] Clearly, there were those who believed that HAPAG had compromised German prestige and identity by employing foreign firms to outfit the *Imperator* in a hodge-podge of foreign historical styles.

Alongside those who claimed that "Germanness" had been betrayed aboard the liner were those who expressed the less ardent opinion that it amounted to a failed cultural politics. Taking the *Imperator* as an example, the cultural critic Arthur Moeller van den Bruck believed that, by adopting the art and design of other nations, Germany had neglected to promote its own culture and failed to represent its economic and political power through specifically German artistic forms.[149] The *Neue Hamburger Zeitung* believed the *Imperator*, *Vaterland*, and *Bismarck* offered excellent opportunities to showcase contemporary German interior design to the world.[150] In fact, they were ideal venues in which to do so: passengers had more time to consider their surroundings than they had in the galleries and museum exhibitions through which they often hurried. It was even possible that travellers would decide to have their homes decorated in a style similar to one of those encountered on HAPAG's liners. And yet the paper asserted that news of how the *Vaterland* was to be decorated was distressing: as with the *Imperator*, it seemed French historical styles would dominate its spaces and there would be nothing of contemporary German interior design. What an irony, the author stated, that the liner should be christened *Vaterland*.

The editor of *Kunst und Künstler*, Karl Scheffler, was in agreement with these sentiments. He championed Impressionism as the epitome of modern painting and was an important supporter of the *Werkbund*.[151] The open letter to Ballin that he published in the journal in November 1913 gave, what he claimed, was expression to what many believed. Scheffler wanted to go aboard the *Imperator* and see the interiors that had attracted so much positive comment in the German and Anglo-American press. But HAPAG refused him permission to do so and, as a result, his knowledge of the liner's interiors was limited to what could be discerned in illustrations that accompanied publicity material forwarded by the company.

The long letter begins by describing Ballin as a national icon. It claims he is known throughout Germany as "the model of a modern man" and a "representative of our globally-minded business spirit." It is true that while Ballin's aesthetic tastes tended towards the traditional, his business vision was progressive and constituted a break from conservative management at HAPAG. He recognized and understood the implications of economic globalization occurring in the two decades before the First World War. Scheffler described Ballin's achievements as symbolic of German endeavours and claimed that a ship like the *Imperator* was built not only by HAPAG, "but more properly by the entire nation." Consequently, Scheffler believed, the right was granted his countrymen to expect that the highest achievements of "German skill" would be represented aboard the liner. Yet while this was the case in terms of marine engineering and technology, an opportunity to showcase the best in modern German art and design had been lost.

Scheffler was astounded that "a man of such modern sensibility" was not disturbed by the "unbearable contradiction" between the vessel's magnificent technical achievements and the petty artistic accomplishments of its interior design. Did Ballin not recognize that the *Imperator*'s "so-called art" appeared tacked onto the ship instead of seeming to have grown organically from it? Indeed, it appeared as if the first-class interiors were designed to make passengers feel they were accommodated in a palace instead of aboard an ocean liner. The *Imperator* was a technological wonder of the modern age, but everything about the historicizing and palatial first-class public rooms was out of sync with the ship's essence. As such, its interior design was "founded on a lie." Appealing to Ballin's moral and patriotic sentiments, the author asked "do you actually think it sensible and artistically moral – you the man of commercial *Realpolitik* – that the ship's architect should artificially insert a royal French palace into an iron construction?"[152] The Greek aesthetic "was never more prostituted" as it was by HAPAG's "pseudo-artists" in the Pompeian-style bathing hall; the first-class smoking room, with its Tudor-style half-timbering and stone fireplace, was ridiculous; the lounge, with its bow windows and painted ceiling was indicative of the "unreality" that characterized the interior decoration.

"In seriousness," Scheffler asked Ballin, "do you consider this art of deception beautiful or simply dignified; or were you guided by the tastes of the international clientele and against your convictions? One reason would be as objectionable as the other." As I have suggested, the *Imperator*'s interiors were both a reflection of Ballin's tastes and the product of a sound business decision. But Scheffler found it hard to imagine that HAPAG's managing director could combine the political and cultural particularism of Hamburg with the ambitions of large industrialists and merchants who aped the aristocracy by purchasing noble houses or built new homes in the style of palaces. It was as if they sought to deny their modern, middle-class lifestyles and regarded their achievements and leadership as of no worth. "I cannot imagine that the upstart's game with historical art forms, played by many members of the upper-middle classes, affords you any satisfaction." People like Ballin who had "revolutionized life so profoundly" must of necessity desire an art that corresponds to their life's work. Ballin's particular achievements as a shipping magnate, and those of his class more generally, Scheffler is saying, are not represented by the aesthetic of the ship's interiors. Even if HAPAG was simply pandering to the tastes of the travelling public, it should remember that it has a duty to maintain a standard of good taste. The author exhorted Ballin not to forget that the *Imperator* is "a floating world exhibition of German workmanship for an international public."

Unfortunately, the liner's cabin-class public rooms were indicative of the fact that little attention was being paid to attempts to formulate new artistic forms that corresponded to the experiences of modern life. Had Ballin not heard of those progressive artists and designers who were inspired by the beauty of iron cranes, ship turbines, propellers, and engineering designs; in short, all the forms that so impress the viewer aboard the *Imperator* where they are not hidden by "fake art?" The design of the vessel's interiors should have been entrusted to Henry van de Velde, Heinrich Tessenow, Peter Behrens, August Endell, Hans Poelzig, and others of their ilk. HAPAG should have learned from NDL's experiments with Bruno Paul and Joseph Olbrich, as well as from the AEG's employment of Peter Behrens. It should have organized a standing advisory commission on the arts long ago. This could have worked with the best modern artists and taken advantage of the advice of Alfred Lichtwark and Justus Brinckmann.[153] What progressive trends in art and design needed above all was large-scale commissions through which they could come to maturity. "The role once played by princes as patrons of the arts has passed, quite naturally, to men like yourself or Krupp and to the great merchants and industrialists." But unfortunately, Ballin and HAPAG "remain well behind the demands of the times."

In keeping with the intended audience of *Kunst und Künstler* and the *Werkbund* – urban, upper-middle class Germans – Scheffler's letter is concerned only with first and second-class accommodation aboard the *Imperator*. In a brief passage, the author criticizes the fact that while so much space is afforded first-class passengers, comparatively little is provided for those in steerage. But the letter makes no mention of the fact that the design of the cabins and public spaces in third-class and steerage accommodation conformed much more to the engineering and machine aesthetic of the ship, if only because much less effort was expended on decorating these quarters.

By characterizing Ballin as a national icon, and "representative of our globally-minded business spirit," and describing the *Imperator* as a national monument, Scheffler was at one with much of the German and Anglo-American press coverage. The author was genuinely impressed by the liner as a product of modern engineering and shared the view of Peter Behrens that "the most impressive achievements of our time are the products of modern technology."[154] But the letter to Ballin was concerned with the design of the vessel's interiors and here Scheffler gives frank and focused expression to the critical opinion of a small group of intellectuals at odds with the bulk of German and foreign reporting on the vessel. More importantly, he channels larger currents of thought on the form and function of German art and design in the modern world.

The letter recalls themes and issues that occupied Scheffler especially during the early stages of his career when he was more concerned with design than fine art. In a society increasingly shaped by visual stimuli, his remarks were prompted by the conviction that the creation of art and design commensurate with an age of rapid industrialization was a "moral task, with the aim of reconnecting the realms of the practical and the beautiful which had been separated in the modern era."[155] Central to this undertaking was the figure of the engineer who concerned himself entirely with the creation of functional forms, but whose technical creations evinced an aesthetic character that was the starting point on the way to artistry in keeping with the times.[156] In his first published essay, Scheffler expressed the view that "the hard power of mechanical forms, the locomotive and the steamship produce new forms of beauty that arise, without being predetermined, only from necessity and expediency."[157] He also showed great interest in the construction of the *Hochbahn* in Berlin, seeing it as an excellent example of how "the requirements of modern technology established a new language of form out of mundane functional considerations."[158]

Of course, Scheffler's preference for, and promotion of functional and constructional design criteria was not unusual. The German government, at the local and national level, was involved in attempts to improve design training and government-sponsored educational institutions were formed to deal with the challenges of the machine age. Machine aesthetics were celebrated not only in the writings and speeches of *Werkbund* members, but in publications like the popular conservative magazine the *Illustrirte Zeitung*, published in Berlin. As Mark Jarzombek has indicated, photographs of machines, factories, steel plating, and ships under construction were commonly featured in its pages by 1904; in 1907, the magazine even published an article entitled "The Steam Turbine and Its Cultural Significance" that discussed the history and beauty of the turbine engine.[159] Scheffler's contempt for the dishonesty and irrelevance of historical revival in architecture and design was also widely shared and he re-iterates frequently expressed concerns about the discrepancy of appearance and reality with respect to architecture.[160] Furthermore, his fundamental desire for "a new cultural synthesis in tune with the realities of contemporary life," and for the creation of a distinctly national style in an age of machine production, was one of the professed aims of the *Werkbund*.[161] What is so interesting about Scheffler's letter, however, is that unlike any other commentator on the subject, he explicitly views the *Imperator* through the lens of these issues and indicates the vessel's importance for progressive critics and cultural reformers.

In 1903, Hermann Muthesius boldly asserted that "the wind that today blows across our culture is middle class." "We want to live in middle-class rooms," he claimed, "whose essence and goal is simplicity and straightforwardness."[162] In keeping with these sentiments, Scheffler's letter makes the particular accusation that the *Imperator*'s interiors fail to reflect the social and economic realities that both shaped and characterized Ballin's achievements as a self-made, middle-class entrepreneur and the forward-thinking managing director of a quintessentially modern, middle-class enterprise. Whether architectural historians are justified in labelling German historicism as reactionary, and a propaganda tool for the politics of the Imperial government, is questionable. Maiken Umbach has argued that "historicism was anything but conservative" and that it gave "visual expression to a sense of the past that was characterized by insecurity, friction and ruptures."[163] She claims that "late historicists," by transforming and recasting historical forms, contributed as much as modernist critics "to the demotion of the alleged unity of academic historicism."[164] Nonetheless, what commentators like Scheffler saw in historicism was the desire to live in the past, not the present, and a denial of Germany's commitment to the future.[165]

This perspective is clearly evident in Scheffler's letter, as is the strong nationalistic impulse that characterized much of German modernism; in particular, he echoes the national agenda of the *Werkbund* and its appropriation of visual culture for political ends. Scheffler hoped that, through a process of education in aesthetics, the middle classes "could be built into a powerful, political unit with an agenda that at least could appear to look beyond the self-serving politics of the reactionaries and the socialists."[166] He was one of many who believed the economic and political future of Germany was dependent upon the ability of the upper-middle class to secure a coherent visual identity for itself. Given the importance of the *Imperator*, and the publicity and public interest surrounding it, Scheffler saw the liner as a means of contributing to the establishment of this identity. But the opportunity had been missed, and his criticism echoes that of many others who took aim at historicism in art and

design. In 1904, Muthesius clearly stated in *Der Kunstwart* the concern that
motivated Scheffler's criticism. Here he wrote that the choice of a historicist
aesthetic entailed forcing oneself "to rise into a pseudo-aristocracy." "We seem
to be ashamed," he continued, "of the very thing which should make us proud,
our *Bürgertum*." "We want to be aristocrats," the author lamented, "at the very
moment when the *Bürgertum* has become the basis of our economic, social and
political life" and "is able to determine the culture of our time."[167]

Scheffler may not have expressed himself as pointedly as Muthesius, but his
criticism of Ballin was clearly informed by fear that a process of
feudalization – or the uncritical adoption of the values, social practices, and
political attitudes of the nobility – was concomitant with the economic success
of Germany's upper middle classes. More particularly, he expresses disbelief
that a native son of the Free and Hanseatic City of Hamburg – built on trade,
shipping, and industry, governed by businessmen and lawyers, and proud of its
republican traditions – could have any desire to ape the nobility whether in his
home or aboard the ships built by his company. Here, Scheffler demonstrates
his misunderstanding of Ballin's character and convictions. As Lamar Cecil has
suggested, Ballin was more a cosmopolitan than a Hamburger or even
a German; he was not a member of the city's chamber of commerce and
viewed local patriotism as stultifying.[168] Also, despite his relationship with the
Kaiser, his social conservatism, and his anti-democratic sentiments, Ballin could
not tolerate narrow-minded conservatism and believed the nobility provided
unsuitable leadership for Germany. In his opinion, government's role was to
maintain domestic harmony, avoid foreign conflicts, and produce the best
possible conditions for the success of German business. Furthermore, the
feudalization theory itself has been proven incorrect as a means of describing
the social and political character of the German middle classes. Most members
of the bourgeoisie did not take their cue from the aristocratic elite; they
supported the state on their own terms and not in subordination to another
class. This was especially the case with Jewish businessmen.[169]

More particularly, the middle-class taste for historical styles in art and design
provides no indication that that the bourgeoisie was becoming feudalized. As
Matthew Jefferies explains, "companies in the chief growth sectors of German
industry – the electrical industry, quality manufacturing industries, food and
drink producers, the chemical industry – abandoned the styles of the past." Yet
historicism in architecture and design – even in the case of factory facades –
remained common throughout Europe and America and it is very difficult to
know the extent to which such architecture was employed as a deliberate
instrument of company policy.[170] As I have suggested, the decision to install
historical revival interiors aboard the *Imperator* was most likely taken as the
result of sound business deliberation that understood the appeal of a grand-hotel
style, and Old-World sophistication, for the many wealthy American passengers
who sailed to and from the United States aboard the vessel.

Part and parcel of establishing a coherent visual identity for the middle
classes was the need to export and market this identity worldwide, thus creating

a visible presence for Germany in global trade. Ensuring the success of German industry through the production of good design, and promoting the nation's economic interests in the international marketplace, was fundamental to the purpose of the *Werkbund*. Fritz Schumacher's keynote address at the association's founding in 1907 argued that quality products would strengthen Germany's competitive position in world markets.[171] A distinctive national style could successfully challenge the established cultural identities of France and England and might in future, as Muthesius hoped, dictate good taste to the world.[172] Scheffler was keenly aware of the *Imperator*'s potential as a floating exhibition of German workmanship, and although it does not appear as an explicit issue in his letter, economic concerns could not have been far from his mind when discussing the liner's interiors. Simply put, the vessel held considerable marketing potential for German art and design, and Scheffler believed it should function like the products that carried Germany's growing reputation for quality and reliability in manufactured goods around the globe. After all, the best German passenger liners were already admired by the Anglo-American travelling public. Why would HAPAG not go a step further and, following the lead of AEG and NDL, hire progressive artists in a move that would benefit both the company and forward-looking trends in art and design struggling to come to maturity?[173]

Of course, the story of Wilhelmine reform movements and modern German culture in general is one of both "bright prospects" and "shadows."[174] Some of the responses to the *Imperator* remind us that Germany's attempts to generate a sense of national identity and national unity – whether in paint, print, stone, or steel – incorporated a great deal of anti-French sentiment. Scheffler objects to the insertion of "a royal French palace" into the *Imperator*'s hull and is in keeping with critics who took particular aim at the employment of French styles.[175] As we have seen, *Der Kunstwart* also decried the use of French labour.[176] But to what extent were Scheffler's criticisms born of anti-French sentiment? Early in his career, he was critical of both French and German Impressionism. Andreas Zeising maintains this was partly motivated by patriotism and attendant reservations about French achievements in the arts.[177] But Scheffler was increasingly reconciled to Impressionism between 1902 and 1905. At the same time, he came to dislike Neo-Romanticism in the work of German painters like Arnold Böcklin, Max Klinger, Franz von Stuck, and Hans Thoma.[178] He also criticized publicists like Ferdinand Avenarius who, in the pages of *Der Kunstwart*, called for an autonomous German modernity in art that would give expression to supposed national qualities such as introspection.

In contrast, Scheffler believed that a national German painting could only arise on the foundations of French achievements.[179] This is not to say that his opinions, and those of liberal-bourgeois art criticism more generally, were devoid of national sentiment. In *Der Deutsche und seine Kunst* (1907), Scheffler castigated the "idiots and the unworthy" – or German Expressionists – whom he believed threatened his cultural, moral and political ideals, and the very spirit of nation.[180] We should also remember that the *Werkbund* was formed as a response to the perceived threat that modernity posed to Germany's national culture, and for many this threat came not simply from industrialization, but from foreign influences. During the First World War, Scheffler published several articles in which he described a vision of Europe dominated politically, intellectually, and culturally by Germany. Of course, such patriotic fervour was not unusual in the extenuating circumstances of war, and it must be emphasized that Scheffler maintained his understanding of French Impressionism as a significant impetus to the development of German art and culture, even if he claimed Germans appreciated and understood French art better than the French themselves.[181]

The point to be made, however, is that, similar to Aby Warburg's dislike of "Frenchifying elegance," Scheffler's criticism of the *Imperator*'s interiors was not born of an antipathy to French culture or a belief that the taste for foreign art was weakening German *Kultur*.[182] As Joan Campbell explains, the call for a national German style by the *Werkbund* "had little in common with the extreme chauvinism or aggressive nationalism of the Pan-Germans."[183] In the particular case of the *Imperator*, Scheffler may have felt that cosmopolitanism was undercutting a specific expression of national identity. But he was no cultural pessimist decrying the effects of modernity on German culture; instead, Scheffler emphasized the international dimensions of modern art's development, and acknowledged the pioneering role played by France in this respect. He is exemplary of what one scholar has described as "moderate and cosmopolitan patriotism (which was happy to recognize the virtues and contributions of other nationalities)."[184]

VI

In the face of criticism mounted by Scheffler and others, Ballin finally had a change of heart. In fact, as early as September 1913, Max Warburg reported to his brother Aby that he had convinced HAPAG's managing director to outfit a passenger liner as a showcase of contemporary German art and design. He also noted that the company had been in contact with Fritz Schumacher in this respect.[185] In a letter from the *Werkbund* in December 1913, Ernst Jäckh inquired whether Aby Warburg would renew his membership given that HAPAG "was beginning to move more in the direction of the German Werkbund."[186] In fact, the *Deutsche Werkstätten* in Hellerau were commissioned by HAPAG to work on new liners less than half the size of the *Imperator*. Richard Riemerschmid, Karl Bertsch, and Adelbert Niemeyer were engaged to design the first class-interiors of the *Admiral von Tirpitz* (launched in December 1913) along with the *Johann Heinrich Burchard* and *William O'Swald* (both launched in early 1914). Yet their work was a compromise between historical revival styles and the modernism of the *Deutsche Werkstätten*.[187] Meanwhile, the keel of the *Bismarck* was laid down in April 1913 and the liner launched on 20 June of the following year. A letter from Hermann Muthesius to Ballin, written in August 1914, indicates that he was tasked with designing one of the imperial suites aboard the liner and had completed all of the preparatory work. *Kunst und Künstler* also reported this fact.[188] The contract that

HAPAG signed with the firm with which Muthesius was working, Hermann Gerson of Berlin, stipulates that it was to exhibit a model of the suite designed by Muthesius at the *Werkbund* exhibition in Cologne in 1914.[189]

Despite these advances, Max Warburg admitted to his brother that progress on a HAPAG liner devoted to contemporary German art and design would be slow. He even suggested Ballin was stalling. Construction of the vessel that the company thought suitable for interiors entirely designed according to modern taste – one intended for the East Asian service – was too far advanced to be altered in any significant way.[190] In any case, HAPAG's tepid change of heart came too late; the First World War would put a stop to the construction of passenger liners including the *Bismarck*. More ominously, it would devastate HAPAG and German merchant shipping.

It would be incorrect to suggest that the matter of the *Imperator*'s interior decoration played a major role in the discourse of contested understandings of German national identity before 1914. A limited number of commentators were critical of the liner and expressly viewed it as a means of asserting their particular vision of the German Empire. The real importance of Karl Scheffler's letter resides in the concise intervention it affords into broader currents of thinking about the form and role of art in modern Germany, and in the fact that it demonstrates how and why progressive ideas were applied to an ocean-going steamship. While others turned their attention to architecture, the applied arts, and consumer goods, a small group of important figures saw the *Imperator* as a vehicle for expressing, through aesthetic form, the tangible impact of modernization and modernity on German society and culture.

Ultimately, Karl Scheffler, Aby Warburg, Fritz Schumacher, and Bruno Paul were frustrated by their inability to influence decision making at HAPAG. But as we turn, in the following chapters, to examine the response to the *Imperator*-class liners in Britain and America, we find that they were often construed and discussed as monuments to the German Empire, its achievements, and its ambitions. In spite of Karl Scheffler's reservations, and what he and others saw as the *Imperator*'s failings, there is no doubt that, along with the *Vaterland*, the liner played an important role in representing Germany to the Atlantic world. It broadcast the image of a modern nation distinguished by a thriving industrial society and economy and an enterprising middle class.

Notes

1 Edgar Horstmann, *Innenausbau von Schiffen* (Lübeck, n.d.).
2 Max Osborn, "Über Zweck, Form und Schmuck. Bemerkungen zu Ilse Dernburgs 'Imperator' Kabinen", *Innen-Dekoration: Die Gesamte Wohnungskunst in Bild und Wort* 24 (December 1913), 470f.
3 Susanne Wiborg, *Albert Ballin* (Hamburg, 2000), 98.
4 Christof Mauch, "Oceans Apart? Paradigms in German-American History and His-toriograpy", in Thomas Adam and Ruth Gross, eds., *Traveling between Worlds: German-American Encounters* (College Station, TX, 2006), 8.
5 Robert Haven Schauffler, *Romantic Germany* (New York, 1909), xv.

6 The letter receives a short bibliographical note in Andreas Zeising, *Studien zu Karl Schefflers Kunstkritik und Kunstbegriff. Mit einer annotierten Bibliographie seiner Schriften* (Tönning, 2006); see also Mark A. Russell, "Picturing the *Imperator*: Passenger Shipping as Art and National Symbol in the German Empire", *Central European History* 44 (2011), 227–56.

7 These are too numerous to list here. An overview of the cultural and artistic history of the German Empire, with bibliography, is found in Matthew Jefferies, *Imperial Culture in Germany, 1871–1918* (Houndmills, 2003).

8 Jefferies, *Imperial Culture*, 221. For a concise overview of middle-class reform movements, see Edward Ross Dickinson, "The Bourgeoisie and Reform", in James Retallack, ed., *Imperial Germany 1871–1918* (Oxford, 2008), 151–73.

9 James Retallack, "Looking Forward", in Retallack, ed., *Imperial Germany*, 268.

10 Bernhard Rieger, *Technology and the Culture of Modernity in Britain and Germany, 1890–1945* (Cambridge, 2005), 176.

11 HAPAG, *Across the Atlantic* (New York, n.d.), 14.

12 A.M. Broadley, *The Ship Beautiful: Art and the Aquitania* (Liverpool, 1914), 34.

13 Rieger, *Technology*, 178.

14 Dagmar Bellmann, *Von Höllengefährten zu schwimmenden Palästen. Die Passagierschiffahrt auf dem Atlantik (1840–1930)* (Frankfurt and New York, 2015), 297f.

15 Hans Ossig, "Die erste Imperatorfahrt – II", *Neue Hamburger Zeitung*, 16 June 1913.

16 "More 'Last Words' in Ocean Steamship Marvels", *The Washington Post*, 11 June 1911.

17 "Von der Jungfernreise der 'Vaterland'", *Hamburger Fremdenblatt*, 19 May 1914.

18 "Innenkunst auf deutschen Schiffen", *Neue Hamburger Zeitung*, 10 July 1913.

19 Philip Dawson and Bruce Peter, *Ship Style: Modernism and Modernity at Sea in the Twentieth Century* (London, 2010), 23; see also Günter Heiderich, "Ein Vierteljahrhundert Innendekoration auf See: Der Schiffsausstatter Johann Georg Poppe", in Volker Plagemann, ed., *Übersee. Seefahrt und Seemacht im deutschen Kaiserreich* (Munich, 1988), 176–9.

20 Heiderich, "Ein Vierteljahrhundert", 179.

21 John Malcolm Brinnin, *The Sway of the Grand Saloon* (New York, 1971), 311.

22 Dawson and Peter, *Ship Style*, 23.

23 Rieger, *Technology*, 176.

24 Rieger, *Technology*, 177.

25 Kurt Junghanns, *Der Deutsche Werkbund: Sein erstes Jahrzehnt* (Berlin, 1982), 37.

26 HAPAG, *Die Hamburg-Amerika Linie: Im Sechsten Jahrzehnt Ihrer Entwicklung 1897–1907* (Berlin, 1907), 69.

27 See Günter Heiderich, "Hier wähnt man sich tatsächlich nicht auf dem Meere: Die Vereinigten Werkstätten und die Neue 'Raumkunst an Bord'", in Plagemann, ed., *Übersee*, 180–3.

28 For photographs, see *Jahrbuch Des Deutschen Werkbundes, 1914, Der Verkehr*, 83–6; Arnold Kludas, *Die Geschichte der deutschen Passagierschiffahrt* (Hamburg, 1988), vol. 3, 212–3.

29 Karl Schaefer, "Der Norddeutsche Lloyd Und Die Moderne Raumkunst", *Die Kunst* 11 (1907), 79; see also Heiderich, "Hier wähnt man" and Kludas, *Die Geschichte der deutschen Passagierschiffahrt*, vol. 3, 200–2.

30 Quoted in Dawson and Peter, *Ship Style*, 28.

31 Dawson and Peter, *Ship Style*, 28.

32 Dawson and Peter, *Ship Style*, 28.

33 See Heiderich, "Hier wähnt man", 181f.

34 R., "Vom Innen-Ausbau des Dampfers 'Imperator'", *Innen-Dekoration: Die Gesamte Wohnungskunst in Bild und Wort* 24 (July 1913), 322.

35 See *Jahrbuch Des Deutschen Werkbundes, 1914, Der Verkehr*, 83–6.
36 L.D., "Studio Talk", *The International Studio: An Illustrated Magazine of Fine and Applied Art* 35 (1908), 154.
37 Mark Jarzombek, "The Discourses of a Bourgeois Utopia, 1904–1908, and the Founding of the Werkbund", in François Forster-Hahn, ed., *Imagining Modern German Culture: 1889–1910* (Washington, DC, 1996), 131.
38 Heiderich, "Hier wähnt man", 180.
39 Clas Broder Hansen, "Dampferarchitektur", in Plagemann, ed., *Übersee*, 174.
40 Dawson and Peter, *Ship Style*, 27.
41 Staatsarchiv der Freien und Hansestadt Hamburg (hereafter St.A.H.) 621–1 HAPAG – Reederei 2656 Band 3. Verträge und Vereinbarungen zu Schiffsneubauten Band 3: D "Imperator" 1910–1914. MUG 128A 04 05, G – Ausstattungsarbeiten.
42 St.A.H. 621–1 HAPAG – Reederei 2656 Band 3. Verträge und Vereinbarungen zu Schiffsneubauten Band 3: D "Imperator" 1910–1914. MUG 128A 04 05 A – Bau-Offerte und Bauvertrag.
43 Philip Dawson, *The Liner: Retrospective and Renaissance* (New York and London, 2005), 57.
44 "Die innere Ausgestaltung des Risenschiffes 'Imperator'", *Hamburgischer Correspondent*, 13 December 1911.
45 Douglas R. Burgess, *Engines of Empire. Steamships and the Victorian Imagination* (Stanford, CA, 2016), 94.
46 William H. Miller, *The First Great Ocean Liners in Photographs* (New York, 1984), 66.
47 St.A.H. 621–1 HAPAG – Reederei 2656 Band 3. Verträge und Vereinbarungen zu Schiffsneubauten Band 3: D "Imperator" 1910–1914. MUG 128A 04 05 – A – Bau- Offerte und Bauvertrag.
48 See Stephen Calloway, *Twentieth-Century Decoration* (New York, 1988), 59–139.
49 Dawson, *The Liner*, 58.
50 St.A.H. 621–1 HAPAG – Reederei 2656 Band 3. Verträge und Vereinbarungen zu Schiffsneubauten Band 3: D "Imperator" 1910–1914. MUG 128A 04 05 A – Bau-Offerte und Bauvertrag.
51 Osborn, "Über Zweck", 460–78.
52 Osborn, "Über Zweck", 471.
53 Osborn, "Über Zweck", 473.
54 Max Osborn, "Innenräume von Ilse Dernburg-Berlin", *Innen-Dekoration: Die Gesamte Wohnungskunst in Bild und Wort* 23 (23 July 1912), 265.
55 Dawson, *The Liner*, 57.
56 Dawson and Peter, *Ship Style*, 25.
57 Alastair Service, *Edwardian Interiors* (London, 1982), 121.
58 Clas Broder Hansen, "Dampferarchitektur", in Plagemann, ed., *Übersee*, 173.
59 John Malcolm Brinnin, *The Sway of the Grand Saloon*, 2nd edn. (London, 1986), 319f.
60 "A New Ocean Greyhound", *The New York Times*, 23 September 1901; "To Be the New Sea King", *The Washington Post*, 23 September 1901.
61 "New Ship a Monster", *The Washington Post*, 1 October 1905.
62 St.A.H. 621–1 HAPAG – Reederei 2656 Band 6. Verträge und Vereinbarungen zu Schiffsneubauten Band 3: D "Vaterland" 1912–1914. MUG 128A 04 05.
63 St.A.H. 621–1 HAPAG – Reederei 2656 Band 6. Verträge und Vereinbarungen zu Schiffsneubauten Band 3: D "Vaterland" 1912–1914. MUG 128A 04 05.
64 St.A.H. 621–1 HAPAG – Reederei 2656 Band 6. Verträge und Vereinbarungen zu Schiffsneubauten Band 3: D "Vaterland" 1912–1914. MUG 128A 04 05.
65 *Catalogue of the Costly Appointments Furnishings and Panelling of S.S. Leviathan.* Auction Catalogue of Hampton & Sons (London, 1938), 71.

66 St.A.H. 621–1 HAPAG – Reederei 2656 Band 6. Verträge und Vereinbarungen zu Schiffsneubauten Band 3: D "Vaterland" 1912–1914. MUG 128A 04 05; *Catalogue of the Costly Appointments*, 71.

67 St.A.H. 621–1 HAPAG – Reederei 2656 Band 6. Verträge und Vereinbarungen zu Schiffsneubauten Band 3: D "Vaterland" 1912–1914. MUG 128A 04 05. One of these was illustrated in the Hamburg press; see "Morgenstimmung auf der Reede von Stralsund", *Hamburger Fremdenblatt*, 29 May 1914.

68 St.A.H. 621–1 HAPAG – Reederei 2656 Band 6. Verträge und Vereinbarungen zu Schiffsneubauten Band 3: D "Vaterland" 1912–1914. MUG 128A 04 05.

69 *Catalogue of the Costly Appointments*, 177–80.

70 Warburg Institute Archive (hereafter WIA). General Correspondence (hereafter GC). Warburg to HAPAG (Schiffbautechnische Abteilung), 30 June 1913.

71 WIA.GC. Warburg to HAPAG (Schiffbautechnische Abteilung), 30 June 1913.

72 WIA.GC. Warburg to Sachse, n.d. (between September and November 1912).

73 "Shwimmende Kunstaustellungen", *Hamburgischer Correspondent*, 5 July 1913.

74 Frederick A. Talbot, *Steamship Conquest of the World* (London, 1912), 80.

75 WIA. Family Correspondence (hereafter FC). Warburg to Mary Warburg, 9 or 10 July 1912.

76 WIA.GC. Warburg to HAPAG, 2 July 1913. Warburg described the interiors of the *Cincinnati* as lacking a unity of artistic vision; see WIA.GC. Warburg to Sachse, 14 June 1912.

77 Johannes Merck, "Meine Erinnerungen an die Hmburg-Amerika Linie und an Albert Ballin, 1896–1918" (1920). St.A.H. 622-1/62 Merck II, 8, Konv. 2b, 110.

78 WIA.GC. Warburg to Sachse, 6 September 1912.

79 WIA.GC. Sachse to Warburg, 17 June 1912.

80 WIA.GC. Sachse to Warburg, 6 September 1912.

81 WIA.GC. Warburg to Sachse, 6 September 1912.

82 WIA.III.52.6.1, fo. 1.

83 WIA.GC. Warburg to Sachse, 7 June 1912.

84 WIA. Kopierbuch (hereafter KB) IV, 351–2. Warburg to Sachse, 19 August 1912; WIA.KB.V, 128–30. Warburg to Ballin, 30 March 1913.

85 WIA.IV.36: Hamburg-Amerika Linie (Imperator and Vaterland); WIA.III.2.1: Zettelkasten 57 (Hamburg) HAPAG; and St.A.H. 621–1. HAPAG – Reederei. 2656 Band. 3.

86 Carsten Meyer-Tönnesmann, *Der Hamburgische Künstlerklub von 1897* (Hamburg, 1985), 151.

87 Meyer-Tönnesmann, *Der Hamburgische Künstlerklub*, 151f.

88 Meyer-Tönnesmann, *Der Hamburgische Künstlerklub*, 214.

89 See for example WIA.KB.V, 128–30. Warburg to Ballin, 30 March 1913.

90 WIA.KB.V, 128–30. Warburg to Ballin, 30 March 1913.

91 WIA.GC. Warburg to Sachse, 6 November 1912.

92 St.A.H. 621–1 HAPAG – Reederei 2656 Band 3. Verträge und Vereinbarungen zu Schiffsneubauten Band 3: D "Imperator" 1910–1914. MUG 128A 04 05 A – Bau-Offerte und Bauvertrag.

93 WIA.GC. Warburg to Sachse, 6 November 1912.

94 WIA.GC. Warburg to Sachse, 10 April 1913.

95 WIA.GC. Warburg to HAPAG, 6 June 1913.

96 WIA.GC. Warburg to Sachse, 10 April 1913.

97 WIA.KB.V, 349. Warburg to Gustav Pauli, 28 February 1914.

98 WIA.GC. Ballin to Warburg, 1 April 1913.

99 WIA.KB.V, 136–7. Warburg to Ballin, 7 April 1913.

100 WIA.FC. Warburg to Mary Warburg, 21 September 1913 and 19 July 1914.

101 WIA.GC. Warburg to Sachse, 6 November 1912 and 6 September 1912.

102   WIA.KB.V, 141. Warburg to Hans Olde, 9 April 1913; WIA.GC. Albert Ballin to Warburg, 9 April 1913.
103   WIA.KB.V, 141. Warburg to Hans Olde, 9 April 1913.
104   WIA.GC. Ballin to Warburg, 9 April 1913.
105   WIA.GC. Warburg to HAPAG, 20 June 1913.
106   WIA.GC. Warburg to HAPAG, 30 June 1913.
107   WIA.KB. V, 349. Warburg to Gustav Pauli, 28 February 1914.
108   WIA.GC. Ballin to Warburg, 6 July 1913.
109   WIA.GC. Warburg to HAPAG, 2 July 1913.
110   WIA.KB. V, 136f. Warburg to Ballin, 7 April 1913.
111   Warburg explained that illness prevented him from accepting Ballin's invitation; see WIA.GC. Warburg to HAPAG, 30 June 1913.
112   WIA.KB. V, 185. Warburg to Felix von Eckardt, 18 June 1913.
113   WIA.KB. V, 141. Warburg to Hans Olde, 9 April 1913.
114   WIA.FC. Mary Warburg to Warburg, 20 September 1913.
115   Fritz Schumacher, "Aesthetische Kultur", *Hamburgischer Correspondent*, 28 January 1913.
116   WIA.GC. Fritz Schumacher to Warburg, 9 February 1913.
117   Warburg cancelled his membership early in 1913; see WIA.GC. Ernst Jäckh (Deutscher Werkbund) to Warburg, 10 December 1913.
118   For the German Werkbund, see amongst others Joan Campbell, *The German Wekbund: The Politics of Reform in the Applied Arts* (Princeton, NJ, 1978); Lucius Burckhardt, ed., *The Werkbund: History and Ideology* (Woodbury, NY, 1980); Elisabeth Domansky, "Der Deutsche Werkbund", in Lutz Niethammer, et al., eds., *Bürgerliche Gesellschaft in Deutschland: historische Einblicke, Fragen, Perspektiven* (Frankfurt a. M., 1990), 268–74; Wolfgang Hardtwig, *Nationalismus und Bürgerkultur in Deutschland, 1500–1914* (Göttingen, 1994), 246–73; Matthew Jefferies, *Politics and Culture in Wilhelmine Germany: The Case of Industrial Architecture* (Oxford and Washington, DC, 1995); Jarzombek, "The Discourses"; Frederic Schwartz, *The Werkbund: Design Theory and Mass Culture Before the First World War* (New Haven, CT and London, 1996).
119   Dickinson, "The bourgeoisie", 154.
120   Campbell, *The German Wekbund*, 3.
121   Jefferies, *Politics*, 113.
122   Jefferies, *Politics*, 127.
123   See *Jahrbuch Des Deutschen Werkbundes, 1914, Der Verkehr*.
124   See Peter Paret, *The Berlin Secession: Modernism and Its Enemies in Imperial Germany* (Cambridge, MA, 1980).
125   See Jefferies, *Imperial Culture*, 218.
126   Mark Jarzombek, "The *Kunstgewerbe*, the *Werkbund*, and the Aesthetics of Culture in the Wilhelmine Period", *Journal of the Society of Architectural Historians* 53 (1994), 11.
127   "Ballin to Organize a German Exhibit", *The New York Times*, 3 September 1913.
128   Quoted in Dawson and Peter, *Ship Style*, 25f.
129   Bruno Paul, "Passagierdampfer Und Ihre Einrichtungen", *Jahrbuch Des Deutschen Werkbundes, 1914, Der Verkehr* (1914), 55–8.
130   F.R., "Ein Gemälde von Professor Schnars-Alquist, Hamburg", *Hamburger Fremdenblatt*, 19 March 1913.
131   "Die Malerei im Dienste der Riesendampfer", *Hamburger Nachrichten*; undated newspaper clipping found in WIA.IV.36.1–2.
132   "The S.S. 'Vaterland' Establishes New Records", *Old Bay Line Magazine* 4 (June 1914), 11.

133 See for example "Die innere Ausgestaltung des Risenschiffes 'Imperator'", *Hamburgischer Correspondent*, 13 December 1911.
134 See for example "Die innere Ausgestaltung des Risenschiffes 'Imperator'", *Hamburgischer Correspondent*, 13 December 1911; F.R., "Die Inneneinrichtung des 'Imperators'", *Hamburger Fremdenblatt*, 10 June 1913.
135 F.R., "Die Inneneinrichtung".
136 F.R., "Die Inneneinrichtung".
137 "Zum Stapellauf des Imperator", *Hamburger Nachrichten*, 23 May 1912.
138 See for example Philipp Berges, "Eine schwimmende Insel – das größte Schiff der Welt", *Hamburger Fremdenblatt*, 19 March 1911; "Die Luxuszimmer auf dem Riesendampfer Imperator", *Neue Hamburger Zeitung*, 22 June 1913.
139 F.R., "Die Inneneinrichtung".
140 Hans Ossig, "Die erste Imperatorfahrt – II", *Neue Hamburger Zeitung*, 16 June 1913.
141 "The Vaterland: Maiden Voyage to New York", *The Morning Post* (London), 16 May 1914.
142 "The Imperator: World's Largest Liner: Her Maiden Voyage", *The Daily Telegraph* (London), 13 June 1913.
143 Rieger, *Technology*, 165.
144 "Ausländerei", *Hamburger Nachrichten*, 29 April 1913.
145 "'Imperator' und 'Vaterland'", *Der Kunstwart* 26 (1913), 67–8.
146 "Imperator Too French?" *The New York Times*, 20 July 1913.
147 "Affairs in Berlin", *The Observer* (London), 20 July 1913.
148 Otto Grautoff, "Albert Ballin und die Deutsche Kunst", *Kunst und Künstler* 12 (1914), 609.
149 Arthur Moeller van den Bruck, "Herrschaft durch Stil", *Hamburger Nachrichten*; undated newspaper clipping found in WIA.IV.36.1–2.
150 "Innenkunst auf deutschen Schiffen", *Neue Hamburger Zeitung*, 10 July 1913.
151 For a recent overview of Scheffler's career and ideas see Zeising, *Studien*.
152 The ship was built principally of steel, not iron.
153 Lichtwark was Director of Hamburg's Kunsthalle from 1886 to1914 and Brinckmann was Director of Hamburg's Museum für Kunst und Gewerbe from 1877 to 1915.
154 Quoted in Jefferies, *Politics*, 112.
155 Zeising, *Studien*, 194.
156 Zeising, *Studien*, 194.
157 Karl Scheffler, "Plastische Natur", *Die Gegenwart* 47 (1895), 298.
158 Zeising, *Studien*, 121; see Karl Scheffler, "Die Berliner Hochbahn als Kunstwerk", *Der Lotse* 2 (1901/02), 82–7; Karl Scheffler, "Hochbahn und Ästhetik", *Deutsche Bauhütte* 6 (1902), 109–11.
159 See Jarzombek, "The Discourses", 131.
160 See Jefferies, *Politics*, esp. chap. 1.
161 Campbell, *The German Werkbund*, 10.
162 Quoted in Matthew Jefferies, "'What We May Learn from It': Cultural Contacts and Transfers in Architecture", in Dominik Geppert and Robert Gerwarth, eds., *Wilhelmine Germany and Edwardian Britain: Essays on Cultural Affinity* (Oxford, 2008), 337.
163 Maiken Umbach, "Memory and Historicism: Reading between the Lines of the Built Environment, Germany c. 1900", *Representations* 88 (2004), 29 and 49.
164 Umbach, "Memory", 49.
165 Rudy Koshar, *From Monuments to Traces. Artifacts of German Memory, 1870–1990* (Berkeley, CA, 2000), 58 and 62.
166 Jarzombek, "The *Kunstgewerbe*", 10.
167 Muthesius quoted in Jefferies, *Politics*, 50–1.

168   Cecil, *Albert Ballin*, 38.
169   For an important challenge to the feudalization thesis, see Dolores L. Augustine, *Patricians and Parvenus: Wealth and High Society in Wilhelmine Germany* (Oxford, 1994).
170   Jefferies, *Politics*, 24.
171   See Campbell, *The German Werkbund*, 10.
172   See Campbell, *The German Werkbund*, 15.
173   See Frederic Schwartz, "Commodity Signs: Peter Behrens, the AEG, and the Trademark", *Journal of Design History* 9 (1996), 153–84.
174   Kevin Repp, *Reformers, Critics, and the Paths of German Modernity: Anti-Politics and the Search for Alternatives, 1890–1914* (Cambridge, MA, 2000), 16.
175   See for example "Ausländerei", *Hamburger Nachrichten*, 29 April 1913.
176   "'Imperator' und 'Vaterland'", *Der Kunstwart* 26 (July 1913), 67–8.
177   Zeising, *Studien*, 175.
178   Böcklin was Swiss but was adopted by the German public as one of their own and championed by German critics.
179   An especially important expression of Scheffler's ideas is found in Karl Scheffler, "Der Deutsche und seine Kunst", *Der Kunstwart* 19 (1905/06), 177–82; 251–67; and 312–5.
180   Quoted in Jarzombek, "The *Kunstgewerbe*", 16.
181   Zeising, *Studien*, 60.
182   Mark A. Russell, *Between Tradition and Modernity: Aby Warburg and the Public Purposes of Art in Hamburg, 1896–1918* (New York and Oxford, 2007), 75.
183   Campbell, *The German Werkbund*, 77.
184   Dickinson, "The Bourgeoisie", 171.
185   WIA.GC. Max Warburg to Warburg, 18 September 1913.
186   WIA.GC. Ernst Jäckh (Deutscher Werkbund) to Warburg, 10 December 1913.
187   Dawson and Peter, *Ship Style*, 32.
188   St.A.H. 621–1 HAPAG – Reederei 2656 Band 3. Verträge und Vereinbarungen zu Schiffsneubauten Band 1: D "Bismarck" 1909–1921. MUG 128A 04 05 / A941 ZAS D. Bismarck; see also Grautoff, "Albert Ballin", 609.
189   St.A.H. 621–1 HAPAG – Reederei 2656 Band 1. Verträge und Vereinbarungen zu Schiffsneubauten Band 1: D "Bismarck" 1909–1921. MUG 128A 04 05.
190   WIA.GC. Max Warburg to Warburg, 18 September 1913.

5 Outdoing Britain at what it did best?

The *Imperator*-class liners in the
context of Anglo-German relations

I

The *Imperator* received an enthusiastic welcome when it first called at
Southampton on 12 June 1913. Before its arrival in the Solent, the English
journalists travelling on board as guests of HAPAG dispatched a telegraph to
Albert Ballin expressing the "extraordinary pleasure the beautiful ship had
given them" and extending their best wishes for its career.[1] When it anchored
just off Ryde on the Isle of Wight, several hundred curious spectators sailed out
in tenders to greet the vessel. It even received a civic reception when the Lord
Mayor of Southampton and a party of city officials were ferried aboard and
conducted on a tour of the ship. The Mayor's brother piloted the liner when it
departed Spithead for Cherbourg before commencing its crossing to New York.

White Star's London manager and the entire local staff of the shipping line
were also welcomed aboard the *Imperator*. It was reported that they found it
more sumptuously outfitted than the *Olympic*, "although, perhaps, not so
majestically arranged."[2] As Southampton was the home port of the latter, it was
often the measure by which English commentators evaluated its new German
rival. *The Morning Post*, for example, published a glowing report on HAPAG's
flagship admitting that it "out-Titans" the *Olympic* and *Titanic*. It claimed that
one "could spend days describing her luxurious appointments" and described
the *Imperator* as "stupendous – overpowering almost." In colourful and
evocative language, the paper also spoke of "a monstrous mechanism that had
swallowed us and disgorged us again." But it emphasized that, from a distance,
"she became a thing of living beauty."[3] One English observer, astounded by the
Imperator's size, exclaimed that the "Germans are on the top!"[4] Britain's
continental rival had seemingly outdone it at what it did best.

The *Vaterland* was greeted in similar fashion when it first called at
Southampton on 15 May 1914. It was reported from London that the liner's
progress down the English Channel was "as slow and stately as an imperial
procession."[5] *Shipbuilding and Shipping Record* published a large, full-page
illustration of the liner in the Solent. This was specially created for the journal by
Harold Wyllie, later a member of the Royal Society of Marine Artists.[6] The large
format of the image, and the fact that it is a drawing and not a photograph, is an

indication of the importance of the vessel and the occasion. As in many other representations, Wyllie employed a low-angle view of the prow as the *Vaterland* steams towards the viewer, dwarfing the craft around it. The liner "completely dominated" all other vessels in the Solent, making the *Amazon* of the Royal Mail Steam Packet Company seem like "a pigmy." In fact, given the presence of the *Kaiserin Auguste Victoria* and the *Cincinnati*, 100,000 tons of HAPAG shipping "peacefully occupied" the Solent on that May afternoon.[7] Once again, the English journalists aboard the liner sent a telegraph to the Kaiser congratulating him on the fact that "the greatest ship of peace the world has ever seen" was built in Germany during his reign.[8] This was just three months before the outbreak of the First World War.

Historians have traditionally and correctly seen Anglo-German relations in the decades prior to 1914 in political, diplomatic, military, and economic terms. In numerous works of scholarship published over the past several decades, the master narrative has been that of increasing antagonism and the deterioration of the relationship between Britain and Germany. A number of political, economic, and military realities have been identified as contributing to this. After unification in 1871, Germany's rapid industrial and economic growth meant that the new continental superpower quickly came to outdo Britain in areas such as industrial production and gross domestic product. Despite the fact that both countries expanded economically at this time, Germany's export of advanced industrial products reversed a favourable trade balance that served to highlight Britain's relative economic decline. And there was a keen awareness in Britain that such economic advantage would result in strategic superiority in an age of imperialism. Following the dismissal of Otto von Bismarck from the Chancellorship in 1890, Germany's embarkation on a course of *Weltpolitik* and its quest for world power status – involving the creation of a colonial empire and the expansion of its navy – threatened the foundations of British foreign policy. Its challenges to the Triple Entente – the alliance formed by Britain, France, and Russia in 1907 – further provoked the deterioration of the Anglo-German relationship. But Paul Kennedy has claimed that, "so far as contemporary opinion was concerned, it was the naval question above everything else which exacerbated Anglo-German relations."[9] According to many scholars, it was not the abstract prospect of an increase in German maritime power that bothered Britons. Instead, it was the way this increase was to occur, namely, the building of a North Sea battle fleet. The construction of this fleet was a perennial topic in the English press which, it has been argued, contributed in its own right to the worsening of relations between the two nations.

Recently, some scholars have suggested that the Anglo-German antagonism was an illusion, one created by British officials and the Foreign Office to make their nation's rapprochement with France and Russia more acceptable.[10] This perspective is not widely shared. Instead, while not ignoring the political, economic, and military realities that have informed the antagonism paradigm, recent scholarship has sought to nuance it with an emphasis on the various social, economic, and cultural points of contact that informed relations between Britain and Germany.[11] A growing interest in transnational and global history has prompted the analysis of interdependencies not "captured by 'the nation' as a category, such as the transfer of ideas, technologies, and cultural practices."[12] Furthermore, a "cultural turn" in the study of Anglo-German relations has resulted in an emphasis on the several ways in which the national cultures of both countries influenced each other and engaged in mutual adaptation.

There is abundant evidence that "the British were not always implacably opposed to all things German" and vice versa.[13] In some respects, Britons felt a long-standing sense of kinship with Germany. In fact, "analogies of kinship and family quarrels dominated public discourse on British-German relations, with 'cousinhood' being the metaphor of choice for many contemporary authors," and historians now emphasize the similarities between the two nations.[14] They point to the "myriad entanglements and transfers" that characterized the Anglo-German relationship; stress that the two countries embraced each other's culture with the intention of emulation; and argue that cultural exchange was particularly intense when the relationship was characterized by rivalry and partnership.[15] As Richard Scully claims, the Anglo-German story cannot be told without accounting for "cultural affinities, intellectual cross-fertilizations, social connections, and mutual admiration."[16] Hamburg, the city in which HAPAG was founded and headquartered, has often been described as the most English city on the continent. With direct commercial links dating back to the Middle Ages, most of Hamburg's trade was with Britain while that with the United States was a distant second until 1914. This served to foster an Anglophilia among the city's patrician merchant families and middle classes, including Albert Ballin, that expressed itself linguistically, in consumer culture, clothing, food, and sports.[17]

The intention of more recent scholarship is not, however, to overturn the master narrative of antagonism. Instead, it is to avoid privileging it at the expense of an evaluation of the transnational connections and affinities that the First World War and its legacy served to obscure. It is now argued that "entanglement and antagonism were opposite sides of the same coin" and that growing economic, financial, and cultural integration strengthened national ideologies in both countries, along with the need to define one's own identity against the other.[18]

Where do the *Imperator*-class liners fit into this picture of "entanglement and antagonism"? This chapter seeks an answer in the medium through which most Britons encountered them: the popular press. Many studies have explored the way in which the two nations perceived each other, and newspaper reporting was only one facet of a wide range of textual and visual conceptions of Germany in magazines, literature, travel reports, school textbooks, and other forms of printed matter.[19] Nonetheless, the press played an important role in disseminating images of Germany and the following pages turn first to a succinct, general assessment of its function. Newspapers and popular journals published in London and elsewhere presented their readers with a complex amalgam of multiple and often ambivalent images of Germany. These were shaped by particular and changing circumstances, were constantly evolving, and must not be simplified nor reduced. It is now clear that the role played by the English media in Anglo-German relations was more complicated and equivocal than was long recognized.[20] Moreover, in the two years before the outbreak of war, it even demonstrated "unusual harmony and readiness for peace" with Germany.[21]

The building of a German battle fleet was perhaps the most striking and most publicized aspect of the Empire's challenge to British military, colonial, and commercial supremacy. Yet the expansion of the German merchant marine from the 1880s, including the building of transatlantic passenger liners, also contributed to the way in which Britons understood their continental rival through the medium of the press. The following pages demonstrate this with a concise discussion of the way in which Germany's merchant marine, HAPAG, and Albert Ballin were presented to the English public. The chapter then turns to examine the manner in which the *Imperator*-class liners were construed in trade publications and newspapers. Given the volume of reporting on the liners, it cannot provide an exhaustive catalogue of all that appeared in numerous articles and must offer a partial picture, although one focused on major organs. Furthermore, we must be careful not to overstate the extent to which transatlantic passenger liners featured in Anglo-German cultural relations and the role they played in shaping the way Britons viewed Germany. And yet, in spite of what Karl Scheffler and other German critics saw as the *Imperator*'s failings, and no matter the fact that the press did not address it, nor the *Vaterland*, in terms of his particular aesthetic concerns, HAPAG's new liners were often construed and discussed as monuments to the German Empire, its achievements, and its ambitions.

Demonstrating this, the chapter offers a concise intervention into the way press reporting on a particular subject provided material for popular perceptions and interpretations of the German Empire. More particularly, it provides a focused study of the manner in which many features and characteristics of Germany functioned as ambivalent symbols in Britain, providing reference points by and around which journalists constructed both positive and negative images of their continental rival. Newspaper reporting on the *Imperator*-class liners was often informed by an anxiety that expressed concern about the future of Britain's economic, industrial, and technological supremacy. Yet it also voiced admiration for German achievements in shipping, engineering, and technological development. Moreover, media coverage of HAPAG and its liners often presented an image of positive intercourse between the two nations. In sum, reporting on the *Imperator*, *Vaterland*, and *Bismarck* helped the English public to conceptualize the German Empire and reflected its changing attitudes and perceptions. Ultimately, an analysis of the attention these vessels were afforded in the English print media is a succinct way of demonstrating the complicated nature of the Anglo-German relationship.

II

Lamar Cecil claims that British businessmen and politicians felt threatened by the growth of German merchant shipping and that "an irresponsible press made use of the fact to alarm the public."[22] Many historians have attributed a great deal of the antagonism that existed between the nations to malicious newspaper reporting and the pressure of public opinion on politicians.[23] The vogue for patriotism, imperialism, and war-reporting sharpened differences between the nations and, in a context of growing enmity and radical nationalism prior to 1914, the press in many nations "abused their country's rivals, glorified the art of war," and "referred ominously to the need to defend their 'national interests.'"[24] The many negative images of German political and social life in the English media contributed to an atmosphere of belligerence and confrontation with the continental superpower. Wilhelm II was an especial object of criticism for the way he expressed and conducted himself on the international stage. There is little doubt that he had a detrimental influence on the Anglo-German relationship. Furthermore, there was a strong streak of Germanophobia in English newspapers. Journalists employed an array of stereotypes in the process of defining and maintaining British identity through comparison and contrast with foreigners. As William Bertolette has shown, stereotypes provided a convenient means of projecting negative aspects of the British national self-image onto the Germans.[25]

With its scare stories about German invasions and campaigns against Germans working in Britain, the *Daily Mail* has been singled out as particularly Germanophobic.[26] This popular newspaper sold 945,919 copies per day in 1914 and was in the forefront of incitement against Germany since its founding in 1896.[27] From that time, and for the next fifteen years, it conducted a campaign against German clerks working in Britain, accusing them of taking British jobs and being industrial spies. In 1897, the paper published a series of articles about life in Germany by George Warrington Steevens entitled "Under the Iron Heel"; in 1906, it serialized William Le Queux's novel, *The Invasion of 1910* about a German military assault on Britain predicted for that year; and, in May 1909, it published a number of reports concerning alleged sightings of German airships and incited fears of an attack by air.[28]

Yet the impetus behind this Germanophobia was not as straightforward as it may seem. In England, as elsewhere, newspaper publishers were businessmen who made the commercial success of their ventures a priority. Papers that were independent of political parties, were financed by advertising, and sold on the streets drew attention to themselves to increase circulation. Patriotic posturing, scare stories, and press campaigns worked well in this respect.[29] But they could also work to the detriment of a newspaper. When the *Daily Mail* became concerned that its anti-German attitude was damaging its continental advertising business, it "experimented with a more conciliatory stance in foreign affairs."[30] Newspapers are also indicative of an important fact about Anglo-German relations: their publishers were businessmen who understood the value of international cooperation. In fact, the popular press in England led the way in establishing close business contacts with its counterparts in Germany: the imperialist *Daily Express* provided Ullstein's *BZ am Mittag* with news from London while the *Daily Mail* had a similar arrangement with the *Berliner Lokalanzeiger*.[31] As Dominik Geppert has emphasized, newspapers operated across national and ideological boundaries; the nationalization and internationalization of the press supplemented and did not exclude one another.[32]

It is also true that many in England were critical of the *Daily Mail's* sensationalism and warmongering. But the important point to be made is that published opinion about Germany was not predominantly negative prior to the First World War, as has often been claimed since 1914. Singling out individual newspapers, or "accounting only for moments of crisis and the final break-down, but not the long-term development," results in a distorted image both of the English press and of the complicated Anglo-German relationship.[33] Speaking about the English media in general, Martin Schramm emphasizes that it was by no means monolithic, did not speak with one voice, and was governed by a wide range of forces including the disparate motivations of publishers, practical business concerns, and opportunism.[34] It produced no single, homogeneous image of Germany, but offered many different perspectives comprising a heterogeneous picture. While conservative newspapers such as *The Times* and *The Daily Telegraph* were more critical of Britain's continental rival, reporting in their liberal counterparts, including *The Manchester Guardian*, reveals considerable variation and nuance along with much positive assessment.

In fact, a close examination of the English media suggests that the Anglo-German relationship actually experienced a period of rapprochement just prior to the outbreak of war in 1914. Clearly noticeable is an increase in articles claiming good relations between the two nations and wishing for their continuation. In particular, the Haldane Mission of 1912, by which the British government sought an agreement with Germany that would recognize the former's naval superiority, marks a point from which improved relations were reported in hundreds of articles. This was especially the case in liberal newspapers, but also in *The Times* and *Daily Mail*, even if most conservative publications were more cautious in their evaluation of the international situation.[35] Of course, the potential for conflict was clear to journalists. But there was hope for the workings of diplomacy, and the Triple Alliance and Triple Entente were seen as guarantors of peace.[36] As Schramm concludes, there was more real fear of war between the great powers in 1912 than in 1914. If anything, the last two years before the war were, in the English press, ones "of unusual harmony and readiness for peace" with Germany.[37] And many prominent politicians including the Foreign Secretary, Edward Grey, the First Lord of the Admiralty, Winston Churchill, and the Chancellor of the Exchequer, David Lloyd George, spoke of good and improved relations with their continental counterpart.[38] This positive assessment was partly due to the relatively peaceful international circumstances in the immediate pre-war period.[39] German foreign policy in the year preceding August 1914 was cast by the English press "as markedly peaceful."[40] Its stance on military conflict in the Balkans was seen as peace-seeking and adroit. While its relationship with France was not understood as friendly, the time of serious conflict was perceived to be in the past.

In addition to presenting a picture of improved relations with Germany, there was little talk of the nation's backwardness in the English press. In fact, many commentators upheld it as a model to be emulated. In June 1913, *The Manchester*

Guardian stated that "far from being a Conservative country, Germany as a whole is in many respects the most Liberal in Europe."[41] Its economic, industrial, and technological progress was often admired and it was widely viewed "as one of the world's most culturally progressive, dynamic, and innovative nations."[42] English newspapers also spoke of the modernity of the German state and did not consider the nation's militarism to be unusual.[43] Many positive assessments in both the liberal and conservative press pointed to its efficient bureaucracy and highlighted its social welfare legislation as particularly progressive. Emphasizing that "checks on popular participation, the relative weakness of parliamentary controls, and the privileges of the titular nobility" were common in Europe before 1914, Geoff Eley has written that contemporaries frequently pictured Germany as "an exemplary 'modern' state." The reasons for this assessment were to be found

> in the technocratic efficiency of its bureaucratic and military machines, in its more interventionist relationship to the economy and society, in the vaunted excellence of its municipal governments, in its system of social administration, and … in the existence of universal male suffrage and the extent of popular political mobilization.[44]

It is well known that both liberal and conservative newspapers criticized the Kaiser as a result of the bellicose manner in which he expressed and conducted himself in foreign affairs. But views of Wilhelm II fluctuated according to political developments up to 1914. He was often pictured as a positive force in Europe and his "modernity" was noted as an important personal trait.[45] The *Daily Express* described the Kaiser as "the safest bulwark of European peace" in 1913, and *The Observer* claimed he was "the most modern and progressive of rulers."[46] In June 1913, the *Daily Mail*, *Daily Express*, and *Sketch* announced they would "extend the warmest of welcomes" to the Kaiser should he visit England in the year of his silver jubilee.[47]

Of course, the German Navy was also a subject of considerable interest for the English press. This was especially the case as it developed in accordance with the strategic vision of Admiral Alfred von Tirpitz and the Imperial Naval Office. The passing of five Navy Bills by the Reichstag between 1898 and 1912 authorized the expansion of the German battle fleet with the aim of forcing Britain to make diplomatic concessions. The two years following the passage of the fourth Naval Bill, in March 1908, marked a high point of tension between the nations. With it, the German government authorized an increase in the rate of battleship construction from three to four per year. This caused considerable alarm in the British government, and fears that Germany was secretly accelerating its construction of dreadnoughts to overtake the Royal Navy in their numbers by 1911 resulted in the outbreak of what is often called a "naval scare" in 1909. The Liberal government's decision to increase dreadnought production constituted a significant acceleration of the naval arms race. After 1909, it became evident that Germany could not challenge the Royal Navy's superiority and tensions shifted from naval rivalry to the continental arms race. As Jan Rüger has indicated, both nations had "a shared interest in finding new forms of cooperation and détente which led them to defuse a number of international crises."[48] To be sure, the extent to which the German naval build-up contributed to the long-term causes of the First World War is still a matter of considerable debate. Many historians continue to emphasize the importance of the German naval threat for British policy-makers. But as Rüger explains, "the direct causal link between Anglo-German naval confrontation and the First World War appears decidedly less compelling" than it once did.[49]

The Royal Navy was also a popular topic in the English press. As in Germany, reporting contributed to a naval cult in popular culture "that blended questions of power and deterrence with representations of collective identity and national prestige."[50] The naval arms race constituted a large part of this coverage. All newspapers, from liberal broadsheets like *The Manchester Guardian* to the arch-conservative *John Bull*, saw the necessity of maintaining British sea power and understood its centrality to the survival of Britain and its Empire. And yet the conservative and liberal press took different positions concerning the nature of Britain's response to the construction of a German battle fleet. Most conservative papers called for increased armament and the expansion of the country's naval forces. And promoters of a strong British navy did not shy away from distorted representations: the *Daily Mail*, for example, published misleading figures about Germany's naval strength.[51]

Most liberal newspapers, however, saw the current superiority of the British fleet as sufficient or called for a policy of moderate spending. Some saw the German Navy Laws as modest and no cause for alarm, while others acknowledged that Germany was only doing what Britain had done in the past.[52] There were newspapers that even claimed it was Britain, and not Germany, that was responsible for accelerating the arms race, especially through scare mongering.[53] In July 1912, the *Star* reported that "the plain fact of the matter is that every single statement made by our Admiralty in 1908 in regard to German shipbuilding has proved untrue"; it also claimed that the Germanophobia of the Foreign Office was "leading us swiftly and surely towards war with Germany."[54] Liberal newspapers often called for an end to such scaremongering; the *Star*, *Daily Chronicle*, and the *Daily News* warned against the provocative politics of the government and the excessive expenditure of financial resources.[55] As Martin Schramm argues, "moderate voices were so numerous that it can in no way be said that the entire British press – or public opinion – stood behind further massive naval armament."[56]

Moreover, positive reporting on the German Navy appeared in newspapers that normally adopted a critical stance. In 1913, a conservative paper like *The Observer* could even describe it as "one of the greatest achievements of its kind in history."[57] It should be remembered, however, that positive reporting on the Imperial Navy appeared more often as it became clear that Britain had secured naval superiority.[58] This was certain at the beginning of 1913 when Admiral Tirpitz made a speech to the Reichstag in which he acknowledged the illusory hope of challenging the naval power of Britain. One of the tangible symbols of the latter's superiority was the battleship HMS *Queen Elizabeth* which was launched in October 1913. Powered by oil and more powerful than all pervious dreadnoughts, it was read as a clear symbol of British naval dominance. Newspapers that continued to call for increased armament justified this not in terms of a German threat, but from the standpoint of Britain's responsibility to the wider world.[59]

Ultimately, the point to be made is that, taken as a whole, the English press betrayed a more changeable, open-minded, and even positive attitude towards Germany than has long been acknowledged. In fact, it is very difficult to "see a linear development of antagonistic sentiment from the turn of the century to 1914."[60] And the press provides one insight into the complex relationship that existed between the two countries. There were several economic, social, and cultural points of contact and a good deal of cross-cultural fertilization in the law, academic life, women's movements, music, architecture, literature, and popular culture.[61] Britons expressed considerable admiration for Germany and vice versa, and cultural exchange between the nations was particularly intense when their relationship was characterized by rivalry and partnership.

III

Germany's merchant marine, and particularly HAPAG, attracted considerable press attention in England and helped shape the image that Britons had of their continental counterpart. Of course, this occurred in a culture that took considerable interest in the maritime affairs of its own nation and those of its competitors. In early 1912, Britain could claim to have a monopoly on the largest, fastest, and most luxurious passenger liners on the North Atlantic: in addition to Cunard's *Lusitania* and *Mauretania*, the White Star Line had launched the *Olympic* and *Titanic*. But this situation changed with the launch of the *Imperator* and *Vaterland*. Alexander M. Carlisle, sometime managing director of the *Titanic*'s builder, Harland & Wolff, said that the *Imperator* "surpasses everything so far in the way of marine construction. There is no possible comparison between her and the other big steamships."[62] In fact, the growth and development of Germany's merchant marine was the subject of public commentary in Britain long before the *Imperator*'s launch. This is hardly surprising given that merchant shipping contributed to a sense of national identity and was a source of national pride in Britain much more so than in Germany. Shipping lines like Cunard and White Star were the object of national sentiment, and their premier transatlantic liners were construed as national symbols. Their construction as such took form, and exhibited itself in ways much like those that turned the *Imperator*-class liners into national monuments in Germany.

As noted in chapter three, the purchase of the White Star Line by America's International Mercantile Marine Company in 1902 caused a sensation in Britain and the press gave voice to a feeling of wounded national pride. The *Pall Mall*

Gazette, for example, said it was not creditable to the nation that its steamship lines should be owned by Americans. The *Daily Mail* declared that "the birthright of British shipping seems to have been sold for something very like a mess of pottage."[63] And when the IMM engaged in unsuccessful attempts to purchase the Cunard Line, the press expressed considerable concern about the possibility of its premier line of Atlantic steamers passing into foreign ownership. As Bernhard Rieger notes, many "feared that the world's foremost maritime power was about to lose economic control of its commercial fleet."[64] As a result, the British government provided Cunard with construction subsidies in order to ensure the company remained in British hands. Subsidizing the line was the result of the "need to avert a perceived threat to a central foundation of British power."[65]

Britons displayed considerable interest in the launch of their nation's premier transatlantic liners. As in Germany, these occasions were designed as public events and routinely represented in the press as "impressive" and "magnificent" sights and interpreted as "spectacle."[66] The vision of the *Titanic* sliding down the ways in 1911 was described as a "wonderful and awe-inspiring sight" that "can never fade from the memory of those who witnessed it."[67] The crowds of spectators that attended these events, such as the one gathered to witness the launch of the *Mauretania* in 1906, were described as "enormous" and enthusiastic.[68] In fact, facilities were sometimes inadequate to accommodate all who wished to participate. This was precisely the case at the launch of the *Titanic*.[69] Press reports also emphasized the large number of political and naval dignitaries, as well as foreign officials, who attended these ceremonies. Describing the launch of the *Lusitania* in 1906, the *Daily Mail* reported that

> at no previous launch of a merchant ship had there been a gathering of so many people distinguished in the scientific and maritime world. They came from all parts of Britain and the colonies, while Naval and Mercantile Marine representatives from France, Germany, Italy, Japan, and Russia were also present.[70]

Considering that these occasions were covered by the foreign press, it is clear that the launch of a major British passenger liner was enacted for an international, as well as for a national audience. And public interest in these vessels continued well after their launch. The maiden voyage of the *Lusitania* in 1907 brought approximately 200,000 spectators to Liverpool.[71]

The speeches that accompanied the launch of a new Cunard or White Star liner were similar to those made at the christening of the *Imperator*, *Vaterland*, and *Bismarck*: they represented the vessels' builders, the companies that commissioned them, and the cities in which they were constructed in terms of national and international self-assertion. Speakers construed the liners themselves as actual and symbolic expressions of British technical and maritime ingenuity, economic virility, and political power. Saxon J. Payne, the Assistant Secretary of Harland & Wolff, described the *Titanic* as a pre-eminent example "of the vitality and the progressive instincts of the Anglo-Saxon race" and said "Belfast could lay no small share in the maintenance of the prosperity of the British Empire."[72] Lord Tweedmouth, First Lord of the Admiralty, toasted the *Mauretania* stating that it "added a great strength to this great nation." He praised the company's late chairman, Lord Inverclyde, for "great services to the country." The British, he emphasized, depended for their existence on the sea and, consequently, "great companies like the Cunard Company deserved all the praise and all the encouragement that our population could give them."[73] On the same occasion, Sir William White, former director of naval construction for the Admiralty, stated that Cunard "was from the first an Imperial company, conceived and worked out in an imperial spirit."[74] At the launch of the *Lusitania*, Sir Charles McClaren, chairman of its builder, John Brown & Co., asserted that

> no one present would be satisfied that for capacity and speed of the Atlantic liners the record should be held by Germany. Britain was the mistress of the seas ... and there was not a Briton who ought not to feel proud that this launch had once more placed Great Britain in the forefront of maritime architecture.[75]

This architecture was often discussed in nationalistic terms. Frederick A. Talbot described the interiors of the *Mauretania*, for example, as "British in style, treatment, and workmanship, solid and durable, so that it fulfills national traditions."[76] This was in spite of the fact that its cabin-class interiors were decorated in foreign historical styles: the main lounge and library/writing room were completed in a French Rococo aesthetic while the smoking room was distinctly Italianate. It is worth remembering, however, that French interior decoration, especially of the eighteenth century, had long been associated with aristocratic elegance in the minds of wealthy Britons. Rich patrons "went on commissioning many of their grandest rooms in the French classical styles, especially Louis Seize, already long associated with elegant splendour in England."[77] But this was not always the case aboard British liners and it was easier to celebrate the *Aquitania*, for example, as "a floating museum of British history," as its cabin-class interiors were designed in a range of English historical styles.[78]

Given the actual and symbolic status of Britain's merchant marine, it is no surprise that the growth of Germany's shipbuilding industry was keenly observed and often provoked anxious commentary. In 1914, *The Observer* reported the opinions of the shipping magnate Sir Owen Philipps who believed that, "fascinated by the meteoric rise of German naval power," Britons had forgotten that their own merchant navy "was increasing by equally impressive leaps and bounds."[79] Yet press reporting suggests this was not the case. Indeed, many Britons knew they need not fear German competition in merchant shipbuilding. Even with the rapid growth of Germany's merchant marine, Britain remained well in advance of its rivals on the Atlantic. Between 1901 and 1913, the German merchant marine grew from 1,941,000 to 3,153,000 net tons, while that of Britain grew from 9,608,000 to 12,119,000 net tons.[80] In early 1914, the journal *Shipbuilding and Shipping Record* stated that while the tonnage of British-owned vessels had doubled in the last forty years, the size of Germany's merchant marine had trebled. It claimed that this fact was regarded "as evidence of the comparative decadence of this country and the healthy state of the German Empire."[81] However, the journal proceeded to correct this view by demonstrating that, despite the rapid growth of Germany's merchant marine from 1870, Britain still built and owned many more vessels. Furthermore, German yards were as yet unable to construct as many ships as that country's shipping lines required, and this deficiency was made up by shipbuilders in Britain and Holland along with the purchase of second-hand vessels. And even if Germany's shipyards were able to meet domestic demand, they did not receive the same relative number of foreign orders as their British counterparts, nor were they able to build vessels as cheaply. This is why HAPAG still had numerous ships built in Britain in the years immediately preceding the First World War.[82]

In addition to certainty about their maritime pre-eminence, Britons could be confident in the knowledge that they enjoyed many positive points of contact with their continental rival. For example, the nations enjoyed considerable scientific and technological exchange. Readers of the English press were informed that the *Imperator* was fitted with the "Stone-Lloyd" system of water-tight bulkheads.[83] Some British manufacturers were proud that their products were employed aboard German liners and used images of the *Imperator* and *Vaterland* to advertise and promote their wares through association with the vessels. W.S. Laycock, for example, published a large image of one of the *Imperator*'s promenade decks to advertise its frameless sash windows in *Shipbuilding and Shipping Record*. Claiming that they were fitted aboard several transatlantic liners, the advertisement listed ten of these, six of which were HAPAG and NDL steamers.[84] William Briggs & Sons published a full-page advertisement in the same journal for its bituminous solutions and enamels that were used to coat the *Vaterland*'s bunkers. Stating that "quality counts – merit wins," more than half the page is devoted to a large image of the vessel at sea under an equally large title announcing the *Vaterland* as the world's largest liner. The text devoted to the products of Briggs & Sons is easily overlooked such that, flipping through the magazine, the reader might think that what is being advertised is actually HAPAG's newest liner.[85] And, of course, Germany "produced goods and technical know-how (particularly … in the fields of chemistry, physics, engineering, machine-building, technical education, and electro-technology) that were immediately adopted in Britain."[86] As noted in chapter one, Germany was manufacturing the world's largest harbour cranes in the early 1900s, and these were employed in the construction of White Star's *Olympic* and *Titanic*.

Furthermore, the economies of the two nations were a complex amalgam of rivalry and exchange. In many ways, their activities in trade and industry were complementary and "Britain did not have to fear German competition any more than that of other nations." In fact, economic considerations "bound the two countries together more closely than others."[87] Germany was the most important country for British exports and it was "rarely the bankers, industrialists, and traders" who argued that economic rivalry would lead to war.[88] A large part of the German merchant marine – including HAPAG and NDL vessels – was insured by Lloyd's of London, an insurance market that became recognized as the centre of the world's insurance industry. In fact, its profits "were boosted by the rise of Germany to a great commercial power."[89] HAPAG vessels appeared on Lloyd's Register of British and Foreign Shipping which recorded details of the construction and condition of ships and made this data available to merchants, underwriters, and ship owners. When the London-based Institution of Naval Architects held its first meetings in Germany in 1896, its president opened the proceedings with these words: "The British people and the German people divide the honour of being the two great commercial races of the world." He continued:

> We earnestly pray that it may always remain a friendly and peaceful rivalry. We regard you as our cousins; the two nations are descended from the same stock; their languages are derived from the same root, and have a common origin. We have always been allies in the past ... Surely the world is large enough to hold us both.[90]

In actuality, despite rising tension between Britain and Germany in international affairs, "imperialism on the ground was often more internationalist than nationalist, more cooperative than competitive."[91] English and German colonists often cooperated peacefully with one another and learned from each other's experience and expertise. In fact, "British and German imperial officials were friendly, cooperating in a joint colonial endeavour."[92] In addition, Germany remained a popular destination for British travellers until the outbreak of war and "British authors continued to produce positively-themed memoirs and accounts of their journeys therein."[93]

In this context, it is really no surprise that English commentators had many positive things to say about German shipbuilding and often gave credit where it was clearly due. In particular, the rapidity with which Germany developed its shipbuilding industry was considered remarkable and praiseworthy. Press reporting on the *Imperator*-class liners was often accompanied by laudatory accounts of the fact that not so long ago – in the 1880s – large German vessels were built in British shipyards and such shipbuilding as existed in Germany relied on British technology and know-how. Yet with the launch of the *Imperator*, the continent's new industrial superpower seemed to be outdoing Britain at one of the things it did best. Consequently, it is difficult not to read into positive assessments of German shipbuilding what one correspondent to the *Daily Mail* stated explicitly in 1909:

> it is just because [the Germans] are so great that the danger is great: they have every qualification for taking our place and are bound to aspire to it more and more ardently as time goes on and their trade and wealth and fleet expand together.[94]

While perceptions of Germany were not always negative, it was not difficult to see its strengths as dangerous and even to incorporate them into anti-German sentiment. In fact, Germany was regarded as "an especially dangerous foe because ... Germans had so many admirable qualities."[95]

Ultimately, as much as Britons had reason to be confident in their nation's pre-eminence as a maritime power, and as much as their nation enjoyed several positive points of contact with Germany, competition in merchant shipping was a concern for many and conjured up the spectre of decline.[96] This was "after having enjoyed the unparalleled economic and political supremacy of mid-Victorian times."[97] To be sure, Germany was not the only source of these challenges. English commentators regularly spoke of the fact that their nation faced "novel competition and challenges," both technological and economic, from rivals including the United States.[98] Nevertheless, it was Britain and Germany, in particular, that regarded each other as a technological competitor.[99] As Bernhard Rieger has demonstrated, "British observers frequently considered technologies as instruments to stabilize an international *status quo* favorable to their nation."[100] More particularly, "British debate about technology and the nation tended to adopt defensive motifs."[101] Many Germans, on the other hand, viewed products of engineering "as tools to transform the international environment that stifled their political ambitions."[102] The commissioning of ever faster, ever larger, and ever more luxurious passenger liners by German steamship companies was sometimes keenly felt as an assault on a pillar of British identity and influence. They clearly contributed to English concerns about technological, industrial, and economic decline. In his book *"Made in Germany"*, published in 1896, Ernest Edwin Williams described the rapid growth of German shipbuilding and declared that Britain was simply "glad and thankful to get the German's leavings." These "leavings" were the orders for ocean-going vessels that German yards could not fulfil as the result of the nation's great demand.[103]

In fact, anxiety about the potential eclipse of British maritime supremacy on the Atlantic was sometimes expressed in dramatic terms. *The Times* asked the following questions in 1900:

> if, then, the Germans know how to build record-breaking Atlantic steamships and run them at a profit, have the English lost the art? Do the English lines mean to contend with the Germans, or do they leave them to their present supremacy on the Atlantic unchallenged?[104]

Speaking of NDL's *Kaiser Wilhelm II*, which was launched in 1902, one journalist combined praise of German progress and innovation with criticism of British conservatism:

> It is little less than remarkable that a nation which in the eighties was more or less dependent on this country for the construction of her mail ships should have so rapidly developed her shipbuilding talents ... The Germans have got rid of a good deal of that rigidity in the matter of life on

shipboard which too often seems a sort of inevitable by-product of British ownership. The explanation is, perhaps, that we have played the game on certain lines for so many years, and with such marked success, that anything which does not quite conform to tradition is perforce regarded with a certain amount of resentment ... They [the Germans] started out hampered by no traditions, and with eager and receptive minds, and to-day we see them not only beating us soundly on the Atlantic, but doing it practically unaided.

The article continued with the dramatic statement that "We have two German lines contending for supremacy – not over us, for we are 'out of it,' but over each other – in this very respect, and doing it practically without state assistance."[105]

Looking back from 1910, one of Cunard's directors, William Forwood, said that "it appeared as if the whole Atlantic trade was destined to pass into the hands of the Germans and Americans."[106] In that same year, the maritime author Edward Keble Chatterton charted the development of the German merchant fleet, saying its development was almost without parallel.[107] For him, it was a matter of honour and pride that Britain should do whatever it could to regain its title as mistress of the seas, a title it seemed to have lost to Germany by 1900. Also in 1910, Ballin sent a letter to the Kaiser in which he stated that

the English really cannot keep up with us anymore, and if they did not have the power of capital, and if a stream of gold did not still continually pour from the extensive colonies into the small motherland, their satiated and conservative way of life would, as a result, soon be a "quantité négligeable" for us in competition in the world market.[108]

And it was not unusual for commentators in the popular press and elsewhere to construe this competition in terms of a military conflict. Writing about the *Titanic*, one English newspaper described what it called "the battle of Transatlantic passenger service." It spoke of the vessel taking high honours "in the fight during the coming season" in which "there will be a scent of battle all the way from New York to the shores of this country."[109] Organs of the American press also spoke of a "great struggle" between Britain and Germany for supremacy on the North Atlantic.[110]

In this context, the achievements and performance of individual liners held considerable symbolic importance for observers in Britain and Germany. German newspapers had taken little notice when NDL's *Kaiser Wilhelm der Große* captured the Blue Riband in 1897. Yet the English press "immediately detected an assault on Britain's leading economic position."[111] For many, the event was powerfully symbolic of the fact that the days of British pre-eminence were over. Looking back from 1936, Humfrey Jordan claimed that the passing of the Blue Riband to Germany was particularly difficult for England "with the jubilee mood still warming her citizens to a fine self-satisfaction in being Britons."[112] The commissioning of the *Kaiser Wilhelm der Große*, he believed, came "at a moment peculiarly unacceptable to the English public." With the launch of HAPAG's *Deutschland* in 1900, some believed that Britain's merchant navy no longer ruled the waves, especially because the new German liner was faster than anything Britain possessed.[113] In 1907, *The Times* reported the "greatest jubilation" in Germany when the *Mauretania* failed to capture the Blue Riband from NDL on its first Atlantic crossing. It claimed that, in the German press, there was "an unfortunate absence of any display of the spirit of sportsmanship which is usually associated with occasions of this kind." In Germany, *The Times* explained, "instead of a determination to do better, there is often a childish exhibition of bad temper." The paper also stated that this had been encouraged by Ballin who delivered a speech in Hamburg celebrating Germany's maritime achievements. Referring to what he saw as the misguided and detrimental government subsidies paid to Cunard in order to facilitate the building of the *Mauretania*, Ballin stated that

> in England, in 1861, it was considered impossible that Germans would ever become sailors. To-day the British government had been compelled to depart from the principle of fair and free play for all, which had made England great, and to pay a heavy subsidy to a single company in order to achieve a slight advantage over German shipping.[114]

When the *Lusitania* finally regained the Blue Riband in 1907, "British journalists assumed an air of ostentatious self-confidence." *The Times* expressed relief that no German ship "could in any way compare with the *Lusitania*." *The Manchester Guardian* even "considered British maritime pre-eminence secure for years to come."[115]

HAPAG was of particular interest to the English media. Many Britons encountered the company as a modern, sophisticated, highly successful German enterprise well before the *Imperator* first called at Southampton. Its British headquarters were located at 15 and 16 Cockspur Street near Trafalgar Square in London. Several major shipping companies were headquartered here and HAPAG was housed in one of its most impressive structures. The multi-story building, with its Neo-Baroque façade, was built in 1906 to designs by Arthur Thomas Bolton (1864–1945). Its sculptural ensemble was created by William Bateman Fagan (1860–1948). A figurehead of Neptune decorates the pediment which also includes female figures cradling ships. The bay windows are decorated with sculptural reliefs of figures from Greek mythology: Dionysus, Europa, and Icarus. The decorative sculpture also includes mermaids, anchors, and the prow of a ship. The impression created by the façade is one of a sophisticated and successful enterprise. The building was seized and sold at auction on 31 July 1917 to the Peninsular & Oriental Steam Navigation Co.[116]

Details of the company's business were reported in the press and professional journals. *Shipbuilding and Shipping Record*, for example, provided considerable information from HAPAG's annual reports and summaries were published in various newspapers.[117] British agents represented the firm in London, Manchester,

Liverpool, Southampton, and Plymouth. Prospective passengers were offered schedules detailing the company's services to America and information on its cruises. Advertising for the English market also described the *Imperator* and *Vaterland*.[118] Photographic postcards depicting the former and its interiors were available from the company's offices in Cockspur Street.[119] Moreover, both HAPAG and NDL liners called at Southampton for passengers.

Yet HAPAG was the target of particular criticism in the press for encroaching upon British power and prestige. For many English commentators, the company's motto, "Mein Feld ist die Welt," proclaimed a disquieting aspiration.[120] The dignitaries that spoke at the launch of Cunard and White Star liners were well aware that HAPAG challenged British steamship lines, commerce, and interests of state in important respects and this was reported in the English press. In the late 1880s, the company waged a successful campaign to remove British shipping from Hamburg's indirect emigrant trade. That is, it took on the direct shipping of emigrants from Germany to overseas destinations instead of having them transported via Britain in British vessels. HAPAG also captured a large share of the carrying trade from Britain. By including continental ports in its sailing schedules, such as in Belgium and the Netherlands, it was able to move German imports and exports without relying on shipment through Britain as it previously had. Challenges to British supremacy also included the opening of a mail and freight service to China and East Asia in 1898; the establishment of a headquarters in Hong Kong, along with docks and warehouses at Shanghai; the inauguration of a steamer service from East Asia to the west coast of North America in 1905; the decision to run a fleet of steamships on the Nile in the same year; and the opening of the company's Arab-Persian Service in 1906.[121] Furthermore, HAPAG's lower rates for freight wrested several contracts from British lines, and the fact that the German government granted rail rebates on exports carried in German vessels provoked frequent protest from British shipping firms.

Alarm was expressed in the English press when it was announced, in May 1914, that HAPAG and NDL had arrived at an agreement whereby they would cooperate in future. *The Manchester Guardian* spoke of a "weapon ... of tremendous strength ... that may prove a formidable antagonist to the British companies."[122] By this point, HAPAG also controlled a small portion of British shipping. In 1912 and 1913, it purchased two smaller British companies: the MacIver Steam Ship Company and the Gulf Transport Company of Liverpool. While the directors of both remained British, HAPAG "stipulated that in all respects they had to follow the views and instructions of the German company."[123] Ballin also sought to purchase the Nelson Line in 1912 but was blocked by HAPAG's board partly because it believed the price of approximately one million pounds was too high.[124]

Ballin was often taken as synonymous with HAPAG in the English press. His opinions on international shipping and trade were often published, as were his letters to the editor of *The Times*.[125] His negative response to the British government's decision to subsidize Cunard in the wake of White Star's amalgamation into the International Mercantile Marine Company in 1902 was well known. In his opinion, the government was practically giving Cunard new ships. *The Manchester Guardian* reported him as saying that he regretted the decision, not because he feared the competition of Cunard, "but on account of the bad example set to other countries."[126] It claimed Ballin believed that subsidies would not make Cunard a more successful competitor. The line's failure to come to an agreement with the IMM demonstrated that it "failed to recognize the new condition of things and how necessary it was to act in co-operation with other lines nowadays." Ballin also praised the lower prices of German shipbuilders, and their more reliable building schedules, noting that, "as the result of labour conditions, the great English shipbuilding yards are reluctant to fix any time at all within which vessels can be supplied."[127]

It was not unusual, however, for journalists to write about HAPAG's managing director in admiring terms. *The Manchester Guardian* even lamented the fact that "the shipping genius of the century," who may have taken up a position in Britain's shipping industry as the result of his employment by the Carr Line, had been "lost to this country." The paper praised the intelligence and industry Ballin displayed in restoring HAPAG's fortunes after 1886. Although it presented him as devoted to expanding his company, the *Guardian* also described Ballin as always working to mitigate competition between the lines of various nations and as a "supporter of the pool system."[128] This is in keeping with Lamar Cecil's assessment that, in parallel with the growth of Anglo-German friction in international shipping, there existed "a well-intentioned and remarkably successful attempt on the part of shipping leaders on both sides to find solutions to their problems."[129] Ballin, he argues, "worked hard to promote good feeling and mutually advantageous agreements among competitors" in international shipping which was, he claims "one area in which Anglo-German rivalry was mitigated by adroit compromise."[130] In August 1914, organs of the American press even reported that Ballin had been expelled from Germany on account of his Anglophile sentiments and pro-British utterances.[131]

Unsurprisingly, following the outbreak of war, HAPAG's managing director was pilloried in the English press. According to Bernhard Huldermann, Ballin was anxious to defend himself against accusations that his attitude towards Britain before August 1914 had been one of indulgence and compliance in the hope of maintaining peace. The author quotes a letter penned by Ballin in 1915 in which he states that, although taken as an Anglophile, "yet I am the only German who can rightly say that he has lived in a state of war with England for supremacy in the field of commercial shipping for thirty years." I have taken "one trench after another" from the English "and have always attacked again as soon as I could gather the means."[132] Despite the admiration it often expressed for Ballin, this was exactly the way much English journalism cast him long before the outbreak of war: as ruthlessly pursuing the interests of the company he had done so much to build.

Ballin was described as supporting cooperation and syndicates when it interested him, but advocating free competition when this better served HAPAG. *The Times* reported in February 1914 that he believed "a long-continued system of syndicates is unhealthy, and that free competition may clear the air." It stated that, as "the *Frankfurter Zeitung* points out, these remarks are very interesting when they come from a man who has made his company what it is through an elaborate system of syndicates."[133] Furthermore, if competition between the shipping lines of Britain and Germany was often described in terms of military conflict, Ballin was blamed as the instigator. As *The Times* also reported in February 1914,

> unfortunately for the prospect of peace the feeling among the other companies is that Herr Ballin has been preparing for a 'war' by building up a large fighting fund for years and thinks that, though a fight to the finish would be extremely costly for the line, it could better stand the expense than the other companies.[134]

In the same month, the paper reported that Ballin was instrumental in efforts to establish a "German Association for World Trade" and a semi-official scheme to provide reports "coloured in accordance with German views" to foreign newspapers. Germany, it explained, was attempting to extend its influence over the world's press.[135]

It was not a stretch from seeing HAPAG under Ballin's direction as a powerful antagonist to British business interests to portraying its ambitions and objectives as synonymous with those of the German Empire, and even to presenting the company as an instrument of the German state. HAPAG was represented by the Imperial government around the globe and Ballin's relationship with the Kaiser was well known. Meetings and published communications between the two, along with honours awarded the former by Wilhelm II, were reported and commented upon in the English press.[136] As noted in chapter two, Ballin was a member of the Navy League and publicly expressed his support for Admiral Tirpitz and the building of a German battle fleet. Furthermore, company vessels were frequently chartered as troop carriers.[137] And, in an official history published in 1907, HAPAG even described itself as "an important national weapon in the hands of the military authorities." It explained how it regularly undertook "relief transports to overseas military stations and, in 1905, had built a vessel especially for troop transport, the double-screw steamer *Borussia*." In the event of war, it stated, HAPAG

> has committed itself – without receiving government subsidies as do the English shipping companies – to provide the navy with use of its suitable steamers free of charge. The speed of the steamers and their precision crews promise to make such assistance effective; furthermore, the company's ships are commanded by captains and officers who are, for the most part, reserve officers in the navy, and most of the crew members have served in the navy.[138]

It is not surprising that English anxiety about dramatic advances made by its continental rival in merchant shipbuilding was powerfully informed by "the potential military consequences of technological decline."[139]

Germany's express steamers, in particular, had important naval implications of which the British government and Royal Navy were well aware. From 1901, British Naval Intelligence monitored the development of Germany's transatlantic liners.[140] To be sure, passenger liners in both countries were designed for quick conversion to auxiliary cruisers in time of war when they would make "powerful commerce raiders."[141] Lamar Cecil has pointed out that HAPAG's express steamers were built according to naval specifications, "with their coal bunkers situated so as to protect their engines and otherwise arranged so that armor and other structural improvements could be quickly added."[142] With the most important features for this conversion already in place, these vessels simply required outfitting with guns. Fast enough to outrun Britain's armoured cruisers, several German passenger liners were seen as posing a real threat to Britain's seaborne commerce and influenced the nation's trade defence policy in the years before 1914.[143] And, in fact, by 1906, plans existed whereby German auxiliary cruisers would raid British commerce in the Americas.[144] As Matthew Seligman indicates, these cruisers destroyed over 427,000 tons of Allied shipping during the First World War.[145]

Knowledge of this situation reached the English public through the medium of the press. Given that the *Kaiser Wilhelm der Große* and the *Deutschland* were the two fastest liners on the Atlantic in 1900, *The Times* lamented Britain's loss of the "championship of the seas" in these specific terms: "the swiftest Cunarders can neither catch the Germans nor run away from them, still less can the White Star ships."[146] The Secretary of the Admiralty asked the following rhetorical question in the House of Commons: "What would be the position of the Admiralty and of the country if, in a naval war, no vessel carrying the British flag could cope with merchant cruisers as those we might find employed against us?"[147] And what caused greatest concern with respect to the IMM's takeover of the White Star Line in 1902 was the fact that "the change in ownership rendered it unclear whether the British Admiralty would be able to use White Star liners as troop transports in case of war."[148] *The Westminster Gazette* insisted that the "vital interests of the empire in time of war may be jeopardized by the new arrangement."[149] Commenting on the agreement signed between the German lines and Morgan's Anglo-American syndicate, it said that the Germans had struck a good bargain because their "government was wide awake, while the British government ignored warnings and laughed at threatened peril. It is high time ... that both the nation and the government awoke to their peril." The British military had employed commercial vessels as troop carriers during the South African War (1899–1902) and the necessity of maintaining its ability to do so was also a subject of discussion in the House of Commons in light of the IMM's control of White Star.

It was clear to many commentators that, among those vessels to be employed against Britain in time of war were those of the *Imperator*-class. Matters were not helped by the fact that HAPAG projected mixed messages about its transatlantic liners. In one brochure, the *Imperator* was described as a symbol of peaceful international exchange, but compared to a warship. "What could be more peaceable," the text suggested, "than the travels of a commercial ship between different parts of the world?" Indeed, the *Imperator* was a symbol of a "modern cultural community" and the exchange of goods and people between nations.[150] Yet it was also a "giant, heavily armoured knight;" its size and power lent it the appearance of a warship; and it was an actual warship in as much as it did battle against the sea. "Even a dreadnought does not bear heavier weapons against the sea as this giant, fortified ship of peace."[151] In September 1914, *The Shipbuilder* magazine published plans of the liner, along with particulars about its construction, in "view of the possible use of the ship as an armed cruiser."[152]

IV

The construction, launch, and career of the *Imperator*-class liners attracted considerable interest in Britain. Unsurprisingly, Cunard paid particular attention to its new competitors and the company archive preserves a twenty-page report on the *Imperator* dated 17 June 1913.[153] This was probably prepared for the board of directors and is signed by two company officials who appear to have sailed aboard the vessel on its maiden voyage. Although one name is illegible, the other is that of C.W. Garrard who was superintendent of Cunard's Furnishing Department. The report discusses several features of the liner including its engines and the design and decoration of its first-class cabins and public rooms. Cunard's *Aquitania* is frequently employed as a point of comparison. In addition, suggestions about the manner in which the *Aquitania* might be outfitted are derived from what the authors found aboard the *Imperator*. For example, they felt that too much space was devoted to the latter's swimming pool and considered the pitch of the water it held to be dangerous. As a result, the authors recommended fitting the *Aquitania* with a Turkish bath. But they approved of HAPAG's decision to provide second-class passengers with their own gymnasium and recommended the same aboard the *Aquitania*.

Much of what the authors provide is a neutral enumeration of fact. However, they were clearly impressed by some of what they found aboard the *Imperator*. The first-class lounge is described as the "masterpiece of the vessel" and its proportions "extraordinary." The writers were particularly struck by the fact that "traditions have been abandoned" in as much as there were no columns to disrupt the large space. They also found the accommodation provided third-class passengers to be of a good size, well-ventilated, and generally "very excellent." The public rooms provided for those travelling in this class are described as "very much in advance of that arranged for the Aquitania." And the sanitary facilities for both third- and fourth-class passengers were found to be "much in advance" of those provided third-class passengers aboard Cunard's liner.

At the same time, the authors found many things they did not like about the *Imperator*. Unfortunately, they do not always provide specific reasons for their judgement. Yet the method in which the liner's main electrical cables were fitted is described as "the worst ever seen on board a ship" and some of the wood on its decks was considered "very poor." The public rooms in second-class "do not seem as good" as those aboard the *Aquitania*. As for the first-class public rooms, while the grill room is "not particularly good," the ladies drawing room is described as "dark and low." In addition, its situation is described as poor, as it functions as a "highway to the Smoking Room." The authors found that the "general effect" of the first-class dining room was not impressive and said it was, in fact, "one of the least successful rooms." What are described as the painted panels of the "post-impressionist school" that decorated its walls were found to be "very unsuitable." First-class cabins are described as poor copies of those aboard the *Mauretania* and the "general finish is bad." The Imperial suites could not compare in finish and completeness with the royal suites aboard the *Lusitania*.

Another report on the *Imperator*, prepared for Cunard in 1921, stated that the accommodation provided the liner's crew "is good from the point of view of quantity and quality." But it found that the positioning of cabins for stewards and firemen "in a place so low down in the ship is bad in the extreme." The alleyway on which the crew's accommodation was situated "was filthy" and the author failed to see how a steward could go on duty "in a clean condition when he lives in a room where firemen are continually coming up from below shaking the coal dust from their clothes in the alleyway adjacent to his room."[154]

The *Imperator*-class liners were keenly covered in professional publications and these took a much more favourable view of the vessels than Cunard. The tone of their reporting is captured in a line published in *Shipbuilding and Shipping Record*. Writing of the *Imperator*, it said "our friends, the Germans, are entitled to full credit for her."[155] The journal *Engineering* offered considerable coverage of the liner which it described as near "to a modern palace as is possible."[156] It published two substantial articles rich in technical detail, as well as photographs and diagrams. It also described the *Vaterland* as the "epitome and culmination of the shipbuilder's art." The journal credited German "industry and technical skill" as "in many respects unexcelled elsewhere" and acknowledged that Britain had learned much from German shipbuilding. But it also stated that the British need not be envious of such a vessel as "the very foundations of her being were laid in this country."[157] This opinion was also voiced in the popular press. While German commentators emphasized what their shipbuilding industry had achieved, English observers often pointed out that this was the result of international exchange and what Germany had learned from them.

The Marine Engineer and Naval Architect followed the *Imperator* from the time its keel was laid down through to 1914, providing its readers with technical details and photographs. And it gave credit where credit was due, pointing out innovation in construction and excellence in outfitting. The journal said of the *Vaterland* that its "many unique features are a revelation of the shipbuilder's art." It concluded that the liner's accommodation "had been arranged on a most superb scale and there is so much wonderful elegance."[158] In keeping with its practice of providing highly detailed coverage of the design, construction, and features of important new liners, *The Shipbuilder* magazine was also full of facts and figures. It mostly did not engage in explicit praise, but described the *Imperator* as a "splendid embodiment of German skill and industry."[159] The several articles it devoted to the liner were richly illustrated with photographs of its exterior and interior.[160] The article it published on the *Vaterland* was accompanied by several photographs that provide a striking impression of the luxury of the vessel's interiors.[161] *Shipbuilding and Shipping Record* published a range of photographs and plans, particularly of the *Vaterland*.[162] In many instances, much more space was provided images than text in these journals and several offered impressive photographic spreads.[163]

The Syren and Shipping Illustrated proclaimed the *Imperator* as its ship of the year.[164] In an engaging, mostly non-technical, and richly illustrated article including several artists' impressions of the first-class public rooms, the journal said there was no room for jealousy "in the great world of shipping." In fact, it was grateful that the liner put English shipbuilders "on their mettle."[165] Focusing on "the vastness, the magnificence, and the security of the great liner," the article offered a glowing tribute and employed phrases such as "the quintessence of elegance and artistry" in its description of the first-class public rooms.[166]

Many organs of the popular English press – both liberal and conservative, broadsheet and tabloid – also followed the career of the *Imperator*-class liners with considerable interest. Several congratulated HAPAG on the launch of the first of the trio. The account of this occasion in *The Daily Telegraph* declared that "nothing marred the beauty of the spectacle."[167] Some newspapers reported on every stage of the *Imperator*'s development from its launch and commissioning to its maiden voyage and beyond. The interest of a few was very keen and readers were provided with reports on particulars such as its grounding in the Elbe and rumoured trouble with its turbines during sea trials in April 1913.[168] Much less press attention was given the *Vaterland*. Some papers, like the *Daily Chronicle*, *The Sunday Times*, and *The Westminster Gazette* reported on the launch of the *Imperator* but not on that of the *Vaterland*. Many did not report on the first call of either at Southampton and some seem to have afforded the liners no attention at all.

Most press reporting came not in the form of lead articles but appeared as anonymous correspondent reports, many of which were neutral enumerations of fact. The titles employed in English newspapers were more sober than those in American ones and English articles were much less illustrated. Many detailed the features of the *Imperator* in a dry, reference-like style with minimal, although mostly approving commentary.[169] They published few, if any, photographs of the liner's interiors. And there was much misinformation and speculation in the press. In fact, as *The Times* described the situation, "in the case of all new ships, fanciful reports have been in circulation."[170] HAPAG was extremely sensitive to the role played by the international media in the success of its vessels and attempted to keep a tight control of information that might damage the *Imperator*'s image. It denied reports of mishaps and complications with the liner, and blamed the foreign press for deliberately attempting to injure the ship's reputation when such reports appeared in English and American newspapers.

To be sure, there was much criticism of HAPAG's new liners in the popular press and elsewhere.[171] *The Manchester Guardian* drew attention to the *Imperator*'s old-fashioned clipper bow and figure head, noting that most vessels constructed in the last forty years were built with a straight stem.[172] Particular attention was given the difficulties the liner encountered, such as when it grounded in the Elbe off Altona on 22 April 1913.[173] Rumours about problems with the vessel, such as with its turbines, were also published.[174] And it was noted that the *Imperator*'s size should not be regarded as ensuring safety. The *Guardian*, for example, suggested that, given the large number of passengers carried by the liner, it would be unlikely that all would escape safely in an emergency.[175]

Despite this criticism, much English reporting clearly treats the *Imperator*-class liners as national monuments put to sea by the German Empire. And, where space was given to commentary, one of the responses of the press was patriotic posturing and anti-German sentiment in different forms and to different degrees. This reinforced an image of Germany that, if inferior, was nonetheless an ambitious and sometimes pernicious rival to Britain and its Empire. While the speed of transatlantic liners preoccupied the imagination of the Atlantic world, it was a source of anxiety for many English commentators. Some newspapers added fuel to the fire of national rivalry simply by erroneously emphasizing that the *Imperator* and *Vaterland* were intended to take the record for the fastest Atlantic crossing from Cunard's *Mauretania*.[176] To be sure, others correctly acknowledged that the German liners had no intention of taking the record; indeed, it was well known that they were not designed to do so.[177]

If speed was a source of anxiety, so was size. The colossal dimensions of the *Imperator* and *Vaterland* – described as "monster ships" – were repeatedly emphasized.[178] Referring to the *Imperator*, the journal *Syren and Shipping Illustrated* claimed that it was as if HAPAG "had carved off a large tract of Germany and sent it afloat."[179] And, in this respect, both liners were frequently compared, in word and image, to British ones: the *Imperator* to White Star's *Olympic*, and the *Vaterland* to Cunard's *Aquitania*.[180] Some reporters assured their readers that, while the *Imperator* guaranteed German supremacy in size and luxury for the moment, this would soon come to an end. *The Daily Telegraph* reported "rumours" coming from the Clyde and Tyne that British engineers were simply waiting to see the new German ship before building something larger.[181] *The Manchester Guardian*, among others, was more specific, reporting that British dominance would be restored with the launch of Cunard's *Aquitania* which would surpass the *Imperator* in length and tonnage.[182] In actual fact, the British liner was more than 6,000 tons lighter and eight feet shorter than its German rival.

Still other publications praised, but simultaneously deprecated German innovations by setting them into a narrative that emphasized the pioneering achievements of Britain. This was done with varying degrees of subtlety. *Syren and Shipping Illustrated* rather bluntly suggested that British ship owners and builders "may well claim that they have brought the *Imperator* into being" because it was the German response to their latest efforts.[183] *The Morning Post* conjured the English pioneers and visionaries of commercial shipping when it explained that "the designers of the old *Great Eastern* were excellent people, who dreamed dreams and saw visions of great ships that they could not build as they would." Had they returned to earth and been escorted aboard the *Imperator*, "they would have seen the heavens opened." They would have found "a city set upon the waters." The paper went on to explain that "it was not until we saw the Imperator with an English background of sky and shore that we fully realized the beauty of her lines."[184]

Other authors, like Frederick A. Talbot, were bluntly disparaging. In *Steamship Conquest of the World*, published in 1912, Talbot described the *Imperator* as simply a larger version of White Star's *Olympic* and criticized Germany for once again "resting content with a design several years old."[185] Moreover, it was English know-how that had built other major German liners including the *Kaiser Wilhelm der Große* and the *Deutschland*. Talbot insisted that

> the Germans have followed slavishly in British footsteps, but this is only in accordance with Teuton traditions. The German is a magnificent copyist, but a poor pioneer. This is the sole reason why German mercantile shipbuilding has not produced a pattern to be copied universally.[186]

Even when Talbot acknowledged the high quality of German shipbuilding yards and their machinery, he was determined to cast Germans in a negative light. "Placed beside an English or American workman," he argued, "the Teuton artificer is sadly deficient. He does not possess the stamina or physique of his rivals, so accordingly Nature must be supplemented by mechanical effort."[187]

Perhaps most dramatically, the *Daily News* announced that in launching the *Imperator* and *Vaterland* HAPAG had "declared war on the world ... and if our claim to rule the waves is threatened, this threat comes not from the German dreadnoughts but from Herr Ballin."[188] To be sure, the vast majority of English reporting was less alarmist and pugnacious. But clearly, many voices in the English press were unable to treat the *Imperator*-class liners, and what *The Observer* described as "the mighty present" and "the ambitious future of the German merchant navy," as distinct from Germany's pretension to world-power status and what this meant for Britain.[189]

Yet despite instances of critical and anxious commentary, much of the English reportage on the *Imperator* and *Vaterland* expressed admiration, congratulation, and positive astonishment. The *Daily Chronicle*, a liberal newspaper, described the *Imperator* as "one of the marvels of modern ship-building."[190] This kind of praise also appeared in conservative dailies like *The*

Times, The Morning Post, and *The Daily Telegraph.*[191] The latter, for example, congratulated HAPAG on "this most magnificent ship."[192] *The Morning Post* claimed that the luxury of the *Vaterland* was "indescribable."[193] *The Times* opined that

> to take proper care of nearly 5,000 souls housed in a vast moving hotel … is a problem requiring more than ordinary organizing powers, and it must be admitted that it has been carried out by the Hamburg-Amerika Line with a success that deserves unqualified praise.

It even stated that the liner embodied many improvements upon the *Titanic.*[194]

And even if often expressed in reserved tones, it is clear that the press took great interest in the *Imperator* and *Vaterland* as feats of engineering. This was in keeping with the reception that the vessels received in professional journals. In this respect, the size of both liners was cause, not only for alarm, but for fascination. *The Manchester Guardian,* for example, took a special interest in the size of the *Imperator* or, as *The Daily Telegraph* reported, what HAPAG officers had named "'The Little Dugout.'"[195] Over a period of several months, it published a number of large photographs, not only of the vessel under construction and docked at Cuxhaven but also of various particulars: one of its "gigantic" funnels lying in the Vulcan yard; a "monster" mooring buoy constructed especially for the liner and weighing twenty tons; and an "enormous" fender of rope used to prevent it from striking the landing stage.[196] All of these large photographs are formatted to emphasize the enormity of their subjects; these fill the picture plane and are sometimes juxtaposed against other objects to emphasize their giant proportions. When the *Vaterland* had trouble leaving its pier in New York harbour in May 1914, sinking two small barges in the process, *The Manchester Guardian* published a very sympathetic report on the difficulties encountered by ships of such size.[197]

English journalists also took an interest in the liners' steadiness and lack of vibration, as well as the exhaustive precision with which they had been built.[198] *The Manchester Guardian,* for example, said that the minor details of the *Vaterland* "have been thought out to an extraordinary degree of thoroughness."[199] There was also much emphasis on the safety of both liners, both in terms of their construction and the equipment, especially lifeboats, with which they were outfitted. High praise came from *The Daily Telegraph* when it claimed, although incorrectly, that HAPAG had scrutinized the plans of the *Imperator* in the wake of the *Titanic* disaster and found that no alterations were required. The paper emphasized the ability of the ship to reach New York even if it faced the same trouble as the ill-fated White Star liner.[200]

Press commentary sometimes went beyond the liners themselves to reflect upon the achievements of HAPAG and German merchant shipping and to marvel at the industrial and technological progress that the nation had made since the 1880s. This reinforced a positive image of Germany as a society on the cutting edge of scientific and technological innovation. *The Sunday Times* noted that

German newspapers made the *Imperator*'s launch the occasion for reflection on the progress of German shipbuilding and confirmed that "they have ample cause for satisfaction."[201] *The Daily Telegraph* described the event as a beautiful spectacle and acknowledged Germany's supremacy in the construction of passenger liners.[202] *The Times* stated that the *Imperator* marked "an important stage in German shipbuilding skill and enterprise." It noted that, as recently as 1886, the Vulcan shipyard considered it an achievement to build three steamers, each of 4,500 tons.[203] *The Daily Telegraph* noted the astonishing progress embodied in the *Vaterland* in more poetic terms. "From the Vanderdecken to the Vaterland," it wrote, "from the greatest ship of German mythology to the greatest ship of Germany's vast mercantile marine – that was the contrast that came unbidden to mind." "The antithesis seems the more permissible," the paper continued, "when it is considered that when Wagner was first captured by the legend of Der Fliegende Holländer – beloved of German poets – there was no German mercantile marine on the Atlantic worth speaking of."[204]

Also noteworthy is the fact that the English press sometimes described the *Imperator*-class liners as the product of more than one nation, but not with the intention of denigrating German achievements. *The Westminster Gazette*, a liberal paper, emphasized the rivalry between the *Imperator* and the *Aquitania*, but wished both vessels success and described them as "triumphs of a courage and commercial enterprise that have not been daunted by the disaster of the *Titanic*."[205] At least one paper – *The Manchester Guardian* – emphasized that the competition that had produced the *Imperator* and *Aquitania* "has brought British and German ship owners into conference and resulted in an understanding between them which regards the peace of Europe as the chief condition of their continued prosperity. Viewed in this light, every ton and foot of the *Aquitania* and *Imperator* was a guarantor of peace."[206] This sentiment was in keeping with the considerable amount of positive coverage of Germany that appeared in the English media immediately before the outbreak of war in 1914, itself indicative of a complex relationship characterized by partnership and rivalry.

V

Many of the *Imperator*'s first-class passengers travelled from London to board the liner for its maiden voyage to New York on 12 June 1913. HAPAG arranged for train travel from Waterloo Station to Southampton where passengers were transferred to the vessel by tender. Following a stopover in Cherbourg, the *Imperator* covered the 3,153 miles to New York in six days, five hours, and fourteen minutes. There it was greeted by a scene of great excitement and a press that embraced HAPAG's liners more enthusiastically than the English media did.

Reviewing England's popular print media from the decade preceding 1914, what is clear from the volume of positive reporting is that published attitudes toward Germany were not always, nor greatly affected by the unpropitious diplomatic climate and international situation. Consequently, anti-German published and public opinion seems not to have been an important impetus to military conflict. In fact, popular hatred of Germany was more the product of the First World War than its cause. The propaganda used to unite and mobilize Britons against their enemy during the struggle served to partially erase the memory of significant connection and affinity between the nations before it.[207] Yet even the events of 1914–1918 did not mark a decisive break in Anglo-German relations. This occurred more completely after the Second World War. Of course, during the first conflict, the English press offered a more uniform and consistent image of Germany as the enemy than it previously had. And yet relations between the nations resumed after 1918, and many Britons continued to express admiration for their sometime foe.

What is certain is that Britons had a "complex sense of Germany" before 1914.[208] The English press clearly represented an ambivalent force in Anglo-German relations as commentators "debated in various ways the potential benefits and dangers posed by the developing German Empire."[209] The press never passively received images of its continental counterpart as a future military opponent.[210] Moreover, it was a force that was more open-ended than antagonistic. It contributed to simultaneous processes of internationalism and nationalism as the economic and cultural integration of a more globalized world increased the need to define one's national identity against others.[211]

Ultimately, there are several reasons why Britain and Germany went to war in 1914 despite multiple points and instances of economic, social, and cultural contact and entanglement. Not least of these is the crisis on the continent following the assassination of Archduke Franz Ferdinand, heir to the Austro-Hungarian throne, on 28 June 1914 and the series of political, diplomatic, and military decisions that turned a localized conflict into a global one. Germany's decision to declare war on Russia and France in early August, and Britain's determination to honour the Treaty of London and defend Belgium against German aggression, were made in the context of an unstable international situation and a polarized state system. This was characterized by a complex web of alliances hardened by political, economic, and territorial conflicts and the pursuance of confrontational policies that eventually led nations into war. Increased competition and conflict stemming from imperial ambition, nationalism, and the militarism of several nations also played a role in the outbreak of war.

As for the naval arms race, it is clear that it damaged Anglo-German relations. However, as we have noted, there are historians who now argue that its role in precipitating the First World War is much less direct and much less substantial than once believed. The extent to which German advances in the construction and commissioning of transatlantic passenger liners contributed to real and significant tensions between the nations was minimal. And yet, what is important is that, capturing the interest of the English print media, the *Imperator*-class liners played a role in representing Germany to Britons. Clearly, Germans themselves did not agree on what these vessels represented or should represent. Yet even before they steamed across the North Sea into the English Channel, the *Imperator* and *Vaterland* played a role in fashioning, reinforcing, and repeating the image that Britons derived of Germany from various sources – an image that was multiple, varied, changing, open-ended, and often positive.

Notes

1 "Erste Reise des Dampfers Imperator", *Zeitschrift der Hamburg-Amerika Linie* 12 (20 June 1913), 84.
2 "Imperator Touches at Southampton", *The New York Times*, 13 June 1913.
3 "The Imperator", *The Morning Post* (London), 13 June 1913.
4 HAPAG, *Imperator Auf See: Gedenkblätter an die erste Ausfahrt des Dampfers am 11. Juni 1913* (Hamburg, 1913), 26.
5 "Vaterland on Way across Atlantic", *The New York Times*, 16 May 1914.
6 "The Vaterland in the Solent", *Shipbuilding and Shipping Record* 3 (21 May 1914), 619.
7 "Vaterland on Way across Atlantic", *The New York Times*, 16 May 1914.
8 "Congratulations for Kaiser Sent from Vaterland", *The Christian Science Monitor* (Boston), 8 June 1914.
9 Paul M. Kennedy, *The Rise of the Anglo-German Antagonism, 1860–1914* (London, 1980), 416.
10 See for example, John Charmley, *Splendid Isolation? Britain, the Balance of Power and the Origins of the First World War* (London, 1999); Niall Ferguson, *The Pity of War: Explaining World War I* (New York, 1999).
11 See Dominik Geppert and Robert Gerwarth, "Introduction", in Dominik Geppert and Robert Gerwarth, eds., *Wilhelmine Germany and Edwardian Britain: Essays on Cultural Affinity* (Oxford, 2008), 13.
12 Jan Rüger, "Revisiting the Anglo-German Antagonism", *The Journal of Modern History* 83 (2011), 581.
13 Patrick Major, "Britain and Germany: A Love-Hate Relationship?" *German History* 26 (2008), 457.
14 Geppert and Gerwarth, "Introduction", 11.
15 Geppert and Gerwarth, "Introduction", 3f.
16 Richard Scully, *British Images of Germany: Admiration, Antagonism and Ambivalence, 1860–1914* (Houndmills, 2012), 3.
17 See Andrew Francis Bell, *Anglophilia*: *The Hamburg Bourgeoisie and the Importation of English Middle Class Culture in the Wilhelmine Era* (Ph.D. diss., Brown University, 2001).
18 Geppert and Gerwarth, "Introduction", 13.
19 See, for example, Scully, *British Images*.
20 On this point see Martin Schramm, *Das Deutschlandbild in der britischen Presse 1912–1919* (Berlin, 2007).
21 Dominik Geppert, *Pressekriege. Öffentlichkeit und Diplomatie in den deutsch-britischen Beziehungen (1896–1912)* (Munich, 2007), 27.
22 Lamar Cecil, *Albert Ballin: Business and Politics in Imperial Germany, 1888–1918* (Princeton, NJ, 1967), 94f.
23 Wolfgang J. Mommsen, "Public Opinion and Foreign Policy in Wilhelmine Germany: 1897–1914", *Central European History* 24 (1991), 381–401; A.J. Anthony Morris, *The Scaremongers: The Advocacy of War and Rearmament 1896–1914* (London, 1984); Kennedy, *The Rise of the Anglo-German Antagonism*; Fritz Fischer, *Krieg der Illusionen: Die deutsche Politik von 1911 bis 1914* (Düsseldorf, 1969).
24 Kennedy, *The Rise*, 361.

25 William F. Bertolette, *British identity and the German other* (Ph.D. diss., Louisiana State University and Agricultural and Mechanical College, 2012).
26 See Dominik Geppert, "'The Foul-visaged Anti-Christ of Journalism'? The Popular Press between Warmongering and International Cooperation", in Geppert and Gerwarth, eds., *Wilhelmine Germany*, 369–89.
27 Geppert, "'The Foul-visaged Anti-Christ'", 380.
28 Geppert, "'The Foul-visaged Anti-Christ'", 374f; see also Twells Brex, *Scaremongerings from the Daily Mail 1896–1914: The Paper that Foretold the War* (London, 1915).
29 Geppert, "'The Foul-visaged Anti-Christ'", 374.
30 Geppert, "'The Foul-visaged Anti-Christ'", 382 and 388.
31 Geppert, "'The Foul-visaged Anti-Christ'", 381.
32 Geppert, "'The Foul-visaged Anti-Christ'", 388f.
33 Lothar Reinermann has warned against the dangers of such a narrow perspective in attempting to understand the Kaiser's image in the British press in Lothar Reinermann, "Fleet Street and the Kaiser: British Public Opinion and Wilhelm II", *German History* 26 (2008), 470.
34 Schramm, *Das Deutschlandbild*.
35 Schramm, *Das Deutschlandbild*, 183f.
36 Schramm, *Das Deutschlandbild*, 196 and 198.
37 Geppert, *Pressekriege*, 27.
38 Schramm, *Das Deutschlandbild*, 17.
39 Schramm, *Das Deutschlandbild*, 86.
40 Schramm, *Das Deutschlandbild*, 146.
41 Schramm, *Das Deutschlandbild*, 130.
42 Geppert and Gerwarth, "Introduction", 6.
43 Schramm, *Das Deutschlandbild*, 129f.
44 Geoff Eley, "German History and the Contradictions of Modernity: The Bourgeoisie, the State, and the Mastery of Reform", in Geoff Eley, ed., *Society, Culture and the State in Germany, 1870–1930* (Ann Arbor, MI, 1996), 93.
45 Schramm, *Das Deutschlandbild*, 83.
46 Schramm, *Das Deutschlandbild*, 76 and 130. For English impressions of the Kaiser see also Reinermann, "Fleet Street".
47 Schramm, *Das Deutschlandbild*, 82.
48 Jan Rüger, "The Navy and the Sea", in Matthew Jefferies, ed., *The Ashgate Research Companion to Imperial Germany* (Farnham, 2015), 407.
49 Rüger, "The Navy", 407.
50 Geppert, *Pressekriege*, 297.
51 Schramm, *Das Deutschlandbild*, 89.
52 Schramm, *Das Deutschlandbild*, 95 and 99.
53 Schramm, *Das Deutschlandbild*, 94.
54 Schramm, *Das Deutschlandbild*, 94 and 95.
55 Schramm, *Das Deutschlandbild*, 95.
56 Schramm, *Das Deutschlandbild*, 96.
57 Schramm, *Das Deutschlandbild*, 89.
58 Schramm, *Das Deutschlandbild*, 102.
59 Schramm, *Das Deutschlandbild*, 102.
60 Rüger, "Revisiting", 589.
61 Geppert and Gerwarth, eds., *Wilhelmine Germany*. In this collection see especially David Blackbourn, "'As Dependent on Each Other as Man and Wife': Cultural Contacts and Transfers", 15–37.
62 "The Imperator, Greatest Steamship Afloat, Ends Half of Her Maiden Voyage Amid Ovation of Sister Craft", *New York Herald*, 20 June 1913.

63 Quoted in "See Peril in Deal", *The Washington Post*, 22 April 1902; see also "Terms of the Ship Merger", *The Washington Post*, 28 April 1902.
64 Bernhard Rieger, *Technology and the Culture of Modernity in Britain and Germany, 1890–1945* (Cambridge, 2005), 236.
65 Rieger, *Technology*, 236.
66 "Launch of Liners", *The Times* (London), 21 September 1906.
67 "Launch of the Titanic", *Belfast Newsletter*, 1 June 1911.
68 "Launch of Liners", *The Times* (London), 21 September 1906.
69 "Launch of the Titanic", *Belfast Newsletter*, 1 June 1911.
70 Quoted in Douglas R. Burgess, *Seize the Trident: The Race for Superliner Supremacy and How It Altered the Great War* (New York, 2005), 105.
71 Burgess, *Seize the Trident*, 115.
72 "Launch of the Titanic", *Belfast Newsletter*, 1 June 1911.
73 "Launch of Liners", *The Times* (London), 21 September 1906.
74 "Launch of Liners", *The Times* (London), 21 September 1906.
75 "Launch of the Lusitania", *The Times* (London), 8 June 1906.
76 Frederick A. Talbot, *Steamship Conquest of the World* (London, 1912), 79.
77 Alastair Service, *Edwardian Interiors* (London, 1982).
78 Burgess, *Seize the Trident*, 189.
79 "Affairs in Berlin", *The Observer* (London), 7 June 1914.
80 S.G. Sturmey, *British Shipping and World Competition* (London, 1962), 302.
81 "The Rise of German Shipbuilding", *Shipbuilding and Shipping Record* 4 (7 January 1914), 16.
82 "What's Wrong with German Shipbuilding?" *Shipbuilding and Shipping Record* 3 (23 April 1914), 504f.
83 "World's Biggest Liner", *The Daily Telegraph* (London), 16 May 1914.
84 "The Rise of German Shipbuilding", 15.
85 "The Rise of German Shipbuilding", 22.
86 Geppert and Gerwarth, "Introduction", 6.
87 Rüger, "Revisiting", 607.
88 Rüger, "Revisiting", 607.
89 Kennedy, *The Rise*, 295.
90 Quoted in Stephen Fox, *Transatlantic: Samuel Cunard, Isambard Brunel, and the Great Atlantic Steamships* (New York, 2003), 378.
91 Geppert and Gerwarth, "Introduction", 8.
92 John M. MacKenzie, "'Mutual Goodwill and Admiration' or 'Jealous Ill-will'? Empire and Popular Culture", in Geppert and Gerwarth, eds., *Wilhelmine Germany*, 94.
93 Scully, *British Images*, 46.
94 Quoted in Geppert and Gerwarth, "Introduction", 12.
95 Geppert and Gerwarth, "Introduction", 12.
96 Rieger, *Technology*, 227.
97 Rieger, *Technology*, 225.
98 Rieger, *Technology*, 225.
99 See Aaron L. Friedberg, *The Weary Titan: Britain and the Experience of Relative Decline, 1895–1905* (Princeton, NJ, 1988); David Edgerton, *Science, Technology and British Industrial "Decline," 1870–1970* (Cambridge 1996); Peter Clarke and Clive Trebilcock, eds., *Understanding Decline: Perceptions and Realities of British Economic Performance* (Cambridge, 1997).
100 Rieger, *Technology*, 18.
101 Rieger, *Technology*, 226.
102 Rieger, *Technology*, 18.
103 Ernest Edwin Williams, *Made in Germany* (London, 1896), 49.

104 "London to New York", *The Times* (London), 6 November 1900.
105 Quoted in John Malcolm Brinnin, *The Sway of the Grand Saloon* (New York, 1971), 335.
106 William B. Forwood, *Recollections of a Busy Life* (Liverpool, 1910), 178.
107 Edward Keble Chatterton, *Steamships and Their Story* (London and New York, 1910).
108 Quoted in Gerhard Ahrens and Renate Hauschild-Thiessen, *Die Reeder: Laeisz, Ballin* (Hamburg, 1989), 58.
109 Quoted in Brinnin, *The Sway of the Grand Saloon*, 2nd edn. (London, 1986), 365.
110 "Seeking Supremacy in Atlantic Traffic", *The New York Times*, 2 March 1913.
111 Rieger, *Technology*, 228.
112 Quoted in Brinnin, *The Sway*, 2nd edn., 316f.
113 "London to New York", *The Times* (London), 6 November 1900.
114 "The Lusitania's Voyage", *The Times* (London), 16 September 1907.
115 Quoted in Rieger, *Technology*, 228.
116 Les Streater, *Berengaria: Cunard's "Happy Ship"* (Charleston, SC, 2001), 52.
117 See for example "Hamburg-Amerika Line", *Shipbuilding and Shipping Record* 3 (19 March 1914), 371.
118 See National Maritime Museum. Caird Library. Ephemera Collection, 43. Foreign Shipping Companies: Hamburg-America Line. HA 14.
119 "Aeroplane Inventions", *The Observer* (London), 27 July 1913.
120 See for example "The Hamburg-Amerika Liner 'Imperator'", *Engineering* 95 (20 June 1913), 827.
121 See Cecil, *Albert Ballin*, 67–80.
122 "Great Shipping Changes", *The Manchester Guardian*, 7 May 1914.
123 Frank Broeze, "Shipping Policy and Social-Darwinism: Albert Ballin and the Weltpolitik of the Hamburg-America Line, 1886–1914", *Mariner's Mirror* 79 (1993), 425.
124 Broeze, "Shipping Policy", 425.
125 See for example "North Atlantic Steamship Tracks", *The Times* (London), 7 September 1898; "The German Merchant Marine", *The Times* (London), 31 August 1901; "The Cunard Company and the German Government", *The Times* (London), 16 May 1904.
126 "Shipping Subsidies", *The Manchester Guardian*, 30 January 1903.
127 "German Trade Handicap", *The Manchester Guardian*, 17 April 1914.
128 "Herr Ballin and His Rival", *The Manchester Guardian*, 4 February 1914.
129 Cecil, *Albert Ballin*, 93.
130 Cecil, *Albert Ballin*, 94.
131 "Kaiser Exiles His Friend Ballin for English Leaning Says Report", *The Washington Post*, 12 August 1914; "Ballin Expulsion Denied", *The Wall Street Journal* (New York), 13 August 1914.
132 Quoted in Bernhard Huldermann, *Albert Ballin* (Oldenburg and Berlin, 1922), 324.
133 "Cheaper Atlantic Rates in Force", *The Times* (London), 2 February 1914.
134 "Peace Overtures to Her Ballin", *The Times* (London), 3 February 1914.
135 "Germany and the World's Trade. Herr Ballin's Scheme", *The Times* (London), 7 February 1914.
136 See for example "The German Emperor and Herr Ballin", *The Times* (London), 17 February 1914.
137 See Cecil, *Albert Ballin*.
138 HAPAG, *Die Hamburg-Amerika Linie: Im Sechsten Jahrzehnt Ihrer Entwicklung 1897–1907* (Berlin, 1907), 145.
139 Rieger, *Technology*, 235.

140 See Matthew S. Seligmann, "Germany's Ocean Greyhounds and the Royal Navy's First Battle Cruisers: An Historiographical Problem", *Diplomacy and Statecraft* 27 (2016), 162–82.
141 Seligmann, "Germany's Ocean Greyhounds", 164.
142 Cecil, *Albert Ballin*, 235.
143 Matthew S. Seligmann, *The Royal Navy and the German Threat, 1901–1914: Admiralty Plans to Protect British Trade in a War against Germany* (Oxford, 2012).
144 Seligmann, *The Royal Navy*, 11–17.
145 Seligmann, "Germany's Ocean Greyhounds", 165.
146 "London to New York", *The Times* (London), 6 November 1900.
147 Quoted in Rieger, *Technology*, 236.
148 Rieger, *Technology*, 236.
149 Quoted in "See Peril in Deal", *The Washington Post*, 22 April 1902.
150 HAPAG, *Turbinen-Schnelldampfer Imperator* (Hamburg, n.d.), 8.
151 HAPAG, *Turbinen-Schnelldampfer*, 8.
152 "The Quadruple-screw Atlantic Liner 'Imperator'", *The Shipbuilder* 11 (September 1914), 125–35.
153 Cunard Archive. D42/C1/2/215. Chairman's correspondence. "Imperator".
154 Cunard Archive. D42/C1/2/215. Chairman's Correspondence. "Imperator", 4.
155 "Leviathan Liners", *Shipbuilding and Shipping Record* 3 (7 January 1914), 3.
156 "The Hamburg-Amerika Liner 'Imperator'", *Engineering* 95 (20 June 1913), 828; "The Hamburg-Amerika Liner 'Imperator'", *Engineering* 97 (12 June 1914), 797–802.
157 "The Hamburg-Amerika Liner 'Vaterland'", *Engineering* 97 (22 May 1914), 712.
158 "The Quadruple Turbine Liner 'Imperator'", *The Marine Engineer and Naval Architect* 35 (July 1913), 469.
159 "The Quadruple-screw Atlantic Liner 'Imperator'", *The Shipbuilder* 9 (August 1913), 249.
160 "The Hamburg-American Liner 'Imperator'", *The Shipbuilder* 7 (Summer 1912), 26–8; "The Launching of the 'Imperator'", *The Shipbuilder* 7 (October 1912), 75–83; "The New Hamburg-Amerika Liners", *The Shipbuilder* 8 (May 1913), 334–40; "The Quadruple-screw Atlantic Liner 'Imperator'", *The Shipbuilder* 9 (August 1913), 235–49.
161 "The Quadruple-screw Atlantic Liner 'Vaterland'", *The Shipbuilder* 10 (June 1914), 346–59.
162 See for example "The Hamburg-Amerika Liner 'Vaterland'", *Shipbuilding and Shipping Record* 3 (23 April 1914), 508; "The Hamburg-Amerika Liner 'Vaterland'", *Shipbuilding and Shipping Record* 3 (7 May 1914), 560–7; "The Biggest Hamburg-Amerika Liner", *Shipbuilding and Shipping Record* 3 (18 June 1914), 742–5 and 747.
163 "The Hamburg-Amerika Liner 'Vaterland'", *Shipbuilding and Shipping Record* 3 (7 May 1914), 560–7.
164 "The Ship of the Year. The Imperator", *The Syren and Shipping Illustrated* 66 (8 January 1913), 95–102.
165 "The Ship of the Year", 95.
166 "The Ship of the Year", 98.
167 "World's Biggest Liner: Launch of the Imperator", *The Daily Telegraph* (London), 24 May 1912.
168 See for example "The Imperator Aground", *The Manchester Guardian*, 23 April 1913; "Some Turbine Trouble", *The Manchester Guardian*, 29 April 1913.
169 See for example "The Imperator", *The Times* (London), 13 June 1913; "The Vaterland's Voyage", *The Times* (London), 16 May 1914.
170 "The Imperator", *The Times* (London), 12 June 1913.

171 See for example "Hamburg-Amerika Line", *The Observer* (London), 9 November 1913.
172 "Largest Liner Launched at Hamburg", *The Manchester Guardian*, 24 May 1912.
173 See for example "The Imperator Aground", *The Manchester Guardian*, 23 April 1913.
174 See for example "The Imperator's Trials", *The Manchester Guardian*, 29 April 1913.
175 "The Growth of the Liner", *The Manchester Guardian*, 24 March 1913.
176 "Largest Liner Launched at Hamburg", *The Manchester Guardian*, 24 May 1912; "Ocean Rivals. Vaterland Starts on Her Maiden Voyage. Race of Supremacy. Britain's Reply to the German Challenge", *Evening Standard and St. James Gazette* (London), 15 May 1914.
177 See for instance "The Imperator", *The Times* (London), 12 June 1913.
178 "The Growth of the Liner", *The Manchester Guardian*, 24 March 1913.
179 "The Ship of the Year. The Imperator", *The Syren and Shipping Illustrated* 66 (8 January 1913), 95.
180 See for example "Largest Liner Launched at Hamburg", *The Manchester Guardian*, 24 May 1912; "World's Biggest Liner", *The Daily Telegraph* (London), 16 May 1914.
181 "World's Biggest Liner", *The Daily Telegraph* (London), 16 May 1914.
182 See for example "Longest Liner Launched at Hamburg", *The Manchester Guardian*, 24 May 1912; "The Making of Great Liners", *The Manchester Guardian*, 24 March 1913.
183 "The Ship of the Year. The Imperator", *The Syren and Shipping Illustrated* 66 (8 January 1913), 95.
184 "The 'Imperator'", *The Morning Post* (London), 13 June 1913.
185 Talbot, *Steamship Conquest*, 336.
186 Talbot, *Steamship Conquest*, 331.
187 Talbot, *Steamship Conquest*, 334f.
188 Quoted in Cecil, *Albert Ballin*, 95.
189 "Affairs in Berlin", *The Observer* (London), 7 June 1914.
190 "The Imperator", *Daily Chronicle* (London), 13 June 1913.
191 "The Imperator", *The Times* (London), 12 June 1913; "The Imperator: World's Largest Liner: Her Maiden Voyage", *The Daily Telegraph* (London), 13 June 1913; "The Imperator", *The Morning Post* (London), 13 June 1913.
192 "The Imperator: World's Largest Liner: Her Maiden Voyage", *The Daily Telegraph* (London), 13 June 1913.
193 "The Vaterland. Maiden Voyage to New York", *The Morning Post* (London), 16 May 1914.
194 "A Voyage in the Imperator", *The Times* (London), 29 August 1913.
195 "The Imperator: World's Largest Liner: Her Maiden Voyage", *The Daily Telegraph* (London), 13 June 1913.
196 "A Gigantic Funnel for the New German Liner Imperator"; "The World's Biggest Liner at Her Specially Constructed Pier at Cuxhaven"; "The Imperator, The Largest Ship Afloat"; "A Monster Buoy for the Imperator"; "The Imperator's Giant Fender", *The Manchester Guardian*, 11, 18, and 31 March 1913; 1 July 1913; 14 March 1914.
197 "Giant Liners", *The Manchester Guardian*, 28 May 1914.
198 See for example "The 'Imperator'", *The Morning Post* (London), 13 June 1913.
199 "The Vaterland's Voyage: Ingenious Planning and Contrivances", *The Manchester Guardian*, 16 May 1914.
200 "The Imperator: World's Largest Liner: Her Maiden Voyage", *The Daily Telegraph* (London), 13 June 1913.
201 "Launch of the Imperator", *The Sunday Times* (London), 26 May 1912.
202 "World's Biggest Liner: Launch of the Imperator", *The Daily Telegraph* (London), 24 May 1912.

203 "The Imperator", *The Times* (London), 12 June 1913.
204 "World's Biggest Liner", *The Daily Telegraph* (London), 16 May 1914.
205 No title, *The Westminster Gazette* (London), 16 May 1914.
206 "The Aquitania and After", *The Manchester Guardian*, 22 April 1913.
207 See Sven Oliver Müller, *Die Nation als Waffe und Vorstellung: Nationalismus in Deutschland und Großbritannien im Ersten Weltkrieg* (Göttingen, 2002).
208 Scully, *British Images*, 6.
209 Scully, *British Images*, 319.
210 Scully, *British Images*, 317.
211 Geppert, *Pressekriege*, 388.

6 Masterpieces "Made in Germany"

The *Imperator* and *Vaterland* as ambassadors to the United States

I

When the *Imperator* steamed into New York harbour for the first time on the morning of 19 June 1913, it was greeted by a scene of great excitement. In Germany, this was described "as a frenzy, as one seldom experiences, even in America."[1] "Throngs" crowded the waterfront of Brooklyn and Richmond; 2,000–3,000 people gathered along the Battery sea wall to admire the liner; and "legions leaned from the towers of Manhattan."[2] Even the flags on the city's skyscrapers were dipped in salute as it passed upstream.[3] Merchants selling pennants and postcards with the *Imperator*'s image were overwhelmed, and advertisements published by the large department stores incorporated pictures of the vessel. People also took to the Hudson River and Upper New York Bay in ferries and sight-seeing yachts, while ships in the harbour welcomed Germany's new ambassador with "a deafening diapason of steam."[4] The tugboat *R.J. Barrett* circled the vessel carrying photographers and men operating moving-picture cameras. Thousands also streamed into Hoboken, where the *Imperator* docked at 11:12 a.m., crowding the piers, the streets abutting the river, and even some of the rooftops. It seemed to one observer "as if every man, woman and child" in the New Jersey city had turned out.[5]

Newspapers described the occasion in terms that sometimes verged on the poetic. *The New York Times*, for example, stated that "the bright morning sun lit up the towering white superstructure of the Imperator, and also shone on the gold lace of Capt. Hans Ruser."[6] *The Washington Post* wrote that "New Yorkers referred to the event in a vein of boastfulness that was unusual, even to them."[7] It published a large photograph of the liner steaming to its pier and described the vessel both as the "new Queen of the Ocean" and as a "monster."[8] *The Newark Star* announced that the *Imperator* was "a veritable floating city" and had been given a record reception in New York harbour. Sightseers were "amazed" by its "palatial appointments."[9]

The construction, launch, and maiden voyages of the *Imperator* and *Vaterland* attracted considerable attention in the American press. As in Britain, this was the medium through which most Americans encountered them. Yet many also travelled aboard the liners. As early as 1872, the *Milwaukee Sentinel*

Figure 6.1 The *Imperator* entering New York harbour.
Source: Bain Collection, The Library of Congress, Washington, D.C.

described the United States as "a nation of travelers" who crowd steamships departing from New York and Boston and think little of crossing the Atlantic.[10] In 1897, *The New York Times* claimed that the popularity of transatlantic passenger steamships was "striking evidence of the immense interest of Americans in ocean travel."[11] And, from the late 1890s, it was HAPAG liners that enjoyed considerable acclaim with America's travelling public as the result of their speed, technical sophistication, luxurious cabin-class interiors, and the quality of their food and service.

As we have noted, American and German commentators often ascribed the impetus behind developments in transatlantic transportation to the demands of Americans. In 1913, *The Washington Post* wrote that "the American tourist is the most exacting traveler in the world. He is not content with the ordinary vehicles of travel, and new and more luxurious methods of conveying him from place to place must be developed."[12] An article in *Current Opinion* explained that "the American, not content with luxury at home, insists on carrying the advantages to which he is accustomed with him on his travels." "It is undoubtedly due to the American," the author explained, "that traveling to-day is more sumptuous and certainly more comfortable than it was even for Cleopatra."[13] In 1905, the *Hamburg-American Gazette* reported that, in the previous year, approximately 500,000 Americans had spent $36,000,000 in fares.[14]

One of the principal motivations behind the construction of the *Imperator*-class liners was HAPAG's concern to continue attracting the patronage of America's nouveau riche by providing them with floating versions of Belle Époque hotels. They appealed to the taste of wealthy Americans for luxury and the historical, European styles of architecture and interior design that also found expression in the New York mansions of magnates like J.P. Morgan and Henry Clay Frick. In the words of the *Boston Daily Globe*, the *Imperator* offered "elegance and comfort enough" to satisfy those American millionaires travelling to Europe to "recuperate or to capture Dukes for their daughters."[15] Yet the liner undoubtedly appealed for other reasons as well. As one German commentator noted, Americans could not sit idle for an entire voyage but yearned to be active. Consequently, one of the many attractions of the *Imperator* and *Vaterland* was their size and extensive promenade decks that allowed passengers to "walk miles."[16]

Nonetheless, most Americans only read about these vessels and saw pictures of them in newspapers and popular magazines. As in Britain, newspaper reporting was only one aspect of a wide range of textual and visual conceptions of Germany in journals, literature, travel reports, school textbooks, and other forms of printed matter. Perceptions of Germany were also shaped by personal encounters with immigrants and German-Americans.[17] Yet reporting on Germany in the American press was extensive and, examining information transmitted principally through newspapers on the eve of the First World War, Jörg Nagler has emphasized that the American populace was "ambivalent toward that paradoxical country."[18] As the relationship between these two rapidly developing nations "came to be characterized by feelings of competition, rivalry and suspicion, processes of image formation themselves grew increasingly complex."[19] In short, the American public was presented with a multi-faceted and mixed picture of Germany, and this chapter begins with a succinct presentation of this fact.

It then turns to examine press reporting on German transatlantic liners, HAPAG, and Albert Ballin before analysing the particular attention afforded the *Imperator*-class vessels. As with their reception in Britain, we must be careful not to overstate the extent to which commercial shipping played a role in shaping the way Americans viewed Germany. And yet, given the volume of reporting on the liners, this chapter cannot provide an exhaustive catalogue of all that appeared in the numerous newspapers catering to all regions, and all facets of the American public. Consequently, it offers a partial picture and one that concentrates on major newspapers and journals in the eastern United States purchased by a mostly middle-class public.

In so doing, the following pages offer a concise intervention into the way press reporting on a particular subject provided material for popular perceptions and interpretations of the German Empire. Similar to their reception in the English press, the American media addressed neither the *Imperator* nor the *Vaterland* in terms of the specific aesthetic concerns that occupied Karl Scheffler.[20] And yet, American journalists construed the liners as monumental symbols, literally and figuratively, of the German Empire and did so in the manner that Scheffler feared the liners' historicist interiors would not permit: as astonishing feats of modern technology, engineering, and maritime architecture produced by "one of the world's most culturally progressive, dynamic, and innovative nations."[21] Along with the many products that carried Germany's reputation for quality and reliability in manufactured goods around the globe, the *Imperator* and *Vaterland* were mostly construed in the United States as the creations of a thoroughly modern, technologically advanced society and economy. These monumental steel vehicles of transportation and commerce, driven by the most advanced propulsion machinery, and boasting the latest technology of various sorts, put a very modern face on the German Empire. They conjured the image of a nation driven by an industrious and progressive middle class that was constructively engaged with the Atlantic world. Presenting them as such, the press complemented and sustained the image that HAPAG projected of itself, and Germany, to the American public, especially through the medium of company advertising.

What is immediately obvious is that English reporting was reserved in comparison with the reception that the *Imperator* and *Vaterland* received in the United States. Across the Atlantic, newspaper coverage displayed an enthusiastic interest in German innovation. In contrast to English views, American perceptions were less coloured by anxiety about Germany's growing status as a maritime and world power. Newspaper coverage in the United States was also less informed by the sense that Germany's merchant marine was a threatening extension of a giant military complex commanded by the Kaiser.

Ultimately, this chapter makes a concise contribution to the history of American–German relations just prior to the First World War. These relations have been the subject of considerable scholarly interest in recent years. Invigorated by, and participating in the growth of transnational approaches to the writing of history, several studies have appeared that explore the processes and variety of transatlantic exchange. As a whole, there has been increased sensitivity to, and awareness of the extent to which German–American relations were interactive on many levels.[22] Some scholars have focused on the impact that American politics, economic growth, and culture had on Germany. They have explored the role played by the United States in the German imagination, especially as a point of reference for self-definition, and examined how discourses about America were harnessed for political purposes in the Empire.[23] Others have investigated the German influence on American society and culture through immigration, as well as academic and institutional exchange.[24] There has also been an interest in the changing patterns of American perceptions of Germany and, more generally, the way in which group opinions and stereotypes were generated and expressed.[25] Yet absent from this increasingly sophisticated picture of German–American relations is an understanding of how the steamships that facilitated transatlantic communication featured, in their own right, in the ways Americans perceived Imperial Germany. The subsequent pages make a concise contribution to correcting this deficiency.

II

In May 1914, one of HAPAG's directors, Dr. Carl Bunz, made a speech in New York to a group of public officials, journalists, and advertising men. He explained that in commissioning the *Imperator*-class liners for the New York service, his company was expressing "unbounded confidence in the future development of the business of the port, in the political and economic future of the United States and in the continuance of the intimate relations between our two countries."[26] If these relations were not exactly intimate, American press reporting "shows very clearly how intensive transatlantic exchanges had become before 1914."[27] It also reveals that Bunz's optimistic view of America was reciprocated by many commentators in the United States who turned their attention to Germany.

To be sure, there were many negative images of the latter in the American media. This was in keeping with the growing alienation of the two nations, especially following the removal of Bismarck from the Chancellorship in 1890.[28] As the economy of both countries grew rapidly, they increasingly saw each other as competitors in trade and became embroiled in disputes over commerce and tariffs. Some Americans feared that Germany possessed the advantage "in the struggle for the trade of the world."[29] As its productivity increased, so the volume of American imports expanded and the sale of its goods to Germany decreased. *The Century Magazine* reported that, between 1908 and 1910, German sales to the United States increased by nearly fifty percent.[30]

Furthermore, as both nations moved beyond regional interests and sought world-power status, they found themselves confronting each other in the Pacific, East Asia, and Latin America. German colonial ambitions were of special concern for American expansionists and a particular source of tension was the fact that Germany sought greater influence in Brazil and the West Indies. HAPAG's acquisition of property in the Danish West Indies was particularly troubling in this respect. Press reporting often sounded a distinct note of anxiety about America's international position vis-à-vis Germany and cast the relationship of the two nations in terms of competition. It was claimed that the Kaiser had the "fixed determination to ignore point by point our Monroe Doctrine until he makes a veritable sieve of that whole fabric."[31] In addition, the business community in the United States feared rising international tensions, recognized the dangers of the Anglo-German naval race, and was increasingly moved to side with Britain.[32]

Particular concern was expressed about the Imperial Navy. In the decade before 1914, newspaper and magazine articles warned of Germany's naval buildup and speculated about the nation as a potential enemy. *The Washington Post* stated that the Kaiser was "raising one of the finest packs of all-steel sea dogs in the world, creatures whose hunting yelp, let us hope, never shall be heard on the face of the waters."[33] Writing in early 1914 in the *Chicago Daily Tribune*, the journalist Frederic William Wile warned his readers that the German navy was larger than that of the United States and, providing facts and figures on the number of vessels, overall tonnage, and the quality of crews, demonstrated that it was also "superior at every point." In fact, it would be more than twice the size of the American fleet by 1920 if Germany maintained its rate of construction. Wile explained that his intention was to "startle self-satisfied patriots" and suggested the establishment of an American naval law, similar to the German laws, and the building of a fleet that would deter any nation from challenging the Monroe Doctrine.[34]

Concentrating on the views of public officials and politicians, Jörg Nagler has demonstrated that positive American responses to Germany in the 1870s underwent a critical change by 1900. By that time, elite opinion in the United States was marked by increased concern about German militarism and authoritarianism, a sense of the incompatibility of the German national character with America's democratic ideology, and suspicion aroused by the fact that both countries were competing for world power status.[35] By 1913, press reporting betrayed a sense that relations were deteriorating; economic assessments became increasingly intertwined with political perspectives that included concerns about German militarism and an aggressive foreign policy that was disturbing international peace.[36] In addition to reasoned assessment and sensible concern came an outpouring of anti-German sentiment. As Nagler explains, "epithets such as 'Hun' began to appear in articles on Germany as frequently as did references to Goethe and Beethoven."[37] Newspapers and magazines described "all the negative aspects of Germans and their culture."[38] Published in 1913, Price Collier's *Germany and the Germans - From An American Point of View* found fault with German politics, foreign policy, the press, and aspects of the national character.[39]

Yet this is only part of the picture. In fact, the image of Germany in the American media was far from uniformly critical or negative. Many positive, even admiring, assessments appeared in the years immediately preceding 1914. Some newspapers explicitly attempted to rebut false and deleterious reporting about the nation. In 1913, *The Wall Street Journal* stated its desire to counter "insidious press attacks" that reported the failure of German crops, a slump in its construction industry, unemployment, and the financial failure of its transatlantic passenger steamers. The paper pointed to the inaccuracy of these views and praised the state of German finances.[40] In other organs of the press, experienced observers offered evaluations that were generally positive. These often applauded Germany's economic and scientific achievements and sometimes described a peace-loving nation with an army that served as a guarantor against conflict in Europe.[41]

One notable example among many is the article written by the author James Davenport Whelpley that appeared in the *The Century Magazine* in 1912. This was a forum for the work of historians and high-ranking government officials. In it, Whelpley stated that German diplomacy and commerce were clearly "aggressive, jealous, tenacious, and disturbing."[42] But the military spirit was being tempered by the spirit of industry; Germans were tolerant of, rather than enthusiastic about their armed forces. In fact, Whelpley claimed that English public opinion was much more militant than anything found in Germany.[43] Business interests predominated in German life "and the conception of Germany as a 'mailed fist' seeking to wrest territory by armed force" was far from the truth. "Neither the German Emperor nor his advisors desire war," the author stated, "for the very good reason that the German people abhor it."[44] Whelpley clearly admired the way in which the government facilitated the nation's foreign trade which he deemed "the marvel of the twentieth century."[45] Germany was a nation bound to the world by ties of commerce for which war could only mean "gloom, destitution, serious disturbances, and riot of all descriptions."[46] Emphasizing the close interaction of the country's trade and diplomacy, Whelpley claimed that everything the Foreign Office does is for the benefit of trade and industry.

Commodore W.H. Beehler, America's naval attaché in Berlin, Vienna, and Rome from 1899 to 1902, struck a similar note in the same magazine also in 1912. On the one hand, Germany was "virtually a nation in arms both on land and at sea." But on the other, Germans "most diligently strive to maintain peace by being more powerful than those who would disturb it."[47] They fully understood that war would disrupt commerce, and thus it was their "paramount policy" to avoid it. Unfortunately, jealous rivals had imputed all kinds of motives to Germany's naval policy. But the Kaiser's "real object is to promote commercial interests. He is much more a *'trade lord'* than a *'war lord.'* He does not wish war."

Germany became evermore important for American business especially after 1900 and the latter increasingly turned its attention towards Central Europe as a competitor and partner. Of course, there was commercial rivalry and tension as the result, for example, of the tariff policies of both nations. But as Volker Berghahn notes, "after 1900 business contacts and trade took place in an atmosphere that was in principle amicable."[48] German companies ventured into the American market, while American firms manufacturing agricultural equipment, sewing machines, office equipment, consumer goods, sophisticated machinery, and machine tools, invested in Germany. Some established production facilities in the Empire. There was also a significant exchange of information concerning industry and infrastructure: Germans travelled to America to study Taylorism and Fordism, while American businessmen went to Germany to evaluate local methods and practices and to analyse the education of skilled workers, managers, and scientists involved in research and development. They also went in search of opportunities for cooperation and participation.[49] And while many American entrepreneurs were struck by British conservatism and the way in which "British industry had lost its drive," they were impressed by German "attitudes toward modern production technology and organization."[50] When back in America, they offered their many positive impressions of Germany to associations, clubs, and the American press. *The New York Times* and *The Wall Street Journal* published articles on the lessons that could be learned from German businesses and what Americans thought should be avoided, such as the formation of cartels that limited competition.[51] While American businessmen envisioned their country as a "highly dynamic and modern industrial and financial power," they saw Germany in much the same way.[52]

From the time of Wilhelm II's accession to the throne in 1888, perceptions of Germany often focused on him. In fact, for many Americans, the Kaiser became synonymous with Germany.[53] To be sure, his image and speeches enhanced the impression of the nation's militarism and its expansionist aims. But Wilhelm II was often treated favourably in the American media and was described as displaying "marked cordiality" to Americans visiting Germany.[54] Upon meeting J.P. Morgan on the latter's yacht at Kiel, the Kaiser reportedly told the financier that "I think we can learn something from all peoples, and most from the Americans."[55] Yet several commentators in the United States saw the relationship the other way around. Claiming that Americans had learned much from Germany, and especially from its scientific and economic achievements, the author Price Collier even described the Kaiser as being "of the stuff that would have made a first-rate American."[56]

In 1904, *The Washington Post* published a substantial article emphasizing his interest in trade and commerce, and describing him as "a leading spirit in all kinds of industries."[57] It portrayed the Kaiser as a forward-thinking monarch, keenly interested in matters of industrial and technological progress. The adoption of wireless telegraphy in Germany, the United States, and other countries, was said to be largely due to his interest and support; the same claim was made with respect to the laying of a direct Atlantic cable between Germany and America. In 1913, the *Post* declared that "The Kaiser is a builder, not a destroyer."[58] He had the shrewdness to surround himself with men like Albert Ballin who helped transform the country into "the admiration and envy of Europe." That same year, *The Wall Street Journal* even referred to Wilhelm II as "the greatest business man in Germany." It emphasized that, while posing as a warlord, he was "in reality a lineal descendent on his mother's side of the manufacturing, trade and commerce which has made England great."[59] The Kaiser, it claimed, was at the heart of all German business to an extent greater than John D. Rockefeller stood at the centre of the American oil industry. Wilhelm II was also portrayed as intensely interested in the commercial and industrial affairs of foreign countries, particularly those of the United States, and in promoting commercial treaties with other powers. In fact, he was construed as a monarch who understood the realities and importance of globalization and who was determined to adapt Germany to changing global circumstances.

When it came to German shipbuilding, the Kaiser was seen as an enthusiastic promoter. *The Washington Post* even described him as a "salesman," saying that he "never misses an opportunity to do a stroke of business for his people's industry." It was reported that he told the Russian government that "if you want really good ships and in quick time, you can't do better than order them in Germany." It was also claimed that he was responsible for the Greek government's order of torpedo boats and a cruiser from Vulcan.[60] Furthermore, there was speculation that the Kaiser was one of HAPAG's largest stockholders.[61]

Many American commentators showed keen interest in the development and rapid expansion of Germany's merchant fleet. Their assessments were neither always favourable nor accurate. Some were unimpressed by the achievements of German shipbuilding in general and saw them simply as an imitation of British innovation.[62] In his book *The Ocean Carrier*, J. Russell Smith described German shipping companies as "more nearly a part of the government than are any other important lines in the world." He explained that they received direct and indirect government assistance and benefited from Germany's desire to be a great sea power as well as "the lively interest of the German Emperor."[63] But he offered an erroneous image of the Empire's merchant marine when he described its shipping companies as working in agreement with one another, as opposed to British lines that were in constant competition. Smith also traded in stereotypes when he provided the explanation: while the British loved their independence, the "German has submitted to the national will, has received military drill, has obeyed orders and has moved in companies and masses. He is thereby trained to common action."[64]

In contrast to this view, the policies that the German government had adopted to encourage domestic shipbuilding, and the resulting successes, were sometimes praised by members of the American government and held up as a model for the United States.[65] And the press often took admiring notice of the great advances in German shipbuilding. *The Christian Science Monitor*, for example, reported that the industry was "advancing rapidly" driven by "enterprising firms" that had established shipyards that are "up to date." These were "of vast extent and prodigious equipment" and were noted for the speed at which they constructed vessels.[66] It was sometimes said that German methods and resources could be studied to American advantage.[67] In his book *The Port of Hamburg*, Edwin J. Clapp argued that "the much-needed modernization of our ocean and Great Lakes terminals must be along the lines followed in Hamburg."[68]

These opinions were presented in the context of reporting that often expressed anxiety about the inadequacies of America's merchant marine. After the Spanish–American War of 1898, there were increased calls for the expansion of the nation's merchant fleet; for government subsidies to shipping lines and builders; and for an increased share of imports and exports to be carried on American vessels. Yet substantial efforts to push pertinent legislation through Congress were not successful. And it was noted that American shipbuilding lagged behind that of Germany. This was due, in part, to technical obsolescence in its shipyards as well as high construction and operating costs.[69] Figures published in *The American Economic Review* demonstrate how far America remained behind its principal competitors on the Atlantic in 1914. The journal calculated ocean-going steam tonnage in the United States at 2,027,000 tons; Germany at 5,135,000 tons; and United Kingdom at 18,892,000 tons.[70]

The Washington Post claimed there was no record of any country as powerful and advanced as the United States having no merchant marine engaged in foreign commerce.[71] While the ships of Britain and Germany "swarm in every port," America sits "supine" and confesses "our impotence to compete." Especially galling was the fact that the ships of many nations were a common sight in the ports of South America, while American vessels were rarely seen in a part of the world where "we are entitled to a controlling interest" in trade. Commentators felt it was absurd to spend such large sums on the construction of harbours and the Panama Canal purely for the convenience of foreign shipping. More seriously, lack of a merchant marine would "cripple" America in the circumstances of war, as the nation would not possess sufficient transports to carry troops, nor coaling vessels to supply its navy. Just over a week after the *Imperator*'s first call in New York, the *Post* quoted one commentator who stated that

> it makes an American sore to ride around on German boats spending good American money, when American men and American shipowners might just as well be receiving the benefits. From a patriotic standpoint alone it would be well worth the money to have our own boats.[72]

Deploring the small size of the American merchant marine the author explained that, on a trip from San Francisco to Naples, he had not seen the American flag on the ocean more than half a dozen times. "If it wasn't for John D. Rockefeller, American sewing machines, and a certain brand of infants' food, the majority of foreigners would not know there is such a country as America."

Concern was also expressed about American port facilities, including those of New York. In 1907, *The New York Times* published an article by Albert Ballin entitled "Growth of the Port of New York as a Shipping Centre."[73] Here, he praised the "magnificent natural harbor" of the city with its extensive facilities. But Ballin felt two factors were retarding its development and, clearly, his company's trade with the United States. One was the high cost of pier rental in New York. A more serious problem was the insufficient depth of the harbour channels for vessels of great draught. This meant HAPAG liners, including the *Amerika* and *Kaiserin Auguste Victoria*, had to travel to America loaded several thousand tons short of their capacity in order to ensure they could enter the port. Some voices in the press speculated that, unless HAPAG received permission to extend its Hoboken piers, the *Imperator* would be too big for the company's docks. Consequently, along with White Star's *Olympic*, it would have to make Boston its port of call.[74]

III

Many American enterprises had reason to see HAPAG not only as a formidable competitor, but also as an unwelcome foreign incursion into their domain. Several commentators were critical of the company's business ambitions, especially vis-à-vis American trade and commerce. Some of this criticism took the form of maritime nationalism, and the press took notice when HAPAG pursued interests that would be detrimental to the United States.[75] In chapter one, we saw that the Philadelphia-based firm of Peter Wright & Sons accused the German line of maintaining monopolies injurious to American businesses. The American company claimed that, utilizing a system of rebates and financial penalties, HAPAG had control over what merchandise was shipped from Europe to the United States; the freight rates that were charged; the steamship lines that were contracted to carry goods; and the routes that their vessels travelled. In many cases, HAPAG even determined the choice of inland carrier by which goods were forwarded from American ports to their final destination.[76] In the opinion of Wright & Sons "a company, foreign in its control, dictates the rates, the line, the manner, the method, the routes, and every other condition of trade and traffic, to which the United States producer, manufacturer, or shipper must humbly submit."[77]

Furthermore, as in Britain, the American press took note of what it perceived to be the close relationship between the German merchant marine and the Imperial Navy.[78] Commodore Beehler emphasized "the intimate connection" between the two in his article for *The Century Magazine*.[79] He claimed that all German merchant ships were "virtually vessels of the German navy."[80] This "intimate connection," he stated, was

> emphasized by the law that places all vessels, stores and other property of any German steamship company or owner, at all times, in peace or war, subject to the orders of any German naval commander who is authorized to take possession.[81]

"All German merchant vessels," he asserted, "have crews that have been trained in the German navy, and all these steamers are thus virtually vessels of the German navy, and might all be brought into service in case of war."[82] Senator J.H. Gallinger of New Hampshire made especial mention in *The Washington Post* of the fact that the German merchant marine was of great value as a naval reserve in time of war.[83] The particular relationship between HAPAG and the Imperial Navy was also a subject of interest. *The New York Times* reported that the company had committed to provide the Navy with the use of its steamers. It also explained that its ships "are commanded by captains and officers who are, for the most part, reserve officers in the navy, and most of the crew members have served in the navy."[84] Thus, it is no surprise that the *Imperator*-class liners were written about from this perspective. It was noted, for example, that the *Imperator* could be used as a troop transport in time of war.[85] Reporting on the *Vaterland*, *The Washington Post* emphasized that it had been "built especially for a cruiser under plans supervised by the German board of naval strategy."[86]

Yet it is also clear that HAPAG enjoyed a positive image in the United States as a modern, sophisticated, highly successful German enterprise long before the *Imperator* sailed into New York harbour on its maiden voyage. The company's positive public profile was one of the ways in which a favourable image of

Germany was provided to Americans. Known more commonly in the United States as the Hamburg–America Line by the late 1890s, the company was a familiar entity to many Americans for several reasons: it did a great deal of business in the United States; Americans were among its shareholders; and its New York service was the most important of the many that it operated around the globe. In fact, it claimed to have "perfected in its magnificence" that "highway and boulevard of global transportation" and to have "substantially drawn all passenger routes nearer to the model of the New York route."[87] Consequently, HAPAG had a considerable physical presence in America. By 1914, its ships could be found in the ports of Baltimore, Boston, Galveston, New Orleans, New York, Philadelphia, and San Francisco. It also occupied offices in several American cities including Boston, Chicago, Minneapolis, New Orleans, Philadelphia, Pittsburgh, Saint Louis, and San Francisco. And it was represented by numerous passenger agents such as C.B. Richard & Co., which had offices on Broadway in New York and on La Salle Street in Chicago.

New York was the headquarters of American operations and the company was a visible and impressive presence in Manhattan. In 1889, it established its offices at 35–37 Broadway and, in 1906, purchased new premises in a ten-story building at 41–45 Broadway for six million marks. These were opened in 1908 and occupied three floors that were converted "with the use of considerable means into an effective palace of business."[88] More imposing than elegant, the two lower stories of the façade were designed in the Neo-Romanesque style with rusticated stone and large rounded-arches. In 1908, *Harper's Weekly* published an illustrated article in which it described HAPAG's offices as taking "front rank in magnificence and elegance among the ornate palaces of business in the Western Hemisphere."[89] It also claimed that "the offices are the finest occupied by any steamship company in the New World, and it is doubtful if they are surpassed by any other commercial organization." The premises were indeed palatial and the photographs published in *Harper's* bear this out. French and Italian marble was used throughout the public spaces, and the floor of the entrance hall bore the company's motto in marble mosaic. The first- and second-class passenger offices occupied a large, imposing hall measuring 80 × 180 feet. This was designed in the "French Renaissance" style, was richly decorated with marble and mahogany, bore sculptural decoration with maritime iconography, and was capped by a large dome of stained glass. It was reported that HAPAG had paid $25,000 just for the furniture.[90] Large-scale models of the company's newest liners were exhibited in wooden and glass vitrines.

By 1907, the New York operation employed 130 company officials in offices for cabin and steerage passengers, divisions dealing with freight and equipment, a tourist office, as well as a book-keeping department.[91] Nearly all the clerks and stenographers were American-born.[92] The German-born Emil Boas (1854–1912), who had been living in New York since the 1870s, held the position of general manager and resident director from 1892 until his death. Boas was heavily involved in the business life of the city, the New York Chamber of Commerce, the

Civic Federation, and efforts to improve the trade and traffic facilities of the harbour. The press often sought his opinion on issues related to trade, economics, and the international shipping industry.[93] When he died of pneumonia at age fifty-eight, *The New York Times* eulogized him as "perhaps the most prominent figure in the steamship business in this port" and "one of the foremost men in the business life of this city."[94] He was replaced by his assistant, Emil Lederer, who shared management duties with vice directors Julius P. Meyer and William G. Sickel.

HAPAG also had a large presence in Hoboken, New Jersey where docks for its Hamburg, West Indian, and East Asian services were located just across the Hudson River from West 10th Street in Manhattan. Having previously shared the same landing place with NDL, the company acquired its own quay facilities in Hoboken in 1881 where, at a cost of about three million marks, it constructed wharfs, warehouses, offices, and accommodation for employees.[95] It owned these pier facilities from 1897 and, along with its Bremen rival, was among the few shipping companies to claim ownership of its docks in New York Harbour. HAPAG also acquired docking facilities on the Manhattan side of the Hudson at West 25th Street. By 1910, a new set of piers at Hoboken – over 1,000 feet long – had been especially designed and constructed for the *Imperator*-class liners. As William Miller emphasizes, these piers were part of an entire complex including

> workshops and storerooms, an engine plant with a boiler house, a coal shed, a smithy, a storeroom for cordage and other loading and discharging tackle, a storeroom for lamps and other lighting articles, a cooper's shop, a storeroom for coaling gear, a painter's shop, a sailmaker's shop, a large baggage room, fifteen offices representing different steamship departments, a separate railway system and a superintendent's apartment that included a portable rooftop swimming pool for summer afternoons.[96]

For the administration of these facilities, HAPAG founded an American company under the title Hamburg American Line Terminal and Navigation Co., the overall direction of which was controlled by HAPAG.

In addition to its substantial and growing physical presence in America, and especially New York before 1914, news of HAPAG's affairs was often in the press.[97] Gleaning its information from the company's annual reports, *The Wall Street Journal*, in particular, reported its earnings, dividends paid, increases in capital stock, interest paid on preferred loans, amounts spent on constructing new vessels, depreciation in the value of ships, and numbers of passengers carried. Articles appeared in the paper comparing the company's figures with those of NDL, Cunard, and the International Mercantile Marine Company.

A subject of particular interest for the American media was Albert Ballin. He was well-known to New York's business community and visited the city on several occasions, the first being in 1887 to reorganize relations with HAPAG's American agents. Bernhard Huldermann claims that the New York newspapers were so interested in his presence that Ballin was able to "escape the journalists" only "by summoning all his cunning."[98] When not physically present in New York, HAPAG's managing director was often spoken of in the newspapers and his opinions were quoted on a range of issues including disputes and agreements regarding transatlantic passenger traffic, the International Mercantile Marine Company, the North Atlantic Steamship Association and, of course, the business of his company. His name and opinions also appeared in reporting on German–American trade, economic conditions prevailing in Europe and America, and Germany's domestic politics. Articles were occasionally devoted solely to reporting his views or, when relating news on global shipping, seemed more interested in detailing his movements and intentions.[99] Reporting even extended to discussion of his health. One newspaper noted that Ballin was "in splendid physical trim" for a dispute over transatlantic passenger rates in which HAPAG was embroiled. Just over a week earlier, the same paper announced his health had been undermined by efforts to organize an independent German delegation to the Panama–Pacific International Exposition in San Francisco.[100]

Of course, not everything that appeared about Ballin in the American press was positive. Some commentators and politicians took a negative and even hostile view of his influence and intentions. Claiming that ninety percent of American commerce was carried by a giant monopoly of foreign ships with Ballin at its head, Republican representative William Ewart Humphrey told the House of Representatives that HAPAG's managing director

> sits in Germany and absolutely fixes the price that the American merchant, manufacturer, and farmer must pay on every pound of freight sent to Europe or South America. This is the Herr Ballin whose company voluntarily withdrew two of its fastest and best ships and sold them to Spain to sink, burn and destroy American commerce. This is the man, and this is the company that to-day absolutely dictates how and on what terms this great nation shall transport $3-500,000,000 worth of commerce annually.

Humphrey went on to state that shipping service between the United States and South America was "grossly discriminatory" against America in favour of European countries. He also claimed that Ballin and Boas had frequently used American newspapers to denounce efforts made by Congress to assist in the development of the American merchant marine. In his opinion, Ballin had even affected the integrity of the Associated Press by means of a hired representative on its staff – Jerome J. Wilbur – who was assigned to the State, War, and Navy Departments.[101] The press also noted what it perceived as unfriendly action on Ballin's part, as when, in 1901, *The New York Times* speculated that he had entered into arrangements with several British shipping companies with the intention of shutting the United States out of trade with China.[102]

Yet, at the same time, HAPAG'S managing director received very favourable, even admiring coverage in the American media far beyond New York. Ballin felt that Americans were "unexcelled in energy, industry, and inventiveness."[103]

And many commentators in the press felt the same of him. The portrait was often painted of an energetic, self-made, progressive entrepreneur who had much in common with his American counterparts. At a concert in the *Vaterland*'s ballroom while it was docked at Hoboken in May 1914, John A. Sleicher, editor of *Leslie's Weekly*, made a speech that was reported in the press and in which he praised Ballin in the following manner:

> no matter what our flag may be, we take off our hats to that which flies over the Vaterland and we take it off again to the virile, vigorous, earnest, commanding personality that has led the German Empire to its foremost place in the commercial and industrial world. Our country might well emulate his patriotic example.[104]

A glowing, even sensational picture was presented of Ballin's standing and role in Germany. *The Wall Street Journal*, for example, described him as one of the "heroes of Germany today above princes and potentates."[105] It extolled him as "the founder of German commercial power" and the man who, along with the Kaiser, had made the Empire "a great sea-power." In his book *Men Around the Kaiser: The Makers of Modern Germany*, the journalist Frederic William Wile praised Ballin as the greatest German of his day.[106] He was described as being "on terms of close intimacy" with the Emperor and, quite incorrectly, as having enormous influence on German politics.[107] It was said that Wilhelm II described him as "a bold adventurer" who had made "peaceful conquests, whose fruits our grandchildren will reap."[108] Americans read that the agreement HAPAG's managing director struck with the International Mercantile Marine Company had immensely increased his reputation in Germany and that the Kaiser might be thinking of appointing him to the Chancellorship to replace Bernhard von Bülow.[109] They were also informed that Wilhelm was criticized at home for keeping Ballin's company and that of other "men who are making industrial and commercial Germany."[110] It was said that German commentators feared the supremacy of the "American idea" in their nation along with the social and political elevation of the men who contributed most to its wealth.

When it came to his relationship with the United States, Ballin was often described in the press as having positive views of America and possessing a keen interest in improving Germany's relationship with it. Americans read that he was chairman of the executive committee of the German–American Economic Association, formed in March 1914, and devoted to cultivating business and economic relations between the two countries.[111] Given the large volume of trade conducted by HAPAG with America, one commentator in *The Wall Street Journal* ventured that "Herr Ballin is not only the greatest German but the greatest American."[112] This statement points to something that is particularly interesting about the way in which the American press often pictured Ballin: as not only possessing extensive knowledge about their country, but also having the attributes of an American businessman.

For example, in the wake of his agreement with the International Mercantile Marine Company, the *St. Louis Post-Dispatch* described Ballin as the J. Pierpont Morgan of Germany.[113] In a glowing portrayal that celebrated him as a self-made man and "democratic pillar of the Fatherland," the paper emphasized that he not only understood American business methods but "the American mind," a subject he had studied closer than any other. Not only did the ships launched under his direction serve cordial relations between Germany and America; they were a product of the extent to which Ballin understood both the economic needs of his own country and those of the United States. He was a man of "progressive methods and far-seeing eye," and it was through Ballin, who stood at the right-hand of the Kaiser, that the latter was learning positive lessons from the New World. Frederic William Wile clearly perceived an affinity with America's captains of industry and saw in Ballin qualities that he considered American. Describing him as "one of the real Makers of Modern Germany," he emphasized that HAPAG's general manager was "a thoroughly self-made man."[114] Wile also stressed that Ballin had renounced titles and honours and was much more proud to be known as a "pioneer" of German commerce and export trade.[115] He had brought progressive ideas to a company dominated by "greybeards" and an old-fashioned vision.[116] Wile praised Ballin's energy, vision, industry, and hands-on approach. He emphasized that the managing director arrived at the office punctually every morning at 9 a.m. and was usually the last to leave in the evening. He was "a managing director who manages and directs."[117]

Something that Ballin recognized the necessity of, and took a directing interest in was public relations and advertising.[118] As noted in chapter one, he established the first public relations department to be found in any major German company: HAPAG'S literary bureau.[119] In keeping with other transatlantic shipping firms, the company conducted sophisticated and extensive advertising campaigns in the United States. Much of this consisted of advertisements in magazines and newspapers. But as one commentator noted in 1913, these were mostly a means of

> stimulating the curiosity of a large number of persons, not a few of whom will write to the company for an illustrated leaflet describing the accommodation of the class on board in which they would like to travel. No one dreams of showing newspaper advertisements to his friends, but an illustrated booklet or pamphlet will be shown to dozens.[120]

These company publications presented Americans with the image of a shipping line that stood at the forefront of high-speed communication, maritime engineering, and technological innovation. They also fostered the image of a firm responding positively to, and facilitating the growth of consumerism, commodity culture, and the "habits of consumptive individualism" on both sides of the Atlantic.[121] Furthermore, they promoted HAPAG as an agent of globalization and modern, international communication.

HAPAG provided the American public with a wide range of literature detailing the company's history and the services it provided. Some of these publications were elaborate, as was the attractive booklet published in New York in 1906 in commemoration of the sixtieth anniversary of the company's founding.[122] This is full of eye-catching illustrations, many of which depict the line's steamers as a means of visually documenting its rapid progress. The text also repeatedly stresses the incredible strides made by HAPAG in the past sixty years. Several other publications were rich in images of its ships, their interiors, their captains, the company's Broadway premises, and its headquarters in Hamburg. Various small booklets detailed the mechanical and technological sophistication of the company's transatlantic liners; the innovations in engineering that they embodied; the latest in communication technology with which they were outfitted; the advanced safety measures and apparatuses they employed; and the power and speed of their engines and propulsion systems. Company literature, including *The Hamburg-American Gazette*, also provided practical advice on travelling across the Atlantic and information on engaging passage, acquiring passports, procuring foreign monies, handling baggage, distributing gratuities to ship stewards, selecting appropriate clothing, dealing with seasickness, selecting European hotels, posting letters from Europe, and travelling by rail. It also offered hints on what not to do before sailing and while on board ship. Passengers were advised, with a good deal of humour, not to flirt with girls travelling to get married; not to quarrel with "the fat man" who always takes someone else's deck chair; not to submit "nervous old ladies" to tales of disaster at sea; not to recite poetry, even on moonlit nights; and not to forget to keep a diary as "the leading publishers may be after it one of these days."[123]

There were guides providing information on London as well as details of railway travel in Europe including timetables and routes.[124] There was a guide to Hamburg with practical information on transportation and hotels. Describing the city as proportionally more affluent than Berlin, it spoke of the picturesque nature of Hamburg and its setting; suggested tourist itineraries with descriptions of quarters, churches, and public buildings; and provided a foldout map of Hamburg-Altona. There were also souvenir booklets for HAPAG'S clientele, some of which had a generic character appropriate to any number of voyages. Others offered humorous cartoons of life on board ship and "thumb-nail sketches" from different trips; photographs of famous places and sites such as Sandy Hook, the Statue of Liberty, and Niagara Falls; reproductions of sentimental artworks; maps and notes on distinguishing ships at sea and time keeping on shipboard; explanations of ciphers and phrases for cablegrams; and numerous advertisements for hotels, clothes, hats, jewellery, confectionary, guns, pianos, railways, and travel agents.[125]

In addition to promoting its transatlantic services, much of HAPAG's advertising in the American market was dedicated to its cruises. The company offered an impressive range of these in the years immediately preceding the First World War. Its destinations included South America, Scandinavia, the

Mediterranean, and India. Round-the-world voyages carrying only first-class passengers were also offered. These sailed to Japan, China, the Philippine Islands, Java, Burma, India, Egypt, and Europe. Between 1911 and 1913, these so-called Cruises de Luxe could be undertaken for a minimum of $650 per person; they travelled both eastward and westward, departed from New York and San Francisco, and lasted approximately 110 days. Many Americans took advantage of the range of cruises offered by HAPAG. In 1913, *The Washington Post* reported that with the approach of winter, "a remarkable migration of a quarter of a million tourists is started from all points of the country toward milder climates."[126]

Company publicity claimed that "so closely has modern cruising become identified with the Hamburg-American Line that it is hard to think of one without thinking of the other."[127] In several of its booklets, and in advertising that appeared in forums such as *Harper's New Monthly Magazine* and *Scribner's Magazine*, this paragon of a modern, global enterprise promoted itself as a conduit away from the stresses and strains of modern life. One brochure suggested that HAPAG had made cruising so comfortable and convenient that it was easier than staying at home, as "life in our modern cities is not free from complexity."[128] The doctor could forget the real and imagined symptoms of his patients; the lawyer could escape "the unwholesome atmosphere of a crowded court-room" and "the dusty folios at the law library;" and the merchant could abandon accounts, invoices, and bills of lading.[129] Aboard some of the most advanced forms of transportation, the harried modern city dweller could be transported for recreation and diversion into the past and to lands of ancient grandeur. The company proclaimed that pleasure travel was "an art" developed by HAPAG and that "the whole world is the itinerary."[130] Travel to locations that could previously be undertaken only at great inconvenience and expense was now rendered easy, affordable, and comfortable. In evocative language, these brochures promised stimulating, well-organized, and even "ideal" itineraries undertaken with ease and "attended with the utmost comfort."[131] In one publication, a client who had travelled aboard the *Augusta Victoria* to Rome, Constantinople, and Cairo in 1897 praised the luxuries and comfort of the vessel as well as the professionalism of the tour itinerary. He added that

> to be carried in this manner to the scenes of the most stirring events of the human race and to the fountain-head of art and culture, without sacrificing your personal comforts and habits is an experiment I cannot too strongly urge you to try.[132]

HAPAG produced several brochures that made much of the romantic and exotic appeal of its cruises' destinations. These, and the many advertisements that appeared in magazines, were designed to be visually appealing and featured photographs, illustrations, and maps. Dealing in tropes and stereotypes, they pictured the exotic sights that awaited the traveller to the West Indies and Venezuela; to Italy and the "Oriental Wonderlands" of Turkey, Palestine, and Egypt; and to the "Land of the Midnight Sun" including Norway, Iceland, and the Orkney and Faroe Islands.[133] For example, a booklet entitled *Winter Cruise to the Mediterranean and the Orient*, published in 1898, included a photographic portrait of an Arab man on its cover along with several photographs captioned "A Café in Algiers"; "Greek Theatre, Syracuse"; "The Tombs of the Mamelukes, Cairo"; "An Oriental Juggler"; "Oriental Devotion"; and "The Parthenon."[134] A good deal of space was also devoted to evocative textual descriptions of exotic destinations including "mysterious Egypt," China's "celestial empire," and the "flowery kingdom" of Japan.[135] While trumpeting its liners as monuments of modern engineering, technology, and design, HAPAG suggested to prospective American travellers that viewing the ruins of ancient Greece offered a lesson in "the decay of earthly power."[136]

What this material demonstrates is that much of the advertising published by HAPAG in the United States did not project an image of Germany per se. Yet it emphasized the global dimensions of the company's business and its ability to bring the entire world within reach of the modern traveller. HAPAG construed itself as an agent of international travel, migration, and trade. Its advertising demonstrated to Americans the extent to which Germany participated in the various processes of globalization and the degree to which the Empire was positively engaged in the world.

Associated with world travel, HAPAG was especially known in the United States for its transatlantic services. As we have seen, just as the label "Made in Germany" came to stand for the quality and reliability of a range of manufactured products, the company's passenger liners were admired by the American travelling public for their technical sophistication, speed, luxurious interiors, and the quality of their food and service. This admiration extended to German passenger liners in general and they enjoyed great popularity, especially from the late 1890s. In fact, it has been said that many of these vessels were better known in America than in Germany.[137]

Describing his experience aboard HAPAG's *Fürst Bismarck* in the early 1890s, Edward S. Wilson said that the "meals are served in the most elaborate style, and the food seems to have been provided without regard to cost." He also found the service to be excellent, while the discipline of the crew and stewards was "rigid, and yet there is a dignity and courtesy that is very agreeable."[138] In 1898, the Presbyterian clergyman and author, John Henry Barrows, stated his belief that the "Germans certainly make excellent purveyors to American voyagers." To them he owed "the most restful of all my seven trips across the Atlantic." Barrows described NDL's *Havel* as "the most comfortable and satisfactory boat on which I have ever crossed the Atlantic." He said it was "scrupulously clean" and "beautiful in its decoration."[139] Praising the vessel for its sturdiness in rough seas, Barrow's advice to fellow Americans was not to fear the ocean; in fact, he claimed, "it is more perilous to cross Broadway."[140] In 1910, the American author Albert Bigelow Paine was impressed by the "regal furnishings" he found aboard NDL's *Großer Kurfürst*.[141]

While garnering praise from those who travelled aboard them, Germany's premier transatlantic liners attracted considerable public attention in New York. The scene that accompanied the *Imperator*'s arrival in June 1913 was not unusual. The New York press had been enthusiastically reporting on the arrival of steamships from across the Atlantic since two British vessels, the *Sirius* and *Great Western*, sailed into the harbour – the former from Cork and the latter from Bristol – in April 1838. HAPAG claimed that the luxury appointments of its *Allemania* drew a large crowd when it first sailed into New York in 1865.[142] It was estimated that nearly 30,000 people visited the *Augusta Victoria* upon its arrival in May 1889.[143] Several NDL liners received a similar welcome. Thousands turned out to greet the *Kaiser Wilhlem der Große* as it completed its maiden voyage from Bremerhaven in September 1897. *The New York Times* reported that the liner presented "a splendid spectacle" and described its opening to public inspection as "an occasion probably unparalleled of its kind in the history of this port's shipping." Invitations in the number of 30,000 were issued and the bearers, with their families and friends, taxed the Hoboken ferries and "overran the vessel."[144] "The great size of the crowd which went to view the *Kaiser Wilhelm der Große* on the day previous to her departure from this port," the paper reported, "is a striking evidence of the immense interest of Americans in ocean travel."[145] The first call of NDL's *Kaiser Wilhelm II*, in April 1903, "consisted of such a great press effort, promoting her size, speed and magnificent interiors that some 40,000 visitors came on board for inspection during the initial call."[146] This group of persons was larger than the entire population of Hoboken where the liner was berthed. And it should be noted that public interest in German passenger liners was not restricted to maiden voyages. Crowds of sightseers wanting to visit HAPAG ships were often so large that, as one newspaper explained in 1914, "officials have been obliged to restrict visitors to the largest vessels on sailing days to relatives and friends of passengers."[147]

Yet for all the enthusiasm that accompanied their arrival in New York harbour, most Americans never saw these ships with their own eyes. Instead, they could admire models exhibited in the company's offices. And, as noted above, there was a great deal of company advertising, a large proportion of which focused on the liners themselves. But as in Germany, HAPAG and NDL vessels were encountered by a wider audience through several media other than advertising. Their liners featured, for instance, in the pages of *The Scientific American Handbook of Travel*, as well as in the many works of travel literature that often commented on life aboard ship.[148] They also appeared in several popular books such as E. Keble Chatterton's *Steamships and Their Story*, Frank Talbot's *Steamship Conquest of the World*, and R.A. Fletcher's *Traveling Palaces*.[149] This literature often mixed admiration for what German shipbuilders had achieved in a short span of time with criticism that they simply adapted British design and innovation.[150]

Yet it was in newspapers and popular journals such as *Harper's Weekly*, *Current Opinion*, and *Scientific American* that HAPAG appeared most often and most extensively, and through which it reached its largest audience.[151] The company and its liners were often in the American press, especially from 1900. In that year, the *Deutschland* captured the Blue Riband for attaining the highest average speed for a transatlantic crossing in the westbound direction. This attracted the attention of the American media, as did its launch at Stettin on 10 January of that year. As noted in chapter three, launch ceremonies were designed for foreign consumption and the speech that Bernhard von Bülow – then German Foreign Secretary – made in honour of the *Deutschland* called upon God to protect the friendship and commerce that existed between Germany and the United States. A summary of the speech with translated excerpts was published in New York and Washington the very next day.[152] And Americans often attended these launch ceremonies. The Consul General at Hamburg, Harry H. Morgan, and several other officials attended the launch of the *Bismarck* on 20 June 1914.[153]

As German liners grew in size and luxury, so they featured ever more prominently in newspaper reporting. Articles were often accompanied by photographs, especially in the *New-York Tribune*. The *Kaiserin Auguste Victoria* received high praise from President Theodore Roosevelt in *The New York Times* in 1910. In a letter to Ballin, Roosevelt explained that:

> I hardly feel that I am at sea, for it is like living in a perfectly appointed and perfectly managed modern hotel. Yesterday I went through the ship with Capt. Ruser, and I was particularly struck with what has been done for the health and comfort of the stokers and engineering force. I am also especially pleased with the arrangements for the third-class passengers, and I hope all immigrants will soon travel as such.[154]

The use of hyperbole, especially to describe the luxury of the latest liner's interiors, was not unusual. In 1906, *The Washington Post* claimed that the *Kaiserin Auguste Victoria* was "the wonder of the century."[155] The *Ohio State Journal* reported that a German newspaper had published a list of the world's seven modern wonders that included the *Imperator*.[156]

American journals and newspapers often discussed the interior decoration of German liners. There were critics, like Count Ernst von Reventlow, who wrote that "looked at from an artistic point of view, these may be considered overdone."[157] He noted that such luxury had made it more difficult for these vessels to turn a profit. But praise was more common than criticism. In 1897, *The New York Times* described the interiors of NDL's *Kaiser Wilhelm der Große* as being "of rare beauty."[158] In 1905, the same paper and *The Washington Post* praised the "lavish" interiors "fashioned by famous artists" aboard HAPAG's *Amerika*.[159] Newspaper reports would also discuss the interior fittings of the *Imperator* and *Vaterland* in considerable detail.[160]

As noted above, HAPAG appealed to the taste of wealthy Americans for luxury and historical, European styles of architecture and interior design. In fact, the *New-York Tribune* described the *Vaterland* as "a floating museum."[161] But when NDL employed progressive German designers – including Bruno Paul, Joseph Olbrich, Richard Riemerschmid, and Rudolph Alexander

Schröder – to design interiors aboard the *Kronprinzessin Cecilie* (1906) and the *George Washington* (1908), this was noted with approval in the United States. As we saw in chapter four, *The International Studio* admired the fact that these ships had been "fitted up with modern ideas" and saw NDL's decision to do so as opening "a new and important field for German art and design."[162]

IV

With respect to the *Imperator* and *Vaterland*, extensive publicity campaigns accompanied their commissioning and potential American passengers were provided with a wealth of information about the new vessels. Sophisticated brochures detailed, in text and image, the luxurious cabin-class accommodation aboard both liners.[163] One publication was devoted solely to photographs depicting the *Imperator*'s first-class cabins.[164] Before the *Vaterland*'s maiden voyage, the company published a large-format booklet containing elaborate artists' impressions of its cabin-class interiors that emphasized their spaciousness and decorative detailing.[165]

The reminiscences of Jack Lawrence, a reporter for the *Evening Mail* in New York, provide insight into the type and nature of the material that the company circulated to news outlets to promote the *Imperator*-class liners and, in the offices of his newspaper, its fate:

> Our old friend Matthew B. Claussen, press agent of the Hamburg-American Line, launched a publicity campaign calculated to astonish the world. He announced from the housetops that these three new ships would make the *Olympic*, *Mauretania* and *Lusitania* look like so many mechanical toys in Central Park lake. He flooded the Ship News office with literature, blueprints, cleverly concocted photographs and endless statistics and Jimmy Lynch tossed the stuff into the old iron stove as fast as it arrived. He even sent us a huge oil painting showing the giant *Imperator* skimming gracefully over the waves. And the artist hadn't neglected to paint in a British liner looking forlorn and insignificant and all but lost in the shadow of the *Imperator*'s towering bows. On the ship's lofty bridge one could make out the plump and haughty figure of the captain. In his fingers he was holding a fat cigar and had just flipped the ashes down on the deck of the passing Britisher. Another of Mr. Claussen's publicity items was a large composite photograph showing the *Imperator* standing on her stern beside the Woolworth building, then the world's tallest structure. Her bow, of course, rose far above the Woolworth tower.[166]

Lawrence also recalled how Claussen issued personal invitations to reporters to travel to Germany with him as guests of HAPAG and return aboard the *Imperator* when she made her maiden voyage. Several accepted the invitation and had "the time of their lives."[167] The *Imperator* had hardly begun its regular transatlantic service before Claussen launched "a publicity campaign promoting the *Vaterland*."[168]

As in Britain, both liners, along with numerous HAPAG vessels and German shipbuilding in general, were featured in the pages of several trade publications. Journals like *The Nautical Gazette*, *The Marine Review*, and *"Shipping" Illustrated* greeted the *Imperator* and *Vaterland* with great interest and admiration. Articles often provided considerable technical detail about the liners and, in the case of *"Shipping" Illustrated*, photographs of them under construction.[169] In addition to the sober enumeration of details and statistics, these journals were interested in the *Imperator* and *Vaterland* as record-breakers of various sorts. They described the former as a "leviathan" of "monster proportions" and explained that it would be 200 feet taller than the Woolworth Building if stood on its stern.[170] The *Old Bay Line Magazine* highlighted the records set by the "super liner" *Vaterland* in terms of it size, detailed the huge amount of provisions required for a single crossing, and stressed that the ship boasted the largest kitchen personnel ever put to sea.[171] It also emphasized the completeness of its safety measures and equipment. To be sure, provisions for safety were often given extensive coverage in professional journals. *The Marine Review* made the particular point that, like the *Lusitania* and *Mauretania*, the *Imperator* would have withstood the shock that sank the *Titanic*, but also provided considerable detail on its lifeboats.[172] In addition, much emphasis was placed upon measures to prevent fire.[173] Reporting also appeared in magazines like *Harper's Weekly* where most space was given to photographs of the exterior and interior of new ships with small captions often emphasizing the innovation, comfort, and convenience of a vessel's appointments.[174]

The Marine Review considered the *Imperator* to be of "trim" and "sightly" appearance.[175] But more extensive discussion was afforded the interiors of the liners focusing on their unprecedented size and luxury. In advance of the *Imperator*'s completion, *"Shipping" Illustrated* reproduced several artists' impressions of the vessel, some of which made its interiors seem larger than they actually were.[176] This coverage served to promote the vessels as destinations in themselves. The *Imperator* was described as "a splendid hotel, in which it is possible to live for a week without any reminder that one is not on dry land." "The busy traveler," *"Shipping" Illustrated* explained, "can utilize the voyage by undertaking a 'cure' under advice of one of the three medical officers."[177] The *Vaterland*'s first-class dining room was compared with those of the best hotels and its menus were described as no less varied and abundant.[178] The liner was presented as offering so many novel and attractive features "that the week spent in crossing the Atlantic scarcely suffices for one to become familiar with the great ship."[179] In contrast to German critics, the *Old Bay Line Magazine* claimed that the *Vaterland*'s interiors had been designed by the "leading decorators of Europe" and praised the vessel as "a floating museum of the decorative arts." It noted that the ship was adorned with paintings by Italian masters, including landscapes by Giovanni Battista Pittoni, as well as "works of many notable contemporary artists" of which it named Hugo Schnars-Alquist and Waldemar Kolmsperger.[180] Yet it was not only first-class interiors that received such attention. Although it provided little detail, *The Marine Review* noted that much could be said in praise of the *Imperator*'s second-class dining room, reading room, music salon, and smoking room and noted the increase in spaciousness and comfort offered third-class and steerage passengers.[181]

This professional interest was exceeded by popular fascination. The New York press anticipated the *Imperator*'s maiden voyage to the city well in advance. *The New York World* greeted its launch with a large artist's impression of the vessel and headlines announcing that "Luxuries Will Be Provided in Abundance" aboard the liner.[182] This anticipation grew more intense during its maiden voyage as newspapers published wireless dispatches from the *Imperator* describing the nature of the crossing well before it appeared in New York harbour. As it prepared to do so, *The New York World* published a headline reading "Sea's New Giant, Imperator, Is At Gate of America."[183] *The Nautical Gazette* claimed that "all New York is planning to turn out to see" the liner. Describing it as the "ship of the year" and "the greatest marine creation thus far of the twentieth century," it stated that its arrival "is likely to mark the most important epoch in the marine history of this port since Robert Fulton steamed up the Hudson."[184]

American newspapers also related the importance of the launch of the *Imperator*-class liners for Germans. It was reported in *The New York Times* that the maiden voyage of the *Vaterland* was seen in Germany as "an event of both national and historic magnitude."[185] It is interesting to note that many of those who turned out to greet the *Imperator* and *Vaterland* may have been Americans of German origin. The *Boston Daily Globe* claimed that the 10,000 people who greeted HAPAG's *Cincinnati* when it first arrived at that city on 1 June 1913 were mostly German. The celebration, which marked the initiation of a new passenger and freight line from Hamburg, was said to have "a decided German tone." A band played mostly German music and some of the speakers who addressed the gathering used the "Teutonic tongue." The festivities ended with the singing of *Deutschland, Deutschland, Über Alles.*[186]

Apart from the celebrations that accompanied its first arrival, 80,688 people paid fifty cents apiece to go aboard the *Imperator* and view its interiors during its six days in port.[187] Of the monies collected, $5,000 were sent to Mayor Gaynor and to the Mayor of Hoboken for distribution among charitable institutions. The remainder was donated by HAPAG to American charitable foundations and to the German *Seemannsheim* and Hospital.[188] On 20 June, 1,200 steamship and railroad agents, as well as businessmen, inspected the ship at the company's invitation; a reception on the following day included an opportunity for guests to try the ballroom's floor.[189] HAPAG's New York offices gave a luncheon in honour of Mayor Gaynor aboard the *Imperator* on 24 June at which he made a speech complimenting German shipbuilders and promising to improve the city's harbour facilities.[190] Crowds continued to visit the HAPAG piers to view the liner until the day before its departure for Europe on 25 June.[191] Again, it seemed to one observer as if all New York descended on Hoboken for the occasion, and it was reported that 5,000 visitors went on board that very morning.[192] Still larger crowds greeted the *Vaterland* when it made its first call at New York accompanied by headlines such as the one that appeared in the *The New York World*: "$6,000,000 Sea Monster *Vaterland* to Move Majestically into This Harbor Today."[193] Other headlines were much less sensational such as the one that featured in *The Evening Post*: "Vaterland, 950 Feet, Greatest."[194] Once again, the liner's arrival had been anticipated by the New York press in the form of published telegraph reports from the ship stating that it "was proving a great success in every particular" and that "all the passengers are delighted."[195] On 24 May 1914, 17,000 visitors went aboard it at its Hoboken berth.[196]

It is important to note that public interest was not restricted to maiden voyages. During its second call at New York in July 1913, company officials attempted to limit the number of people visiting the *Imperator* immediately before its departure for Europe. Passes were issued admitting a limited number of friends and relatives of passengers onto the pier. But as the *The New York Times* reported, the plan failed and, by 10 a.m. on the day of departure, an estimated 3,000 people were on the pier and 1,000 aboard the liner. The paper surmised that 2,000 individuals without passes had evaded the gatemen and many "fought their way onto the ship" to look around. There was considerable confusion aboard the vessel itself and the result was "a jamming, crushing, irritated crowd that sweltered, swore, pushed and fussed, while the baggagemen struggled trying to get the state room luggage on board before sailing time."[197] *The New York Times* claimed that the number of visitors to the *Imperator* dwindled after the *Vaterland* was put into commission.[198] But in July 1914, it also reported that "so great are the crowds of sightseers who want to see the big ships of the Hamburg–American Line that the officials have been obliged to restrict visitors to the largest vessels on sailing days to relatives and friends of passengers."[199]

As in Germany and Britain, it was through the press that information about HAPAG's new liners was most widely disseminated. Reports about the *Imperator* appeared in the American press from the early days of its construction in 1910. While coverage was concentrated in newspapers published on the eastern seaboard, and especially New York, it was not limited to this part of the country. The *Imperator* and *Vaterland* attracted the attention of the media in New York, Baltimore, Boston, Chicago, Cleveland, Detroit, Kansas City, Newark, Philadelphia, Pittsburgh, San Francisco, and St. Louis among other cities. News items also appeared as far away as Hawaii.[200]

As with English reporting, we must be sensitive to the form and nature of the coverage afforded the *Imperator* and *Vaterland* in America. Much of this did not appear as lead articles and a good deal involved the reiteration of themes and tropes that typified press reporting on transatlantic passenger shipping in general which we encountered in chapter two. There was also considerable misinformation in the press: for example, more than one report claimed that the *Imperator*'s eagle figurehead had space for a bow lookout.[201] Furthermore, much reporting on the liners was not accompanied by explicit commentary on the nature of the German Empire. Ultimately, they formed a relatively small item of news, especially during 1914. To be sure, many newspapers of record – including *The New York Times*, the *New-York Tribune*, *The Wall Street Journal*, and *The Washington Post* – devoted considerable attention to the *Imperator*-class liners, HAPAG, and the business of international shipping. And yet they did so in the context of many articles treating the German Empire in its political, economic, social, and international dimensions. It is also important to note that some reporting did not treat the *Imperator* and *Vaterland* as German vessels. Many articles made no mention of the fact that the *Imperator* was German. *The Washington Post* stated that New Yorkers did not seem to recognize that the liner was the product of a foreign nation; they spoke of it "as if she were their own creation – a fine specimen of marine architecture, but not the best that New York could turn out if New York were really in earnest."[202]

The *Imperator* and *Vaterland* also attracted negative commentary in the same newspapers that greeted them with admiration. This came in many forms and degrees of seriousness. At least one reporter became unpopular in Hoboken when he wrote that "the *Imperator* looked like Grand Central Station afloat and had none of 'the slender, feminine beauty to be found in such ships as the *Mauretania* and the *France.*'"[203] Both liners encountered various technical difficulties and some newspapers were ready to highlight what they considered as their failings. When the *Vaterland* took four hours to dock in Hoboken at the completion of its maiden voyage, the *New York Herald* described it as "an unhappy bumbler from the start."[204] And when it sank a coal barge while backing from its pier on its first departure from the harbour, the *New-York Tribune* proclaimed it the "terror of North River."[205]

It is also clear that not all journalists approved of the image projected by the ships. Jack Lawrence remarked upon the air of superiority and arrogance that he felt the *Imperator* exuded. Speaking of the eagle that adorned its prow, Lawrence said he felt that he had "never seen anything quite so supercilious, haughty and generally arrogant. But to the corpulent German steamship officials who went down the bay with us on the Revenue Cutter it seemed to be a splendid symbol of superiority."[206] Standing on the bridge as the *Imperator* steamed slowly to its pier, it seemed that "the golden eagle looked down disdainfully on Manhattan Island and the fleet of welcoming craft that swarmed about like sea-going ants in the shadow of the massive hull."[207] Lawrence also claimed that the vessel's arrival was accompanied by a change in the demeanour of the HAPAG officials and German nationals whom he regularly encountered in his work:

> It has always seemed to me that the launching of the *Imperator* and her slightly larger sistership, the *Vaterland*, worked a mysterious and unfathomable change among the many Germans with whom we came in almost daily contact covering ship news. We began to notice that ships' officers who once had been jovial and unfailingly courteous had now become pompous and puffed up. The affable German purser who was once glad to hand the ship news reporter a passenger list and recount anything of interest that may have occurred during the voyage was now frequently too busy to be annoyed and was often rude. The deck officers who once had been glad to see us aboard were now given to passing us by with their chins in the air.[208]

Of course, we must remember that these impressions were recorded in 1940 and in very different circumstances from those prevailing before the First World War. In fact, there is little doubt that Lawrence's views were coloured by subsequent events. Writing about HAPAG's motto – "My Field is the World" – he opined that this was "a sentiment that Hitler himself could hardly have improved upon."[209]

Similar impressions found their way into reporting of the time. *The Wall Street Journal*, for example, poked fun at a chief steward who "pompously" led invited guests on a tour of the *Vaterland* and blustered "with much pride" about having served the Kaiser a glass of wine in the first-class lounge.[210] The vessels also afforded some journalists the opportunity to trade in caricatures and pejorative stereotypes, principally those about German efficiency and thoroughness. In 1913, at least one article presented the well-worn image of the German *Untertan*. In its report on the Kaiser's inspection of the *Imperator* in early July of that year, *The New York Times* explained that when Wilhelm visited the ship's swimming pool every bather "drippingly attempted to come to the stiff salute every loyal Teuton is accustomed to give when in the presence of the supreme war lord."[211]

More interesting is reporting that, if not deliberately pejorative, provided a glimpse of the harsh realities behind the vaunted sophistication and luxury of the liners and that characterized a society undergoing rapid economic and social change. As we saw in chapter three, *The New York Times* reported that some of the *Imperator*'s crew members, dissatisfied with working conditions on board, had committed acts of "irreparable damage" to its furnishings and water system before the vessel departed on its maiden voyage.[212] It noted that there were complaints about inadequate and unsanitary quarters for crew members.[213] In Canada, *The Globe* related that, during the *Imperator*'s first call at New York, 1,000 crew members held a meeting in Hoboken and adopted a resolution denouncing working conditions aboard the vessel.[214] The *New-York Tribune* reported on rumours of dissatisfaction amongst stewards aboard the *Vaterland* with respect to wages, food, and quarters.[215] HAPAG protested that these reports had no foundation, and even claimed that negative reporting about the liner was intentionally designed to damage its image.[216]

Yet negative reporting on the *Imperator* and *Vaterland* was not the norm. In keeping with this, the headlines printed in the American press, especially in New York, were often dramatic and sensational in a way that those in English newspapers were not. The *New York Herald* reported on the arrival of the *Vaterland*, for example, with eye-catching headlines extolling it as the "Greatest of Ocean Liners" and "Queen of the Seas."[217] Reporting on the fire that occurred aboard the *Imperator* when docked at Hoboken in August 1913, the English journal *Shipbuilding and Shipping Record* claimed that, as usual, the New York press exaggerated the incident. Contrary to reports in the latter, it claimed that the liner's steerage passengers were landed without even being aware of the fire.[218] Whether this was or was not the case, what is interesting is the English journal's criticism of what it saw as the tendency of the New York press to dramatize and overstate, at least when it came to reporting on the

Imperator-class liners. And there is truth in this observation: generally speaking, English press reporting on the *Imperator* and *Vaterland* adopted a more sober tone, while that which appeared in New York and other American cities, whether or not journalists engaged in hyperbole, employed more excited and enthusiastic language.

The sensational *New York Herald*, with its large distribution, reported on the arrival of the *Imperator* with a collage of photographs on its front page. These depicted the liner making its way to its Hoboken pier, the eagle figurehead, the swimming pool, and Commodore Ruser and his captains.[219] It stated that the vessel entered the port "with the dignity of a Roman conqueror in the Appian Way." While describing the ship as a monster, it said that the Ritz-Carlton restaurant was "an apartment of rare beauty" and offered a glowing report on its interiors. Commenting on the manner in which it was commanded by Commodore Ruser and his captains, the paper described the liner as a "German principality afloat." It also gave direction on how to pronounce its name. Ruser was quoted at length describing the fine performance of the *Imperator* and the paper also related the "enthusiastic" praise of J. Bernard Walker, editor of *Scientific American*, who travelled on its maiden voyage and described the vessel as the steadiest ship aboard which he had ever crossed the Atlantic.

The New York World had no hesitation announcing in a headline that the *Imperator* was the "Greatest Ship In The World."[220] Employing especially colourful and evocative language, it said that if Noah and his family had floated in an ark of such size and luxury they would never had sent a dove in search of dry land. The *Imperator*'s provisions, the paper explained, "would have sustained the first houseboat party for the remainder of the members' lives and there would have been more than enough wine for a half dozen generations of the house of Noah." *The Pittsburgh Post* claimed that the liner was the "Queen of the Ocean" and the "new monarch of the seas."[221] *The Kansas City Star* suggested that, if one went aboard the *Imperator* without a guide, he may well find that "the insurance companies have paid his policies to his widow before he can find his way out again."[222] Promenading on the decks, it said, one could easily believe oneself to be on Broadway. At the time of its launch, *The Detroit News* stated the liner would be equipped with "scores of new and novel features" including tennis courts and a skating rink.[223] Newspapers in New York and elsewhere sometimes published the opinions of those who had travelled aboard the *Imperator*. William Grecht described the liner to *The Baltimore Sun* as a "dream" and said it was "the finest thing I have ever seen afloat."[224] The *New-York Tribune* quoted Rear Admiral Winslow's opinion that "she is a magnificent ship, splendidly run" and noted that the many people on board with "critical eyes" agreed that the *Imperator* exceeded anything that had previously docked in New York.[225]

Given this praise, it is no surprise that American advertisers employed the image of the *Imperator* and *Vaterland* to their advantage. In several newspapers, Steinway Pianos placed advertisements emphasizing that its instruments were to be found aboard both vessels; the world's finest passenger liners were equipped with the world's finest pianos.[226] Stating that "progress, service and efficiency" were characteristic of the *Imperator*, and as the best of everything was lavished on the ship, the choice of Steinway Pianos was "a necessity."[227] The John Wanamaker department store sent a wireless message of congratulations to the *Imperator* and published the thanks it received from Commodore Ruser in a newspaper advertisement. Under a photograph of the liner accompanied by a sizable caption reading "Greetings From The World's Largest Ship," Wanamaker's boasted that it conducted the largest men's clothing business in New York.[228]

Many American newspapers published impressive visual representations that capture the reader's attention. In some cases, more space was devoted to images – be they photographs or artists' impressions – than text. And this was not simply the case with the New York press. At the time of its launch, the *Boston Daily Globe* published a large artist's rendering of the *Imperator*, much larger than the minimal text that focused on the vessel's size.[229] It employed the same arrangement when it printed a large photograph of the *Vaterland* on its stocks in the Blohm & Voss yard and another as it steamed into New York harbour.[230] *The Philadelphia Inquirer* published three large photographs on its front page depicting the *Imperator* in the same harbour.[231] It called the liner a "monster" but said it was in perfect control of itself and moved "majestically." Its engines were "delicately adjusted" and the vessel was "wonderfully sensitive" to direction from the bridge. It also printed a photograph of the *Vaterland* docking in Hoboken that covered almost half of its front page.[232]

Visual imagery played an important role in casting the *Imperator* and *Vaterland* both as emblematic of German modernity and as national monuments. As we saw in chapter two, this was often achieved by matching them with and against widely recognized symbols of modernity, as well as iconic German and American monuments. One visually arresting example from *Scientific American* that was published in *The Washington Post* and elsewhere pictured the *Imperator* towering over the 750-foot bulk of the Woolworth Building in New York. In an inversion of the liner, a historicist exterior clad the most advanced steel-frame construction constituting a masterpiece of twentieth-century architecture and technology. Quickly dubbed the "Cathedral of Commerce," the Woolworth Building remained the world's tallest skyscraper until 1930.[233] The result of this comparative illustration with the *Imperator* was "Brobdingnagian and well calculated to impress the man on the street" who would be "staggered to learn" that the liner would rise 150 feet above the building. It also served to visually emphasize, as was so often the case in text, the modernity of HAPAG's new flagship.

The *New York Herald* chose the Capitol Building and the Washington Monument as points of comparison, telling its readers that the *Imperator* was 160 feet longer than the former and, if stood on its stern, 326 taller than the latter.[234] Americans were used to seeing German liners compared to their iconic structures. NDL's *Kaiser Wilhelm der Große*, launched in 1897, was pictured standing on its stern beside Trinity Church in New York, the Capitol Building, and the Washington Monument.[235] *The Washington Post* used the latter, in 1905, to demonstrate the increasing length of HAPAG liners.[236] It chose the

LENGTH OF "IMPERATOR" 919 FEET   HEIGHT OF WOOLWORTH BUILDING 750 FEET

Figure 6.2 Postcard published by the Cunard Line. 1919–1920.
Source: The Hoboken Historical Museum.

Statue of Liberty as a measure for understanding the size of the *Vaterland*, writing that "if the largest statue in the world were set down on the deck of the great liner the torch in the upraised arm would be below the American flag at the main mast."[237] It provided an image of how such an arrangement would look. The *Cleveland Plain Dealer* bluntly stated that the *Imperator* made the Statue of Liberty look like "a miniature reproduction of itself."[238] These comparisons to some of America's most iconic structures and recognizable national monuments effectively conjured the very same status for HAPAG's *Imperator*-class liners.

Sensationalism and eye-catching imagery, however, were accompanied by a great deal of serious commentary. Although much of this addressed the vessels' modernity, some observers focused on the way in which their cabin-class interiors recreated the atmosphere of the Old World. As previously noted, both the *Imperator* and *Vaterland* bore the symbolism of monarchical power: prominent among their iconography were painted portraits and sculptural busts of the Kaiser. In addition, their cabin-class interiors were designed in a range of historical European styles. And these clearly appealed to American travellers and commentators. In fact, for many Americans travelling to Europe, "evidence of modernity was cause for chagrin, as the Old World was supposed to look old." These views reflected "a binary distinction between a Europe of the past and an America of the future."[239] As Rudy Koshar has noted, American tourists gained a well-deserved reputation for chasing after every trace of royal or feudal pomp they could find. Their enthusiasm for such symbols bordered on "aristo-mania," as the romantic Old World of Europe was contrasted (nostalgically or critically) with the American New World of gleaming modernity.[240]

According to Christof Mauch,

> the focus on (and in some cases the obsession with) symbols, sites and ceremonies of bygone times was rooted in what one might call the voyeurism of the New World. Because aristocracy had no place in the United States, getting a glimpse of its splendor was intriguing to American visitors.[241]

Some travel literature, like Robert Schauffler's *Romantic Germany* of 1909, assured its readers that

> Germany still remains the land of the *Nibelungenlied* and of Grimm's Fairy Tales, of gnomes and giants, storks and turreted ring-walls, of Gothic houses in rows, and the glamour of medieval courtyards. One must merely know where to look for these things.[242]

"Many of the towns," Schauffler explained,

> like Rothenburg, Danzig, and Brunswick, have preserved almost intact their Old World magic, and a touch of real romance is to be found as well in almost every one of those larger cities which we have been taught to consider hopelessly prosaic.[243]

These quotations reveal Schauffler's concern, however, not to sustain a particular vision of Germany, but to recover it. He implies that literature treating the Empire's politics, history, sociology, commerce, and science had led to a de-romanticized picture of the nation.

At the St. Louis World's Fair of 1904, the Kaiser had insisted that the German Pavilion be a copy of Charlottenburg Palace in Berlin with accurate reconstructions of several of its rooms, as well as some of those found in Berlin's City Palace. As Paul Michael Lützeler has indicated, Wilhelm's aim was to highlight a connection between the German Pavilion, the architectural style of absolutism (being the Baroque), the Prussian monarchy, and the Hohenzollern dynasty. Of course, while progressive German achievements in the fine arts were not represented in the official contribution to the fair, this was not the case with science and technology. Nor was it the case with interior design and applied art. In fact, the most recent work of Peter Behrens, Max Länger, Joseph Olbrich, and Bruno Paul was exhibited in the Palace of Varied Industries. Furthermore, the German Pavilion was not unusual; several other countries chose to model their national pavilions on famous historic palaces. As Lützeler explains, what it did was merely represent Germany "as a conservative country that was focused on a glorified past."[244] This was enhanced by the fact that only officially sanctioned academic art was exhibited in the Pavilion. To a certain extent, the interior decoration of the *Imperator* and *Vaterland* contributed to this image of Germany.

Yet it was not this aspect of the *Imperator*-class liners that attracted most attention in the American press. Instead, it was their modernity and the progressive nature of the nation and society that built them. It is well known that Germans took America as a measure of what was new in the early twentieth century and that they looked to the United States because it embodied forces that were transforming the world.[245] Germans saw achievements like the Brooklyn Bridge and New York's skyscrapers as symbols of progress and indications of how the future would transform Europe. Yet much reporting on the *Imperator* and *Vaterland* evinces a similarly strong American interest in German innovation.[246] Just as the growth of individual German industries was cited daily in the press as an example of German prosperity, HAPAG's new liners were touted as symbols of the nation's modernity and its industrial and technological prowess.

Press coverage was dominated by praise for the *Imperator* as a feat of maritime architecture, engineering, and modern technology. This was especially the case with *The Washington Post*. It published illustrated excerpts from *Scientific American* that combined sober enumeration of technical detail – about the liner's rudder post or funnels, for example – with unreserved astonishment at the scale of the vessel and its fittings.[247] This interest in particular details was not uncommon. *The Kansas City Star* published a lithograph depicting the *Imperator*'s rudder. The accompanying text informed readers that it weighed ninety tons, was as tall as a five-story building, and "is so finely hung that it responds to the slightest turn of the steering wheel."[248] *The Wall Street Journal* quoted Alexander M. Carlisle – former chairman of the board and managing director of the Harland & Wolff Shipbuilding Company – who travelled on the maiden voyage: "The Imperator is a marvel of efficiency, and good steady action." He explained that no one "could wish to travel in greater luxury or apparent safety. Every appliance known to the mechanical, scientific or world of luxury has been adopted and applied in the construction of this vessel."[249] The *San Francisco Chronicle* praised the *Imperator* as "a striking tribute to the genius of German engineering."[250] The *Vaterland* was described by *The New York Times* as such "a notable triumph of German engineering and construction, industry and commercial enterprise as to justify international tributes."[251] The paper also published an interview with Dr. Ernst Foerster, one of HAPAG'S naval architects and designer of the *Vaterland*'s hull, in which he described the construction of the vessel in detail.[252]

The nature and scope of German achievements represented by the *Imperator* and *Vaterland* was occasionally reinforced by highlighting the deficiencies of American harbour facilities and shipbuilding that both vessels served to emphasize. The port of New York was singled out for criticism. The *Vaterland* encountered problems docking at Hoboken and when it departed its pier on 26 May 1914, it reversed so rapidly towards the Manhattan shore that the backwash sunk the *Ulster*, a barge with almost 800 tons of coal aboard. Two other barges were badly damaged in the upheaval of water caused by the ship's propellers and "bobbed up and down like corks."[253] While some papers criticized the liner as a result, *The Wall Street Journal* saw this as a consequence of the inadequacies of the city's harbour facilities and the Hudson River, so far as the traffic of large ships was concerned.[254] The subject was also taken up by the *New-York Tribune* which insisted that the city must adapt to the world's commerce and make itself fit to receive the largest ships by constructing adequate piers and channels of travel.[255] More damning was an article in *The Washington Post* stating that the arrival of the *Imperator*, "instead of celebrating the greatness of New York, actually signalized the impotence and inferiority of that port as a builder of mighty ships." "When New York or any other American port can turn out a ship like the Imperator, let it brag; but until it does something creditable, let it give credit to the Germans, where credit is due."[256]

To the image of Germany as a modern, industrial society and economy was added that of a peaceful nation shaped by its enterprising middle classes. *The New York Times* described the *Vaterland* as "a mighty engine for the development of commerce and the promotion of peace."[257] It also quoted one of HAPAG's directors who claimed the Kaiser considered the growth of German shipping to be a great impetus to world peace. "Inter-communication between the nations," the article stated, "facilitated by the present possibilities of comfortable, even luxurious, travel made for that better knowledge of one another which Emperor William believes will minimize the dangers of international friction."[258] The *Vaterland* cost less to construct than a dreadnought and was "much more valuable to mankind."[259] Thus, if the *Imperator*-class liners were symbols of Germany's might, they were also read as a resolution to use that strength peacefully. Commenting on the *Vaterland* as an exemplary product of the nation's enterprising middle classes, *The New York Times* announced that "hearty congratulations are due to the German people for this new symbol of peace and industrial prosperity." "She [the *Vaterland*] fairly represents the genius of the German people, their enterprise and thrift, their determination to do in the best way possible whatever is worth doing."[260]

V

The *Imperator* and *Vaterland* continued to attract the interest of the American press following their maiden voyages for various fortunate and unfortunate reasons. As noted in chapter two, a fire aboard the former while docked at Hoboken in August 1913, which cost the life of one of the ship's officers, received extensive coverage.[261] And yet, with its determination to preserve the liner's image, HAPAG was able to turn the tragedy to its advantage. It published a statement in the New York press explaining that the successful containment of the blaze demonstrated the efficacy of the *Imperator*'s construction in terms of its hull's divisible compartments.[262] The *New-York Tribune* expressed astonishment that the company's post-fire publicity campaign provided such assurances, and allayed all fears, to the extent that no bookings were cancelled.[263] When the *Imperator* sailed from New York on the morning of 27 June 1914, 4,696 passengers and crew were aboard. This was more people than had ever been borne out of the city's harbour aboard a single vessel.[264]

German–American political relations deteriorated towards 1914 as the likelihood of war in Europe increased, a war it was feared would disrupt international trade and destroy the foundations of national wealth. Following the commencement of the conflict in Europe, one ship in particular played an important role in German–American relations and has been central to an understanding of them: the *Lusitania*. Its sinking on 7 May 1915 by a German U-boat had a considerable impact on the American public. As Frank Trommler has indicated, just mentioning the liner's name "conjured a whole world of brutality, barbarism, and betrayal that tainted everything remotely connected with the German cause."[265] It "became a free-floating signifier for malice, war, and evil."[266] This was in complete contrast to the *Imperator* and *Vaterland*.

Diverse American audiences received different images of Germany from a variety of sources. Those that appeared in newspapers, magazines, and popular books on the eve of war were mixed, but "not overwhelmingly unfavourable."[267] This was partly due to the fact that these representations were not static. David Barclay and Elisabeth Glaser-Schmidt emphasize that depictions of Germany were "constantly evolving, constantly in a state of dynamic flux," conditioned by historical circumstances and political and cultural changes within the communities of observed and observer.[268] Ultimately, we are left with "the continuity of ambivalence."[269] As Jörg Nagler argues, Americans were "ambivalent toward that paradoxical country." "Images of Kaiser Wilhelm II, Social Democrats, a welfare state, the army, German education, and German culture," he explains, "presented pictures that were both favorable and unfavorable."[270]

The same was clearly the case with the *Imperator* and *Vaterland*. HAPAG's liners attracted considerable interest and favourable comment that contributed to a positive image of Germany in the American media. As noted above, it was not primarily the monarchical symbolism of the vessels that was embraced by observers, nor did the ships project an image of Germany as the land of the Brothers Grimm. Instead, American press reporting celebrated the *Imperator* and *Vaterland* as modern, peaceful products of a progressive nation and an enterprising middle-class. Historians are well aware that "in the early 1900s Germany was widely viewed as one of the world's most culturally progressive, dynamic, and innovative nations."[271] In spite of Karl Scheffler's reservations, and what he and other prominent Germans saw as the liners' failings, there is no doubt that the *Imperator* and *Vaterland* played a role in disseminating this image to the Atlantic world.

As we have seen, the same can be said of their role in the English press. Here, the dominant tone of coverage was also one of admiration, congratulation, and astonishment even in conservative dailies like *The Times*, *The Daily Telegraph*, and *The Morning Post*.[272] But a survey of reportage in the major English newspapers discloses revealing differences with much that appeared in the United States. First, newspapers of record in America embraced the liners more enthusiastically than their English counterparts and demonstrated a greater interest in the science and technology of the vessels. Second, a readiness to celebrate HAPAG liners as peaceful products of Germany's enterprising middle-classes is more explicit than in English coverage. Third, although a degree of anxiety and self-criticism with respect to the comparative state of the country's merchant marine is evident, American commentary was less coloured by concern about Germany's growing status as a maritime and world power.

The reason for these differences may be attributable to many factors. Less concern about the superiority of German commercial shipping was partly due to the fact that the United States did not feel as threatened as Britain in this particular respect. To a much greater extent than in America, passenger and merchant shipping informed a sense of British national identity and the nation's dominance was felt to be under threat by both German shipbuilding and American money. Furthermore, the images of Germany generated in the American and English media were partly a reflection of the cultural and political outlook of the observers; while sensitive to differences, commentators also appreciated in the German Empire what they valued about themselves. The American press clearly expressed dislike for the authoritarianism and militarism of the German state and was suspicious of its international ambitions. Yet the *Imperator* and *Vaterland* were symbols of a dynamic, innovative nation that had achieved the rank of industrial superpower through the ambitions of its enterprising middle-classes and self-made men like Albert Ballin. Similar examples of positive images based on perceived affinities could be drawn from other media including school textbooks. These presented the German national as "an honest, hard-working, industrious citizen, quite similar to the Yankee."[273] Behind this opinion was the shared experience of expanding industrial economies, global commerce, and international influence that saw both nations surpass Britain. Ultimately, with their enthusiastic interest in German innovation, American journalists were more prepared to celebrate the *Imperator* and *Vaterland* as the products of a progressive, modern nation shaped by an enterprising, forward-thinking middle-class – in other words, a nation much like their own.

Finally, while many Britons were keenly aware of the erosion of their industrial and commercial pre-eminence, many American commentators reveal an express confidence that the United States could compete with Germany in merchant shipping if it desired. An article in *The New York Times* expressed it in the following terms:

> it may be that the builders of the tallest useful structure on earth will never accept the challenge of the longest thing afloat. And yet we doubt it. The genius which was equal to the Woolworth Building can beat the Imperator, if it tries.[274]

Notes

1 Quoted in Peter Zerbe, *Die Grossen Deutschen Passagierschiffe: Imperator, Vaterland, Bismarck* (Hamburg, 1999), 222.

2 "The Imperator, Greatest Steamship Afloat, Ends Half of Her Maiden Voyage Amid Ovation of Sister Craft", *New York Herald*, 20 June 1913; "Imperator Docks", *Boston Daily Globe*, 20 June 1913.

3 "Imperator Minds Helm Like a Yacht", *The New York Times*, 20 June 1913; "Great Ship Imperator Warmly Welcomed on Arrival Here", *The Wall Street Journal* (New York), 20 June 1913.

4 "Imperator Docks", *Boston Daily Globe*, 20 June 1913.

5 "Imperator Minds Helm Like a Yacht", *The New York Times*, 20 June 1913.

6 "Imperator Minds Helm Like a Yacht", *The New York Times*, 20 June 1913.

7 See for example, "Imperator Minds Helm Like a Yacht", *The New York Times*, 20 June 1913; "The Biggest Ship," *The Washington Post*, 20 June 1913.

8 "New Queen of the Ocean Arrives on Maiden Voyage", *The Washington Post*, 21 June 1913.

9 "New Imperator Is a Veritable Floating City", *The Newark Star*, 20 June 1913.

10 Dagmar Bellmann, *Von Höllengefährten zu schwimmenden Palästen. Die Passagierschiffahrt auf dem Atlantik (1840–1930)* (Frankfurt and New York, 2015), 42.

11 "Demands of Ocean Travel", *The New York Times*, 2 October 1897.

12 "Winter Migration Starts", *The Washington Post*, 12 November 1913.

13 "The Sumptuousness of Modern Travel", *Current Opinion* 56 (June 1914), 478.

14 *Hamburg-American Line Gazette* (1905), 4.

15 "Safety before Speed", *Boston Daily Globe*, 20 June 1913.

16 "Innenansichten aus dem Riesendampfer 'Vaterland'", *Hamburger Fremdenblatt*, 10 May 1914.

17 David E. Barclay and Elisabeth Glaser-Schmidt, "Introduction", in David E. Barclay and Elisabeth Glaser-Schmidt, eds., *Transatlantic Images and Perceptions: Germany and America Since 1776* (Washington, DC and Cambridge, 1997), 13.

18 Jörg Nagler, "From Culture to Kultur: Changing American Perceptions of Imperial Germany, 1870–1918", in David E. Barclay and Elisabeth Glaser-Schmidt, eds., *Transatlantic Images*, 152.

19 Barclay and Glaser-Schmidt, "Introduction", 14.

20 *The New York Times*, however, took note of the fact that there were German critics of the *Imperator*'s interiors; see "Imperator Too French?" *The New York Times*, 20 July 1913.

21 Dominik Geppert and Robert Gerwarth, "Introduction", in Dominik Geppert and Robert Gerwarth, eds., *Wilhelmine Germany and Edwardian Britain: Essays on Cultural Affinity* (Oxford, 2008), 6.

22 See for example Barclay and Glaser-Schmidt, eds., *Transatlantic Images*; Frank Trommler and Elliott Shore, eds., *The German-American Encounter: Conflict and Cooperation between Two Cultures, 1800–2000* (New York and Oxford, 2001); Thomas Adam and Ruth Gross, eds., *Traveling between Worlds: German-American Encounters* (College Station, TX, 2006).

23 See Victor Otto, *Deutsche Amerika-Bilder: zu den Intellektuellen-Diskursen um die Moderne 1900–1950* (Munich, 2006); Alexander Stephan, ed., *Americanization and Anti-Americanism: The German Encounter with American Culture after 1945* (New York and Oxford, 2004); Alexander Schmidt, *Reisen in die Moderne: Der Amerika-Diskurs des deutschen Bürgertums vor dem Ersten Weltkrieg im europäischen Vergleich* (Berlin, 1997).

24 See Lynne Tatlock and Matt Erlin, eds., *German Culture in Nineteenth-Century America: Reception, Adaptation, Transformation* (Rochester, NY, 2005).

25 See Nagler, "From Culture".

26 "Vaterland to Sail Without a Stike", *New-York Tribune*, 26 May 1914.
27 Volker Berghahn, "German Industry and American Big Business, 1900–1914", in Sven Oliver Müller and Cornelius Torp, eds., *Imperial Germany Revisited: Continuing Debates and New Perspectives* (New York and Oxford, 2011), 317.
28 Nagler, "From Culture".
29 James Davenport Whelpley, "Germany's Foreign Trade", *The Century Magazine* 83 (1912), 499.
30 Whelpley, "Germany's Foreign Trade", 499.
31 See "Root's Grave Task", *The Washington Post*, 20 November 1905.
32 Berghahn, "German Industry", 320ff.
33 "More 'Last Words' in Ocean Steamship Marvels", *The Washington Post*, 11 June 1911.
34 Frederic William Wile, "German Navy Wins Second Place", *Chicago Daily Tribune*, 29 March 1914.
35 Nagler, "From Culture".
36 Berghahn, "German Industry", 320.
37 Nagler, "From Culture", 136.
38 Reinhard R. Doerries, "Tansatlantic Intelligence in Krieg und Frieden: Die Rolle von Nachrichtendiensten in den Deutsch-Amerikanischen Beziehungen", in Manfred Berg and Philipp Gassert, eds., *Deutschland und die USA in der Internationalen Geschichte des 20. Jahrhunderts* (Stuttgart, 2004), 280.
39 Price Collier, *Germany and the Germans - From An American Point of View* (New York, 1913).
40 "Industrial Germany: United at Home, Expanding Abroad", *The Wall Street Journal* (New York), 20 September 1913.
41 See for example, Price Collier, "Germany and the Germans. From An American Point of View", *Scribner's Magazine* 52 (1912), 513–27 and 662–76; *Scribner's Magazine* 53 (1913), 46–62, 216–33, 283–303, 468–82 and 545–60.
42 Whelpley, "Germany's Foreign Trade", 497.
43 Whelpley, "Germany's Foreign Trade", 486.
44 Whelpley, "Germany's Foreign Trade", 486.
45 Whelpley, "Germany's Foreign Trade", 494. It is interesting to note that the article was accompanied by reproductions of etchings by Joseph Pennell and Fred Gardner depicting industrial installations and German workers at their labour. These represent dark, dingy, bleak, smoke-filled landscapes filled with cranes and smokestacks that, for the twenty-first-century viewer, speak more of the disadvantages of industrial development than its advantages.
46 Whelpley, "Germany's Foreign Trade", 498.
47 W.H. Beehler, "Germany as a Sea Power", *The Century Magazine* 84 (1912), 402.
48 Berghahn, "German Industry", 317.
49 Berghahn, "German Industry", 318.
50 Volker Berghahn, *American Big Business in Britain and Germany: A Comparative History of Two "Special Relationships" in the 20th Century* (Princeton, NJ, 2014), 356.
51 Berghahn, "German Industry", 318f.
52 Berghahn, *American Big Business*, 355.
53 Nagler, "From Culture", 146.
54 Marquise de Fontenoy, "Kaiser Hampered by Social Code", *The Washington Post*, 22 February 1907.
55 "J.P. Morgan Converses with Emperor William", *The New York Times*, 6 July 1902.
56 Collier, "Germany", 527.
57 "Business His Hobby", *The Washington Post*, 30 October 1904.
58 "Men around the Kaiser", *The Washington Post*, 1 November 1913.

59 C.W. Barron, "German Naval Expansion Aid to Commercial Growth", *The Wall Street Journal* (New York), 17 September 1913.

60 "Kaiser A Salesman", *The Washington Post*, 27 September 1912.

61 "News and Gossip of Other Lands", *The Washington Post*, 27 September 1904.

62 See especially Frederick A. Talbot, *Steamship Conquest of the World* (Philadelphia, PA, 1912).

63 J. Russell Smith, *The Ocean Carrier* (New York and London, 1908), 321.

64 Smith, *The Ocean Carrier*, 320f.

65 See for example J.H. Gallinger, "No Free Ships", *The Washington Post*, 9 May 1909.

66 "Germans Develop Big Dockyards", *Christian Science Monitor* (Boston), 2 April 1913.

67 Beehler, "Germany", 398.

68 Edwin J. Clapp, *The Port of Hamburg* (New Haven, CT, 1911), vii.

69 Gerhard A. Ritter, "The Kaiser and His Ship-Owner: Albert Ballin, the HAPAG Shipping Company, and the Relationship between Industry and Politics in Imperial Germany and the Early Weimar Republic", in Hartmut Berghoff, Jürgen Kocka, and Dieter Ziegler, eds., *Business in the Age of Extremes: Essays in Modern German and Austrian Economic History* (Washington, DC and Cambridge, 2013), 22.

70 Abraham Berglund, "The War and the World's Mercantile Marine", *The American Economic Review* 10 (1920), 230.

71 "American Shipping Interests", *The Washington Post*, 9 March 1908.

72 "Chats of Visitors to the Capital", *The Washington Post*, 27 June 1913.

73 Albert Ballin, "Growth of Port of New York as a Shipping Centre", *The New York Times*, 6 January 1907.

74 "Greatest of Ocean Liners May Come to Boston Next Year", *The Christian Science Monitor* (Boston), 12 November 1912.

75 See for example "A 21,000-Ton Liner", *The New York Times*, 31 July 1901.

76 Smith, *The Ocean Carrier*, 312ff.

77 Smith, *The Ocean Carrier*, 315.

78 See for example "Humphrey Attacks the Foreign 'Shipping Trust'", *The Wall Street Journal* (New York), 18 June 1910.

79 Beehler, "Germany", 398.

80 Beehler, "Germany", 399.

81 Beehler, "Germany", 398.

82 Beehler, "Germany", 399.

83 J.H. Gallinger, "No Free Ships", *The Washington Post*, 9 May 1909.

84 "Big Ships Not Likely to Desert New York", *The New York Times*, 14 November 1912.

85 "Imperator Launched; Kaiser Escapes Peril", *The Sun* (New York), 24 May 1912.

86 "Vaterland to Defy Warships of Three Nations in Effort to Carry Reserves to Germany", *The Washington Post*, 5 August 1914.

87 HAPAG, *Die Hamburg-Amerika Linie: Im Sechsten Jahrzehnt Ihrer Entwicklung 1897–1907* (Berlin, 1907), 140.

88 HAPAG, *Die Hamburg-Amerika Linie*, 124.

89 "New Offices of the Hamburg-American Line", *Harper's Weekly* 9 (1908), u.p.

90 "Ballin Will Retire from Hamburg Line", *The New York Times*, 18 July 1908; see also "Denial from Hamburg Line", *The New York Times*, 19 July 1908.

91 HAPAG, *Die Hamburg-Amerika Linie*, 135.

92 "Kaiser Exiles His Friend Ballin for English Leaning Says Report", *The Washington Post*, 12 August 1914.

93   See for example, "Atlantic Steamships", *The Wall Street Journal* (New York), 3 October 1908.

94   "Emil L. Boas Dead of Pneumonia At 58", *The New York Times*, 4 May 1912.

95   HAPAG, *Souvenir of the Hamburg-American Line* (Berlin, 1908), u.p.

96   William H. Miller, *The First Great Ocean Liners in Photographs* (New York, 1984), 30.

97   "Kaiser Exiles His Friend Ballin for English Leaning Says Report", *The Washington Post*, 12 August 1914.

98   Bernhard Huldermann, *Albert Ballin* (Oldenburg and Berlin, 1922), 403.

99   See for example "Views of Herr Ballin", *The New York Times*, 12 November 1901; "Atlantic Rate Conference", *The New York Times*, 5 November 1907.

100 "Ballin Defends Rate War Attitude", *The New York Times*, 2 February 1914; "Ballin in Poor Health", *The New York Times*, 22 January 1914.

101 "Humphrey Attacks the Foreign 'Shipping Trust'", *The Wall Street Journal* (New York), 18 June 1910.

102 "A 21,000-Ton Liner", *The New York Times*, 31 July 1901.

103 Albert Ballin, "Growth of Port of New York as a Shipping Centre", *The New York Times*, 6 January 1907.

104 "Vaterland Arrives Fights Tide 4 Hours", *The New York Times*, 22 May 1914.

105 "Industrial Germany: United at Home, Expanding Abroad", *The Wall Street Journal* (New York), 20 September 1913.

106 Frederic William Wile, *Men Around the Kaiser: The Makers of Modern Germany* (Indianapolis, IN, 1914).

107 "The Newspapers of Germany", *The Wall Street Journal* (New York), 10 August 1907.

108 "Speech by the Kaiser", *The New York Times*, 20 June 1901.

109 "Gossip about the Kaiser", *The Washington Post*, 13 July 1902; see also "Folly of an Alliance", *The Washington Post*, 3 February 1901.

110 "Scold the Kaiser", *The Washington Post*, 25 April 1902.

111 "Germans at Odds over Us", *The New York Times*, 13 March 1914.

112 C.W. Barron, "German Naval Expansion Aid to Commercial Growth", *The Wall Street Journal* (New York), 17 September 1913.

113 "Greatest Man in My Empire", *St. Louis Post-Dispatch*, 20 July 1902.

114 Wile, *Men*, 12.

115 Wile, *Men*, 11.

116 Wile, *Men*, 14.

117 Wile, *Men*, 17.

118 Ritter, "The Kaiser", 19.

119 Susanne Wiborg, *Albert Ballin* (Hamburg, 2000), 31.

120 R.A. Fletcher, *Travelling Palaces: Luxury in Passenger Steamships* (London, 1913).

121 See Bernhard Rieger, *Technology and the Culture of Modernity in Britain and Germany, 1890–1945* (Cambridge, 2005), 166.

122 HAPAG, *Sixty Years of Ocean Navigation and the Half Century Anniversary of the Establishment of the First Line of Steamships Flying a German Flag* (New York, 1906).

123 John H. Gould, *Over the Ocean: An Illustrated Souvenir of the Hamburg-American Line* (New York, n.d.), 34ff.

124 HAPAG, *Hints to Cabin Passengers of the Hamburg American Packet Co.* (New York, n.d.).

125 See for example Gould, *Over the Ocean*.

126 "Winter Migration Starts", *The Washington Post*, 12 November 1913.

127 HAPAG, *Have You Seen the World?* (New York, n.d.).

128 HAPAG, *Have You Seen the World?*

129 HAPAG, *Across the Atlantic* (New York, n.d.), 2.
130 HAPAG, *To the Land of the Midnight Sun* (New York, 1912), 2.
131 HAPAG, *To the Land of the Midnight Sun*, 2.
132 HAPAG, *Winter Cruise to the Mediterranean and the Orient* (New York, 1898), 5.
133 See for example HAPAG, *To the Land of the Midnight Sun* (New York, 1912); *To the Mediterranean: Cabin Rates, Gibraltar, Naples and Genoa* (New York, 1913); *Winter Cruises to the West Indies, the Panama Canal and Venezuela* (New York, 1914); *Winter Voyages to Oriental Wonderlands and to the West Indies* (New York, n.d).
134 HAPAG, *Winter Cruise to the Mediterranean and the Orient* (New York, 1898), 5.
135 HAPAG, *Around the World, 110 Days, S.S. Victoria Luise* (New York, 1911).
136 HAPAG, *Winter Cruise to the Orient* (New York, 1900).
137 Miller, *The First Great Ocean Liners*, 35.
138 Edward S. Wilson, *An Oriental Outing* (Cincinnati, OH, 1894), 13 and 18.
139 John Henry Barrows, *A World Pilgrimage* (Chicago, IL, 1898), 12f.
140 Barrows, *A World Pilgrimage*, 20.
141 Albert Bigelow Paine, *The Lure of the Mediterranean* (New York and London, 1910), 7.
142 HAPAG, *Sixty Years*, 23.
143 HAPAG, *The Hamburg-American Packet Co.* (New York, n.d.), 2.
144 "The Kaiser's Fast Trip", *The New York Times*, 28 September 1897; "Inspecting the Kaiser", *The New York Times*, 30 September 1897.
145 "Demands of Ocean Travel", *The New York Times*, 2 October 1897.
146 Miller, *The First Great Ocean Liners*, 9.
147 "Fewer Big Ship Gazers", *The New York Times*, 21 July 1914.
148 *The Scientific American Handbook of Travel* (New York, 1910); Paine, *The Lure of the Mediterranean*; Robert Urie Jacob, *A Trip to the Orient* (Philadelphia, PA, 1907); Barrows, *A World-Pilgrimage*; Wilson, *An Oriental Outing*.
149 Edward Keble Chatterton, *Steamships and Their Story* (London and New York, 1910); Talbot, *Steamship*; Fletcher, *Travelling Palaces*.
150 See especially Talbot, *Steamship*.
151 See for example "The Latest Type of Transatlantic Liner", *Harper's Weekly* 11 (1905), 1669; "Advancing the Standard of Luxury in Ocean Travel", *Harper's Weekly* 5 (1909), 32.
152 "German Liner Launched", *The New York Times*, 11 January 1900; "Germany's Sea Power", *The Washington Post*, 11 January 1900.
153 "Biggest Liner Yet Takes the Water", *The New York Times*, 21 June 1914.
154 "Roosevelt Makes Denial", *The New York Times*, 1 July 1910.
155 "Monster of Sea in Port", *The Washington Post*, 20 May 1906.
156 See "Seven Wonders of World", *The Washington Post*, 27 February 1914. The others were wireless telegraphy, the Panama canal, the dirigible airship, the flying machine, radium, and the cinematograph.
157 Ernst von Reventlow, "The Shipbuilding Industry of Germany", *Cassier's Magazine: An Engineering Monthly* 40 (1911), 788.
158 "The Kaiser's Fast Trip", *The New York Times*, 28 September 1897.
159 "New Ship a Monster", *The Washington Post*, 1 October 1905.
160 See for example "Imperator, Biggest of Liners, in Port", *The New York Times*, 19 June 1913.
161 See for example "Imperator, Biggest of Liners, in Port", *The New York Times*, 19 June 1913; "Hamburg-American Liner Vaterland the World's Largest Ship Which Will Arrive Here Thursday", *New-York Tribune*, 17 May 1914.
162 L.D., "Studio Talk", *The International Stuido: An Illustrated Magazine of Fine and Applied Art* 36 (1908), 154.
163 HAPAG, *Imperator* (New York, n.d.).

164 HAPAG, *S.S. Imperator. Illustrated Description of First Class Staterooms and Their Equipment* (New York, n.d.).

165 HAPAG, *"Vaterland"* (New York, n.d.).

166 Jack Lawrence, *When the Ships Came in* (New York, 1940), 216.

167 Lawrence, *When the Ships Came in*, 221.

168 Lawrence, *When the Ships Came in*, 224.

169 "Launch of the 'Imperator'", *"Shipping" Illustrated* 38/39 (1 June 1912), 220–2.

170 "Greater than the 'Titanic'", *The Nautical Gazette* 82 (24 July 1912), 3–6; "New Hamburg-American Liner", *The Marine Review* 42 (August 1912), 264f.

171 "The S.S. 'Vaterland' Establishes New Records", *Old Bay Line Magazine* 4 (June 1914), 10 and 12.

172 "New Hamburg-American Liner", *The Marine Review* 43 (July 1913), 245.

173 See for example "The S.S. 'Vaterland' Establishes New Records", *Old Bay Line Magazine* 4 (June 1914), 10–12.

174 See for example "The Latest Type of Transatlantic Liner", *Harper's Weekly* 11 (1905), 1669; "Advancing the Standard of Luxury in Ocean Travel", *Harper's Weekly* 5 (1909), 32.

175 "New Hamburg-American Liner", *The Marine Review* 42 (August 1912), 264.

176 "Launch of the 'Imperator'", *"Shipping" Illustrated* 38/39 (1 June 1912), 221f.

177 "Launch of the 'Imperator'"; see also "The S.S. 'Vaterland' Establishes New Records", *Old Bay Line Magazine* 4 (June 1914), 10–12.

178 "Greater than the 'Titanic'", *The Nautical Gazette* 82 (24 July 1912), 5; "The S.S. 'Vaterland' Establishes New Records", *Old Bay Line Magazine* 4 (June 1914), 11.

179 "The S.S. 'Vaterland' Establishes New Records", *Old Bay Line Magazine* 4 (June 1914), 10.

180 "The S.S. 'Vaterland' Establishes New Records", *Old Bay Line Magazine* 4 (June 1914), 11.

181 "New Hamburg-American Liner", *The Marine Review* 43 (July 1913), 247.

182 "Greatest Ship of All Is Launched for Hamburg Line", *The New York World*, 24 May 1912.

183 "Sea's New Giant, Imperator, Is at Gate of America", *The New York World*, 19 June 1913.

184 "The 'Imperator' Starts To-Day", *The Nautical Gazette: A Journal of Navigation, Shipbuilding, Marine Engineering, Naval Architecture and Commerce* 83 (11 June 1913), 4.

185 "Kaiser Ended Rate War", *The New York Times*, 12 May 1914.

186 "More than 10,000 at the New Pier", *Boston Daily Globe*, 2 June 1913.

187 "Curious Contribute $15,344 to Charity", *The Wall Street Journal* (New York), 4 July 1913.

188 "Erste Reise des Dampfers Imperator", *Zeitschrift der Hamburg-Amerika Linie* 13 (5 July 1913); "Curious Contribute $15,344 to Charity", *The Wall Street Journal* (New York), 4 July 1913.

189 "Inspect the Imperator", *The New York Times*, 21 June 1913.

190 "Imperator Starts Return Trip To-Day", *The New York Times*, 25 June 1913.

191 "Imperator Starts Return Trip To-Day", *The New York Times*, 25 June 1913.

192 "Throng Piers to See the Imperator Sail", *The New York Times*, 26 June 1913.

193 Quoted in Melvin Maddocks, *The Great Liners* (Alexandria, 1978), 63.

194 "Vaterland, 950 Feet, Greatest", *The Evening Post* (New York), 21 May 1914.

195 "Vaterland a Big Success", *The New York Times*, 18 May 1914; see also "Vaterland Like a Yacht", *The New York Times*, 19 May 1914.

196 "Vaterland to Sail without a Stike", *New-York Tribune*, 26 May 1914.

197 "Imperator Delayed by Mob of Visitors", *The New York Times*, 20 July 1913.

198 "Fewer Big Ship Gazers", *The New York Times*, 21 July 1914.

199 "Fewer Big Ship Gazers", *The New York Times*, 21 July 1914.
200 "Mammoth Imperator Ends Her Maiden Voyage without Incident", *Hawaiian Gazette*, 20 June 1913.
201 "Romance and Legend Cling Round the Ancient Figurehead", *New-York Tribune*, 3 August 1913.
202 "The Biggest Ship", *The Washington Post*, 20 June 1913.
203 Lawrence, *When the Ships Came in*, 221.
204 Quoted in Maddocks, *The Great Liners*, 66.
205 "Vaterland Terror of North River", *New-York Tribune*, 27 May 1914.
206 Lawrence, *When the Ships Came in*, 219.
207 Lawrence, *When the Ships Came in*, 219.
208 Lawrence, *When the Ships Came in*, 220.
209 Lawrence, *When the Ships Came in*, 218.
210 "German Financing", *The Wall Street Journal* (New York), 15 August 1913.
211 "Kaiser's Imperator Cruise Is Ended", *The New York Times*, 10 July 1913.
212 "Vandalism on Imperator", *The New York Times*, 31 May 1913.
213 "Imperator Starts Return Trip To-Day", *The New York Times*, 25 June 1913.
214 "Crew of Imperator Demands Better Food", *The Globe* (Toronto), 25 June 1913.
215 "Vaterland to Sail without a Stike", *New-York Tribune*, 26 May 1914.
216 See for example "Vaterland to Sail without a Stike", *New-York Tribune*, 26 May 1914; "Tales about Imperator", *The New York Times*, 3 June 1913; "Imperator Starts Return Trip To-Day", *The New York Times*, 25 June 1913.
217 "Huge Vaterland Has River Fight to Get to Berth", *New York Herald*, 21 May 1914; "The Vaterland, New Queen of the Atlantic, Arrives", *New York Herald*, 22 May 1914.
218 "The Fire on the 'Imperator'", *Shipbuilding and Shipping Record* 2 (11 September 1913), 308.
219 "The Imperator, Greatest Steamship Afloat, Ends Half of Her Maiden Voyage Amid Ovation of Sister Craft", *New York Herald*, 20 June 1913.
220 "Marine Mountain Goes to Her Pier as Easy as a Child", *The New York World*, 20 June 1913.
221 "Great Ship Imperator Arrives in New York", *The Pittsburgh Post*, 19 June 1913.
222 "Yes, It Is Some Big Ship", *The Kansas City Star*, 23 June 1913.
223 "Titanic's Successor Launched Today in Presence of Kaiser", *The Detroit News*, 23 May 1912.
224 "Home on the Imperator", *The Baltimore Sun*, 20 June 1913.
225 "Giant Imperator Is Easily Docked", *New-York Tribune*, 20 June 1913.
226 *The Evening Post* (New York), 21 May 1914.
227 *New-York Tribune*, 19 June 1913; see also *New York Herald*, 19 June 1913.
228 *The New York World*, 20 June 1913.
229 "World's Biggest Vessel Launched", *Boston Daily Globe*, 24 May 1912.
230 "World's Largest Steamship, the Vaterland", *Boston Daily Globe*, 26 April 1914; "Biggest Ship Balks in Docking", *Boston Daily Globe*, 22 May 1914.
231 "Latest Leviathan Liner Steams Majestically to Her Hudson River Pier", *The Philadelphia Inquirer*, 20 June 1913.
232 "Steamer Vaterland Completes Maiden Voayage", *The Philadelphia Inquirer*, 22 May 1914.
233 "Biggest Ship and Building", *The Washington Post*, 22 September 1912.
234 "New Sea Giantess, the Imperator, Is Launched", *New York Herald*, 24 May 1912.
235 Douglas R. Burgess, *Engines of Empire. Steamships and the Victorian Imagination* (Stanford, CA, 2016), 261.
236 "Marine Monsters", *The Washington Post*, 5 March 1905.
237 "Largest Ship and Statue", *The Washington Post*, 17 May 1914.
238 "Giantess Dwarfs All in Big Harbor", *Cleveland Plain Dealer*, 20 June 1913.

239 Rudy Koshar, *German Travel Cultures* (Oxford and New York, 2000), 49.

240 Koshar, *German Travel Cultures*, 52.

241 Christof Mauch, "Oceans Apart? Paradigms in Geman-American History and His-toriograpy", in Adam and Gross, eds., *Traveling between Worlds*, 8.

242 Schauffler, *Romantic Germany*, xv.

243 Schauffler, *Romantic Germany*, xvf.

244 Paul Michael Lützeler and Graduate Students, "The St. Louis World's Fair of 1904 as a Site of Cultural Transfer: German and German-American Participation", in Lynne Tatlock and Matt Erlin, eds., *German Culture in Nineteenth-Century America. Reception, Adaptation, Transformation* (Rochester, NY, 2005), 63.

245 See Alexander Schmidt, *Reisen in die Moderne: Der Amerika-Diskurs des deutschen Bürgertums vor dem Ersten Weltkrieg im europäischen Vergleich* (Berlin, 1997).

246 Wolfgang Helbich, "Different, but Not Out of This World: German Images of the United States between Two Wars, 1871–1914", in Barclay and Glaser-Schmidt, eds., *Transatlantic Images*, 122; see also Schmidt, *Reisen*.

247 See for example "Rudder Post of Imperator", *The Washington Post*, 23 June 1912; "Biggest Ship and Building", *The Washington Post*, 22 September 1912; "Smoke-stack of Ocean Liner", *The Washington Post*, 20 April 1913.

248 "Guides the World's Greatest Boat" *The Kansas City Star*, 15 June 1913.

249 "Great Ship Imperator Warmly Welcomed on Arrival Here", *The Wall Street Journal* (New York), 20 June 1913.

250 "World's Largest Liner", *San Francisco Chronicle*, 17 June 1913.

251 "The Vaterland", *The New York Times*, 22 May 1914.

252 "Designer of Vaterland's Hull Describes Biggest Ship", *The New York Times*, 24 May 1914.

253 "Vaterland Sweeps Ships against Pier", *The New York Times*, 27 May 1914.

254 "Increasing Size of Ocean Vessels in Last 20 Years", *The Wall Street Journal* (New York), 13 June 1914.

255 "The Vaterland in the North River", *New-York Tribune*, 22 May 1914; "Model of North River to Solve Harbor Problems", *New-York Tribune*, 31 May 1914.

256 "The Biggest Ship", *The Washington Post*, 20 June 1913.

257 "The Vaterland", *The New York Times*, 22 May 1914.

258 "Vaterland on Way across Atlantic", *The New York Times*, 16 May 1914.

259 "The Vaterland", *The New York Times*, 22 May 1914.

260 "The Vaterland", *The New York Times*, 22 May 1914.

261 A particularly good account of the incident is "Imperator Fire Costs Life of Second Officer", *New-York Tribune*, 29 August 1913.

262 "Imperator to Go on Time", *New-York Tribune*, 30 August 1913.

263 William C. Freeman, "Advertising Talks", *New-York Tribune*, 7 September 1913.

264 "Hamburg-American Line", *The Wall Street Journal* (New York), 27 June 1914.

265 Frank Trommler, "The *Lusitania* Effect: America's Mobilization against Germany in World War I", *German Studies Review* 32 (2009), 241f.

266 Trommler, "The *Lusitania*", 243.

267 Nagler, "From Culture", 152.

268 Barclay and Glaser-Schmidt, "Introduction", 13.

269 Barclay and Glaser-Schmidt, "Introduction", 14.

270 Nagler, "From Culture", 152.

271 Geppert and Gerwarth, "Introduction", 6.

272 See for example "The Imperator", *The Times* (London), 12 June 1913; "The Imperator: World's Largest Liner: Her Maiden Voyage", *The Daily Telegraph* (London), 13 June 1913; "The Imperator", *The Morning Post* (London), 13 June 1913.

273 Nagler, "From Culture", 151.

274 "Ave, Imperator!" *The New York Times*, 19 June 1913.

Conclusion

Atlantic crossings by the *Imperator* and *Vaterland* came to a halt on 31 July 1914. Fully booked, the former was preparing to sail for New York when HAPAG received a communication from the Imperial Navy advising against this because of the uncertain political situation. As a result, most of its passengers had to make their way to neutral or English ports to find transatlantic passage.[1] The liner would remain laid up at Hamburg for the duration of the conflict. On the same day, the *Vaterland* was preparing to depart from New York when it received news from Germany that British and French cruisers were waiting to seize it.[2] With the outbreak of war, it was interned at Hoboken. Construction of the *Bismarck* ceased just two months after its launch.

The First World War had disastrous consequences for the German merchant marine. Shipping companies cancelled all sailings in August 1914. As in Britain and France, German passenger liners were soon pressed into service as auxiliary cruisers, troop transports, and hospital ships. The Imperial Navy requisitioned several dozen HAPAG vessels; other ships were mothballed. And yet of the company's 175 major freight and passenger vessels, only eighty were in German ports when war commenced. Twelve were seized in enemy ports and eighty-three were tied up in neutral countries, thirty-five in the United States. Almost half of the company's 25,554 employees joined the armed forces; those that did not were employed in the maintenance of vessels laid up in German ports and in HAPAG workshops converting railroad carriages for use in hospital trains.[3] The company's emigrant barracks were converted into a hospital. HAPAG lost 100,000,000 marks in revenue in the first nine months of war, not including the value of vessels requisitioned by the Navy or seized by enemy nations.[4] In addition, it cost two to three million marks a month to maintain an inactive fleet.[5] The company only survived with the aid of government loans, the sale of ships, and the investment of capital amassed before 1914 in department stores, aircraft and zeppelin manufacturing, and the hotel and insurance industries.[6]

In a letter penned on 17 August 1914, Albert Ballin wrote that the "creation of my thirty years of effort lies temporarily in ruins."[7] And yet HAPAG's managing director was not inactive during the war years. He was chiefly involved in lobbying the government for state subsidies to keep German shipping lines afloat, as well as for compensation for the loss of ships in acts of war. With the help of NDL's managing director, Phillip Heineken, he succeeded in having the Shipping Indemnification Law passed on 11 November 1917. This not only provided compensation for lost and damaged vessels, but guaranteed government loans to rebuild Germany's merchant fleet following the cessation of hostilities.[8] While his advice was continuously sought by government officials in Berlin, such influence as he had on the Kaiser declined. Many in Wilhelm's entourage were critical of his Anglophile nature and what they saw as his pacifism. Ballin hoped for a speedy German victory and envisaged post-war cooperation between his nation and Britain to foster the global trade that he believed would constitute the foundation of Germany's post-war economy. But as the war dragged on, he came to believe in the necessity of negotiating peace with the Triple Entente. Wanting to preserve a modernized monarchy, Ballin also believed in the need for constitutional reforms. Yet he would not live to witness Germany's political transformation. On 8 November 1918, the Hamburg Soldiers' Council occupied part of HAPAG's headquarters, threatening him with arrest and bodily harm. At home on that same day, Ballin swallowed a large number of sleeping tablets causing an ulcer in his digestive tract to haemorrhage and his heart to fail. He died early on the afternoon of 9 November, the day the German Republic was born. It is impossible to know whether Ballin intended to take his own life. There are those who are certain it was not his desire.[9] In an official history of HAPAG, the authors claim that Ballin surely would have chosen a less gruesome death if he wished to commit suicide.[10] More recent accounts of his life leave the reason for his demise an open question.[11]

The Armistice stripped Germany of almost all its passenger liners. By 1919, HAPAG and NDL no longer possessed fleets. All German ships displacing over 1,600 gross tons were allocated to the victorious allies, along with half of all vessels displacing between 1,000 and 1,600 gross tons. In possession of the largest passenger fleet on the Atlantic in 1913, Germany was left only with the *Deutschland*, a HAPAG vessel which, renamed *Hansa*, was pressed into service as an emigrant carrier in 1921. And yet, despite this dire situation, the speed with which German merchant shipping rebounded from the catastrophes of war is extraordinary. The remodelling and enlargement of HAPAG's headquarters was completed by the architect Fritz Höger in 1921 and, in 1923, the merchant fleet's new flagship, the *Albert Ballin*, sailed on its maiden voyage to New York. A HAPAG liner displacing 20,185 gross tons, it was less than half the size of the *Imperator*. Nonetheless, it is incredible that, by 1927, under the directorship of Wilhelm Cuno (1876–1933), HAPAG was once again the world's largest shipping line.[12]

However, as German merchant shipping quickly returned to form, the *Imperator*-class liners spent the bulk of their careers in foreign ownership. The *Imperator* was laid up in the Elbe for the duration of the war. On 27 April 1919, it was surrendered to the United States and entered service as a troop transport repatriating American soldiers until it was again laid up in August of that year. In February 1920, it was handed over to Britain's Shipping

Controller and chartered to Cunard. It made its first post-war voyage from Liverpool to New York on 21 February 1920 and was purchased by Cunard in February of the following year. A report on the liner written in January or February of 1921, and presumably prepared for the company's board of directors, describes it as having "the finest Saloon Passenger accommodation of any ship afloat." The author believed it would be worth incurring "considerable expenditure to improve certain arrangements and to increase her earning power."[13] But not all of Cunard's directors were in favour of purchasing the *Imperator*. Sir William Forwood feared the liner would be unprofitable to operate in part because its German origin would likely be an impediment to attracting sufficient custom. The losses that Cunard would incur, he believed, "will be ghastly."[14] Others, like Sir Alfred Booth, felt it was bound to be profitable because of the demand for the type of accommodation it offered. Furthermore, he claimed it would not be possible to build a similarly large and luxurious liner for another ten years.[15] Sir Ashley Sparks, the chief representative of Cunard in the United States, was certain any problems attracting passengers would disappear when the vessel's name was changed and provided it performed well at sea.[16]

In a board meeting held on 16 February 1921, Cunard's directors resolved that the *Imperator* would be rechristened *Berengaria* in honour of Berengaria of Navarre who was Queen of England as the wife of Richard I.[17] Between October 1921 and May 1922, the liner received an extensive refit at Armstrong, Whitworth & Co. at Walker-on-Tyne. Minutes of the meetings of Cunard's executive committee record a host of repairs and renovations. These included re-caulking decks; cleaning carpets; reupholstering furniture; providing lavatories with new enamel; repainting; remodelling some of the state rooms; enlarging the first-class dining room; and re-arranging the crew's accommodation.[18] The most major transformation was the vessel's conversion to burn fuel oil instead of coal.

Rechristened and refitted, the *Berengaria* recommenced transatlantic sailings in the company of the *Mauretania* and *Aquitania*. While the latter were "superb running mates," it was the *Berengaria* that "garnered for Cunard the rich and titled."[19] The company's intention was to keep the vessel in operation until the new *Queen Elizabeth* came into service in 1940. But the liner was plagued by numerous electrical fires and in 1938, following yet another blaze while docked in New York, the *Berengaria* returned to Britain without passengers and was sold to Palmers Shipbuilding and Iron Company at Jarrow to be broken up. Its furnishings were sold at an auction occurring over several days in January 1939. Conducted by Hampton & Sons in conjunction with Anderson & Garland, this took place in the vessel's first-class lounge. The catalogue does not list any paintings or tapestries, but furniture, pianos, light fittings, tableware, sanitary equipment, panelling, bells, lifeboats, and even decks were put up for sale.[20] The demolition of the *Berengaria* began in February 1939 in the Palmers yard and was completed in 1946.

The *Vaterland* remained anchored at Hoboken for nearly three years. It hosted fund-raising banquets and balls mounted by the German-American community in support of Germany's war effort.[21] In March 1917, HAPAG ordered its captains to cripple the engines of all vessels in American ports, including the *Vaterland*.[22] After the United States entered the war in the following month, the liner was seized, along with other German vessels in American waters, and converted into a troop transport. It underwent repairs, was equipped with guns, and was rechristened the U.S.S. *Leviathan*. The largest vessel yet to fly the Stars and Stripes made its first sailing to Britain carrying American soldiers in December 1917. The liner was neglected at Hoboken after the war, but was finally transferred to the United States Lines which was founded in August 1921. Sent to Newport News, Virginia for an extensive refit, it was converted to burn oil fuel and made its maiden voyage to Southampton on 4 July 1923 as the flagship of America's merchant marine. Although it was run mostly at a loss, the *Leviathan* continued to sail the Atlantic until September 1934 before making its last voyage to Britain in 1938 to be scrapped.

The *Bismarck* was launched shortly before the outbreak of war but lay unfinished in Hamburg. It was handed over to Britain's Shipping Controller in 1919 and work on the liner recommenced in the yards of Blohm & Voss under British supervision and according to British specifications. Sold to the White Star Line in February 1921, the world's largest liner became the company's flagship and was rechristened the *Majestic*. It undertook its maiden voyage to New York on 10 May 1922 and served on this route alongside the *Olympic* and the *Homeric*. When White Star and Cunard were forced to merge in 1934 as a result of the serious financial difficulties faced by both lines, the *Majestic* was transferred to the newly-formed Cunard-White Star Line. In 1936, it was sold for scrap. But the vessel was bought by the British Admiralty and refitted for use as a training ship. Rechristened the *Caledonia*, it commenced refitting as a transport vessel upon the outbreak of the Second World War. Unfortunately, a fire that broke out during this conversion caused it to sink at its moorings. Beyond repair, the vessel was finally sold for scrap in March 1940.

Much of the attention afforded the *Imperator*-class liners, and other storied transatlantic passenger steamers of the Belle Époque, has been guided by an attempt to reconstruct these lost vessels, and the experiences they afforded those who travelled aboard them, in text and image. This book has provided tangible evidence for their role as giant objects signifying the German nation and its nature. Monuments of metal and stone were one important means – along with politics, ideology, popular festivals, the arts, the media, and a host of objects in material culture – by which the idea of nation was generated and transmitted and through which it became part of a common understanding in Imperial Germany. And yet, historically speaking, the *Imperator*, *Vaterland*, and *Bismarck* were much more than physical objects; the largest, most sophisticated vehicles built before 1914 were also advertising, media, and cultural constructions that attained notable status as monuments to the German Empire in both a national and international context. This was achieved not with steel and steam, but largely through a variety of ephemeral representations on paper published on both sides of the Atlantic. These loaded their hulls not with passengers and provisions but with a variety of interpretations concerning the nature, achievements, and ambitions of the new continental superpower. In this way, they became "virtual monuments" that spoke not univocally nor only locally, but with several voices and internationally.[23] To be sure, HAPAG's vessels were not unique in this respect. Nevertheless, their story constitutes much more than a case study in the way in which objects are invested with symbolic meaning and the manner in which they mediate nationhood. They demonstrate that the contemporaneous signifiers of these objects – the way in which they were construed and presented to those who never encountered them personally – are as historically real and sometimes as important as the objects themselves, if not more so. It was especially in this respect that the *Imperator*-class liners were truly monumental steamships contributing to the idea and image of the German nation.

Closely analysed as objects that mediated nationhood, these "virtual monuments" foreground several important facts and phenomena not considered in broad-brush narratives that, captivated by the vessels themselves, treat historical context in an impressionistic and uncomplicated manner. Of course, they testify to the ability of representations to circulate widely – during an era that witnessed the rapid expansion of the mass media and consumerism – and their capacity to bring the nation into the everyday lives of ordinary Germans. And yet to say that the latter were proud of the *Imperator*-class liners as national monuments is to say too much and too little. To be sure, it is impossible to precisely formulate the phenomenon of everyday national identity and culture. Yet the *Imperator*, *Vaterland*, and *Bismarck* were often implicitly and explicitly construed as monuments to German achievements and ambitions in the popular media. At the same time, claims to this status were seriously and sometimes vigorously contested. Furthermore, commentators who saw the vessels as emblematic of the German nation did so from a variety of different perspectives and circumstances. This is a reminder that the manner in which Germans understood their nation was not singular, nor uniform. Instead, the national idea was constructed and coloured by a variety of differing perceptions and narrated from a multitude of viewpoints; different sectors of German society – be they defined as Catholic, Protestant, aristocratic, bourgeois, or working class – constructed different ideas of nationhood. As a result, it might even be said that Imperial Germany failed to shape a coherent and stable national identity.

In addition, the *Imperator*-class liners were some of the many objects, representations, and events that prompted Germans to think outside the nation. A particularly notable and visible part of their society's international and transnational orientation and engagement, they participated in feeding the popular imagination about the world beyond Germany's borders and the Empire's positive connections to, and involvement with it. In fact, these vessels, and many others, were repeatedly construed as monuments to the progress and achievements of the leading nations of the Atlantic world taken together; they were often interpreted as emblematic of the international and transnational competition, exchange, and cooperation in business, trade, technology, and culture of which they were born. As such, they were sometimes imagined as indicators, if not guarantors of international peace. Furthermore, they facilitated important encounters with Imperial Germany, both virtual and real, for societies across the English Channel and on the other side of the Atlantic. The manner in which HAPAG's liners were written about and pictured in the popular and professional media of Britain and the United States reflects the multi-faceted image of Germany presented to the populations of both countries in the years shortly before the First World War. More profoundly, their reception is an indicator of the complex relationship both nations had with their soon-to-be enemy, a relationship composed of a variety of political, social, economic, and cultural contacts, interactions, tensions, and transfers, along with a diversity of popular perceptions and projections that embodied everything from bitter antagonism to enthusiastic admiration.

While this book has focused on the *Imperator*-class liners, it is clear that the company that commissioned them also explicitly presented itself, and was often widely construed at home and abroad, as symbolic of Germany's industrial, economic, commercial, and international power and progress. In various ways, HAPAG played an important role in both mediating nationhood and facilitating real and virtual contact and connections with societies around the globe. So did the Norddeutscher Lloyd and other German shipping lines. Exploring this phenomenon is one of the ways in which the maritime history of Imperial Germany – in its political, social, economic, and cultural forms – needs to be expanded and developed. The history of its merchant marine still has much to tell us about the German Empire in its national, international, and transnational dimensions.

Notes

1 Bernhard Huldermann, *Albert Ballin* (Oldenburg and Berlin, 1922), 306f.
2 Milton H. Watson, *Flagships of the Line: A Celebration of the World's Three-Funnel Liners* (Wellingborough, 1988), 115.
3 Lamar Cecil, *Albert Ballin. Business and Politics in Imperial Germany, 1888–1918* (Princeton, NJ, 1967), 215.
4 Cecil, *Albert Ballin*, 237.
5 Cecil, *Albert Ballin*, 218f.
6 Gerhard A. Ritter, "The Kaiser and His Ship-Owner: Albert Ballin, the HAPAG Shipping Company, and the Relationship between Industry and Politics in Imperial Germany and the Early Weimar Republic", in Hartmut Berghoff, Jürgen Kocka, and Dieter Ziegler, eds., *Business in the Age of Extremes: Essays in Modern German and Austrian Economic History* (Washington, DC and Cambridge, 2013), 32.
7 Quoted in Peter-Franz Stubmann, *Ballin: Leben und Werk eines deutschen Reeders* (Berlin-Grunewald, 1926), 261.
8 Ritter, "The Kaiser", 32.
9 See for example Gerhard Ahrens and Renate Hauschild-Thiessen, *Die Reeder: Laeisz, Ballin* (Hamburg, 1989), 65.
10 Susanne Wiborg and Klaus Wiborg, *1847–1997: Unser Feld ist die Welt: 150 Jahre Hapag-Lloyd* (Hamburg, 1997), 207.

11 See Johannes Gerhardt, *Albert Ballin* (Hamburg, 2009).

12 Arnold Kludas, *Die Geschichte der deutschen Passagierschiffahrt* (Hamburg, 1988), vol. 4, 61.

13 Cunard Archive. D42/C1/2/215. Chairman's Correspondence. "Imperator".

14 Cunard Archive. D42/C1/1/32. Chairman's Correspondence. William B. Forwood to Sir Alfred Booth, 5 April 1920.

15 Cunard Archive. D42/C1/1/32. Chairman's Correspondence. Sir Alfred Booth to Sir William Forwood, 1 April 1920.

16 Cunard Archive. D42/C1/2/2. Chairman's Correspondence. Sir Ashley Sparks to Alfred Booth, 16 March 1921.

17 Cunard Archive. D42/B1/10. Board of Director's Minutes, vol. 8 (21 February1917–25 January 1922). Board Meeting of 16 February 1921.

18 See Cunard Archive. D42/B4/55 – D42/B4/55. Executive Committee meetings, vols. 55–9.

19 Watson, *Flagships*, 111.

20 *Catalogue of the Costly Appointments Furnishings and Paneling of R.M.S. Berengaria.* Auction Catalogue of Hampton & Sons (London, 1938).

21 William H. Miller, *The First Great Ocean Liners in Photographs* (New York, 1984), 81.

22 Cecil, *Albert Ballin*, 232.

23 Rudy Koshar, *From Monuments to Traces: Artifacts of German Memory, 1870–1990* (Berkeley, CA, Los Angeles, CA, and London, 2000), 48f.

Bibliography

Archival sources

I Bremerhaven: Deutsches Schiffahrtsmuseum

Deutsches Schiffahrtsmuseum I. 1458/77; III.2.VI.2m; III.95-27.

II Hamburg: Staatsarchiv der Freien und Hansestadt Hamburg

St.A.H. A941. Zeitungsausschnittsammlug (ZAS) D. "Imperator."

St.A.H. A941. ZAS D. "Vaterland" Bj. 1913.

St.A.H. A941. ZAS D. "Bismarck."

St.A.H. 331-3. Politische Polizei, S18765: Bericht Szymanski, 24 May 1912, attachment.

St.A.H. 621-1/95. HAPAG – Reederei 2637 Band 1. Verträge und Vereinbarungen zu Schiffsneubauten, 1899–1924. MUG 128A 04 05.

St.A.H. 621-1/95. HAPAG – Reederei 2637 Band 4. Verträge und Vereinbarungen zu Schiffsneubauten, 1906–1910. MUG 128A 04 05.

St.A.H. 621-1/95. HAPAG – Reederei 2637 Band 5. Verträge und Vereinbarungen zu Schiffsneubauten, 1911–23. MUG 128A 04 05.

St.A.H. 621-1/95. HAPAG – Reederei 2656 Band 1. Verträge und Vereinbarungen zu Schiffsneubauten Band 1: D "Bismarck" 1909–1921. MUG 128A 04 05.

St.A.H. 621-1/95. HAPAG – Reederei 2656 Band 3. Verträge und Vereinbarungen zu Schiffsneubauten Band 3: D "Imperator" 1910–1914. MUG 128A 04 05.

St.A.H. 621-1/95. HAPAG – Reederei 2656 Band 6. Verträge und Vereinbarungen zu Schiffsneubauten Band 6: D "Vaterland" 1912–1914. MUG 128A 04 05.

St.A.H. 621-1/95. HAPAG – Reederei 3176. Zeitungsausschnitt- und Materialsammlung zum Schiffbau in Hamburg, 1911–1924. MUG 128A 04 05.

St.A.H. 621-1/95. HAPAG – Reederei 3251. Graphische Darstellungen der Flotten- und Schiffsgrößenentwicklung der HAPAG sowie des Vergleichs mit anderen Reedereien des In- und Auslandes, 1907–1925. MUG 128A 04 05.

St.A.H. 621-1/95. HAPAG – Reederei 3251. Statistische Übersichten, Zeitungsausschnitte, Beschreibungen u.a. zu HAPAG und anderen Schiffen, 1909–1958. MUG 128A 04 05.

St.A.H. 622-1. Merck, II 8, Johannes Merck, Konv. 2b, "Meine Erinnerungen an die Hamburg-Amerika Linie und an Albert Ballin, 1896–1918" [1920].

III Hamburg: Hapag-Lloyd Archiv

Hapag-Lloyd Archiv: 1.5.14; 8.5.14; 12.4.13; 22.6.14; 25.6.14; 26.5.14.

IV Liverpool: University of Liverpool, Special Collections and Archives: Cunard Archive

D42/B1/10. Board of Director's Minutes, vol 8 (21 Febraury 1917–25 January 1922).
D42/B4/55. Executive Committee meetings, vols. 55–59.
D42/C1/1/32. Chairman's Correspondence.
D42/C1/2/2. Chairman's Correspondence.
D42/C1/2/102. Chairman's Correspondence.
D42/C1/2/215. Chairman's Correspondence. "Imperator."
D42/PR2/1/33. Publicity Material.

V London: National Maritime Museum

Caird Library. Ephemera Collection, 43. Foreign Shipping Companies: Hamburg-America Line. HA 14.

VI London: Warburg Insitute Archive

WIA. FC (Family Correspondence).
WIA. GC (General Correspondence).
WIA. III.2.1: Zettelkasten 57 (Hamburg).
WIA. IV.36: Hamburg-Amerika Linie (Imperator and Vaterland).
WIA. Kopierbuch V.

Published primary sources

I Books and catalogues

Barrows, John Henry, *A World Pilgrimage* (Chicago, IL: A.C. McClurg, 1898).
Brex, Twells, *Scaremongerings from the Daily Mail 1896–1914: The Paper That Foretold the War* (London: Daily Mail, 1915).
Broadley, Alexander M., *The Ship Beautiful: Art and the Aquitania* (Liverpool: Cunard Steamship Co., 1914).
Catalogue of the Costly Appointments Furnishings and Paneling of S.S. Leviathan (London: Hampton and Sons, 1938).
Chatterton, Edward Keble, *Steamships and Their Story* (London and New York: Cassell & Co., 1910).
Clapp, Edwin J., *The Port of Hamburg* (New Haven, CT: Yale University Press, 1911).
Cobb, Irvin S., *Europe Revised* (New York: George H. Doran Company, 1914).
Collier, Price, *Germany and the Germans – From an American Point of View* (New York: Charles Scribner's Sons, 1913).
Dickens, Charles, *American Notes and a Child's History of England* (London, Edinburgh, and New York: Thomas Nelson and Sons, n.d.).

Die elektrischen Kommandoanlagen auf den Schnelldampfer Imperator der Hamburg-Amerika Linie (Berlin: Siemens & Halske AG, 1915).

Fletcher, R.A., *Steamships: The Story of Their Development to the Present Day* (London: Sidgwick and Jackson, 1910).

Fletcher, R.A., *Travelling Palaces: Luxury in Passenger Steamships* (London: Sir Isaac Pitman & Son, 1913).

Forwood, William B., *Recollections of a Busy Life* (Liverpool: Henry Young & Sons, 1910).

Freyer, Walter, *Im Kampf um den Ozean: Seeroman* (Leipzig: Dietrich, 1914).

Gaulke, Johannes, *Im Zwischendeck. Ein Kulturbild aus dem Auswandererleben* (Berlin-Tempelhof: Freier Literarischer Verlag, 1909).

Gauss, Christian, *The German Kaiser as Shown in His Public Utterances* (New York: Charles Scribner's Sons, 1915).

Goetz, Adolph, *Ballin: ein königlicher Kaufmann* (Berlin: Hermann Seemann Nachfolger, 1907).

Goetz, Adolph, *25 Jahre hamburgische Seeschiffahrtspolitk* (Hamburg: Verlagsanstalt und Druckerei-Gesellschaft, 1911).

Gould, John H., *Over the Ocean: An Illustrated Souvenir of the Hamburg-American Line* (New York: Ocean Publishing Co., 1895).

Gould, John H., *Across the Atlantic* (New York: Ocean Publishing Company, 1896).

Haack, Rudolph and Carl Busley, *Die Technische Entwicklung des Norddeutschen Lloyds und der Hamburg-Amerikanischen Packetfahrt-Aktiengesellschaft* (Berlin: Julius Springer, 1893).

Harjes, Philipp, *Eine Reise nach dem Lande wo die Arbeit adelt* (Gotha: Engelhard-Reyhersehen, 1905).

Hayes, Bertram, *Hull-Down: Reminiscences of Wind-Jammers, Troops and Travellers* (New York: Macmillan, 1925).

Himer, Kurt, *Die Hamburg-Amerika Linie im sechsten Jahrzehnt ihrer Entwicklung, 1897 bis 1907. Zum Sechzigsten Geburtstag des Gesellschaft* (Hamburg: Eckstein, 1907).

Himer, Kurt, *75 Jahre Hamburg-Amerika Linie: Geschichte der Hamburg-Amerika Linie*, 2 vols. (Hamburg: Petermann, 1922/27).

Hirschberg, Julius, *Um die Erde: Eine Reisebeschreibung* (Leipzig: Georg Thieme, 1894).

Holitscher, Arthur, *Amerika, Heute und Morgen. Reiseerlebnisse* (Berlin: S. Fischer, 1912).

Holmes, George C.V., *Ancient and Modern Ships* (London: H.M. Stationery Office, 1906).

Holt, Emily, *Encyclopedia of Etiquette* (New York: Syndicate Publishing Company, 1915).

Hopkins, Albert A., ed., *The Scientific American Handbook of Travel* (New York: Munn & Co., 1910).

Horstmann, Edgar, *Innenausbau von Schiffen* (Lübeck: Moll-Winter, 1952).

Jacob, Robert Urie, *A Trip to the Orient: The Story of a Mediterranean Cruise* (Philadelphia, PA: The John C. Winston Co., 1907).

Landerer, Richard, *Geschichte der Hamburg-Amerikanischen Paketfahrt-Aktien-Gesellschaft* (Leipzig: Giesecke & Devrient, 1897).

Lawrence, Jack, *When the Ships Came in* (New York: Farrar & Rinehart, 1940).

Ledoux, Katherine R., *Ocean Notes for Ladies* (New York: G.P. Putnam's Sons, 1877).

Ledoux, Katherine R., *Ocean Notes and Foreign Travel for Ladies* (New York: Cook, Son, and Jenkins, 1878).

Marvin, Winthrop Lippit, *The American Merchant Marine: Its History and Romance from 1620 to 1902* (New York: Charles Scribner's Sons, 1902).

Murken, Erich, *Die großen transatlantischen Linienreedereien-Verbände, Pools und Interessengemeinschaften bis zum Ausbruch des Weltkrieges: Ihre Entstehung, Organisation und Wirksamkeit* (Jena: G. Fischer, 1922).

Norddeutscher Lloyd, *Die Fortschritte des Deutschen Schiffbaus unter besonderer berücksichtigung der entwicklung der flotte des Norddeutschen Lloyd* (Berlin: Hobbing & Co., 1909).

Owen, H., *Ship Economics* (London: G. Phillip & Sons, 1911).

Paine, Albert Bigelow, *The Lure of the Mediterranean* (New York and London: Harper & Brothers, 1910).

Radunz, Karl, *100 Jahre Dampfschiffahrt 1807–1907: Schilderungen und Skizzen aus der Entwicklungsgeschichte des Dampfschiffes* (Rostock: C.J.E. Volckmann Nachfolger, 1907).

Schauffler, Robert Haven, *Romantic Germany* (New York: The Century Company, 1910).

Schröder, Georg, *Fiasko! Die deutsche Politik des Wahnsinns: Ballin gleich Deutschlands Tragödie* ... (Hamburg, n.d.).

Simpson, George, *The Naval Constructor: A Vade Mecum of Ship Design* (New York: D. Van Nostrand Co., 1914).

Smith, J. Russell, *The Ocean Carrier* (New York and London: G.P. Putnam's Sons, 1908).

Talbot, Frederick A., *Steamship Conquest of the World* (London: William Heinemann, 1912).

Weth, H., *Die Orient-Reise der "Augusta Victoria" vom Januar bis März 1891* (Hamburg: Gustav Diedrich, 1891).

Wile, Frederic William, *Men around the Kaiser: The Makers of Modern Germany* (Indianapolis, IN: The Bobbs-Merrill Company, 1914).

Williams, Ernest Edwin, *"Made in Germany"* (London: William Heinemann, 1896).

Wilson, Edward S., *An Oriental Outing: Being a Narrative of a Cruise along the Mediterranean and Visits to Historic Cities* (Cincinnati, OH: Cranston and Curts, 1894).

II HAPAG publications

Across the Atlantic: Photographic Reproductions of the Company's Various Types of Steamers Comprised in the Transatlantic Passenger Services (New York, 1905).

Around The World, 110 Days, S.S. Victoria Luise (New York, 1911).

Die Auswandererhallen der Hamburg-Amerika-Linie in Hamburg (Hamburg, 1907).

Dampfer Imperator: Das Größte Schiff Der Welt (Hamburg, n.d.).

Europe. First Class Cabins (New York, 1914).

Europe: Second Cabin Rates (New York, 1914).

Große Orient-und Indienfahrt 1914 (Magdeburg, 1913).

Hamburg American Line. S.S. Imperator (New York, n.d.).

The Hamburg-American Packet Co. (New York, n.d.).

Die Hamburg-Amerika Linie: Im Sechsten Jahrzehnt Ihrer Entwicklung 1897–1907 (Berlin: Eckstein's Biographischer Verlag, 1907).

Have You Seen the World? (New York, n.d.).

Hints to Cabin Passengers of the Hamburg American Packet Co. (New York, n.d.). *Imperator* (New York, 1913).

Imperator (Siegburg bei Köln, n.d.).

Imperator Auf See: Gedenkblätter an die erste Ausfahrt des Dampfers am 11. Juni 1913 (Hamburg, 1913).

Imperator: The World's Largest Ship, Embodying Maximum Comfort and Safety for All (New York, n.d.).

Jahresbericht für die am 26. März 1912 stattfindende ordentliche Generalversammlung der Aktionäre (Hamburg, 1912).

Marine Monsters (New York, n.d.).

The New Twin-Screw Express Steamers of the Hamburg-American Packet Company (New York, n.d.).

Sixty Years of Ocean Navigation and the Half Century Anniversary of the Establishment of the First Line of Steamships Flying a German Flag (New York, 1906).

Souvenir of the Hamburg-American Line (Berlin: J. Hermann Herz, 1908).

S.S. Imperator. Illustrated Description of First Class Staterooms and Their Equipment (New York, n.d.).

To the Land of the Midnight Sun (New York, 1912).

To the Mediterranean: Cabin Rates, Gibraltar, Naples and Genoa (New York, 1913).

Turbinen-Schnelldampfer Imperator (Hamburg, n.d.).

Turbinenschnelldampfer Vaterland (Hamburg, 1914).

Vaterland (Hamburg, n.d.).

"Vaterland" (New York, n.d.).

Winter Cruise to the Mediterranean and the Orient (New York, 1898).

Winter Cruise to the Orient (New York, 1900).

Winter Cruises to the West Indies, the Panama Canal and Venezuela (New York, 1914).

Winter Voyages to Oriental Wonderlands and to the West Indies (New York, n.d).

III Journals and magazines

Britain

Engineering.
The Marine Engineer and Naval Architect.
The Shipbuilder.
Shipbuilding and Shipping Record.
The Syren and Shipping Illustrated.

Germany

Deutsche Bauhütte.
Die Gartenlaube.
Die Gegenwart.
Die Hamburger Woche.
Hansa: Deutsche nautische Zeitschrift.
Illustrirte Zeitung.
Innen-Dekoration: Die Gesamte Wohnungskunst in Bild und Wort.
Jahrbuch Des Deutschen Werkbundes, 1914, Der Verkehr.
Jahrbuch für Deutschlands Seeinteressen.
Jahrbuch der Schiffbautechnischen Gesellschaft.
Kunst und Künstler.

Der Kunstwart.
Der Lotse.
Schiffbau: Zeitschrift für die gesamte Industrie auf schiffbautechnischen und verwandten Gebieten.
Schriften des Vereins für Sozialpolitik.
Seefahrt: Technische und kritische Zeitschrift für die Seeschiffahrt.
Über Land und Meer.
Zeitschrift der Hamburg-Amerika Linie.
Zeitschrift des Vereines Deutscher Ingenieure.

United States

The American Economic Review.
Cassier's Magazine: An Engineering Monthly.
The Century Magazine.
The Christian Science Monitor.
Current Opinion.
Hamburg-American Gazette.
Harper's Weekly.
The International Studio: An Illustrated Magazine of Fine and Applied Art.
The Marine Review.
The Nautical Gazette: A Journal of Navigation, Shipbuilding, Marine Engineering, Naval Architecture and Commerce.
Old Bay Line Magazine.
Scientific American.
Scribner's Magazine.
"Shipping" Illustrated.

IV Newspapers

Britain

Belfast Newsletter.
Daily Chronicle (London).
Daily Mail (London).
The Daily Telegraph (London).
Evening Standard (London).
The Manchester Guardian.
The Morning Post (London).
The Observer (London).
The Sunday Times (London).
The Times (London).
The Westminster Gazette (London).

Canada

The Globe (Toronto).

Germany

Allgemeine Zeitung (Mainz).
Berliner Tageblatt.
Hamburgischer Correspondent.
Hamburger Echo.
Hamburger Fremdenblatt.
Hamburger Nachrichten.
Kölnische Zeitung (Cologne).
Neue Hamburger Zeitung.
Tägliche Rundschau (Berlin).
Vossische Zeitung (Berlin).

United States

The Baltimore Sun.
Boston Daily Globe.
Boston Herald.
Chicago Daily Tribune.
Cleveland Plain Dealer.
The Detroit Free Press.
The Detroit News.
The Evening Post (New York).
Hawaiian Gazette.
The Kansas City Star.
New York Herald.
The New York Times.
New-York Tribune.
The New York World.
The Newark Star.
The Philadelphia Inquirer.
The Pittsburgh Post.
San Francisco Chronicle.
St. Louis Post-Dispatch.
The Sun (New York).
The Wall Street Journal (New York).
The Washington Post.
The World (New York).

Secondary sources

Adam, Thomas and Ruth Gross, eds., *Traveling between Worlds: German-American Encounters* (College Station, TX: Texas A & M University Press, 2006).
Afflerbach, Holger, *Der Dreibund. Europäische Großmacht-und Allianzpolitik vor dem Ersten Weltkrieg* (Wien: Böhlau, 2002).
Ahrens, Gerhard and Renate Hauschild-Thiesen, *Die Reeder Laeisz, Ballin* (Hamburg: Verein für Hamburgische Geschichte, 1989).

Anderson, Benedict, *Imagined Communities: Reflections on the Origin and Spread of Nationalism* (London and New York: Verso, 1983).

Applegate, Celia, *A Nation of Provincials* (Berkeley, CA: University of California Press, 1990).

Archibald, Edward H.H., *The Dictionary of Sea Painters of Europe and America*, 3rd edn. (Woodbridge: Antique Collectors' Club, 2000).

Armgart, Arno, *Bremen, Bremerhaven, New York, 1683–1960: Geschichte der Auswanderung über die bremischen Häfen* (Bremen: Steintor, 1991).

Augustine, Dolores L., *Patricians and Parvenus: Wealth and High Society in Wilhelmine Germany* (Oxford and Providence, RI: Berg, 1994).

Barclay, David E. and Elisabeth Glaser-Schmidt, eds., *Transatlantic Images and Perceptions: Germany and America since 1776* (New York and Cambridge: Cambridge University Press, 1997).

Belgum, Kirsten, *Popularizing the Nation: Audience, Representation, and the Production of Identity in Die Gartenlaube, 1853–1900* (Lincoln, NE: University of Nebraska Press, 1998).

Bell, Andrew Francis, *Anglophilia: The Hamburg Bourgeoisie and the Importation of English Middle Class Culture in the Wilhelmine Era* (Ph.D. dissertation: Brown University, 2001).

Bellmann, Dagmar, *Von Höllengefährten zu schwimmenden Palästen. Die Passagierschiffahrt auf dem Atlantik (1840–1930)* (Frankfurt a.M. and New York: Campus, 2015).

Berg, Manfred and Philipp Gassert, *Deutschland und die USA in der Internationalen Geschichte des 20. Jahrhunderts. Festschrift für Detlef Junker* (Stuttgart: Franz Steiner, 2004).

Berger, Stefan, Linas Eriksonas, and Andrew Mycock, eds., *Narrating the Nation: Representations in History, Media and the Arts* (New York and Oxford: Berghahn Books, 2008).

Berghahn, Volker, *American Big Business in Britain and Germany: A Comparative History of Two "Special Relationships" in the 20th Century* (Princeton, NJ: Princeton University Press, 2014).

Berghoff, Hartmut, Jürgen Kocka, and Dieter Ziegler, eds., *Business in the Age of Extremes: Essays in Modern German and Austrian Economic History* (Cambridge: Cambridge University Press, 2013).

Bertolette, William F., *British Identity and the German Other* (Ph.D. dissertation: Louisiana State University and Agricultural and Mechanical College, 2012).

Bouvet, Vincent, "Méwès: une révolution esthéthique", *Monuments Historiques* 130 (1984), 44–8.

Bove, Jens, ed., *Oswald Lübeck: Bord- und Reisefotografie 1909–1914* (Dresden: Saxophon, 2011).

Braynard, Frank O., *Leviathan: The Story of the World's Greatest Ship*, 5 vols. (New York: South Street Seaport, 1972–1981).

Brinnin, John Malcolm, *The Sway of the Grand Saloon* (New York: Delacorte Press, 1971) and 2nd edn. (London: Arlington Books, 1986).

Britta, Heitman, "Spitzengastronomie auf hoher See: Ritz-Carlton Restaurants auf HAPAG-Dampfern", *Schiff et Zeit* 70 (2009), 28–36.

Broeze, Frank, "Albert Ballin, the Hamburg-Bremen Rivalry and the Dynamics of the Conference System", *International Journal of Maritime History* 3 (1991), 1–32.

Broeze, Frank, "Albert Ballin, the Hamburg-America Line and Hamburg: Structure and Strategy in the German Shipping Industry (1886–1914)", *Deutsches Schiffahrtsarchiv* 15 (1992), 135–58.

Broeze, Frank, "Shipping Policy and Social-Darwinism: Albert Ballin and the Weltpolitik of the Hamburg-America Line, 1886–1914", *Mariner's Mirror* 79 (1993), 419–36.

Budde, Gunilla, Sebastian Conrad, and Oliver Janz, *Transnationale Geschichte: Themen, Tendenzen und Theorien* (Göttingen: Vandenhoeck and Ruprecht, 2006).

Burckhardt, Lucius, ed., *The Werkbund: History and Ideology* (Woodbury, NY: Barron's, 1980).

Burgess, Douglas R., *Seize the Trident: The Race for Superliner Supremacy and How It Altered the Great War* (New York: McGraw-Hill, 2005).

Burgess, Douglas R., *Engines of Empire. Steamships and the Victorian Imagination* (Stanford, CA: Stanford University Press, 2016).

Calloway, Stephen, *Twentieth-Century Decoration* (New York: Rizzoli, 1988).

Campbell, Joan, *The German Wekbund: The Politics of Reform in the Applied Arts* (Princeton, NJ: Princeton University Press, 1978).

Cecil, Lamar, *Albert Ballin: Business and Politics in Imperial Germany, 1888–1918* (Princeton, NJ: Princeton University Press, 1967).

Charmley, John, *Splendid Isolation? Britain, the Balance of Power and the Origins of the First World War* (London: Hodder and Stoughton, 1999).

Clarke, Peter and Clive Trebilcock, eds., *Understanding Decline: Perceptions and Realities of British Economic Performance* (Cambridge: Cambridge University Press, 1997).

Cohen, Anthony P., *The Symbolic Construction of Community* (Abingdon: Routledge, 1985).

Confino, Alon, *Germany as a Culture of Remembrance* (Chapel Hill, NC: University of North Carolina Press, 2006).

Conrad, Sebastian, *Globalization and the Nation in Imperial Germany* (Cambridge: Cambridge University Press, 2010).

Conrad, Sebastian, *German Colonialism: A Short History* (Cambridge: Cambridge University Press, 2012).

Conrad, Sebastian and Jürgen Osterhammel, *Das Kaiserreich transnational: Deutschland in der Welt 1871–1914* (Göttingen: Vandenhoeck and Ruprecht, 2004).

Conrad, Sebastian and Dominic Sachsenmaier, eds., *Competing Visions of World Order: Global Moments and Movements, 1880s–1930s* (New York: Palgrave Macmillan, 2007).

Dawson, Philip, *The Liner: Retrospective and Renaissance* (New York and London: W.W. Norton, 2005).

Dawson, Philip and Bruce Peter, *Ship Style: Modernism and Modernity at Sea in the 20th Century* (London: Conway, 2010).

Drechsel, Edwin, *Norddeutscher Lloyd, Bremen, 1857–1970*, 2 vols. (Vancouver: Cordillera, 1994–1995).

Drechsel, Wiltrud and Heide Gerstenberger, eds., *Arbeitsplätze: Schiffahrt, Hafen, Textilindustrie, 1880 bis 1933* (Bremen: Bremen University, 1983).

Edgerton, David, *Science, Technology and British Industrial "Decline," 1870–1970* (Cambridge: Cambridge University Press, 1996).

Eley, Geoff, ed., *Society, Culture and the State in Germany, 1870–1930* (Ann Arbor, MI: University of Michigan Press, 1996).

Evans, Richard J., *Death in Hamburg: Society and Politics in the Cholera Years* (London: Penguin, 2005).

Ferguson, Niall, *Paper and Iron: Hamburg Business and German Politics in the Era of Inflation, 1897–1927* (Cambridge: Cambridge University Press, 1995).

Ferguson, Niall, *The Pity of War. Explaining World War I* (New York: Basic Books, 1999).

Fink, Leon, *Sweatshops at Sea. Merchant Seamen in the World's First Globalized Industry, from 1812 to the Present* (Chapel Hill, NC: University of North Carolina Press, 2011).

Fischer, Lewis R., "Are We in Danger of Being Left with Our Journals and Not Much Else: The Future of Maritime History", *The Mariner's Mirror* 91 (2011), 366–81.

Fitzpatrick, Matthew P., "Narrating Empire: *Die Gartenlaube* and Germany's Nineteenth-Century Liberal Expansionism", *German Studies Review* 30 (2007), 97–120.

Fitzpatrick, Matthew P., *Liberal Imperialism in Germany: Expansion and Nationalism 1848–1884* (New York and Oxford: Berghahn Books, 2008).

Forster, Hahn, Françoise, ed., *Imagining Modern German Culture: 1889–1910* (Washington, D.C.: National Gallery of Art, 1996).

Fox, Stephen, *Transatlantic: Samuel Cunard, Isambard Brunel, and the Great Atlantic Steamships* (New York: HarperCollins, 2003).

Freeman, Michael J., *Railways and the Victorian Imagination* (New Haven, CT: Yale University Press, 1999).

Friedberg, Aaron L., *The Weary Titan: Britain and the Experience of Relative Decline, 1895–1905* (Princeton, NJ: Princeton University Press, 1988).

Fritz, Fischer, *Krieg der Illusionen: Die deutsche Politik von 1911 bis 1914* (Düsseldorf: Droste, 1969).

Geppert, Dominik, *Pressekriege. Öffentlichkeit und Diplomatie in den deutsch-britischen Beziehungen (1896–1912)* (Munich: R. Oldenbourg, 2007).

Geppert, Dominik and Robert Gerwarth, eds., *Wilhelmine Germany and Edwardian Britain: Essays on Cultural Affinity* (Oxford: Oxford University Press, 2008).

Gerhardt, Johannes, *Albert Ballin* (Hamburg: Hamburg University Press, 2009).

Gerstenberger, Heide and Ulrich Welke, *Vom Wind zum Dampf: Sozialgeschichte der deutschen Handelsschiffahrt im Zeitalter der Industrialisierung* (Münster: Westfälisches Dampfboot Verlag, 1996).

Geyer, Michael, "Where Germans Dwell: Transnationalism in Theory and Practice", *German Studies Association Newsletter* 31 (2006), 29–37.

Giddens, Anthony, *The Consequences of Modernity* (Cambridge: Polity Press, 1990).

Grigsby, Darcy Grimaldo, *Colossal: Engineering the Suez Canal, Statue of Liberty, Eiffel Tower, and Panama Canal* (Pittsburgh, PA: Periscope, 2012).

Groppe, Hans-Hermann and Ursula Wöst, *Über Hamburg in die Welt. Von den Auswandererhallen zur Ballinstadt* (Hamburg: Ellert & Richter, 2007).

Grüttner, Michael, *Arbeitswelt an der Wasserkante. Sozialgeschichte der Hamburger Hafenarbeiter 1886–1914* (Göttingen: Vandenhoeck and Ruprecht, 1984).

Hardtwig, Wolfgang, *Nationalismus und Bürgerkultur in Deutschland, 1500–1914* (Göttingen: Vandenhoeck and Ruprecht, 1994).

Harlaftis, Gelina, Stig Tenold, and Jesús M. Valdaliso, eds., *The World's Key Industry: History and Economics of International Shipping* (Houndmills and New York: Palgrave Macmillan, 2012).

Höft, Manfred, *Der Vulcan in Stettin und Hamburg: Schiffswerft, Lokomotivfabrik, Maschinenfabrik 1851–1929*, 3 vols. (Bremen: Hauschild, 2013–2015).

Hoerder, Dirk and Jörg Nagler, eds., *People in Transit: German Migrations in Comparative Perspective, 1820–1930* (Washington, D.C.: German Historical Insitute, 1995).

Huldermann, Bernhard, *Albert Ballin* (Oldenburg and Berlin: Gerhard Stalling, 1922).

Jarzombek, Mark, "The *Kunstgewerbe*, the *Werkbund*, and the Aesthetics of Culture in the Wilhelmine Period", *Journal of the Society of Architectural Historians* 53 (1994), 7–19.

Jefferies, Matthew, *Politics and Culture in Wilhelmine Germany: The Case of Industrial Architecture* (Oxford and Washington, DC: Berg, 1995).

Jefferies, Matthew, *Imperial Culture in Germany, 1871–1918* (Houndmills: Palgrave Macmillan, 2003).

Jefferies, Matthew, *Contesting the German Empire, 1871–1918* (Oxford: Blackwell, 2008).

Jefferies, Matthew, *Hamburg: A Cultural and Literary History* (Oxford: Signal Books, 2011).

Jefferies, Matthew, ed., *The Ashgate Research Companion to Imperial Germany* (Farnham: Ashgate, 2015).

Jenkins, Jennifer, *Provincial Modernity. Local Cultural and Liberal Politics in Fin-de-Siècle Hamburg* (Ithaca, NY and London: Cornell University Press, 2003).

Junghanns, Kurt, *Der Deutsche Werkbund: Sein erstes Jahrzehnt* (Berlin: Henschelverlag Kunst und Gesellschaft, 1982).

Kamphoefner, Walter D., Wolfgang Helbich, and Ulrike Sommer, eds., *News from the Land of Freedom: German Immigrants Write Home* (Ithaca, NY: Cornell University Press, 1991).

Kennedy, Paul M., *The Rise of Anglo-German Antagonism 1860–1914* (London: George Allen & Unwin, 1980).

Keppler, Ulrike, *Wahrnehmung der Fremde – Konstruktion des Selbst: Studien zur Bordphotografie von Oswald Lübeck (1883–1935)* (Ph.D. dissertation: Martin-Luther-Universität Halle-Wittenberg, 2007).

Kern, Stephen, *The Culture of Time and Space, 1880–1918* (Cambridge: Harvard University Press, 1983).

Kisch, Egon Erwin, *Reportagen von der Seefahrt 1914–1924* (Oldenburg, München, and Hamburg: Stalling, 1979).

Kludas, Arnold, *Die Geschichte der deutschen Passagierschiffahrt*, 5 vols. (Hamburg: Ernst Kabel, 1986–1990).

Kludas, Arnold, *Die Geschichte der Hapag-Schiffe*, 5 vols. (Bremen: Hauschild, 2007–2010).

Koshar, Rudy, *From Monuments to Traces. Artifacts of German Memory, 1870–1990* (Berkeley, CA: University of California Press, 2000).

Koshar, Rudy, *German Travel Cultures* (Oxford and New York: Berg, 2000).

Layton, J. Kent, *The Edwardian Superliners: A Trio of Trios* (Stroud: Amberley, 2013).

Lenman, Robin, *Artists and Society in Germany, 1850–1914* (Manchester and New York: Manchester University Press, 1997).

Maddocks, Melvin, *The Great Liners* (Alexandria: Time-Life Books, 1978).

Major, Patrick, "Britain and Germany: A Love-Hate Relationship?" *German History* 26 (2008), 457–68.

Matthes, Olaf and Carsten Prange, eds., *Hamburg und die HAPAG: Seefahrt im Plakat* (Hamburg: Museum für Hamburgische Geschichte, 2000).

Maxtone-Graham, John, *The Only Way to Cross* (New York: Macmillan, 1972).

Mertens, Eberhard, *Die HAPAG-Riesen der Imperator-Klasse: die Geschichte der Luxusschiffe Imperator, Vaterland, Bismarck in Bildern und Zeitdokumenten* (Hildesheim and New York: Olms, 1974).

Meyer-Lenz, Johanna, *Schiffbaukunst und Werftarbeit in Hamburg 1838–1896: Arbeit und Gewerkschaftsorganisation im industrialisierten Schiffbau des 19. Jahrhunderts* (Bern: P. Lang, 1995).

Meyer-Tönnesmann, Carsten, *Der Hamburgische Künstlerklub von 1897* (Hamburg: Christians, 1985).

Miller, Michael B., *Europe and the Maritime World: A Twentieth Century History* (Cambridge: Cambridge University Press, 2012).

Miller, William H., *The First Great Ocean Liners in Photographs* (New York: Dover, 1984).

Mohrhof, Folkert, *Der syndikalistische Streik auf dem Ozean-Dampfer 'Vaterland' 1914* (Hamburg: Archiv Karl Roche, 2008).

Mommsen, Wolfgang J., "Public Opinion and Foreign Policy in Wilhelmine Germany: 1897–1914", *Central European History* 24 (1991), 381–401.

Morris, A.J. Anthony, *The Scaremongers: The Advocacy of War and Rearmament 1896–1914* (London: Routledge and Kegan Paul, 1984).

Müller, Sven Oliver, *Die Nation als Waffe und Vorstellung: Nationalismus in Deutschland und Großbritannien im Ersten Weltkrieg* (Göttingen: Vandenhoeck and Ruprecht, 2002).

Müller, Sven Oliver and Cornelius Torp, eds., *Imperial Germany Revisited: Continuing Debates and New Perspectives* (New York and Oxford: Berghahn Books, 2011).

Neider, Charles, ed., *The Complete Humorous Sketches and Tales of Mark Twain* (New York: Doubleday, 1961).

Niethammer, Lutz, et al., *Bürgerliche Gesellschaft in Deutschland: Historische Einblicke, Fragen, Perspektiven* (Frankfurt a.M.: Fischer Taschenbuch, 1990).

Nipperdey, Thomas, "Nationalidee und Nationaldenkmal in Deutschland im 19. Jahrhundert", *Historische Zeitschrift* 206 (1968), 529–85.

Otto, Victor, *Deutsche Amerika-Bilder: Zu den Intellektuellen-Diskursen um die Moderne 1900–1950* (Munich: Wilhelm Fink, 2006).

Paret, Peter, *The Berlin Secession: Modernism and Its Enemies in Imperial Germany* (Cambridge, MA: Belknap Press of Harvard University, 1980).

Plagemann, Volker, ed., *Industriekultur in Hamburg: des Deutschen Reiches Tor zur Welt* (Munich: C.H. Beck, 1984).

Plagemann, Volker, ed., *Übersee: Seefahrt und Seemacht im deutschen Kaiserreich* (Munich: C.H. Beck, 1988).

Pohlsander, Hans A., *National Monuments and Nationalism in 19th Century Germany* (Oxford: Peter Lang, 2008).

Radkau, Joachim, *Technik in Deutschland: Vom 18. Jahrhundert bis zur Gegenwart* (Frankfurt a.M.: Suhrkamp, 1989).

Reinermann, Lothar, "Fleet Street and the Kaiser: British Public Opinion and Wilhelm II", *German History* 26 (2008), 469–85.

Reinke-Kunze, Christine, *Die Geschichte der Reichs-Post-Dampfer* (Herford: Koehlers Verlagsgesellschaft, 1994).

Repp, Kevin, *Reformers, Critics, and the Paths of German Modernity: Anti-Politics and the Search for Alternatives, 1890–1914* (Cambridge: Harvard University Press, 2000).

Retallack, James, ed., *Imperial Germany 1871–1918* (Oxford: Oxford University Press, 2008).

Rieger, Bernhard, "Floating Palaces: Ocean Liners as Icons of Modern Splendour", *History Today* 55 (2005), 37–43.

Rieger, Bernhard, *Technology and the Culture of Modernity in Britain and Germany, 1890–1945* (Cambridge: Cambridge University Press, 2005).

Ritter, Gerhard A., "Der Kaiser und Sein Reeder: Albert Ballin, die HAPAG und das Verhältnis von Wirtshaft und Politik im Kaiserreich und in den Ersten Jahren der Weimarer Republik", *Zeitschrift für Unternehmensgeschichte* 42 (1997), 137–62.

Rosenbaum, Eduard, "Albert Ballin: A Note on the Style of His Economic and Political Activities", *Leo Baeck Institute Yearbook* 3 (1958), 257–99.

Ross, Corey, *Media and the Making of Modern Germany: Mass Communications, Society, and Politics from the Empire to the Third Reich* (Oxford: Oxford University Press, 2008).

Rudolph, Wolfgang, *Das Schiff als Zeichen: bürgerliche Selbstdarstellung in Hafenorten* (Hamburg: Kabel, 1987).

Rüger, Jan, *The Great Naval Game: Britain and Germany in the Age of Empire* (Cambridge: Cambridge University Press, 2007).

Rüger, Jan, "Revisiting the Anglo-German Antagonism", *The Journal of Modern History* 83 (2011), 579–617.

Russell, Mark, "The Building of Hamburg's Bismarck Memorial", *The Historical Journal* 43 (2000), 133–56.

Russell, Mark A., *Between Tradition and Modernity: Aby Warburg and the Public Purposes of Art in Hamburg, 1896–1918* (New York and Oxford: Berghahn Books, 2007).

Russell, Mark A., "Picturing the *Imperator*: Passenger Shipping as Art and National Symbol in the German Empire", *Central European History* 44 (2011), 227–56.

Russell, Mark A., "Steamship Nationalism: Transatlantic Passenger Liners as Symbols of the German Empire", *The International Journal of Maritime History* 28 (2016), 313–34.

Schivelbusch, Wolfgang, *The Railway Journey: The Industrialization of Time and Space in the Nineteenth Century* (Los Angeles, CA: University of California Press, 1987).

Schmidt, Alexander, *Reisen in die Moderne. Der Amerika-Diskurs des deutschen Bürgertums vor dem Ersten Weltkrieg im europäischen Vergleich* (Berlin: Akademie, 1997).

Schramm, Martin, *Das Deutschlandbild in der britischen Presse 1912–1919* (Berlin: Akademie, 2007).

Schwartz, Frederic, "Commodity Signs: Peter Behrens, the AEG, and Trademark", *Journal of Design History* 9 (1996), 153–84.

Schwartz, Frederic, *The Werkbund: Design Theory and Mass Culture before the First World War* (New Haven, CT and London: Yale University Press, 1996).

Schwerdtner, Nils, *German Luxury Ocean Liners. From Kaiser Wilhelm der Grosse to AIDAstella* (Stroud: Amberley, 2011).

Scully, Richard, *British Images of Germany: Admiration, Antagonism and Ambivalence, 1860–1914* (Houndmills: Palgrave Macmillan, 2012).

Seiler, Otto J., *Bridge across the Atlantic: The Story of HAPAG-Lloyd's North American Liner Services* (Herford: E.S. Mittler & Sohn, 1991).

Seligmann, Matthew S., *The Royal Navy and the German Threat, 1901–1914: Admiralty Plans to Protect British Trade in a War against Germany* (Oxford: Oxford University Press, 2012).

Seligmann, Matthew S., "Germany's Ocean Greyhounds and the Royal Navy's First Battle Cruisers: An Historiographical Problem", *Diplomacy and Statecraft* 27 (2016), 162–82.

Service, Alastair, *Edwardian Interiors* (London: Barrie and Jenkins, 1982).

Sondhaus, Lawrence, *Preparing for Weltpolitik: German Sea Power before the Tirpitz Era* (Annapolis, MD: Naval Institute Press, 1997).

Stephan, Alexander, ed., *Americanization and Anti-Americanism: The German Encounter with American Culture after 1945* (New York and Oxford: Berghahn Books, 2004).

Stilgoe, John R., *Train Time: Railroads and the Imminent Reshaping of the United States Landscape* (Charlottesville, VA: University of Virginia Press, 2009).

Straub, Eberhard, *Albert Ballin: Der Reeder des Kaisers* (Berlin: Siedler, 2001).

Streater, Les, *Berengaria: Cunard's "Happy Ship"* (Charleston, SC: Tempus, 2001).

Stubmann, Peter, *Ballin: Leben und Werk eines deutschen Reeders* (Berlin-Grunewald: Hermann Klemm, 1926).

Stubmann, Peter, *Mein Feld ist die Welt. Albert Ballin. Sein Leben* (Hamburg: Hans Christians, 1960).

Sturmey, S.G., *British Shipping and World Competition* (London: Athlone, 1962).

Tatlock, Lynne and Matt Erlin, eds., *German Culture in Nineteenth-Century America. Reception, Adaptation, Transformation* (Rochester, NY: Camden House, 2005).

Tebbe, Jason, "Revision and 'Rebirth': Commemoration of the Battle of Nations in Leipzig", *German Studies Review* 33 (2010), 618–40.

Tebbe, Jason, "Excursions on the 'Middle Sea': Germans Cruising in the Mediterranean", Presentation at the German Studies Association Annual Conference, Louisville, KT, 22–25 September 2011.

Thiel, Reinhold, *Die Geschichte des Norddeutschen Lloyd 1857–1970 in fünf Bänden* (Bremen: Hauschild, 2007).

Tomlinson, John, *The Culture of Speed. The Coming of Immediacy* (Los Angeles, CA: SAGE, 2007).

Torp, Cornelius, *Die Herausforderung der Globalisierung: Wirtschaft und Politik in Deutschland* (Göttingen: Vandenhoeck and Ruprecht, 2005).

Trennheuser, Matthias L., *Die innenarchitektonische Ausstattung deutscher Passagierschiffe zwischen 1880 und 1940* (Bremen: Haushild, 2011).

Trommler, Frank, "The *Lusitania* Affect: America's Mobilization against Germany in World War I", *German Studies Review* 32 (2009), 241–66.

Trommler, Frank and Elliot Shore, eds., *The German-American Encounter: Conflict and Cooperation between Two Cultures, 1800–2000* (New York and Oxford: Berghahn Books, 2001).

Umbach, Maiken, "Memory and Historicism: Reading between the Lines of the Built Environment, Germany c. 1900", *Representations* 88 (2004), 26–54.

Umbach, Maiken, *German Cities and Bourgeois Modernism, 1890–1924* (Oxford: Oxford University Press, 2009).

Väth-Hinz, Henriette, *Odol: Reklame Kunst um 1900* (Giessen: Anabas, 1985).

Watkin, David, *Grand Hotel: The Golden Age of Palace Hotels: An Architectural and Social History* (London: J.M. Dent, 1984).

Watson, Milton H., *Flagships of the Line: A Celebration of the World's Three-Funnel Liners* (Wellingborough: Patrick Stephens, 1988).

Wealleans, Anne, *Designing Liners. A History of Interior Design Afloat* (Abingdon: Routledge, 2006).

Wiborg, Susanne, *Albert Ballin* (Hamburg: Ellert and Richter, 2000).

Wiborg, Suzanne and Klaus Wiborg, *Unser Feld ist die Welt: 150 Jahre Hapag-Lloyd* (Hamburg: Hapag-Lloyd AG, 1997).

Witthöft, Hans Jürgen, *Hapag-Lloyd: über ein Jahrhundert weltweite deutsche Seeschiffahrt im Bild* (Herford: Koehler, 1979).

Witthöft, Hans-Jürgen, *Norddeutscher Lloyd* (Herford: Koehler, 1973).

Zacharasiewicz, Waldemar, *The Image of Germany in American Literature* (Iowa City, IA: University of Iowa Press, 2007).

Zala, Sacha, ed., *Die Moderne und ihre Krisen: Studien von Marina Cataruzza zur europäischen Geschichte des 19. und 20. Jahrhunderts* (Göttingen: Vandenhoeck and Ruprecht, 2012).

Zeising, Andreas, *Studien zu Karl Schefflers Kunstkritik und Kunstbegriff. Mit einer annotierten Bibliographie seiner Schriften* (Tönning: Der Andere, 2006).

Zerbe, Peter, *Die Grossen Deutschen Passagierschiffe: Imperator, Vaterland, Bismarck* (Hamburg: Nautik Historie Verlag, 1999).

Index